Hadrian's Wall

Hadrian's Wall

Everyday Life on a
Roman Frontier

Patricia Southern

AMBERLEY

First published 2016

Amberley Publishing
The Hill, Stroud
Gloucestershire, GL5 4EP

www.amberley-books.com

British Library Cataloguing in Publication Data.
A catalogue record for this book is available from the British Library.

ISBN 978 1 4456 4025 9 (hardback)
ISBN 978 1 4456 4034 1 (ebook)

Typesetting and Origination by Amberley Publishing.
Printed in the UK.

Contents

Preface and Acknowledgements

The accepted protocol for writing yet another book on any popular topic is to apologise. There are lots of books on Hadrian's Wall, so why write another? There are history books, guide books, walking guides, picture books, and scholarly articles in academic journals and conference proceedings. The range of publications is indicative of the range of people who are interested in the Wall at various levels. The Wall means different things to different enthusiasts, tourists, school parties, walkers, photographers, admirers of the countryside, serious students, not to mention archaeologists and historians, but in the latter cases enthusiasm tends to spill over into obsession. When I was twelve the neighbouring grammar school offered our school in Cheshire four spare seats, gratis, on their coach for a trip to Hadrian's Wall. I had read about it and seen the pictures, courtesy of the public library, and become obsessive about it myself, and I saw it for the first time at an impressionable age. Blown away was not a phrase that was in current usage then, except in so far as it tends to be windy on Hadrian's Wall. In those days you could read everything there was on Roman Britain, let alone Hadrian's Wall, save for the aforementioned scholarly articles in academic publications, to which you don't tend to have access when you're twelve. Publication has increased vastly since then, but despite the plethora of books on Hadrian's Wall, some misconceptions still persist: soldiers from Rome shivering on the frontier; the Wall was built to stop the Picts, who had not been invented, so to speak, in Hadrian's day; the Wall is the border between England and Scotland, as exemplified by two small girls full of joy leaping back and forth over the depleted Wall at Banks East turret, shouting 'England, Scotland, England, Scotland' as they landed on what they thought was the appropriate side. You can't squash that degree of enthusiasm with the truth.

I owe thanks to various people over the years for conversations about the Wall, with the late Charles Daniels and Professor Barri Jones, and with Lindsay Allason-Jones, Karen Dixon and Trish and Chris Boyle, to mention a few of them. Thanks also to Jonathan Reeve of Amberley Publishing for persuading (nagging?) me to tread on hallowed ground and write the book. Especial thanks are due, as ever, to Graeme Stobbs not only for conversations, references and ideas, but also for producing the line drawings and plans. Gratitude is also due to Susan Veitch for drawings done from garbled instructions. This is a work of synthesis, hopefully including the salient points, but with no attempt to go into every detail of every bit of Hadrian's Wall that has been investigated, because that would be tedious in the extreme, not to mention impossible. It is an interim statement, because study of the Wall never ceases. As with many Roman subjects, when you have sent the manuscript to the publisher, read the proofs and done the index, received the book, to open it at random and immediately spot a typo, there will also have been half a dozen new articles arguing cogently against long-held theories, or presenting the results of excavations which completely overturn the theories which are dutifully included as part of the old orthodoxy, and are now out of date. The last word on Hadrian's Wall has not yet been written and probably never will be, and some people are always discovering the Wall for the first time. Hence this book, a small part of the perennial fascination of Hadrian's Wall. Eternal Rome, in England.

Patricia Southern
Northumberland
2015

1

Before the Wall: *c.* 55 BC to AD 122

When the Emperor Hadrian toured the province of Britain in AD 122, the Romans had been in the island for nearly eighty years. They had campaigned in Scotland, building forts and a large legionary fortress there, and would perhaps have stayed, had it not been for circumstances elsewhere in the Empire that necessitated the withdrawal of troops for what turned out to be a series of major wars on the Danube, spanning the end of the first century and the opening years of the second. This chapter describes the decades of Roman government that Hadrian inherited.

Romans and Britons had been aware of each other long before Britain became a province. The British tribes in the southern parts of the island had been trading with the Romans for some considerable time when Julius Caesar established direct contact by invading the island in 55 and 54 BC. As proconsular governor of Gaul, he made the excuse that the Britons were aiding the Gallic tribes. He did not attempt to hold Britain, being more focused on the conquest of Gaul and events in Rome. His description of what he found in Britain informs archaeologists and historians about the tribes, their organisation and fighting methods.

In the first century AD it was taken for granted that Britain would one day be added to the Empire. Augustus prepared for an expedition to Britain three times, but never invaded. Claudius achieved it in AD 43. Military glory for the non-military Emperor cannot have been the sole motive for the conquest. The Romans were already benefitting from taxes on luxury goods and wines, and according to the Greek author Strabo they also received hides, hunting dogs and slaves. There were also mineral resources to be gained, lead in abundance, and gold in Wales, and the population could be exploited for manpower in the form of recruits for the army.

Britannia was not a unified country with a united population. The tribesmen and women did not think of themselves primarily as Britons. Their loyalties were to their tribe and their leader, for as long as the leader was strong enough to command them, and as long as the cohesion of the tribe lasted. Tribal society was fluid, and larger federations could absorb some smaller tribes, peacefully or otherwise. Significantly, some of the tribes mentioned by Caesar in the first century BC are no longer heard of in the first century AD. On the other hand, territorial boundaries could remain relatively stable even if the tribal compositions changed, especially in Scotland, where Roman influence was shallow and sporadic. Gordon Maxwell has argued for a high degree of spatial continuum, pointing out that the post-Roman and medieval kingdoms in Scotland can be traced back to the tribal areas of Roman times.[1]

Initially the Romans were fully occupied in subduing the south and west of Britain. Various camps and temporary forts provide traces of the campaigns, attesting continual movement of army groups, usually parts of legions accompanied by various whole or part auxiliary units. The legions did not move as a single entity from battle to battle, and although the forts established by various army groups may have been occupied and reoccupied over a period of time, the legions were not housed in permanent bases until the fortresses at Caerleon, Chester and York were built, starting in the AD 70s. Before this consolidation, the Romans built a fortress at Exeter and another at Lincoln and joined them by a road known in modern times as the Fosse Way. With regard to what Hadrian did later, this road merits a brief discussion, because it has been labelled as a frontier line, implying that the Romans intended to halt their advance, having won the parts of the province that they were interested in. The road was certainly guarded by forts strung out along it, but they are not all aligned to the south of the road, which would have indicated they were intended to form part of a coordinated scheme to watch for movement from areas to the north. The forts were built to guard the communication route between Exeter and Lincoln, not to delineate the boundary between Roman and non-Roman territory. Though it may boil down to technical terms and semantics, the Fosse Way does not approximate to the kind of frontier that Hadrian was to establish in the early second century. The halt on the Fosse Way line can be construed not as a frontier but as a temporary demarcation line behind which consolidation took place.

According to an inscription from Rome celebrating Claudius' conquest, eleven British kings submitted to the Emperor. Their names are not listed, but two of the rulers are generally agreed to have been King Prasutagus of the Iceni, and Togidubnus of the Atrebates, who may have been the occupant of the famous villa at Fishbourne. The rulers of kingdoms and tribes who entered into agreements with Rome were usually designated as 'friends of the Roman people'. Modern historians label them client kings. The Romans provided support and protection, in return for tribal assistance in providing troops on a regular or an ad hoc basis. In the north, another British ruler who submitted to the Romans was most likely Queen Cartimandua of the federation of the Brigantes. Her tribal territory covered the Pennine area from south Yorkshire up to and perhaps beyond the line later occupied by Hadrian's Wall, though the exact boundaries are not known.

Although there may have been diplomatic or mercantile contact with the tribes of northern England, the Brigantes under Cartimandua were initially left in peace. During the early years of the conquest, the rebel leader Caratacus had managed to unite some of the tribes against the Romans but when he was finally defeated and fled to the north, appealing to Cartimandua for help, she refused to shelter him and handed him over to the Romans.[2] Apart from the fact that he was not of her tribe, if she had supported him the Romans would have descended on her kingdom, sooner rather than later. Similarly Cartimandua did not march to join Boudicca, Queen of the Iceni, in the rebellion in 60–61.

Hostile relations between tribes and disputes within the tribes were not infrequent. Recognising this tendency for disunion among the people beyond the Empire, the Romans often supported a tribal leader with gifts of money, prestige goods and food, which helped the ruler to maintain his or her position and to control and reward the tribesmen. In exchange the leader guaranteed to keep the peace within the tribe and to hold off neighbouring tribes, so Roman interests were protected. Tacitus comments that when Cartimandua surrendered Caratacus to the Romans, she acquired her wealth from this action, and the self-indulgent behaviour that goes with it.[3] The Romans helped to shore up the Queen's regime. From about 60, if not earlier, Roman forts were established in south Yorkshire, probably on the southern borders of Cartimandua's kingdom, at Templeborough, and at Rossington Bridge, near Doncaster. A fort of unknown date was built at Osmanthorpe, near Southwell. The units based in these forts may have watched the Brigantian territory, prepared for action if necessary in Cartimandua's realm.[4] The lands to the east of Brigantia were occupied by a tribe called the Parisi, who may have been friendly to Rome and allowed troops to operate in their terrain. This may explain why there seems to have been early Roman activity in the Vale of York, before the fortress at York was founded, though this remains extremely conjectural.[5]

There were squabbles between Cartimandua and her husband Venutius, in which the Romans had to intervene. Tacitus provides a brief retrospective survey of the troubles among the Brigantes. At war with her husband, Cartimandua captured his brother and other members of his family, and Venutius' response was to stir up warriors, perhaps not all of them Brigantes. Tacitus says that the Romans had foreseen this and sent auxiliary cohorts to restore order. There was another battle or series of battles involving a legion commanded by Caesius Nasica, who may have been legate of *IX Hispana*. The governor at this time was Didius Gallus who, according to Tacitus, was content to act through his military subordinates.[6] These events took place over a number of years under two different propraetorian governors, only one of whom is named, and Tacitus explains that he describes them together, because it would lessen their impact to relate them in their proper chronological order.[7] It is not possible to say how far north the Romans penetrated, but useful intelligence will have accrued to the Roman high command when the soldiers were sent to restore order. They would have learned about the terrain, the routes through it, the social organisation of the various factions of the Brigantes, and the strength of their settlements. In the 70s, when the governor Petillius Cerialis embarked on the conquest of the north, the topography of the land and the likely sites for military establishments will not have been entirely unknown.

The most serious episode when the Romans had to intervene in Brigantian affairs occurred during the governorship of Vettius Bolanus at the time of the civil war in Rome. Nero committed suicide in 68, and Galba was declared Emperor by the troops in Spain, but was assassinated. Otho and Vitellius became the next Emperors, but it was Vespasian who won in the end and established an Imperial dynasty that survived from 69 to 96. The legions in Britain were also divided against each other, some of the legionaries favouring Vitellius and others Otho, and yet others declared for Vespasian who had commanded legion *II Augusta* in Britain during the early years of the conquest. Detachments from the legions and auxiliary units of Britain had been sent to help Vitellius, and some of the officers owed their promotions to him. *XIV Gemina* proved somewhat troublesome, and was sent back and forth from Britain to the continent, until part of it was sent to help Vespasian, and the rest of it followed *c.* 70. During the spring of 69, the legate of *XX Valeria*, Roscius Coelius, agitated very strongly for the removal of the unwarlike governor of Britain, Trebellius Maximus, eventually forcing him to leave. A hiatus in the administration and military command ensued, until Vettius Bolanus was appointed as governor in 69, but even after his arrival, concerted action by the legions was still compromised. While the Romans were somewhat preoccupied Venutius seized his chance. Cartimandua had divorced him and married Vellocatus, her armour-bearer. With nothing to lose and everything to gain, Venutius tried to oust his former wife. Cartimandua had to turn to the Romans. Bolanus had not yet properly restored order over the legions, but he assembled troops to rescue the queen. No one knows her ultimate fate.

Tacitus says that after the rescue of Cartimandua, 'the kingdom was left to Venutius, and the war to us' (*regnum Venutio, bellum nobis relictum*).[8] Between 69 and 71 Bolanus probably began to occupy southern Brigantia to secure its borders with Roman territory.[9] The poet Statius, writing towards the end of the reign of Domitian, describes how Bolanus built watchtowers over a wide area and forts 'a long way off', surrounding them with defensive ditches. He also wore a cuirass taken from a British king, usually identified as Venutius.[10] Statius portrays Bolanus addressing his troops in the Caledonian plains, but this is poetic licence combined with an inexact knowledge of Britain, and need not imply that Bolanus carried on into the Highlands in 69 or 70. At the beginning of the reign of Vespasian when the civil wars were ended and the revolt of the Batavian auxiliaries on the Rhine had been put down, northern England and southern Scotland came within the remit of the governors of Britain.

The first of the Flavian governors, Flavian being derived from Vespasian's family name Flavius, was Petillius Cerialis. As legate of *IX Hispana* during the revolt of Boudicca, he had tried to stop the British forces after they had sacked Colchester, but was defeated, hurrying back to his base with his cavalry.[11] This base was perhaps the vexillation fortress at Longthorpe near Peterborough, but it is also possible that Cerialis was at Lincoln, where there are some traces of military occupation before the better-known fortress was built on the opposite side of the River Witham. Cerialis made significant advances in Britain during his term as governor from 71 to 73/74. He moved *IX Hispana* from its fortress at Lincoln to a new one at York, and at some point before 76, *II Adiutrix* occupied Lincoln. In the northwest of Britain, Cerialis was probably the founder of the first fort at Carlisle, built in timber with turf and earth ramparts. Dendrochronological or tree-ring dating shows that the timbers were felled in the winter of 72/73. The fact that Cerialis was able to advance so far into northern England in a relatively short time testifies to the fighting capacity of his troops, and to the previous work of Bolanus.

It is not known how far north Cerialis campaigned, or how he consolidated his hold on the territory overrun. Tacitus, probably in order to magnify the achievements of his father-in-law Agricola, who governed Britain from 77/78 to 83/84, describes how Cerialis contained a great part of the Brigantes by victory or by war: *magnamque Brigantum partem aut victoria complexus aut bello*.[12] Since he refers to the Brigantes rather than the territory, Tacitus implies that Cerialis had not gained the whole of Brigantia.

Cerialis' successor Sextus Julius Frontinus is credited with the subjugation of the Silures of South Wales. Tacitus simply states that in the north Frontinus sustained the burden, evading a description of what had been achieved before his father-in-law Agricola was appointed governor. In the recent past, every fort from the Pennines to the Scottish Highlands was allocated to Agricola, but it is now recognised that Frontinus most likely consolidated the north by establishing forts. Unfortunately evidence is lacking to prove this.

Agricola and the Conquest of the North

While Hadrian was growing up, the Romans were pushing northwards into Scotland, but by the time he was entering into the first stages of his career, the northern conquests had been abandoned. When the Romans entered Scotland, there was no serious pressure on the other borders of the Empire, but by the later first century the Dacians menaced the Danube provinces, and the military focus shifted to that area.

The late first-century conquest of Scotland is described here at some length to provide some idea of what it cost and how long it took, which may explain why Hadrian did not choose to resume the conquest. Tacitus' account of Agricola's campaigns was published *c.* 98, so it would have been available to Hadrian, but no one can say whether he read it, or how much interest he took in the history of the province until he became Emperor and was directly responsible for it.

Agricola's earlier career and his term as governor of Britain is by far the best documented in literary terms, but by contrast there is a dearth of epigraphic evidence. Without Tacitus' biography of his father-in-law, all that would be known of Agricola would consist of a fragmentary inscription from Verulamium, bearing a part of his name, recording the construction of the Forum, and a lead pipe from the fortress at Chester, on which his name is stamped in full. With only these pieces of evidence, historians would not have guessed that Agricola had already served in Britain twice, the first time during the rebellion of Boudicca, when he may have served on the staff of the governor Suetonius Paulinus. He may have been attached to headquarters with the rank of tribune, though it is just as likely that he served with a legion.[13] During the civil war of 68–69, Agricola raised troops for Licinius Mucianus, Vespasian's de facto deputy, and was appointed legate of *XX Valeria*, under Bolanus as governor.[14] Agricola may have had a difficult task in imposing discipline after the legionaries had been stirred up by the previous legate Roscius Coelius. When Cerialis took over from Bolanus, Tacitus says that at first the new governor gave Agricola only a share in the work and the danger, but later gave him independent commands over a part of the army.[15]

Agricola's third term of service in Britain was as governor. This career pattern, serving three times in the same province, was abnormal, in that most men served in different provinces, combining civilian administrative posts with military appointments. Without Tacitus' account, it would have been impossible to discern that as governor Agricola had directed campaigns in Britain for seven seasons. The normal term of office was about three years.

The date of Agricola's arrival is not established. Tacitus describes the whole period in terms of summers and winters of Agricola's seven seasons, with no dates. This problem has occasioned much flowing of ink and pounding of keyboards, resulting in a choice of dates for Agricola's arrival, either in 77 or 78, the earlier date being the favoured one.[16] It was already late in the season, and the troops were expecting to go into winter quarters when Agricola launched his first campaign against the Ordovices of North Wales.[17] In the first winter Agricola attended to civilian government, correcting several abuses, one of which concerned the requisitioning of food supplies, principally grain, where there was plenty of scope for the soldiers and administrators to cheat the natives.

In the second season Agricola turned his attention to the north. Archaeological evidence shows that northern England was already occupied at least as far north as Carlisle and York, and Tacitus writes of the subjugation of a 'new area' of Britain, and hitherto unknown tribes. These were surrounded with forts (*praesidiis castellisque circumdatae*). It is likely that Agricola was operating in the Borders, penetrating into southern Scotland, and he may have been responsible for placing forts on what is now known as the Stanegate, in the Tyne-Solway gap, just south of the line of Hadrian's Wall. The forts at Carlisle, Nether Denton, Vindolanda and Corbridge eventually belonged to the Stanegate system, but only Carlisle and Corbridge have Agricolan associations. The first fort at Carlisle was built by Cerialis, and he may have been responsible for the first fort at Corbridge as a stores base, but this is usually assigned to Agricola. This fort, labelled the Red House, was discovered in 1974 when the then new version of the A69 was being laid out, and it explained the origins of the bath house, found nearly two decades earlier, some distance from the current fort site. Archaeologists, unaware that the baths did not belong to the known fort, puzzled over the scenario of soldiers hiking such a long way with the Roman equivalent of soap and towels. Vindolanda is not yet proven to have been a foundation of Cerialis or Agricola, unless the situation is similar to that of Corbridge, with an earlier fort on a different site, possibly somewhere to the west as Robin Birley has suggested.[18]

In the third season, Agricola met new peoples, and advanced as far as the estuary of the River Tay, which is named: *usque ad Taum (aestuarium nomen est)*, one of the few unequivocal names that Tacitus provides.[19] Tacitus remarks that there was time to build forts, without giving locations. The forts were occupied during the winter, equipped with supplies for at least a year, and the natives were kept under control by frequent sallies (*crebrae eruptiones*). The tribesmen usually relied on being able to recoup their strength during the winter, which made up for the losses in the summer campaigns, but now they were harried all year round.

Marching as far as the Tay and meeting new tribes is not the same thing as occupying the land, so the Romans may have demonstrated their prowess to the natives and then wintered somewhere further south.[20] Several forts of first-century date are known in the Borders and Lowland Scotland, but some of them may have been founded by Petillius Cerialis, or perhaps his successor Frontinus. Not knowing how many forts Agricola inherited in his second and third seasons, it is not possible to say where he built new ones.[21] Fortunately, the fort at Elginhaugh near Dalkeith, discovered in 1979 and excavated in the 1980s, does provide dating evidence for its foundation in 79 or 80, and as the excavator points out, the foundation of this fort must imply that all forts to the south were also established either before this time or contemporaneously with Elginhaugh.[22]

The So-Called Gask Frontier

At some time in the first century the Romans constructed a line of forts and watchtowers running from Ardoch, near the village of

Braco south of Crieff, through Strageath, and then along the Gask Ridge around the western edge of Fife to Bertha on the River Tay. In modern parlance the whole system is known as the Gask frontier, but strictly speaking, the Gask Ridge proper, running roughly east to west, forms only the eastern part of the line. In this chapter the installations are described, while the debate about the possible function of the Gask as a frontier is reserved for a later chapter.

It is possible that not all the component parts of the Gask system are contemporary. On a map, the line looks like a homogenous whole, conceived as part of the same plan, but this may not be accurate. This uncertainty about the dating and the function of the line means that there are several alternative contexts for its establishment, and mention of it must be made in connection with virtually every event of the first-century Roman occupation of Scotland.[23] It is possible that previous governors had established a military presence that Tacitus remains tacit about, in order to enhance the glory of Agricola. One day the Gask system may even prove to be pre-Agricolan.[24]

The watchtowers on the Gask Ridge were each supported on four large timber posts surrounded by a circular ditch and bank. In the south-eastern sector, which does not lie on the ridge line, there were usually two ditches around each tower. In addition there were auxiliary forts, at Ardoch and Strageath, and at Bertha which was built at the point where the River Almond joins the Tay. These forts possibly belong to Agricola's third season.[25] On either side of Ardoch there were fortlets, one to the south at Kaims Castle, and another to the north-east between Ardoch and Strageath. Another fortlet has been found at Midgate, about half way between Strageath and Bertha. There were presumably more of these smaller forts, and quite possibly another large fort in the gap between Strageath and Bertha, as well as more towers to fill the gaps where nothing has come to light. On grounds of spacing, the towers ought to be there, but rigid spacing of Roman installations has lost credibility in recent years, in favour of a more flexible scheme, whereby forts and towers were built where topography dictated a need for surveillance.[26] It used to be thought that the Gask towers were contemporary with the timber towers along the road around the Taunus–Wetterau region, conventionally dated to the reign of Domitian. More recently, dendrochronological dating has shown that the towers belong to the early Trajanic period. This means that the Gask system with its Flavian dates of occupation is the earlier of the two.[27]

The towers, fortlets and forts of the Gask were in existence from *c.* 80 or possibly earlier, to *c.* 90 or possibly later. Some of the timber towers stood for long enough to require rebuilding, possibly more than once. Eighteen towers have been found, but only a few have been excavated. The fine details of rebuilding could not always be detected, but six towers have yielded evidence of repair work and in some cases replacement of the main supporting timbers.[28] The forts at Ardoch and Strageath have two Flavian phases, being finally given up *c.* 90 towards the end of the reign of Domitian, who was assassinated in 96. The first phase may belong to Agricola's campaigns, and the second phase may belong to the governor or governors who came after him. Though the towers and forts appear to have been in continuous existence from Agricola's early years until the withdrawal of the troops from northern Scotland, this does not necessarily imply that there was unbroken occupation and use of the Gask system, but it would have been unusual for the Roman army to decommission military sites without demolishing them tidily, so for the Gask Ridge, long existence without any signs that there was a demolition programme, followed by rebuilding, could mean that there was a similarly long and continuous occupation, not just of the Gask Ridge system but possibly as far north as Strathmore, rendering it difficult to marry up the archaeological findings with the perceived chronology of the conquest and the withdrawal.[29]

The Halting Place of the Fourth Season

According to Tacitus, Agricola's fourth season was spent in consolidating the advance, and the establishment of forts (*praesidia*) in the gap between the rivers *Clota et Bodotria*, the Clyde and the Forth. It has been pointed out that although the words used by Tacitus, *praesidiis firmabatur*, are usually taken to mean that Agricola built forts where none had existed before, a more strict interpretation could imply that he simply refurbished, or firmed up, forts that had already been built.[30]

Tacitus describes this line as a potential *terminus*, which could
have served as the boundary of the province.[31] It is unfortunate
that there are no firmly established dates for Agricola's arrival
and departure in Britain and hence no fixed dates for his seven
seasons in command. If the later dating is preferred, allocating
Agricola's arrival in Britain to 78, it is then possible to argue that
the fourth season belongs to 81, the year when Titus died and
was succeeded by his brother Domitian, so the change of Emperor
could have determined Agricola's decision to find a suitable place
to hold a line and consolidate, while waiting for orders. The
further advance in the fifth, sixth and seventh seasons could then
be seen as the decision of the new Emperor Domitian. However,
the earlier dating for Agricola's campaigns, now mostly accepted,
would mean that the fourth season belongs to 80, when Titus was
very much in power, but this still does not rule out a direct order
from the Emperor to stop the advance.[32] In Tacitus' biography of
Agricola there is no mention of a direct order from either Titus or
Domitian. In his careful choice of word order, before describing
the terminus, Tacitus dismisses the idea of ending the campaign in
Britain because the glory of the name of Rome would not allow for
such a premature halt.

The line chosen by Agricola between the Forth and Clyde would
have been similar to other boundaries established by the Romans in
some provinces, usually consisting of a road guarded by forts and
possibly fortlets and watchtowers between the forts. No evidence
has been found of a palisade or running barrier on Agricola's line,
and more importantly there is very little evidence for Agricolan
forts, or for the postulated road connecting them. The only clues
derive from the first-century finds, but not structures, at some of
the forts of the Antonine Wall, at Mumrills, Castlecary, Cadder,
Balmuildy and Old Kilpatrick, where the building phases are
all Antonine. The fort at Mollins, south of the line of the later
Antonine Wall, has been dated to the late first century, and
Barochan overlooking the Clyde has been suggested as another
Agricolan site.[33] The Agricolan forts would have been built of turf
and timber, not stone, rendering traces of their structures more
difficult to recognise. There may have been some occupied sites
beyond the Forth–Clyde line serving as outposts, and the road and
towers along the Gask Ridge around Fife may belong to the line,

regardless of whether they were built in the third or the fourth season, which would make it more accurately a Tay–Clyde fortified line.

The Advance to the North

In the fifth season Agricola used the navy to make a crossing of some waterway.[34] Tacitus does not name the waterway, but since he ended the description of the fourth season with the army on the Forth–Clyde line, it is thought that the next phase must relate to this, and therefore Agricola crossed the Clyde estuary and operated in the west, because after defeating hitherto unknown tribes he assembled his troops on the coast which faced Ireland. There is no specific mention of fort building, and Tacitus passes quickly on to the sixth season, when Agricola concentrated on the east side of Scotland, reconnoitring the ports and harbours of the east coast and surrounding the tribes beyond the Forth. Later in the same chapter Tacitus says that the people of Caledonia attacked some forts, presumably new ones established in the territory beyond the Forth, since Agricola's officers advised retreat to the south of the river.[35]

The perennial questions concern how Agricola brought the British tribes to battle at all, how far north he marched, and where did he fight the final decisive battle at the site named by Tacitus as Mons Graupius. The terrain in northern Scotland assists the population to resist invaders, and there are attested historical examples where a retreat into the mountains resulted in the withdrawal of the invaders, who were not able to sustain a long-term investment of the whole country. Tribal alliances were not readily made, and it usually took extreme harassment to force the issue and make tribes sink their differences and work together. Tacitus refers to tribal alliances sanctified by sacrifices.[36] The likelihood is that the Romans harried the Britons throughout Agricola's sixth and seventh seasons, and the battle was not fought until late in the final seventh season, implying that the Britons did not combine effectively until the final year.

The battle of Mons Graupius was fought near a mountain, *mons*, which hardly narrows the field in Scotland. The modern name of the Grampians derives from a faulty transmission of the name used by Tacitus, so no clues there. The search for the battle is mostly limited to the area to the east of the Highlands, or even south of the Highland line, because no forts have been discovered in the Highlands or north of them. There are tenuous hints that Agricola was in the far north when he fought at Mons Graupius. Tacitus invents a speech for the leader of the Britons, Calgacus, which means 'the Swordsman', in which the chieftain says that the furthest parts of Britain had been exposed, and there were no more tribes and nothing beyond them but sea and cliffs, which can be taken to mean that the battle was fought in the extreme north.[37] The speech that Agricola makes to his troops in Tacitus' biography may have some basis in reality, perhaps embroidered and embellished by the author. Tacitus reports that his father-in-law praised his soldiers for marching further than all previous governors, and that it would not be inglorious to meet death at the end of the land and nature itself (*in ipso terrarium ac naturae fine cecidisse*). Hyperbole, perhaps, but the language is suggestive of reaching the far north of Scotland, which statement immediately polarises historians of Roman Britain.[38]

Agricola put his legions in reserve and fought the battle with his auxiliary troops. The victory was decisive. Scouts sent out the next day reported no Britons in evidence. Agricola ordered the fleet to sail around Britain, now shown for the first time to be an island, and marched back southwards in a leisurely manner to impress the natives. According to Tacitus, he entered the territory of the Boresti and took hostages. The Boresti are usually interpreted as a tribe possibly located around the mouth of the River Spey, but the word may derive from a copyist's error or a text already corrupted in ancient times, and may not concern a tribe at all. It is odd that only one tribe should be named by Tacitus, and the reference to hostages may in fact refer to arrangements made with several tribes, which would have been more prudent after the final victory. Agricola placed his troops in winter quarters, but Tacitus gives no clues as to where.[39] There are first-century Roman forts at the mouths of the glens leading into and out of the Highlands, one or two of them with two phases, but none of them occupied for very long. They may have been established by Agricola but there is no proof of foundation dates.[40]

There are so many other things that archaeologists and historians would like to know, among them what was the date when Agricola left the province, who was his successor, where were the winter quarters, who built the forts at the mouths of the glens, how was the north of England and most of Scotland garrisoned, what happened to Calgacus and his defeated tribesmen, were there peace treaties between the Romans and some of the British tribes? Were some Britons forcibly recruited into the army?

The Withdrawal from Scotland

Agricola's successor as governor may have been Sallustius Lucullus, but this is not certain since it can only be said that he was in post at some time between Agricola's departure in 84 or 85 and the death of Domitian in 96. Whoever succeeded Agricola would possibly have inherited, or perhaps newly established, the auxiliary forts at the mouths of the glens into and out of the lowlands, with a legion, usually thought to be *XX Valeria*, at Inchtuthil guarding the valley of the Tay. There may have been more forts further north, but although a search for installations around the Moray Forth and Inverness has been made, the results were not conclusive. It is not clear whether the glen-blocking forts were bases for advance into the Highlands, or whether they had a passive role of preventing movement into and out of the mountains. Further south it is not known if the *praesidia* planted by Agricola on the Forth–Clyde line were still in occupation. Given that the Gask system was occupied for several years and kept in repair, perhaps Agricola's successor remodelled it, and was responsible for the second Flavian phase at Ardoch and Strageath.

The occupation of the glen forts was short. The legionary fortress at Inchtuthil was incomplete when it was tidily destroyed. A million nails were buried by the Romans to avoid having to transport them, and to prevent the Britons from obtaining a free supply of iron. The forts at Fendoch and Mollins were also deliberately dismantled, and the sites tidied up, so it can be assumed that all the forts were dismantled in the same way. If there had been any plans for the further occupation of the Highlands and the exploitation of natural and human resources, they were abandoned around 86 or 87, the date being derived from the bronze coins, called *asses*, the staple of soldiers' pay. At Inchtuthil, Strageath, Stracathro and Cardean, *asses* issued in 86 were found in near-perfect mint condition, indicating only a short time in circulation. The coin series at the fort at Elginhaugh also ends with unworn *asses* and *sestertii* of 86.[41] The issue of bronze coins of 87 was extensive, and examples have been found in abundance at other sites in Roman Britain, but not at the glen forts. The conclusion is that the coins of 87 are not found because the soldiers were no longer there to receive them. If this hypothesis is correct, among the main questions are: why were the troops withdrawn, how much of Scotland was abandoned, and was it done in successive stages or all at once?

The reason for withdrawal is most likely the serious trouble on the Danube. The Dacians of what is now Romania had crossed the Danube into the Roman province of Moesia and killed the governor, badly mauling the troops in the process. The Emperor Domitian assembled another army and placed the Praetorian Prefect Fuscus in command. The war went well at first, but then the Romans were defeated. In 86 Domitian was collecting troops for yet another campaign army, and this time he needed more soldiers from other provinces, having probably already taken them from Upper and Lower Germany, Raetia and Pannonia for Fuscus' army. He may have recalled *II Adiutrix* from Britain, where it had been stationed since 70 or 71, though it is not firmly attested in the Danube provinces until 92.

Tacitus' well-worn phrase in the *Histories*, explaining that Britain was conquered and immediately let go (*perdomita Britannia, statim missa*) describes in a nutshell the conquest and abandonment of Scotland.[42] The context for this laconic judgement is an enumeration of all the successful or unsuccessful wars in the period he was about to describe, but Tacitus also possessed an alternative agenda in that his father-in-law Agricola was greatly disappointed at not receiving further commands, and at seeing the whole of his work abandoned. It now seems that Tacitus was not exaggerating. The phrase *statim missa* can be taken at face value, not hyperbole. The only question is whether Britain had been quite so *perdomita* as Tacitus says.

Before Agricola died in August 93 the Romans had withdrawn southwards probably to the southern Lowlands, around Newstead,

Dalswinton and Glenlochar. The first two of these forts were reconstructed and enlarged in the late 80s, and the third was newly built. There is still room for debate concerning the stages of withdrawal. Was Lowland Scotland eventually given up all at once, or in successive phases? At whatever dates the forts in Scotland were given up, the troops would need to be accommodated, some of them possibly going to the Danube, or to other provinces to replace the troops lost in the Dacian wars. The rest would need to find homes in the remaining forts in Britain, and the late Professor Barri Jones thought that they were lodged in the forts of the Stanegate between the River Tyne and the Solway Firth. Aerial photography and excavation shows that some forts on this line were enlarged in *c*. 90, by which time he suggested that all the troops had been brought out of Scotland.[43] A few Lowland forts were occupied after 90, and these could be interpreted as outposts.[44]

Jones' theory sets the withdrawal from Scotland firmly in Domitian's reign, but it now seems more likely that it was Trajan who was responsible for the final abandonment. Domitian's Dacian victory in 88 had not concluded the war satisfactorily, and it was clear that another war would have to be fought. Domitian started to prepare for a war but never undertook it. When Trajan became Emperor in 98 the Danube area soon became a priority. In Britain he reorganised the troop dispositions, and the Romans fortified the Stanegate line.

The Stanegate

The name Stanegate is medieval, not derived from Roman usage. 'Stane' denotes stone, and gate or yate is a medieval term for a road, which means that at some point in its life, not necessarily from the very beginning, the Stanegate was a stone-paved road. Though a route was laid out linking the forts along the Stanegate, the position of the forts dictated where it ran, implying that there was no pre-existing metalled road that instead dictated where the forts were sited. It is likely that the surface of the road may not have been paved until sometime after the forts and fortlets were built.[45] The common conception that all Roman roads were stone-paved is not accurate.

By about 105 the Stanegate line represented most northerly attested Roman occupation, which is not the same as the actual most northerly occupation. The forts on this route at Corbridge, Vindolanda and Carlisle all display signs of rebuilding around 105.[46] It is not known if Nether Denton was also reconstructed at this time.

When Scotland was finally abandoned the Stanegate was strengthened by additional forts, at Old Church near Brampton and Carvoran which may be earlier than the other forts, since it lies at the junction between the Roman road known as the Maiden Way and the Stanegate.[47] Carvoran is close to the line later occupied by Hadrian's Wall, but it is excluded from the Wall by the ditch to the south of the Wall, known as the Vallum. At Burgh-by-Sands four miles to the north-west of Carlisle there are at least three different forts, two of them to the south of Hadrian's Wall, labelled Burgh I and Burgh III, and one lying on the line of the Wall, labelled Burgh II. The area forms a key site on the Stanegate.[48] On the site of Burgh I a timber watchtower with a circular ditch was occupied for a short time, then it was levelled and a two-phase fort was built, one a large fort of about seven acres, and a smaller fort of just over three and a half acres, but the chronology is not certain, so the fort could have been reduced to three and a half acres or vice versa it could have started as a small fort that was later enlarged. Jones and Woolliscroft consider that the large fort was the first and it was later reduced in size.[49] Since the modern village is located half way between Stanwix and Bowness, it is expected that there was a Wall fort.[50] In fact there was a Wall fort, as stated above, in the form of Burgh II, which was built to the north of Burgh I on the line of the Wall, but there are complications, because this fort was probably not Hadrianic in date, and was probably not built until the 160s.[51] The sequence of the forts at Burgh-by-Sands is not yet clear. Burgh I and Burgh III may have been occupied consecutively, and one of them may well belong to the Stanegate, or alternatively to the first scheme for Hadrian's Wall.[52] A possible chronology was proposed in 2009, that Burgh I is the Hadrianic fort, Burgh II was built *c.* 160 when the Hadrianic frontier, which was initially built of turf in this area, was rebuilt in stone, and Burgh III may have been a camp, or an early fort built before the Hadrianic era.[53] As always, when evidence is lacking, theories abound.

Near the western coast, a Roman site at Kirkbride had been known for some time, probably belonging to the late first century, but yielding finds of early second-century date. It was assumed that there would have been a fort somewhere in the vicinity at the western terminus of the Stanegate, where there may have been a port on the River Wampool. The search area was so large that even though excavation showed that there was definitely a fort on the site it did not prove easy to discover its layout or its size. Aerial photography in 1976, a particularly hot dry year, revealed the roads inside the fort and from then onwards it was possible to discover more about it.[54]

Fortlets have also come to light on the Stanegate, one at Haltwhistle Burn between Carvoran and Vindolanda, and the other at Throp between Carvoran and Nether Denton. These have been excavated, and another possible fortlet has been discovered by aerial photography at Castle Hill, Boothby.[55]

Watchtowers were probably part of the system. A tower is known at Pike Hill, predating Hadrian's Wall, but incorporated into the Wall, angled at 45 degrees rather than square-on. Pike Hill is oriented to face Nether Denton to the south-east, and Robin Hood's Butt at Gillalees to the north-east, suggesting that it could communicate with both sites.[56] Another pre-Hadrianic tower was built inside an old British hillfort on Barcombe Hill above Vindolanda, with a clear view to the north that was not obtainable from the fort itself. A second tower, stone-built, was built on a different part of the same hill affording a view to the south. Both towers may have operated simultaneously. Other towers are known at Mains Rigg and Birdoswald.[57] The towers so far discovered are unlikely to have operated in isolation, and it is assumed that there are more towers which have not been found, sited where uninterrupted views of the country could be obtained, and probably not limited to areas to the north of the Stanegate. The towers were presumably intended to watch for unauthorised movement, and having observed such occurrences, would then communicate with the forts, by signals of some kind, using smoke, fire, flag, trumpet, or by sending messengers. The topic of Roman military signalling is covered by D. J. Woolliscroft.[58]

It has been suggested that there may have been a regular pattern of Stanegate forts interspersed with smaller forts and towers, though as already mentioned in connection with the Gask towers, the rigid spacing postulated by archaeologists may not have been adopted by the Romans, who most likely sited their military installations where river crossings and other features demanded surveillance.

There are controversial questions about the Stanegate system, not the least being whether or not it functioned as a frontier, which is more fully discussed in chapter three. Another question is whether it ran from the west to the east coast. It has been unequivocally traced only as far as Carlisle in the west and Corbridge in the east. These sites were founded in the early Flavian period, on the principal north-south routes on the west and east sides of the country. In recent years traces of a road have been discovered from the air, running from Carlisle to the western coast. The earliest fort at Burgh-by-Sands and another fort at Kirkbride, a short distance inland from the Solway estuary, are considered to belong to this western section of the Stanegate.[59] North of the road from Carlisle to Kirkbride there are traces of a road and a ditch with a palisade in front of it.[60] A palisade is difficult to date, and in any case it may not be a military installation; it could have fulfilled an agricultural purpose, possibly of the pre-Roman Iron Age. However it is conceded that the palisade could have been erected to protect the road linking Carlisle, the first fort at Burgh-by-Sands and Kirkbride.[61] Breeze and Dobson, writing before the full report on the road and palisade was produced, are cautious in linking this road to the Stanegate.[62] In the east, a possible fort discovered from the air at Washing Wells near Whickham in County Durham has been claimed as a continuation of the Stanegate road system, but it is admitted that apart from this somewhat doubtful site there still is a dearth of Roman sites east of Corbridge. There is a road running east from Corbridge but this may be later than the establishment of the Stanegate line, possibly linked to the Wall.[63] In the eastern sector, there may be sites which have been ploughed out or destroyed and hidden by industrial premises.

It seems that after c. 105 there were no forts to the north of the Stanegate, serving as outposts like those of Hadrian's Wall, though this is a premise that could be overturned by the discovery of new evidence indicating that more northerly sites were indeed occupied. In the Vindolanda writing tablets, there is mention of the fort at High Rochester (Bremenium), but the reference is dated to the second half of the second century, when it was occupied as an outpost to Hadrian's Wall, so it cannot be said that it served as an outpost to the Stanegate forts in 105.[64]

The authorisation for the withdrawal of Roman troops to this line would have originated with the Emperor himself, via the governor of Britain. The years between the formation of this Stanegate line or boundary in 105 and the building of Hadrian's Wall in the 120s are more or less blank. There was probably not a complete stasis. The minutiae of daily life can be found in the writing tablets from Vindolanda, which illustrate that this most northerly area of the province was considered safe enough for officers to bring their families to the forts, that correspondence between friends in different units was sent and received, there was concern over transport difficulties and the state of the roads, and records of personnel and finances were regularly drawn up and filed.

For the Britons, life was perhaps not so good. Government was carried out by the military, as implied by the presence of Annius Equester, as *centurio regionarius* at Carlisle, in the early years of Trajan's reign, *c.* 103. At a later period two other centurions in charge of a region were based at Ribchester. No source elucidates the responsibilities of a centurion acting as *regionarius*, but it is likely that they were responsible for law and order among the civilian population. Judging from the oft-quoted reference to the derogatory term '*Brittunculi*' for Britons in the Vindolanda tablets, the local Britons were regarded with contempt, so if any of them caused trouble it is likely that the *centurio regionarius* would be responsible for their punishment. In the context of the Vindolanda tablets, the *Brittunculi* may have been recruits for the army, and the derogatory term might be a typical officer's opinion of their performance in training.[65] It is known that Britons were recruited into the Roman army from an early date; there were British tribesmen in Agricola's army at Mons Graupius. In the Trajanic era, there may have been a determined recruitment drive to strengthen the frontiers in other provinces, which would also have served the secondary purpose of removing potential troublemakers from their homelands. The small units called *numeri Brittonum* attested on the German frontier in the Odenwald may have been assembled when the withdrawal from Scotland took place and the

Stanegate became the northernmost boundary.[66] These small units are not fully attested in Germany until the Antonine era, but it is likely that they arrived at their small Odenwald forts under Trajan. The process would have rounded off the reorganisation in northern England and served to protect the German frontier while the armies fought in Dacia.

There is support for such a postulated recruitment drive derived from the census carried out by Titus Haterius Nepos, among the Anavionenses of modern Annandale. This was probably at the end of the first century or at the beginning of the second, though the date is not certain.[67] The tribe of the Anavionenses is also mentioned in the Vindolanda tablets, and the dating evidence from the tablets suggests that Haterius Nepos' activities as *censitor* belong to the 90s, which would mean that he was working some years before the Romans abandoned the lands north of the Stanegate *c.* 105.[68]

War in Britain at Hadrian's Accession?

During the Agricolan conquest and the short occupation of Scotland, the Romans would have learned a lot about the country and the tribes who inhabited it. The topography would have been familiar to them, the potential ports and harbours would have been surveyed; routes, if not properly paved roads, would have been established linking the forts; tribal society and organisation would have been observed, possibly some treaties would have been made with friendly tribes, and hostile ones carefully watched. It is generally agreed that the Votadini in the east were friendly to Rome, largely on account of the quantity of Roman goods found in their territory, beginning with pottery of Flavian date. Some of the artefacts may have arrived as gifts to the Votadini, as was customary when Rome supported friendly kings, and some may have arrived as the result of trading activities. There is a corresponding lack of Roman forts in the lands of the Votadini, indicating that there was no need to be on the alert for potential trouble. Conversely the Selgovae and the Novantae further west are seen as more hostile to the Romans, so the siting of the fort at Newstead, in the immediate vicinity of the stronghold of the Selgovae on the most northerly of the Eildon hills, implies a need for constant watching and policing of this tribe.

The brief occupation of Scotland under Agricola and his successors probably did not allow enough time for pacification of the tribes, and though Agricola may have taken hostages from some tribes and made treaties with others, the nature of the relationship between Romans and natives is not known. The forts at the glen mouths and on the routes in the Lowlands presumably served to keep the peace, and when the Romans ceased to occupy the lands north of the Tyne-Solway by *c.* 105, it is likely that control and influence did not cease abruptly at the boundary line. There were probably patrols in force to watch over native activities, aided by the watchtowers, but without forts in their territory the Britons may have seen an opportunity to discard whatever arrangements had been made with the Romans and rebel against their control. It seems that there was serious trouble in Britain under Hadrian, possibly breaking out just after his accession, or at any rate between the death of Trajan in 117 and the arrival of Hadrian in 122.

Literary sources drop hints about a war in Britain, but without giving the details that would clarify the date or the location. In the biography of Hadrian in the *Historia Augusta* all the troubles of the Empire at his accession are grouped together in a brief list. The peoples conquered by Trajan had begun to revolt, the Sarmatians across the Danube made war, the Moors in Africa attacked, there were riots in Egypt, Libya and Palestine, and the Britons could not be held under Roman control (*Britanni teneri sub Romana dicione non poterant*).[69] There always seemed to be trouble in Britain at the beginning of the reigns of several Emperors, so it is possible to dismiss as merely conventional the statement about the unruly Britons, but another more reliable literary source also mentions warfare in Britain under Hadrian. During the wars of Marcus Aurelius in the later second century, the Emperor's tutor and friend Cornelius Fronto tried to console the Emperor for the great losses in the army, referring to the large numbers of soldiers who had been killed by the Jews and the Britons in Hadrian's reign.[70] Fronto was not given to the sort of sensationalism that the author of the *Historia Augusta* indulged in, and also the events under Hadrian were still within living memory in Marcus' reign, so it would seem that there was definitely a costly war in Britain.

Corroborative evidence derives from epigraphic sources. Two inscriptions recording the careers of soldiers show that there was a British expedition, most probably in Hadrian's reign. One of these inscriptions reveals that reinforcements consisting of vexillations of 1,000 men from each of three different legions, VII *Gemina* based in Spain, and VIII *Augusta* and XXII *Primigenia* in Upper Germany, were brought into Britain under the command of Titus Pontius Sabinus. This man had been *primus pilus*, or chief centurion, of III *Augusta*, and was sent to Britain as *praepositus* commanding the vexillations in an *expeditio Brittannica (sic)*. He was an important officer who had probably already come to the notice of the Emperor, and he went on to serve in Rome as an officer in the *Vigiles* who were part firemen and part police, the Urban Cohorts and the Praetorian Guard.[71] It is not known if the legionaries were brought in to take part in the fighting, or to fill the gaps in the legions of Britain after the war had been concluded. Either of these scenarios, involving large numbers of men under a distinguished officer, indicates a disaster of some considerable proportions. But there is no firm date for the expedition.

The other inscription mentioning Hadrianic operations in Britain shows that an officer called Marcus Maenius Agrippa was chosen by the divine Hadrian as tribune of *cohors I Hispanorum*, and sent on a British expedition (*misso in expeditonem Britannicam*).[72] This does not necessarily involve fighting, since it is just possible that Maenius Agrippa, described in the first part of the inscription as a host of Hadrian, may have accompanied the Emperor to Britain in 122, but more usually an *expeditio* does refer to a military operation, not a visit. It is tempting to relate Agrippa's expedition to that of Pontius Sabinus and his vexillations, and since Agrippa was listed as commander of an auxiliary unit he may have been sent to assist in a war. He served in Britain in several posts, as commander at the fort at Maryport, then as Prefect of the Fleet, and as procurator.[73]

According to an inscription from Vindolanda, Titus Annius, a centurion in a unit of Tungrians, had been killed in a war. Without firm dating evidence the death of this soldier cannot be unequivocally attributed to a war under Hadrian, nor does the inscription prove that the fighting took place around the Tyne-Solway gap, but it does attest to the fact that the Britons could not be kept under control and the Romans did sustain casualties.[74] There may have been resentment because of the recruitment policies of the Romans, who removed potentially troublesome young men from the province and sent them to another province where they could guard the boundaries and protect routes. The activities of the *censitor* among the Anavionenses, referred to above, may have been part of a recruitment drive, and as a cause of revolt, the derogatory description of the Britons as *Brittunculi* may indicate that the British tribesmen were roughly treated as well as despised.[75] There is also a tendency for rebellions to occur when a second generation of young men, who saw their parents subjugated, decide that they can do better. In the first two decades of the second century there would be a supply of aspiring warriors who probably considered that the Roman withdrawal from Scotland signified a grand opportunity to take back what was theirs.

It is not known who was governor of Britain when Trajan died and Hadrian succeeded him in 117. Probably in 118 Hadrian appointed Pompeius Falco, who had governed Lower Moesia from about 116 or possibly earlier. Hadrian visited Moesia in 118 and it seems that he may have made Falco governor of Britain at this time. Falco's career is well illustrated in other provinces, but details of his activities in Britain are not so well attested.[76] Falco was presumably responsible for restoring order. The war was over by 122 when Hadrian visited, and the restoration of the province is recorded on a fragmentary inscription, two sections of which were found in the eighteenth century, built into the Saxon church at Jarrow. The first part of Hadrian's name is found on one of the pieces, and the word *diffusis*, meaning dispersed or scattered, appears in full on the other fragment. Much of the rest of the inscription is restored by modern scholars, but it appears to refer to an enemy being defeated and dispersed, and it records the building of the Wall from coast to coast.[77] The victory over the Britons may be commemorated on coins, showing the personification of Britannia seated, with her right hand held up to her chin in contemplative mode. Opinion differs as to whether the portrait is meant to convey subjection and unhappiness, or alert contentment.[78]

The evidence that has been assembled to support this British unrest seems at first sight to be interrelated and conclusive, but the literary and epigraphic sources do not provide firm dates for the event or events, and no real clues as to where any fighting may have broken out. It is usually assumed that the focus was in the north of England or in southern Scotland, but no tribes are named in the sources, so the fighting could have been in the regions further south of the Tyne-Solway gap. The sources do not enumerate any causes for the trouble. War could have broken out perhaps because the Britons considered that whatever agreements they may have made with Trajan were null and void when Hadrian succeeded him. Tribesmen were accustomed to make alliances or treaties with a ruler, not a state. The trouble may not have been directed against the Romans to begin with. There may have been intertribal warfare, or an incident similar to the Brigantian rebellion against Cartimandua when the Romans had to intervene.

In 122, after visiting the German provinces, Hadrian arrived in Britain, bringing with him another legion, *VI Victrix*. He probably arrived together with the new governor, Aulus Platorius Nepos, previously governor of Lower Germany, where *VI Victrix* had been stationed. This legion was eventually based at the fortress at York, previously the headquarters of *IX Hispana*. The demise of *IX Hispana* used to be linked to some disturbance in Britain, because it seemed to disappear from the record around the end of the first century, so the legend grew that it marched off into a Scottish mist, never to be seen again. It is a good story, as told by Rosemary Sutcliffe, but not true. The legion is last attested at York in 108, where an inscription records the rebuilding of one of the gates of the fortress.[79] It is thought that the legion or part of it went to Lower Germany. It was still in existence in 121 when Aninius Sextius Florentinus was its legate. There are still conflicting theories about the legion's ultimate fate. It may have been annihilated in the Jewish revolt which began in 132, or alternatively it may have been badly mauled in the Parthian war under Marcus Aurelius and Lucius Verus in the 160s.[80]

Hadrian had obviously devoted some time and thought to how to deal with the problem of Britain, which seemed to be subject to endemic unrest in the north, where there may have been fierce fighting. Before he came to Britain he made new arrangements for the protection of the borders of Upper and Lower Germany and Raetia, where rivers did not form the boundary. The *Historia Augusta* does not mention this work in the description of Hadrian's visit to Germany, but in a later passage he groups together all the frontier works, describing how Hadrian closed off the tribes by means of stakes driven into the ground and held together to form a sort of wall.[81] The archaeological evidence from excavations of the frontier palisade in Germany does not always corroborate a Hadrianic foundation, but the timbers would need repair from time to time in the reigns of successive Emperors, making it seem to early archaeologists that these later Emperors had built the fortifications. In Britain it was once thought that the Wall belonged to the reign of Severus, because this Emperor had repaired it so extensively. The Hadrianic frontier in the German provinces was a new idea, an improvement on the borders marked by a road and watchtowers, but controversial in its time because of its implication that the era of territorial advance was over. Arriving in Britain, Hadrian determined to carry out a similar project, and according to the *Historia Augusta* he was the first to build a wall 80 miles long to separate the Romans from the barbarians.[82]

2

The Man Who Put Hadrian into Hadrian's Wall

Hadrian's full name, Publius Aelius Hadrianus, shows that he stemmed from the clan of the Aelii, whose original homeland was at Hadria on the Italian east coast, but Hadrian's immediate ancestors were Italians who had settled in Spain, in the province of Baetica. Their home town was Italica, now known as Santiponce, not far from Seville. The town was founded on the site of a native settlement by Publius Cornelius Scipio in 206 BC, during the war against Hannibal.[1] Scipio would take the name Africanus after he took the war to Africa and defeated Hannibal and the Carthaginians at Zama in 202 BC. Italica was established to house wounded soldiers after the battles against the Carthaginians in Spain, and the men would be Italians from the allied armies rather than Roman citizens. The member or members of the Aelii who had fought in Scipio's army founded a branch of their clan in Spain, becoming wealthy from their lands in Baetica, and eventually reaching senatorial status in the first century BC, when more and more provincials, especially from southern Gaul and from the province of Baetica were gaining entry to the Roman Senate. Hadrian's great-great-great grandfather, Marullinus, was the first Aelius to become a senator. By the time of Hadrian's birth, the Aelii were established Roman citizens with roles to play in the government of the Empire.

The Young Hadrian

Hadrian was born on 24 January 76, in the reign of Vespasian. In the *Historia Augusta*, the lives of the Emperors written probably in the fourth century, it is stated that Hadrian was born in Rome. This was once disputed by modern scholars because in the same biography Hadrian is said to have *returned* to Italica, his native city, when he was in his fifteenth year, implying that he had been born there, then moved with his family to Rome as a child, and returned to Italica as a youth.[2] Since senatorial families were expected to live in Rome, and the Aelii had achieved senatorial status long before Hadrian's birth, it is now thought that the passage in the *Historia Augusta* is correct, and Hadrian was indeed born in Rome.

Hadrian's father was Aelius Hadrianus Afer, who married Domitia Paulina, whose ancestors also came from the ancient city of Gades, modern Cadiz. Hadrianus Afer died when Hadrian was ten years old, and Hadrian became the ward of his relative Marcus Ulpius Traianus, who was later to become the Emperor Trajan, though at the time of Afer's death Trajan was only of praetorian rank.[3] Hadrian's grandfather had married Trajan's aunt, the sister of his father the elder Trajan, who had commanded a legion, *X Fretensis*, stationed in Judaea in 66 when Vespasian began his Jewish campaign. This ended in 70, when Vespasian's son Titus took over the command. The siege of Masada and the destruction of the temple in Jerusalem belong to this final phase of the war. In 69 when Vespasian was declared Emperor, the elder Trajan's loyalty was rewarded. He was made governor of Syria *c.* 75, an important post which indicates the good opinion and the favour of the Emperor. The future Emperor Trajan served under his father in the army as a military tribune. By the time that Hadrian was made his ward, *c.* 86, in the reign of Domitian, Trajan had gained military experience, and was legate of *VII Gemina* in 89, based in Spain. In that year, the commander of the army of Upper Germany, Antonius Saturninus, rebelled against Domitian, backed by at least four legions. In order to finance this venture, Saturninus had seized all the cash in the strongrooms of the legionary fortresses, including the soldier's savings. Trajan ordered his legion to march from Spain to the Rhine in support of Domitian, but by the time he arrived in Germany the revolt had already been put down by the governors of Lower Germany and Raetia.

Although he had not taken part in the fighting, the march from Spain cannot have done Trajan any harm, since he was made *consul ordinarius* in 91. Though there were only two consuls in power at any one time during the Empire, the consulship had undergone a change from the Republican era. In the early days the two consuls were elected by the people, but under the Emperors, from Augustus' reign onwards, the powers of the electorate were severely truncated and elections gave way to Imperial recommendation. The consulship was from then onwards in the gift of the Emperor, and the office was stripped of its automatic right to supreme military power, or *imperium*. This was now reserved for Emperors, who could delegate such power to military commanders. Two kinds of consulship evolved. There was still considerable honour in holding a consulship, but in order to provide administrative experience for a greater number of aspiring senators, the suffect consulship had been instituted. The two *consules ordinarii* took up their appointments before the others, giving their names to the year and remaining in office for one or more months, then they stepped down and the *consules suffecti* took up their appointments, holding the office for another short period. There was ostensibly no limit to the number of suffect consuls who could be rushed through the administrative training period, which is what the office had become; in 190, when Septimius Severus first reached the consulship, there were no less than twenty-four other consuls sharing the office in succession, which indicates that none of the men can have gained more than a month's experience. The practice did at least create enough men with the proper rank and some experience, so that they could then go on to the burgeoning number of further appointments necessitated by Imperial government of the Empire.

The appointment as *consul ordinarius* was a signal honour for Trajan. Usually this office was granted only to members of the extended family of the Emperor, and all other candidates would be granted a suffect consulship. According to the *Historia Augusta*, around this time Hadrian went to Italica in his fifteenth year, but was recalled by Trajan because he was too fond of hunting in preference to his duties.[4] It may be supposed that Hadrian's fifteenth year meant that he was only fourteen when he went to

Italica, but according to Roman standards, he could already have entered manhood at this age, in a formal ceremony in which he exchanged the *toga praetexta* worn by boys for the *toga virilis*, which marked him as an adult. Probably just after Trajan had learned that he was to be consul in 91, he may have travelled to Italica to collect Hadrian and then returned to Rome.[5] The *Historia Augusta* goes on to say that from this time onwards, Trajan treated Hadrian as his own son, and not long afterwards, Hadrian embarked on the lower rungs of a political and military career, entering one of the junior offices known as the *vigintivirate*, literally meaning twenty young men who filled the posts in four magisterial boards (originally six in the Republic) which were responsible for some policing functions, minting of coins and keeping the streets of Rome in order. The most important of these boards was the *decemviri stlitibus iudicandis*, the court dealing with disputed inheritances. Hadrian was appointed one of the ten judges in this court.[6] This may have been early in 94, when Hadrian was about eighteen years old.[7]

In the *Historia Augusta*, only the highlights of Hadrian's early career are presented, moving quickly on from the appointment to the inheritance court to military tribune of *II Adiutrix*.[8] The gap in knowledge is filled by information from an inscription dedicated to Hadrian in Athens in 112. The text omits the appointment to the inheritance court, but shows that Hadrian was *praefectus feriarum Latinarum*.[9] Though the year is not mentioned, it was probably in the early summer of 94.[10] The festival of the *feriae latinae* was a very ancient Roman tradition, so old by the Imperial era that its origins were partly obscured. During their very early history the Romans had conquered the rival city of Alba Longa, and still celebrated the event during the Empire. Every year, in early summer, all the magistrates, including the tribunes of the plebs, left Rome to conduct the ceremonials on the Alban Mount, though the exact location of the ancient city of Alba was not precisely known. Its memory is preserved in the modern name Albano, where Domitian built a huge villa, later converted into Castel Gandolfo, the summer residence of the popes. While the magistrates were absent, the priests took over the functions of the consuls, and a prefect was appointed to oversee public order in the city for the few days of the ceremony. In the early Empire, the office was still called *praefectus urbi* or prefect of the city, but from the reign of Tiberius when the permanent city prefect was established, the title was changed to the more specific *praefectus feriarum Latinarum*. The post was usually awarded to promising young men, who for a short time would become the head of government in charge of legal proceedings. The young men who were chosen were marked out for future promotions. One of the most famous before Hadrian was Gaius Octavius, the future Augustus, appointed at the age of sixteen by his great-uncle Gaius Julius Caesar.

Hadrian's next appointment, detailed on the Athens inscription, was *sevir turmae equitum Romanorum* which probably dates to July 94.[11] There were six *seviri*, each commanding a squadron or *turma* of Roman equites or knights, men of the middle class. In keeping with their ancient name originally meaning horsemen, the young men rode through the city of Rome in an annual parade. The *sevir* in command of each *turma* was usually a young man who had not yet entered the Senate but who aspired to senatorial status, or in some cases had only just achieved it. Hadrian was not yet a senator, but he could look forward to a senatorial career under the guidance of his kinsman Trajan.

In the Roman world administrative and military careers were inextricably intertwined, and most but not all young men who aspired to fame and fortune served as military tribunes in a legion for variable lengths of time. From Republican times there were six of these posts in a legion, one reserved for youths of senatorial status, but not yet members of the Senate. These were described as *tribuni laticlavii*, from the broad stripe on their clothing. The senatorial tribune was nominally second in command after the legionary legate, though the young men who filled these posts had little military experience. After the single senatorial tribune, there were five equestrian tribunes in each legion. These tribunes wore a narrow stripe, and were known as *tribuni angusticlavii*. These young men had more military experience than the senatorial tribunes, usually having commanded a unit of auxiliaries before becoming legionary tribunes.

Hadrian's first taste of legionary life was as *tribunus laticlavius* in *II Adiutrix* in Pannonia. This legion is named in the *Historia Augusta*, but although Hadrian served as tribune on two further occasions, the biography simply mentions the provinces where he served without naming the legions.[12] Pannonia was still a single province at this time, but was divided into two after Trajan's Dacian wars, probably in 106. It is suggested that Trajan was governor of Pannonia, and had appointed Hadrian himself. This was in accordance with Roman practice, since governors regularly put their relatives and friends into various administrative and military posts.[13] Pannonia was bordered on the north and east by the Danube, and the tribes on the other side of the river were not friendly to Rome. Further east, in the Danube province of Moesia, the hostile Dacians had crossed the river and defeated the Romans during Hadrian's youth. The Emperor Domitian lost two armies to the powerful Dacians, but in 88 he won a battle inside Dacian territory, but he had not won the war. He had made terms which the Romans considered far too advantageous to the Dacians, and it was clear that he would have to wage war on the Danube again when he had attended to other problems in the Empire. He was assembling another army for the Dacian war when he was killed in 96, but he had conducted two campaigns in Pannonia, the second one in 92.

II Adiutrix was originally assembled in 70 from men of the Ravenna fleet, just after the civil wars that brought Vespasian to power. On the Rhine, the Batavians who had been recruited as auxiliary soldiers took advantage of the chaos to rebel against Rome, led by their chief Julius Civilis, who had served in the Roman army leading an auxiliary unit, and had been granted Roman citizenship. *II Adiutrix* served with other legions under Petillius Cerialis to quell the revolt, and then in 71 Cerialis was made governor of Britain and took the new legion with him. It remained in Britain until 85, when a detachment was sent to the Danube during the Dacian wars of Domitian. Probably in 86 the rest of the legion followed, and took part on the final battle of 88 that put a temporary end to the wars.[14] It was based at Sirmium (Sremska Mitrovica) which during the Dacian wars was attached to the Moesian provinces, until after Trajan's final victory and then returned to Pannonia, based at Aquincum (Budapest) where the fortress was built on the site of an auxiliary fort in Domitian's reign. The date when *II Adiutrix* arrived there is disputed, which means that it is not certain that Hadrian's first post as tribune was at Aquincum. According to some authors *II Adiutrix* was already there by 89 and may have built the fortress, but some authors have dated its occupation of the fortress to 106 when the Dacian wars ended and Pannonia was divided into two provinces.[15]

In 95 when Hadrian joined the legion, it was probably at Aquincum. The equestrian tribunes would have been able to help him with his duties if they were well disposed towards him, but they would have served only for a relatively short time, and would not be able to tell him much about the past activities of the legion. The centurions and the soldiers would remember the campaigns. Legionaries served for twenty years and then four as reserves, so some of the men would even be able to recall events in Britain, and more of them would know about the Dacian wars. Since Hadrian had a reputation for being able to engage ordinary people in conversation he may have learned about battles, and about other places, from some of the soldiers and centurions. With no military experience of his own, like most of the tribunes he would probably have embarked on a steep learning curve about the legions and their administration in peace and war. He may have read military manuals that outlined the basics but there was no training school in the Roman army to prepare for military command. Young men were expected to know how to be soldiers and how armies worked. There is no surviving information about how Hadrian performed in his first military post.

At some date before 96 Hadrian was sent to Lower Moesia. The large province of Moesia had been split into Upper and Lower provinces by Domitian in 85 or 86, at the beginning of the Dacian wars, and in 96 the two provinces were still under threat from the Dacians. No specific post is mentioned in the *Historia Augusta*, but the inscription from Athens dated to 112 omits the province and names the post as tribune of *V Macedonica*.[16] This legion is attested at Oescus on the Danube. There was probably no gap between the two appointments, and Hadrian may have moved from Pannonia because another tribune had been appointed under a fresh governor.[17] This was probably in the summer of 96, which means that Hadrian had not served for a full twelve months with *II Adiutrix*, but he would have made the acquaintance of a few men whom he would remember well. Birley suggests that one of these new friends was Quintus Marcius Turbo, attested one an inscription as a centurion of *II Adiutrix* at Aquincum. He was Praetorian Prefect for fifteen years during the reign of Hadrian.[18]

Hadrian's tenure as military tribune of *V Macedonica* is not described in any extant source. He could not have been in post for very long before news arrived of Domitian's assassination. The Senate chose the elderly Marcus Cocceius Nerva as Emperor. He reigned for only two years. He faced financial difficulties, and even more seriously, trouble with the army, because the soldiers had been well-treated by Domitian, who was the first Emperor to give them a pay rise. The rates had been set by Julius Caesar and ratified by Augustus at the end of the Republic, and had remained the same for over a hundred years, until Domitian raised pay by one third, probably in 82 or 83. Had he not done so, it may have been more difficult to persuade the soldiers to fight and die for him in the Dacian wars. As part of his policy to pacify the army and its officers, Nerva had a quick reshuffle of military commanders and provincial governors. One of the men who profited was Trajan, who was made governor of Upper Germany. He profited again about a year after the assassination of Domitian, when the Praetorians rebelled against Nerva. They had also been treated well by Domitian, and were resentful because the assassins had not been punished. Nerva was not a military man, and he had no sons. It was clear that his hold on power was shaky without military support, and in an effort to gain it he appointed Trajan as his heir in 97. Trajan had a good reputation, as commander of a legion in Spain, and as governor of the frontier province of Pannonia. He had managed to appear neither opposed to Domitian, which would have offended the army, nor completely in Domitian's pocket, which would have offended the Senate. He was to be *consul ordinarius* for the second time in 98.

On hearing this news, Hadrian was the natural choice of emissary from the troops in Lower Moesia to make the journey to congratulate Trajan. He never returned to *V Macedonica*, but was made tribune of *XXII Primigenia* at Moguntiacum (modern Mainz) in Upper Germany. Julius Servianus, married to Paulina, Hadrian's sister, became governor in place of Trajan. Servianus and Hadrian did not get on well, largely because Servianus reported to Trajan about Hadrian's alleged bad behaviour.

Although it was not unknown for young men to serve for an

extended period as military tribune, as Trajan himself had done, it was unusual to serve in three different legions, as Hadrian did.[19] His total term of service was less than three years, and if Nerva had not adopted Trajan, Hadrian may well have stayed with V *Macedonica*, and then gone on to different administrative and military appointments. As it turned out, Trajan presumably wanted to place his kinsman in positions close to him, but without initially promoting him to a higher command, for which he was presumably not yet considered ready.

In January 98 Nerva died, and the accession of Trajan was assured and uncontested. The messengers from Rome will have reached Mainz more quickly than Cologne, and although the prerogative of informing Trajan really belonged to Servianus, Hadrian raced ahead, possibly accompanied by slaves and a few friends. The *Historia Augusta* reports that Servianus sabotaged Hadrian's carriage, but the story goes that Hadrian abandoned his carriage, completed the journey on foot, and still arrived at Trajan's headquarters before the messenger sent by Servianus.[20]

Hadrian under the Emperor Trajan

The relationship between Trajan and Hadrian improved from this time onwards, facilitated through the agency of Lucius Licinius Sura, according to the *Historia Augusta*.[21] Sura was a close associate of Trajan, and was presumably with him, or arrived shortly after the news arrived that Nerva had designated Trajan as his heir and successor. He was instrumental in persuading the supposedly reluctant Trajan to accept the situation. Precisely how Sura brought Trajan and Hadrian closer together is not elucidated. The bond was strengthened by marriage ties, probably in 100, when Hadrian married Vibia Sabina, who was Trajan's great-niece. Her mother was Matidia, daughter of Trajan's sister Marciana, and her father was Lucius Vibius. If the *Historia Augusta* is correct, quoting the lost work of the author Marius Maximus, it was Plotina who encouraged the marriage, while Trajan had reservations about it.[22] The marriage was not a success. Hadrian's homosexual tendencies were probably already apparent, and according to gossip around the court and in Rome he had got into trouble with Trajan because of his interest in the handsome boys that Trajan included in his circle of friends.[23]

It is not known for certain if Hadrian accompanied Trajan from the beginning of 98 until the Imperial arrival in Rome towards the end of 99. The new Emperor remained in Germany for a while and then went to the Danube, probably to assess the situation within the provinces and beyond them. On the opposite side of the Danube the Sarmatians and Dacians remained more than simply a perceived threat. Trajan appointed Hadrian's brother-in-law Servianus as governor of Pannonia, one of the more vulnerable provinces, and he may have organised the military establishment according to the increased need for defence, but there is no evidence for this.

Hadrian's subsequent career is outlined only sketchily in the *Historia Augusta*. The years from *c.* 100 to 117 when Hadrian became Emperor are covered in a breathless rush in only two chapters. He was quaestor in 101, firmly dated because it was in the year when Trajan held the consulship for the fourth time.[24] The post of quaestor was usually the next step after the military tribunate, and was normally held by young men in their late twenties, so Hadrian's career was following the customary pattern for his age group. The quaestorship had been established in the fifth century BC, to take charge of financial matters, and the number grew in accordance with the acquisition of territorial provinces, where governors usually chose one of the appointees to take care of the provincial finances. In the early Empire the magistrates each had a quaestor to assist him, and the consuls and the Emperor had two. The *quaestores Caesaris* were personally selected by the Emperor, so it is not surprising that Hadrian was chosen.[25] The Emperor's quaestors were usually patricians, but in Hadrian's case he was not elevated to patrician status by Trajan. The quaestorship did however guarantee his entry to the senate, and his plebeian status enabled him to become tribune of the plebs in 105, since patricians were forbidden to hold this office. The *Historia Augusta* laconically states that after the quaestorship Hadrian was put in charge of the acts of the senate, meaning that he was responsible for the *Acta Senatus*, the records of the debates in the senate and its decisions, a Roman equivalent to Hansard, the record of parliamentary debates in the British government.[26] He held this post for only a short time and then accompanied Trajan to the first Dacian war, on intimate terms with the Emperor. Hadrian's part in the war is not known. He probably did not engage in any of the battles. Birley suggests that he served in his capacity as quaestor, and returned to Rome when the office expired.[27] All that the *Historia Augusta* comments on is that he became the drinking partner of Trajan, whose capacity for wine consumption was already legendary. For this compliance, Hadrian was well rewarded; unfortunately no one can say whether this entailed monetary gain or other marks of favour in return for headaches and hangovers.[28] He may have been made praetor in 105. In the *Historia Augusta* the chronology is somewhat garbled, and the praetorship is placed in sequence after the second Dacian war ending in 106, and just before Hadrian was sent to govern Lower Pannonia, but the text states that Hadrian was praetor in the second consulship of Suburanus and Servianus, which cannot be supported by the historical record. Suburanus and Servianus did serve as consul for a second term, but not in the same year. Servianus' second consulship belongs to 102, and that of Suburanus to 104.[29] Birley favours 104 for the elections, so that Hadrian became praetor in 105, only a little younger than the normal age.[30]

The first Dacian war failed to solve the problems of the Danube region, just as Domitian's first victory was only a stopgap. In 105 Trajan mounted another expedition, and this time Hadrian was made legate of *I Minervia* which had been raised by Domitian, and named in honour of his favourite goddess, Minerva. The legion had been moved from the Rhine to the Danube during the first Dacian war and had remained there as part of the build-up of troops to protect the area. The Rhine now lost its supremacy as the most heavily garrisoned region opposite the warlike German tribes. Though some Romans expected that one day the whole of Germany would be conquered, the Emperors never made the effort to do so, and only a short time after the reign of Hadrian they were not given the opportunity, because the greatest and most perennial threats to the Empire began along the Danube and eastern frontiers.

The activities of Hadrian as legionary legate are not recorded. He still held his office as praetor, according to the Athens inscription, at the same time (*eodem tempore*) as his military post,[31] but he presumably did not perform any of the normal duties of the praetors at Rome while he commanded the legion. In the wars he served with honour and performed great deeds, as mentioned in the *Historia Augusta* but the achievements are not described in detail.[32] On the inscription set up at Athens in 112, it is stated that Hadrian was twice awarded military decorations by Trajan.[33]

So far, Hadrian had reached each appointment at more or less the standard age, and had not been promoted by Trajan beyond the accepted norms of the Roman career pattern. The appointment as legionary legate was a sign of Imperial favour, but it was not an extraordinary promotion for a young man who had served three times as military tribune, as quaestor and as tribune of the plebs. There were no unequivocal signs that Hadrian was marked out for the succession. He had plodded through his career in the normal way, but after the end of the Dacian wars in 106, his promotion began to accelerate slightly. He probably did not return to Rome, but stepped straight from his post as legionary legate to be installed as governor of Lower Pannonia. According to the *Historia Augusta* he kept the Sarmatians under control, and maintained (*tenuit* in Latin) military discipline among the soldiers.[34] The choice of wording indicates that discipline had not lapsed, so he did not have to act the martinet to bring the troops to order. Discipline and watchfulness constitute standard activity for generals and governors, but it is less usual for governors to try to curtail the over-zealous activities of the procurators, principally in collecting the taxes. According to the *Historia Augusta* the procurators had gone beyond the boundaries of their powers, not unusual in the Roman world, but Hadrian tried to curb the procurators. As Emperor he continued in the same vein.[35]

The consulship of 108 was a significant appointment in that Hadrian at thirty-two was well under the normal age for the office by at least ten years, but it was tempered by the fact that it was only a suffect consulship. It is at this point that the *Historia Augusta* inserts the story that during his consulship Hadrian learned from Trajan's friend Licinius Sura that he was to be adopted by the Emperor, and he 'ceased to be an object of contempt and neglect to Trajan's friends' (*contemni desiit ac neglegi*).[36] If this is true, and if it is placed in the correct context, it would be the first hint of an adoption. No official announcement designating Hadrian as successor was made during Trajan's reign, until he was on his deathbed. Unlike Vespasian, who declared unequivocally that his sons were to succeed him, Trajan made no definite statement about who was to become emperor after him. His true opinion about Hadrian remains obscure. He seems to have favoured Julius Servianus, Hadrian's brother-in-law. Trajan once asked his friends at a banquet for ten names of men who would be capable of succeeding him, and then reduced the list to nine names because he already regarded Servianus as a likely candidate. This story derives from Dio, but it is controversial.[37] In the Greek text and the English translation of the Loeb edition, the Emperor who says this is Hadrian, logical in a way because this section of Dio's work deals with Hadrian's reign. Other editions prefer to amend Dio's text to make Trajan the author of this statement about Servianus.[38] Hadrian's familial and social relationship with Servianus seems to have vacillated. He did not get on well with his brother in law in his youth, but according to the *Historia Augusta*, when Hadrian was ill and thought he might die, he first thought of Servianus as his successor, which supports the possibility that Dio really did name Hadrian in the anecdote about the dinner party. Late in his reign Hadrian forced Servianus to commit suicide.[39]

Between 108 when he was consul, and 112 when he was in Athens, nothing is known of Hadrian's movements or activities. In only a few lines, the *Historia Augusta* mentions the consulship, the favourable disposition of Trajan's wife Plotina towards Hadrian, the outbreak of the Parthian war, and Hadrian's accession as Emperor. Athens is not mentioned, though in an earlier passage, it is said that Hadrian immersed himself in Greek studies, to the extent that he earned the nickname 'Graeculus', little Greek, or Greekling.[40] Many Roman youths went to Athens to learn from the resident teachers and philosophers, and to enjoy the opportunities for what moderns would call night life. But for Hadrian, already well versed in Greek literature and history, the city of Athens itself with its imposing architecture may have occupied much of his time. No one knows how he spent his days there, but he presumably behaved appropriately, since he was elected *archon* or chief magistrate of Athens, and just as the *consules ordinarii* at Rome gave their names to the year, so the year 112 in modern reckoning was named for Hadrian in Athens. Birley points out the Greek year started in summer not in January, so Hadrian's term of service as archon could have spanned 111–12.[41] The election as *archon* was far from being simply a routine honour that was granted to all and sundry among high-ranking Roman visitors to Athens, and Hadrian perhaps did not wholly owe his appointment to the fact that he was a relative of the Emperor. A statue of him was placed in the Theatre of Dionysus, with an inscription in Greek explaining that the council and people of Athens honoured him, and another inscription in Latin detailing the civil and military posts that he had held up to 112, which serves to fill the gaps in the historical sources about his early career.[42]

The Parthian war was already brewing in 113, and the campaign began in earnest in 114. The Parthians were having troubles of their own, so the internal discord provided an opportunity to intervene, especially since the Roman nominee for the throne of Armenia had been ousted by Chosroes, one of the three rival Parthian kings. Armenia is often described as a buffer state between Rome and Parthia, but perhaps the term political football might be more accurate. Kings were set up in Armenia with either Roman or Parthian backing, and just as frequently ousted by the rival Empire. Parthian domination of Armenia was a perceived threat to Rome, and vice versa the Parthians regarded Roman domination as a threat to the stability of their western borders. The two Empires fought each other throughout the history of Rome, with varying success. The Romans were often the aggressors, at least until the early third century AD, but though they usually reached and took the Parthian capital at Ctesiphon, the Romans could not hold the territory that they had overrun. Parthian threats were limited to Rome's eastern provinces, and no Parthian king invaded the west and marched to Rome.

The Euphrates was for most of Rome's history the eastern boundary of the Empire. The river did not form an impenetrable barrier, but it generally made a clear demarcation between Rome and Parthia, and later between Rome and the more vigorous Persians who superceded the Parthians. Roman attempts to annexe a large part of Mesopotamia to establish new borders beyond the Euphrates were a mixed blessing. At the turn of the second and third centuries, Severus tried it and created more problems for Rome than he solved. In the late third century it could be said that Diocletian did solve the problem, at least for a time.

There had already been some readjustments in Rome's eastern

provinces before the trouble with Parthia began. In 106 Trajan had annexed the client kingdom of Nabataea, with its principal cites at Bostra and Petra. The reason for the annexation was not necessarily aggressive. There seems to have been no bloodshed or conquest as such. It is suggested that the Nabataean king Rabbel II may have died, and it had become customary for the Romans to annexe territory when the client king expired.[43] Trajan reorganised the territory as the new, very large, province of Arabia, not to be confused with the modern Arabia which occupies a larger area than the Roman version. Roman Arabia comprised the Negev desert, Transjordan and the northern part of modern Arabia. A legion was eventually based at Bostra. The first governor, Gaius Claudius Severus, remained in post from 106 through the Parthian wars. The annexation of the Nabataean territories gave the Romans even better access to the Red Sea and the trade between Egypt and India, though the Roman navy had already assured such contact by patrolling the coasts. As preparation for the Parthian campaign, Trajan made more changes. He placed Syria, a key province, under a trusted man as governor. This was Quadratus Bassus, who had governed Cappadocia-Galatia for some time. Though there were several military units already in the east, extra troops were assembled for the campaigns, many of them from the Danube provinces, and on the important route from the Danube to the east, a senior consular governor had been placed in command of Bithynia-Pontus. The appointment of a consular governor raised the status of the province, which was formerly senatorial, not imperial, with the governors appointed by lot for one year only, taking the title of proconsul even though many of them had only reached the lower office of praetor. The younger Pliny had been governor there but had died in post at an unknown date.[44]

At the end of 113, Trajan arrived in Athens, and set off for the east with Hadrian in his entourage, establishing his headquarters at Antioch. According to the *Historia Augusta*, Hadrian was appointed as *legatus* of the Emperor, owing to the influence of Plotina.[45] It is not absolutely certain what this entailed for Hadrian, since the title *legatus* literally means a person to whom some task has been delegated. It is not likely that Hadrian was legate of a legion, and he was not yet governor of Syria. Hadrian was probably attached to Trajan's household and to his staff.

In 114 and 115 Trajan fought battles in Armenia and then attacked Parthia in 116, marching down the Euphrates, eventually arriving at the Persian Gulf. According to Dio, Trajan said that if only he had been younger, he would have made an expedition further east to India, as Alexander the Great had done.[46] Fortunately for the Roman Empire, common sense ruled, and Trajan did not pursue such an ephemeral dream.[47] In Rome the senate began to plan a triumphal arch to celebrate his victories, which seemed to emulate those of Alexander because in his despatches Trajan mentioned peoples and places hitherto unknown to the senators, who did not know how to pronounce some of the names.[48]

Trajan's conquests were not secure. Rebellion broke out almost immediately, while the Emperor was journeying to and from the Persian Gulf. Dio says that almost all the soldiers placed in garrisons in the newly annexed provinces were thrown out or even killed.[49] Trajan had gone to Babylon where the news of the uprising in Mesopotamia reached him. He sent the Moorish general Lusius Quietus with another commander named Maximus to quell the rebellion. Maximus was killed, but Lusius took the city of Nisibis and burned Edessa, while two other Roman commanders burned Seleucia. Trajan pre-empted any reaction by installing a pro-Roman king, Parthamaspates, on the Parthian throne.[50]

Around this time, there was a great rising of the Jewish population in Cyrenaica, Cyprus and Egypt. Dio documents the alleged atrocities and the numbers of people killed.[51] Lusius Quietus features once again. He had rendered sterling service in putting down the rebellion in Mesopotamia, commanding his own units of Moorish cavalry, who were noted for their supreme horsemanship. As a reward in 117 he was made a senator, promoted to suffect consul and sent to govern Judaea.[52]

There remained the rebellious city of Hatra, now a ruined site in Iraq. This desert city was not prosperous like Palmyra, and had meagre supplies of water and timber, but its remoteness and lack of supplies were its best defence. The Romans put it under siege but had to give up, defeated by the summer heat and storms, and flies. One of the defenders shot at Trajan as he was riding around the walls, but missed and killed one of the Emperor's horse guards. The siege was raised.[53] By this time Trajan was ill, and had to abandon any hopes of regaining firm control of Mesopotamia. He set off on the journey back to Rome, and got as far as the city of Selinus in Cilicia in 117, probably during the summer.[54] Hadrian was not with him. He had been designated *consul ordinarius* for 118, and had been made governor of Syria, replacing Julius Quadratus Bassus who had been governor all through the Parthian campaign, and had now been sent to Dacia because war had begun again in the newly acquired territories.

Hadrian as Emperor

Early in August 117 Trajan died, partially paralysed and swollen up with dropsy.[55] Suspicion and controversy now enter the scene, which marred Hadrian's succession and indeed his reign. According to the *Historia Augusta*, Hadrian received the letters of adoption on 9 August, only two days before he received news that Trajan had died.[56] Dio says that Trajan's death was not made public until his wife Plotina, assisted by Caelius Attianus, had secured the adoption of Hadrian, either by persuading Trajan on his deathbed to make the necessary arrangements, or even by forging the documents and writing to Hadrian to inform him that he had been adopted, to ensure the succession. This story, Dio says, derives from his own father Apronianus, who served as governor of Cilicia, where tales were preserved of what went on at Trajan's death. Dio adds more damaging assertions, that the letters of adoption that were sent to the Senate were signed by Plotina and not by Trajan, though she had never been known to do this in previous years.[57] The *Historia Augusta* takes the story to new heights, suggesting that Plotina found a man to impersonate Trajan's voice to persuade anyone trying to speak to the Emperor that he was still alive.[58]

More doubt was cast on Hadrian's succession by rumours. According to the *Historia Augusta* it was believed that Trajan had intended to name Neratius Priscus as his successor, having allegedly said to Priscus that he entrusted the provinces to him in case anything should happen to him.[59] It was also said that like Alexander, Trajan never intended to name anyone who would succeed him. Alternatively some people believed that he had intended to write to the Senate, suggesting that in the event of his death, the senators should choose a successor from an attached list naming several men he considered worthy. If this is true, then he presumably never wrote the letter.

As Dio points out, Hadrian had never been granted any mark of distinction that would have made it clear that Trajan intended him to be his successor.[60] In Dio's work, admittedly fragmentary at this point, there is no mention of Hadrian's activities under Trajan until 117, when he was 'left with the army in Syria' as Trajan prepared to return to Rome.[61]

At his accession, Hadrian was in much the same position as Octavian-Augustus had been after the assassination of his great-uncle Julius Caesar in 44 BC. Octavian, then only Gaius Octavius, had received only a few prestigious appointments owing to his youth, and there had been no firm statement during Caesar's lifetime that he intended to adopt his great-nephew as his son and heir. This intention came to light only when Caesar's will was opened, and even then it was in a codicil, drafted not very long before Caesar's death. One of the main difficulties that Octavian faced was that testamentary adoption, with no previous public statement about the adopter's intentions towards the adoptee, may not have been legal. Octavian had to make two attempts to have the adoption ratified by law. Mark Antony thwarted him the first time, and Octavian succeeded in having the necessary law passed only when he had become consul in 43 BC, still only a teenager, but with troops at his back. From then on he could claim to be Gaius Julius Caesar, never using the name Octavianus by which modern audiences know him, because it signalled his origins among the Octavii and not the Julii Caesares. In Octavian's day at the end of the Republic, it was not possible to bequeath political or military power. Instead he had to fight for both, with the result that he founded the Empire and made it possible for Emperors to inherit such powers along with the family name, lands, property and money, whether the succession was to be secured by natural or adoptive means.

Hadrian would have been aware of the parallel concerning the adoption. He was a dedicated devotee of Octavian-Augustus, and had a bust of Octavian in his bedroom, presented to him by Suetonius Tranquillus, author of the *Twelve Caesars*. Fortunately Hadrian was slightly more secure than Octavian had been, because by this time the Empire was well established, succession by a member of the family had been accepted, and he had the armies behind him. The troops in Syria hailed him as Emperor as soon as they heard that Trajan was dead and that Hadrian was to succeed him as his adopted son. The date when Hadrian was informed of Trajan's death, 11 August, was to be celebrated as his *dies imperii*, the anniversary of his accession. It had become customary to give the soldiers all over the Empire a donative when new Emperors came to power, and Hadrian prudently doubled the usual sum, though the actual amounts are not known. In the third century, failure to provide monetary rewards could be fatal for new Emperors. Presumably Hadrian organised distribution of the cash as quickly as possible, in case someone else tried to buy the loyalty of armies somewhere in the Empire. But although the armies gave him de facto power, only the Senate could officially confer *imperium* on him. The circumstances were unusual because unlike all previous Emperors, Trajan had not died within easy reach of Rome, nor even in Italy. Hadrian could not afford to waste time in sending a message to the Senate and then waiting in Syria, in limbo with no official position, for the Senate's confirmation of his accession to arrive at his headquarters. In his letter to the Senate, according to the *Historia Augusta*, Hadrian asked for confirmation of his powers, apologizing for depriving the senators of their right to decide about his accession. He explained that the soldiers had been somewhat hasty in acclaiming him, because they thought that the Empire should not be without an Emperor during the interval while letters were exchanged.[62] Hadrian also asked for divine honours for Trajan, but he refused honours for himself.[63]

When he was confirmed as Emperor, the ratification of the adoption by Trajan could be taken as read, but to underline it and publicise it to a wider audience, coins were issued with Hadrian on the obverse, and Hadrian and Trajan on the reverse, with hands clasped as though they were sealing some sort of pact, and the legend ADOPTIO at the bottom.[64] Perhaps because of the suspicion and doubt surrounding his own accession, Hadrian made specific arrangements towards the end of his life to ensure that there were two generations to succeed him.

It is clear that there was some opposition to Hadrian as Emperor, but there is not enough evidence to prove that all the men who are named in the ancient sources were acting together. Caelius

Attianus had escorted Plotina and Matidia as they conveyed Trajan's ashes to Rome, and once there he presumably gauged the mood of the senators and the people. He sent a letter warning the new Emperor that he ought to take action against three men, Baebius Macer, prefect of the city, who seemed intent on opposing Hadrian's accession, and Laberius Maximus and Crassus Frugi who had been exiled to separate islands.[65] The latter seems to have been perennially discontented with most rulers, and had allegedly plotted against Nerva. Hadrian does not seem to have taken any overt action, but Crassus Frugi was 'killed while attempting to escape' which may have sounded as hollow in 117 as it does today. Hadrian said he had not ordered such a killing. Laberius and Baebius may have been spared, perhaps with a warning. As Birley points out, Laberius' son-in-law Bruttius Praesens was the governor of Cilicia and was well disposed to Hadrian.[66] The new Emperor had enough to do without finding someone reliable to take over Cilicia at a time when fringes of the Empire were under threat.

More serious was the alleged plot of four senators, probably in 118 and probably headed by Avidius Nigrinus, who was said to have been marked down as Hadrian's successor.[67] The facts are sparse, which means that conjecture is abundant, but the motives, and the relationship of the four senators, are not clear. The others were Palma, Celsus and Lusius Quietus.[68] The last named man was the only one with a personal grievance. As governor of Judaea he had put down the rebellion with tremendous zeal, equalled only by his cruelty. Hadrian removed him from command and sent his famous Moorish cavalry and troops back to Mauretania.[69] The Jews were grateful. The Moors were not. Dio says that Palma and Celsus were accused of conspiring against Hadrian, and that there were certain other complaints against the other two, but he does not mention any trial.[70] In the end they were all killed, Nigrinus, Celsus and Palma in different places in Italy, and Lusius on his way back to Africa. The *Historia Augusta* lays the blame on the senators for the decision to execute the four men.[71] Hadrian insisted that he had not ordered their deaths and included a statement to this effect in his autobiography.[72] The scenario of Henry II of England and the Archbishop Thomas Becket springs to mind. It is alleged that Henry expressed the wish to be rid of Becket, and four knights took it upon themselves to oblige him, but then Henry did public penance, whereas Hadrian did not.

It was not an auspicious beginning to Hadrian's reign. At some unknown date he promised that he would not execute senators without first holding a vote in the Senate. Dio says that he made this promise in a letter, possibly before the deaths of the senators, but this is in a fragmentary passage that may not have been inserted in the correct time slot. The *Historia Augusta* implies that Hadrian was actually in the Senate when he made this promise, implying that this occurred after the four senators had been killed.[73] Fortunately there seems to have been no further incidents like the affair of the four senators. Although Hadrian was quick to take offence and held grudges against people, sometimes falling out with former close friends on a monumental scale, it is not recorded that he had people killed, but towards the end of his reign he forced Servianus to commit suicide.

Before Hadrian left Syria he had to face several problems all at once, as enumerated in the *Historia Augusta* in a laconic passage that prefigures the simultaneous troubles of the third century: the nations conquered by Trajan had begun to revolt, the Moors were in arms in Mauretania, the Sarmatians had started a war on the Danube, the Britons could not be kept under control, Egypt was in turmoil because of riots and rebellion was erupting in Cyrenaica and Judaea.[74] This list makes it seem as though all the troubles had only just occurred, but unrest in the Danube area, and the Jewish revolts in Egypt, North Africa and Judaea were ongoing when Trajan died. In Mauretania, rebellion was probably stirred up by the soldiers of Lusius Quietus who had been sent home from Judaea. Trouble in Britain seems to have constituted a regular feature of any new Emperor's reign, but this time there may have been some serious trouble, which has been discussed in the previous chapter.

The Danube provinces were closer to Rome than either Mauretania or Britain, and occupied Hadrian's full attention as soon as he could leave Syria. He could not hope to hold and pacify the eastern territory that Trajan had annexed while at the same time dealing with the widespread problems in other parts of the Empire, so according to the *Historia Augusta* he relinquished all the new conquests east of the Euphrates and Tigris rivers.[75] This meant that the troops assigned to Mesopotamia and Armenia could be pulled out and sent to endangered provinces. The Roman provinces of the east and their borders with the Parthian Empire were as safe as Hadrian could make them, and he forestalled future trouble for a while by removing the king that Trajan had placed over the Parthians and installing him instead in the smaller territory of Osroene, while the Parthians under the rivals Chosroes and Vologaeses could fight it out over their own Empire for some time. The new Roman governor of Syria was Catilius Severus who met Hadrian at Antioch. Hadrian could now attend to the Danube.

Trajan had sent Julius Quadratus Bassus, who preceded Hadrian as governor of Syria, to take charge of the new province of Dacia, but he died in office. Hadrian may have appointed Avidius Nigrinus in his place as governor of Dacia.[76] In view of the alleged plot and the death of Nigrinus this can only have been a short-lived appointment. In the meantime, having removed Lusius Quietus from Judaea, Hadrian needed a new governor there as well, and he chose Marcius Turbo, who had probably been a centurion in *II Adiutrix* at Aquincum when Hadrian was serving as military tribune, and was favoured by prestigious appointments in Hadrian's reign. After quelling the Jewish rebels in Judaea, Turbo went on to quell yet more rebels in Mauretania, and then was given the command of Lower Pannonia and Dacia.[77] Significantly this meant that both banks of the Danube and the troops stationed on either side were under a unified command. This was an anomalous appointment, not only because it combined two provinces under one governor, but also because it shows Hadrian's high regard for Turbo, who was an equestrian, not a senator, and therefore should not have commanded provincial armies, and certainly ought not to have been put in command of the troops of such a large area comprising two provinces. Some senatorial feathers will have been ruffled by the advancement of this man of a lower social class. But Hadrian chose a soldier he could trust to keep the peace, fitting the qualifications to the requirements of the task in hand. Later in the Empire, equestrian military commanders called *duces* (*dux* in the singular, meaning leader) would evolve with command over the troops of more than one province, mostly on the frontiers, thus obviating the need to coordinate the activities of several military commanders if the trouble affected large areas, or if highly mobile natives, especially on the northern frontiers, carried the war across provincial boundaries.

Hadrian's friends were installed as governors of other important provinces. Lower Moesia and both sides of the lower reaches of the Danube were commanded by Pompeius Falco. Thrace, adjoining the southern borders of Lower Moesia was governed by Aulus Platorius Nepos, who had fought in the Parthian campaign.[78] The chronology of these appointments and of the events around the Danube area is not properly established. After leaving Syria, Hadrian travelled to Moesia and Pannonia, and probably into Dacia, assessing the situation for himself, and most likely conferring with the provincial governors and probably the army commanders as well. His ultimate decisions ran contrary to Roman expectations. The eastern section of Trajan's Dacia was given back to the Sarmatian Roxolani. The lower Danube became the northernmost boundary of the Empire, running from a point between Oescus and Novae to the Black Sea. On the western side the Hungarian plain was also given up, producing a Dacian province like a misshapen bulge north of the Danube and the two Moesian provinces. During the Dacian campaigns, Trajan's architect Apollodorus had built a stone bridge across the Danube, such a marvellous structure in Dio's opinion that he devotes an entire chapter to describing it in the context of Trajan's wars. The bridge was supported by twenty square stone piers, and stood at a considerable height above the river, called the Ister at this point.[79] Dio contrasts Trajan's martial spirit with what he saw as Hadrian's pacifism, explaining that Trajan wished to use the bridge to take troops into Dacia to pre-empt attacks, but Hadrian wanted to prevent the tribesmen from using it to invade Moesia. This bridge was also given up by Hadrian, though Dio says that he removed the superstructure, not that he destroyed it completely. Roman engineers could build another superstructure if it was necessary to do so, whereas the tribesmen of the Danube did not possess the skills. Part of Domitian's ignominious settlement with the Dacians at the end of the first century had involved sending teams of Roman builders to construct strongholds that they could not build themselves. This meant that Trajan's campaigns involved destroying the structures that Romans had built.

The new Dacia consisted of separate provinces of differing status.

Dacia Inferior or Lower Dacia, facing Upper Moesia to which the territory had once belonged, was an unarmed province governed by an equestrian procurator. Another small province, also governed by a procurator, was carved out of the northernmost lands and called Dacia Porolissensis after its town called Porolissum. Upper Dacia centered on the old native capital at Sarmizegethusa, and had one legion whose legate was also the governor.[80] When the Danube provinces were settled, and an active programme of Romanization was established to upgrade various settlements with local government on the Roman model, Hadrian returned to Italy.

In order to deal with the problems in Britain, Hadrian appointed Quintus Pompeius Falco, probably in 118, sending him directly from Lower Moesia where he had been governor. Falco's career is recorded on inscriptions from different provinces, and he is mentioned by Cornelius Fronto and Pliny in their letters.[81] He has no place in Dio's work, but as already mentioned, it is probable that not all of Dio's work covering this period has survived. In Britain, not much is known of the new governor's activities or achievements. The arguments for serious trouble and many casualties in the province at the beginning of Hadrian's reign have been described in the previous chapter, but to recap briefly, there are certain pieces of evidence which have been combined to form a possible overall scenario. An inscription from Italy, most probably belonging to Hadrian's reign, records Titus Pontius Sabinus, who led an expedition to Britain bringing vexillations from three legions, three thousand men in total.[82] Another inscription records a war in Britain in which Gaius Julius Karus received military decorations.[83] Literary references include the statement in the *Historia Augusta* that the Britons could not be controlled at the outset of Hadrian's reign, and Fronto's letter to Marcus Aurelius mentions great losses in Judaea and Britain.[84]

By 118 or 119 the various wars and skirmishes were over. When he returned to Rome Hadrian put into effect several measures designed to alleviate hardship among the people of Rome and the provinces. He cancelled debts to the state treasury (*fiscus*), which could hardly have been an unpopular move: imagine having debts to the Inland Revenue in Britain revoked even for one year. Dio says that Hadrian remitted debts from 104 to 118, going back fifteen years.[85] Inside the reconstructed Senate House in the Forum in Rome there are two marble reliefs, which originally stood on plinths in the Forum itself. One of the reliefs shows men marching in procession from the left, carrying documents, probably tax records, to be burnt. The temple of Saturn, where the treasury was housed, appears just behind them. Stylistically, the reliefs date to around 120, but this is not without dispute, and Marcus Aurelius also cancelled debts, so the reliefs could belong to his reign.

Among other crowd-pleasing measures, Hadrian celebrated the deification of Trajan, and organised a triumph for the dead Emperor, whose effigy was carried in the procession. He put on games and shows, gave the people handouts, continued and supplemented the *alimenta* scheme that Trajan had established to help feed the children of impoverished families, and supported senators who had lost their wealth, giving money to some men, not just his friends to enable them to hold office, and also to some women who were in need.[86]

In 121 he began his series of journeys to many of the provinces, so that his biography becomes less of a political and military history and more of a list of places.[87] He started with Gaul and Germany. The armies of Upper and Lower Germany were thoroughly inspected, as were the garrisons in the other provinces that he visited. In the pages of Dio and the *Historia Augusta* his methods are described in general, thus avoiding repetition for each province. Some of the actions with which he is credited could simply be standard attributes of good Emperors and commanders, but there is probably some worth in outlining what the ancient sources say. Hadrian set the example for the soldiers by walking or riding everywhere and not using a carriage, eating the same food as they did, not bothering with a head covering whether he was in snows of the north or the hot sun of Egypt. He retained and tightened up discipline, and examined all aspects of the camp, the state of the fort buildings and the equipment and weapons, and the well-being of the soldiers, enquiring about their private lives. He gave orders that no soldiers should be enlisted before they were old enough, or retained beyond their capacity in old age. On the other hand he frowned on soldiers asking too often for leave of absence, for giving gifts to officers which were presumably bribes, and for their propensity for luxurious living. He went into the cost of the army, examined stores, inventories and receipts, in other words leaving no stone unturned.[88] A visitation from the Emperor probably exhausted and exasperated the governors and the fort commanders, because after all, having served in and commanded various legions, Hadrian would know all the scams and schemes that soldiers got up to.

After travelling around Germany, where his new palisade frontier was probably being built before he left, he went to Britain in 122. Returning to Gaul he journeyed to Spain.[89] At Tarragona, according to the *Historia Augusta*, a slave ran at him with a sword, but Hadrian did not punish him because he was merely deranged, so he sent him to a doctor.[90] From 123 to 125 Hadrian travelled through the province of Asia and the Greek islands, and came to Athens, a city which he loved. From there he went to Sicily, and climbed Mount Etna to see the sunrise.[91] He was clearly pursuing his own interests on these tours, but he also benefited the cities and other communities in the provinces, and according to the *Historia Augusta* he examined the conduct of the governors and procurators, no doubt chastising them for abuses that he discovered.[92] In modern slang he would be 'marking their cards' as employers would do for their workers.

Returning to Rome probably in 125, Hadrian stayed for not quite two years. Rome was full of building works, with new structures still in progress, like the massive temple of Venus and Rome situated between the Forum and the Colosseum. Some structures may have been completed, like the Pantheon, which was dedicated somewhere between 126 and 128. The front of the original temple built by Marcus Vipsanius Agrippa still bears his name, not Hadrian's. Other buildings were being repaired. Hadrian was a great builder, not only in Rome but in the provinces too, where he did not confine building work to the frontiers. At Tivoli he constructed a lavish villa, still visible today, where he could retreat into his library across a miniature moat, though he cannot have spent much time there. By 127 he was travelling again in Italy, which he now divided into four regions in charge of a consular legate, but the scheme was dropped by Antoninus Pius.[93]

In 128 Hadrian travelled by way of Sicily to Africa, and went on from there to the eastern provinces.[94] Somewhere in the east he met a young man called Antinous from Bithynia, and was instantly smitten. From then on Antinous travelled in Hadrian's entourage, more than just a friend. The meeting is not mentioned in the extant ancient sources. The great passion that Hadrian developed for the young man never faded, but the object of his affection was drowned in the Nile during the trip to Egypt in 130. No one knows whether Antinous simply fell in by accident or was intent on suicide, or whether he was pushed. According to the ancient sources, which become somewhat cryptic at this point, Antinous offered himself as a willing sacrifice to the gods, in order to assist Hadrian's projects which demanded such measures. A city named after him was built on the site of the tragic death. Antinous himself was deified, as was customary in Egypt after drowning in the Nile.[95]

In 131–32 the first signs of unrest broke out in Cappadocia and Judaea. The governor of Cappadocia was Flavius Arrianus, more commonly cited as Arrian, who dealt with the threat from the Alani, a tribe from the lands beyond the Caucasus. They had attempted to cross into the Roman Empire on more than one occasion before Hadrian's reign. Arrian wrote an account of his order of battle against the Alani, called *Acies Contra Alanos*, which is highly useful for studies of the Roman army. The other source of trouble, the most serious of Hadrian's reign, broke out in Judaea. Before describing the revolt, Dio notes the Jews were deeply offended because Hadrian founded a new city on the ruins of Jerusalem and built a temple to Jupiter on the site of the great Jewish temple, which had been totally destroyed in 70 by Titus. The building works were probably only in the first stages when the revolt broke out, and perhaps were only completed after its suppression. According to Dio this is what caused the revolt, but in the *Historia Augusta* the cause is attributed to the fact that the Jews had been forbidden to practice circumcision, and there the account ends with no further mention of the Jewish revolt.[96] The rebellion seemed a minor problem at first, because the Romans underestimated the hatred and the determination of the Jews, under their leader known as Bar Kochba, though there are several versions of his name. The Jews did not risk open battle but waged a successful guerrilla war, occupying the most advantageous positions and hiding themselves and supplies in tunnels with air shafts at intervals which also let in light. Julius Severus was made governor of Judaea, sent there straight from Britain. He did not try to bring about a battle, but rounded up small groups whenever possible, and hemmed in the rebels, cutting off their food supplies and hounding them down until they were exhausted. It took a long time, and the result was devastation over most of Judaea. Dio's estimate of the Jewish death toll is 580,000 men killed and an unknown number of casualties from disease and famine.[97] The number of Roman dead is not known, except that Fronto's letter to Marcus Aurelius indicates that there were great losses. The revolt is not forgotten in modern times, and the Jews still refer to Hadrian in highly uncomplimentary terms.

By 134 Hadrian had returned to Rome. He had started to suffer from nosebleeds, which by 136 had worsened considerably, and Hadrian began to make preparations for the future. He adopted Lucius Ceionius Commodus as his son and renamed him as Lucius Aelius Caesar, but it was not a sound choice because the new Caesar's health was no better than the Emperor's. He probably suffered from tuberculosis and was said to cough up blood.[98] In January 138, Lucius Aelius Caesar died.[99] Hadrian, by now seriously ill himself, adopted Titus Aurelius Fulvius Boionius Arrius Antoninus, better known as Antoninus Pius, on condition that Antoninus also adopted two boys. One was the son of Lucius Aelius Caesar, and was now renamed Lucius Aelius Aurelius Commodus, and the other was Marcus Annius Verus, who was betrothed to Ceionia Fabia, daughter of Aelius Caesar, and also the nephew by marriage of Antoninus Pius.[100] Annius Verus became the Emperor Marcus Aurelius. Hadrian had been at a disadvantage when he became Emperor because the adoption by Trajan was suspect, and he clearly wanted to ensure that for two generations at least there should be no doubt as to the legitimate successors.

The adoptions probably caused trouble within Hadrian's family. It was said that Julius Servianus, now a very old man, and his grandson Fuscus had ambitions to take over from Hadrian, and being foiled they were going to usurp him. Both were eliminated, Servianus being forced to commit suicide.[101] Hadrian's reign ended as it had begun, under a cloud. Shortly before he died, he wrote the short, brilliant poem, wondering where his soul would go, with the well-known first line, *animula vagula blandula,* followed by four more lines that have occasioned many more lines of debate about the correct text, the meaning and even the authorship. One hopes that Hadrian's soul did not go to the dark and cold place that he

predicted. He died at the seaside resort of Baiae on 10 July 138. He
probably had heart disease.[102] The Emperor was buried at Puteoli
on the site of a villa once owned by Cicero. His remains were
eventually transferred to the mausoleum on the bank of the Tiber,
now known as Castel Sant'Angelo.

Dio says that Hadrian was hated by the people, even though
his reign was mostly good.[103] He refers elsewhere to Hadrian's
mild and dignified rule.[104] Compared to the upheavals that Dio
witnessed at the turn of the second and third centuries, Hadrian's
reign was indeed mild. The golden age of Antoninus Pius owes a
lot to Hadrian's capacity for establishing peace and prosperity and
his interest in the welfare of the people of Rome and Italy, and
the provinces. The only serious wars were in Britain and Judaea.
If the pressures on the Danube had begun under Hadrian instead
of Marcus Aurelius, then armies would have been assembled and
wars fought, but it may be that Hadrian's methods of diplomacy
and subsidies, backed up by his frontier forces, kept the tribes at
peace.

Hadrian was not made in the strict mould of his predecessors.
Even his physical appearance differed from the norm, since he
went against the clean shaven look, sporting a curly beard which,
it was said, was grown to hide blemishes on his face. It started a
fashion for facial hair that was to last for decades. He was also
homosexual in a more open manner than his predecessors. Though
Trajan was reputedly fond of handsome boys, Hadrian is famous
or infamous, depending on one's point of view, for his relationship
with Antinous, who is known from the surviving statues of him
that were put up all over the Empire, virtually over the whole
world, as Dio says.[105]

Hadrian displayed a complex personality, combining generosity,
compassion and open-handedness with parsimoniousness, cruelty
and deceit. He was stubborn and quick to anger and to take
offence, bearing grudges for life, but not always exacting revenge,
but he persecuted some men for reasons unknown, and the *Historia
Augusta* supplies a list of victims.[106] He was kind to his friends and
acquaintances, sometimes giving them money without waiting to
be asked, and often dined with them and stayed in their houses.[107]
He put on games and shows, gave the people handouts, continued
and supplemented the *alimenta* scheme that Trajan had established

to help feed the children of impoverished families, and supported senators who had lost their wealth.[108]

Among his household staff and close friends he inspired loyalty, and Dio says that none of these people took money in return for divulging secrets about him.[109] He was devoted to art, architecture, literature and philosophy, and liked to enter debates, but it was difficult for anyone to contradict him, as revealed by the story of the rhetorician Favorinus from Gaul, who accepted criticism from Hadrian without protest, commenting to his friends that one had to accept a man as the most learned in the Empire if he controlled thirty legions.[110]

3

Protecting the Empire

Hadrian's Problems and Possible Solutions

The situation of the Roman Empire when Hadrian succeeded Trajan in 117 provided him with much food for thought about its future and the way to control it. As already mentioned there was trouble in several parts of the Empire. Trajan's conquests had not been consolidated and revolts had begun, and as always there were the troublesome Britons.[1]

No one even among his contemporaries could know all that was in Hadrian's mind, and modern historians and archaeologists can see only what he did, not how he arrived at his decisions. Hadrian's subsequent actions after 117–18 do not necessarily suggest that when he travelled from Syria to the Danube and then back to Rome he formulated a complete policy to be implemented in stages to deal with provincial government, the borders of the Empire and the peoples beyond them. It is impossible to say whether he discussed any of this with his friends and advisers, though he would have assembled a group of trusted officials and probably military commanders to form part of his *consilium*, for which the English word council is not an exact description. From Republican times, Roman senators had always assembled such a body of men, drawn from different backgrounds, and a similar group had grown up surrounding each Emperor. The *consilium* was not an official body of the government. Membership was neither closely defined nor permanent, and could vary from time to time, though by the second century the *consilium* had crystallized a little; the

Praetorian Prefect was always a member, and legal experts were invited. Probably under Marcus Aurelius these legal advisers of the *consilium* received salaries.

Hadrian and his friends would have been perfectly capable of analysing the problems that faced the Empire. They were on the spot, and they had access to information that is denied to modern scholars. In assessing the implications of the Trajanic conquests, Hadrian as the new Emperor lost no time in abandoning territory that had only just been annexed. To continue to add more and more provinces when the latest ones were not thoroughly settled was not viable, unless a greatly expanded army could be assembled to hold the new conquests and keep them pacified until the natives willingly embraced Romanization and began to govern their own communities within the larger framework of the Empire. This process could take a long time. In the past, the Romans had sometimes assumed far too early that conquests were completed and pacification could begin, but found that the people considered to be thoroughly subdued were not in fact subdued and further wars had to be waged to complete the process. In the German territories of Augustus' day, forts were being converted to civilian use and a governor had been installed with more civil and legal experience than military expertise. This suggests that the Romans thought that the German tribes were ready for Romanization and there was room for Roman traders and businessmen to move in. The result was not progressive pacification and development, but the uprising that wiped out three legions in the Teutoburger Wald, at Kalkriese. In Britain in 60–61 a tribe that was considered ripe for exploitation after the death of the king suddenly revealed a talent for war under their queen, who also managed to unite other tribes to her cause. Less than a decade after Boudicca's rebellion, the Batavian auxiliaries of the Rhine showed their lack of commitment to the Roman world by staging a rebellion that was put down only with hard fighting. Initial conquest was often followed by an uprising, and Trajan's two major Dacian wars were no exception. The trouble that broke out at the end of his reign seems to have been quickly put down, but not without shuffling troops around and appointing new governors.

The creation of a larger army to hold new conquests may have been possible in the short term, but it would have been expensive to run and difficult to maintain. The recruitment problem alone, for the initial creation of new units, and afterwards for replacing losses caused by warfare, disease and desertion, would have stretched manpower resources, and although the silver and gold from the Dacian mines may have solved the problem of pay and pensions for the soldiers, this source would not be infinite or inexhaustible. This meant that the Romans had to rely on the time-honoured ways of waging war without continually establishing new legions and auxiliary units. Campaign armies had to be assembled from troops in different provinces to fight in wars that were taking place elsewhere, sometimes by extracting detachments or vexillations from legions and auxiliary troops, and sometimes by removing whole units. Not all of the units returned to their original bases. On occasion troops were shunted along, for instance units from the Rhine could be sent to trouble spots on the Danube further east, and other units and vexillations from Britain or other provinces could be sent to the Rhine to replace them. There were not enough soldiers to go round when large scale campaigns had to be mounted, or most especially when the Empire was threatened on several fronts at once, a problem which became more frequent in the third century. The Romans always packaged their wars as justified, in response to some real or perceived threat, but nonetheless, despite the self-justificatory propaganda, they had also waged aggressive wars which often yielded great profits for Rome. The majority of Romans probably did not recognise it yet, but the era of proactive wars was coming to an end, in favour of reactive wars when real or perceived threats loomed. Sometimes the wars resulted in a permanent reorganisation, and the garrisons of some provinces could be reduced, while others could be increased. In the early Empire the focus was on the Rhine, guarded by several legions, but the focus and the numbers of legions and auxiliary units shifted to the Danube as time went on. All this could be accommodated during the early Empire, even if there were wars on more than one front. Domitian attacked the Chatti in Germany while Gnaeus Julius Agricola was advancing to the north in Britain. Then at the end of the first century, the Dacians entered Roman history, violently and persistently. Two Emperors and four serious wars were required to subdue them, and then another war was waged after the conquest to quell a rebellion.

The solution to the strain on manpower and resources, in Hadrian's reign, was to give up territories newly acquired and not yet pacified, especially if they were not going to be profitable and assimilation was going to take a long time. The central parts of Dacia yielded precious metals, but the eastern and western areas on either side of Dacia may not have been worth the costs of controlling and administering them. Hadrian gave up the lands on either side of Dacia, and he rejected the territory that Trajan had newly acquired in the eastern campaigns, to reduce the Empire to what could be successfully held and controlled. This enabled him to concentrate the armies in the provinces that he retained instead of distributing them over huge distances where they would have been vulnerable for some considerable time until complete pacification had been achieved. Pulling back from further and further conquest reduced the distances that the army would have had to march to trouble spots, so with a more compact Empire, which even so was vast enough in an age of slow communications, it would be quicker to assemble campaign armies, mostly in response to internal rebellions or external threats. In Hadrian's reign there were no further conquests to expand the Empire, and the only wars, serious enough and involving losses and bloodshed, were in Judaea when the Jews rebelled, and in Britain, most probably in northern England and southern Scotland, possibly more than once.

No one can say whether Hadrian devoted some time and contemplation to the needs of the Empire, but his actions suggest that he did. He visited as many provinces as he could, travelling more rapidly over more territory and visiting more cities than any other Emperor.[2] It could be argued that he was simply a privileged tourist, but he seems to have listened to people and genuinely tried to help them. It is recorded that he gave ready assistance to cities, whether or not they were in difficulties, and provided help after disasters.[3] Perhaps he tried to analyse what the provincials wanted, and concluded that their priorities were food and shelter, peace and prosperity that would enable them to obtain and retain these essentials, and for all this they required law and order and protection, most especially if they lived near the borders of the Empire where non-Roman peoples lived, who might not be friendly. Later on, when the fortunes of the Roman Empire changed in the middle of the third century, the groups of provinces that broke away and fought for themselves showed what could happen when the central government could not protect them.

Similarly, Hadrian probably asked what the soldiers wanted. The priorities of the armies probably revolved around regular pay, extra donatives and routes to promotion. Regrettably, soldiers could usually be motivated by the thought of gaining wealth at somebody else's expense, so if wars were not being fought very often, the opportunities to get rich quickly by means of plunder and booty would be withdrawn, therefore pay and donatives would assume even greater importance in soldiers' lives. If the soldiers were to protect the Empire without constantly engaging in wars of conquest, they required recompense, without crippling the treasuries or causing resentment among tax payers, who generally wanted protection as cheaply as possible. The soldiers would have to be properly disciplined, or else everything would fall apart, and they would also need to feel that they were valued, carrying out tasks that were worthwhile, and to be able to look forward to retirement with pensions and the opportunities to set up businesses and farms. When continual movement of troops slowed down, some soldiers set up businesses while they were still in service, which ensured for them a more prosperous retirement. In his travels Hadrian reviewed the armies and praised them for their displays that they put on for him. He made a long speech to the troops in Numidia, which was recorded on stone, singling out some units for especial praise, but not castigating any of them.[4] When he inspected the military units in other provinces he most likely made similar speeches, so one day more records may be discovered attesting to his praise of the soldiers, and possibly of the achievements of towns and cities in other parts of the Empire.

Outside the boundaries of the Empire, especially in the north opposite the Rhine and the Danube, the tribes had become increasingly aware of the Romans, as the Romans had always been aware of them. It would facilitate Roman dealings with them if there was also an awareness of what the various tribesmen wanted. Food and security would probably feature largely in their list of priorities, like the provincials. Tribal society was held together by time-honoured customs but it was fluid. Tribesmen seem to have been free to join other tribes, and there was as yet no sense of states or nationhood. Even tribal names could change, and smaller groups could be absorbed by larger ones and disappear from the record. A leader by whatever title was only as strong as his own right arm, but with Roman backing he could last longer. In return for Roman support, a tribal ruler might be asked to contribute warriors if campaigns were to be fought near their regions, or to send regular batches of recruits for the Roman army, according to whatever terms had been arranged with the leader of the tribe. Recruitment of tribesmen into the auxiliary units was one way of absorbing the energies of the men who just wanted to fight. The Romans had been doing this for some time, for instance sending Britons to Germany, probably in Trajan's reign, forming them into small units called *numeri*, which guarded the less populated areas in broken country. Recruitment of tribesmen was carried out on an increasing scale in the later second century and into the third, some tribesmen being absorbed separately into existing units, and others kept together in units like the *numeri*.

There were different methods of controlling the tribes. The most effective but costly method entailed warfare, either by invasion of tribal territory, followed by annexation if possible, or in defensive warfare if tribes crossed into the Empire. War did not always result in immediate success for the Romans, so other methods had been developed to try to prevent the tribesmen from damaging Roman territory. If a chief seemed to be a strong leader, amenable to Roman influence, he could be supplied with subsidies in various forms, such as food or money, which he could then distribute among his people in return for keeping them in order. The tribal gift-culture bound the important men to the leader, and though it did not always work as the Romans intended, for the most part the tribesmen probably realised that the assassination of their leader was tantamount to killing the goose that laid golden eggs. Gifts and subsidies were already in place when Hadrian became Emperor, and he continued the practice, giving magnificent presents to kings of eastern states as well as to the tribes.[5] At the outset of his reign, when he came to the Danube, he investigated personally the case of the Roxolani, who complained that the subsidy, called *stipendium*, the same word that was used for the soldiers' pay, had been reduced. It is not stated that Hadrian increased the payment, but he made peace, which suggests that the amounts had been properly negotiated and promises made for the future, presumably on both sides.[6]

When he came to rule the Empire, Hadrian faced choices about how to protect it. He could have embarked on conquests as Trajan had done, shielding the existing provinces by adding extra ones further out, but Hadrian renounced continual expansion. Having given up even the newly formed provinces, he could have continued in the old way, meeting challenges as they occurred, beating off attacks and maintaining the status quo. Or he could develop the protective measures already in place to make the Empire more secure. Nothing that the Romans could do would ever prevent a large scale invasion into any part of the Empire if the participants were determined and desperate enough. The best method was to pre-empt this as far as possible. Subsidies to the tribes and small kingdoms on the periphery of the Empire would serve to keep the peace, by removing some of the motives for invading the Empire. Starving tribesmen with only exhausted lands had nothing to lose, but if food was supplied they did not need to go and find it on the other side of their agreed boundary with Rome. Much of Roman control relied on psychology and overtly advertised power. Armies in constant readiness to fight and kept loyal by pay and rewards could help to deter any aggressive action on the part of fire-eating warriors who were not hungry but wanted adventure and booty. Hadrian and his entourage would not have found it difficult to conclude that influencing and controlling the peoples facing the Empire by subsidizing them was cheaper than going to war, and the whole process would be more effective if the armies were maintained at peak proficiency, presenting a demonstration of strength backed up by the combined weight of the whole Empire. Dio comments that most natives saw Hadrian's state of preparation and kept the peace, aided by subsidies.[7]

These components of defence could be considerably enhanced if movement across the boundaries could be impeded. Rivers not only delineated the boundaries but protected them up to a point. The great rivers such as the Rhine and Danube could not prevent all movement, since modest numbers of intrepid men in boats could make the attempt to cross, and larger numbers could walk into Roman territory when the waters were frozen, but river boundaries in general could concentrate movement at bridging points where people could be observed, checked for weapons, and as an added incidental advantage they could be taxed as well, though the soldiers probably only stood guard while civilian officials dealt with the proceedings. Rankov concluded that rivers do make good frontiers and are easily defensible if a major power holds one bank in strength, removes most of the bridges except those that can be defended and controls river traffic.[8] The German tribesmen of the Tencteri dwelt on the right bank of the Rhine, opposite the Romanized city of Cologne where the pro-Roman Ubii lived. The complaints made by the Tencteri serve to illustrate how the Romans had closed access across the rivers and the lands, so that the tribesmen were allowed to come into Cologne only if they shed their equipment, weapons and most of their clothing, and they had to pay for the privilege as well.[9] Going through modern airport controls separated from luggage and without belts, shoes, watches and anything metal is the nearest parallel, but the object is the same: to maintain security.

Land boundaries were more vulnerable than rivers to penetration, so control of these areas would be assisted if solid barriers could be erected to mark the end of fully administered Roman territory and the zones where Roman influence and watchfulness, but not total control, began. Running barriers such as those established by Hadrian in Britain and Germany can be seen as attempts to take the function of controlling movement one step further than the more simplistic road fortified by forts and watchtowers. It is possible for small numbers of people to slip through a line of watchtowers unobserved, and a small number of warriors on the loose can cause a lot of damage, as demonstrated by the problems caused by a limited number of aggrieved Native Americans pursued by General Crook in the nineteenth century. A wall or a timber palisade would render it difficult, but not impossible, to cross the frontier zone except in designated places, where people travelling in either direction, into or out of Roman territory, could be supervised. Their goods and possessions could be examined, and incidentally the taxes that were levied on most Roman borders, including internal borders between provinces, could be applied. Roman frontiers of the second century functioned as administrative barriers and customs posts as well as military installations. Roman soldiers took on many of the tasks that are now performed by a variety of modern uniformed officials, such as police, customs officers, border guards, security guards, bodyguards and, in a sense, traffic wardens. If they did not carry out these tasks directly, soldiers usually escorted the officials who did, such as the provincial procurators when assessing and collecting taxes.

Probably with these considerations in mind Hadrian started out on his travels a few years after his accession. In these early years, the Romans would not yet know of the full extent of his revolutionary ideas, for the creation of running barriers to mark the frontiers was indeed revolutionary. As far as was known, in about 118, Imperial policy had become somewhat irritating because it consisted of giving up conquests that could quite possibly have been exploited by trading companies, usually controlled by senators, who were not supposed to engage in work, but operated through the middle-class equestrians, both of which groups were already wealthy. Not only that, but Hadrian apparently did not intend to conquer other areas to extend the Empire, whereas the Emperors who did engage in conquests had always been regarded as heroes. There would be such men in the future, like Septimius Severus, hailed as *propagator imperii* for his achievements in expanding the Empire. Hadrian's non-expansionist policies would have been anathema to those Romans whose concept of Empire was to go on and on, extending their power without end, spreading Roman ideology, extending trading contacts, extracting minerals and precious metals, and exploiting territories and peoples at will. But as Hadrian's reign progressed it would get worse for these Imperialists. Instead of increasing Roman wealth by conquering more and more lands, Hadrian expended wealth on giving subsidies to tribesmen beyond the Rhine and Danube, and to tribal rulers on the borders of the African provinces, and to petty kings of small territories bordering the eastern provinces. Then after making it clear that he was not going to wage wars of conquest, and would be content to buy peace as far as possible, he made his non-expansionist policies clearer still by creating running barriers at the edges of Roman territory.

Hadrian probably did not have a blueprint in mind for all the frontiers of the Empire, and when he started to erect frontiers he did not follow a one-size-fits-all policy. Consideration was given, as far as possible, to the needs of the particular frontier province or groups of provinces, their demography and geography, and the nature of the lands and peoples beyond them. But in some places, most especially in Britain, the geography and geology of parts of the new frontier line would dictate where the barrier was to run, and the tribal boundaries may have been disregarded, creating a situation not unlike the shock of the Berlin Wall which separated families and friends. The tribe that occupied a vast part of northern Britain was called the Brigantes, but it is disputed whether or not the line of the Wall marked their northern boundary. A dedication to the goddess Brigantia was found at Birrens, one of the outpost forts north of the Wall, by a man called Amandus, described on the inscription as an *architectus*, which proclaims him as a legionary with special skills as a builder.[10] The inscription has been used as evidence that part of the tribe of Brigantes lived outside the frontier, but it has to be acknowledged that anyone can make a dedication to a tribal or territorial goddess even though he or she is not actually in the tribal territory at the time. This evidence is therefore suggestive but not conclusive.[11]

Not all boundaries in and after Hadrian's day were delineated by solid frontiers, but some were simply marked by a road with forts and towers. The frontiers were not built to exactly the same pattern, and were not all of stone. Even when running barriers were erected, the location of forts, fortlets and towers in relation to the barriers was not uniform across the Empire. In Germany and Raetia, forts were placed some short distance behind the frontier line, while in Britain, the early plans may have embraced this idea, but within a short time the forts were attached to the Wall itself. Some frontiers were not even continuous, but barriers were placed where control of movement was necessary, particularly in the African provinces where seasonal transhumance routes crossed cultivated lands. The barriers were placed alongside these routes, and did not prevent movement but channelled it into controllable areas, which kept the peace between the pastoralists and the agriculturalists.

Once the frontiers had been established and the forts and garrisons had become static, modern historians accuse the later Roman Emperors of laziness or inertia, paralyzed into being unable to think of anything else, and the frontiers themselves have been labelled ineffective, as though we moderns know exactly what they were intended to do at all periods of their existence. If the Romans had thought the frontiers ineffective, why would succeeding generations have repaired them, as Severus, Constantius and Theodosius did? Or if they did not repair existing works, sometimes Emperors abandoned parts of the old frontiers and re-erected similar fortified lines in a different location, such as the fourth-century Danube–Iller–Rhine frontier, when the Upper Danube regions had been given up. This new frontier is usually attributed to Valentinian I, but Diocletian and Constantine may also have had a part to play in creating it, while Valentinian probably repaired and strengthened it. On the whole, it could be said that Hadrian's policies were the correct ones for preserving and protecting the Empire. Attempts to add more territory after Hadrian's reign were not always successful. Severus tried to annexe part of Mesopotamia as Trajan had done, but it created more problems than it solved. Subsidies to the tribesmen were no doubt resented, but when they were stopped, war usually ensued, as when Philip the Arab stopped payments to the Goths in 248 and invasions followed. Aurelian refused to reinstate payments to the Alamanni, and he and his successors spent years fighting them. The comparison is not exactly fair, since Hadrian's reign and that of his successor Antoninus Pius were not noted for enormous pressures on the frontiers that began under Marcus Aurelius and continued through the third century, but the decades of peace enjoyed for most of the second century can probably be attributed to Hadrian's methods of ruling the Empire.

Frontiers in Britain before Hadrian?

About forty years before Hadrian chose to build his Wall in Britain, it can be construed that Agricola had pre-empted him in the conception of a fortified frontier by means of the forts on the Forth–Clyde line and the forts and towers of the Gask. The physical form and the installations of this system are described above in chapter one, while this section is concerned with its function as a possible frontier. The controversy over what constitutes a frontier has been referred to above, in connection with the Fosse Way. A major problem is that there is a lack of consensus as to the precise definition of what the word implies. It has different connotations for different authors of different generations, so some clarification is required to explain how the word is interpreted in this book. In general a frontier is defined in the *Oxford Popular English Dictionary* as a border between two different states or countries, including the districts between the two. Moving from the general to the specific, with reference to frontiers as established by Hadrian, a frontier is taken to define not just the line defined by a running barrier, but the zone beyond and behind the line. Inside the Roman territory demarcated by the line, Roman government, administration and law applies in full, and beyond the line Roman control and influence is maintained in a variety of ways, by friendly relations with some tribes, possibly by subsidising some of the natives, possibly by patrolling either from the frontier itself or from outposted fortified bases, and the areas well beyond the frontier could be monitored and watched to gather intelligence and give early warning of potential trouble. The debate could continue, distinguishing finer and finer detail. The frontier can be marked out in some way by a clearly defined road or by a running barrier of timber or stone, together with fortifications in the form of towers, forts and fortlets. It need not be entirely permanent, and adjustments, in the form of advancements or withdrawals, can be made to parts, or all, of the frontier zone. The frontiers were designed either to prevent or to control movement, which has occasioned long-term discussion with regard to Hadrian's Wall. Frontiers of the Empire may have been tailored to the circumstances prevailing beyond them, but no frontier, however strongly guarded, can withstand a determined assault, and probably no Roman frontier was ever intended to do so.

Archaeologists and historians recognise several potential frontiers in Britain prior to Hadrian's reign, but the concept of a long-term or permanent halt behind a fortified line anywhere in Britain between 43 and 122 is questionable.[12] In describing Agricola's fourth season and his establishment of a fortified line between the Forth and the Clyde, Tacitus' choice of the word 'terminus' in Latin, which in English summons up train stations and bus depots as well as an end in the territorial sense, hints at the cessation of further conquest, which in Tacitus' day at the end of the first century AD was counter to the Roman ethic of *Imperium sine fine*, power or rule without end, in both the territorial and temporal spheres. The Empire would go on expanding until there was nothing left to take in, and it would last forever. The ideology of perpetual conquest died hard. In connection with Germany, Tacitus himself imagined that conquest would be completed at some point, complaining that it was taking a long time, despite the fact that when he was writing, at the turn of the first and second centuries, the likelihood of another advance into Germany was remote.[13]

The Gask 'Frontier'

Discussion of the Agricolan, or Flavian period forts and watchtowers of the so-called Gask frontier could fill far too many pages for a book on Hadrian's Wall, but because it is sometimes seen as a forerunner of the Hadrianic frontier, it is worth a small amount of diversionary verbiage.[14] As mentioned in chapter one, the system takes its name from the eastern part of the line running along the Gask Ridge, but this obscures the fact that the whole line ran from Ardoch to Bertha on the River Tay, around the western edge of Fife. The watchtowers of the Gask system were presumably intended to observe movements of unauthorised people, and report what they had seen to the fort commanders. The towers are very close together, so it has been suggested that they were not necessarily used as signal towers. Signalling could function well enough if the towers had been spaced much further apart.[15] More probably the main function of the installations was to watch for movement across the line represented by the towers and forts. This use of such closely spaced installations is illustrated by the arrangements made by one of Napoleon's officers who split up his forces into small packets and strung them out in a line with only small gaps between them. Napoleon examined the dispositions and said to the officer 'It's beautiful. What d'you want to do, prevent smuggling?'

One of the main problems with the Gask Ridge system is that its function is not outlined in Roman literature, or on a building inscription such as the useful examples from *burgi* or large watchtowers in the Danube region, dating from the 180s during the reign of Commodus. Two inscriptions were set up in different years of Commodus' reign, one near Intercisa (Dunaujvaros) and one near Aquincum (Budapest).[16] The inscriptions display virtually the same wording, explaining that the *burgi* along the river were newly built from the ground up, to control the places where robbers or bandits could try to cross the frontier (*per loca opportuna ad clandestinos latrunculorum transitus oppositis*). These towers were free-standing, like those of the Gask, and no *burgi* have been found attached to any of the running barriers on the northern frontiers, so it is possible that the late first-century towers in Britain and late second-century towers on the Danube fulfilled some, but not all, of the same purposes. It is not to be expected that Agricola or his successors erected similar explanatory inscriptions, so in the absence of such helpful evidence from the Gask system, it is not clear to modern observers how it was intended to work. Which way did it face? Was it to guard the area of Fife from attacks from the west, thus protecting the tribesmen who lived there, while also protecting the lands to be appropriated and exploited by the Romans? Was there an alliance between the people of Fife and the Roman government?[17] Was it a tribal boundary? Probably not. Or was it an arbitrary line drawn by the Romans and manned while they advanced, probably from Agricola's third season onwards, to stop anyone coming across the Tay estuary into Fife and then coming up behind the Roman forts? Was it occupied and in use while the second line of forts at the mouths of the glens were being built, and even after they had been established? It has been shown that the towers and forts were in existence for some considerable time, and that there are two detectable Flavian phases at the forts, but it is not known if there was a gap in occupation, or whether the whole system was manned continuously throughout the Flavian contact with Scotland, starting with the advance into northern Scotland, the establishment of the glen-blocking forts, and then the withdrawal to the Tyne–Solway line marked by the Stanegate. If the Gask system was in fact occupied at all stages of the first-century Roman contact with Scotland, did it fulfil the same functions throughout? There are several interpretations of the use of the Gask system, which may have changed with the different circumstances of the advance into Scotland, the conquest, the partial settlement, and the sudden withdrawal.

It could be said that another definition of a frontier is that it marks the limit of the Empire. For much of its life the Gask frontier did not mark the most northerly limits of the province of Britain, but was well within the territory where Agricola was campaigning and his successor or successors were also operating. The possible occasions when the Gask could be said to be on the furthest edge of the Roman province, satisfying one of the definitions of a frontier, was when Agricola was in the process of advancing to the Tay, or when he was consolidating behind the Forth–Clyde line, or sometime later when the troops were being removed from the forts lying to the north of the Gask. The Gask could have been used by Agricola while he advanced, and then the line could have been left redundant for a short time, and put back into commission when the withdrawal from Scotland took place, though the archaeological evidence cannot yet prove this. Nor can it be proven beyond doubt that the Gask system stood at the edge of the province at any time in its existence, since even during the consolidation process behind the Forth–Clyde line, it is not impossible that there were forts to the north of the *praesidia* of the fourth season.[18]

Although the importance of the fortified line round Fife is demonstrated by its use in the first century and the reoccupation of the forts during the Antonine period, it is not certain that it was intended to be a permanent fortified boundary. Hadrian's Wall on the other hand marked the limit of Roman administered territory, with outposts providing for Roman influence and policing beyond it. To all intents and purposes the effort put into building the Wall would suggest that it was intended to be permanent, even though the next Emperor, Antoninus Pius, decided to move north. The new Antonine frontier from the Forth to the Clyde does not seem to have been intended to act as a launching pad for further military conquest of the north of Scotland, though as with all statements about Roman frontiers, this one could provoke howls of protest. It is probable that the new line was intended to help keep the peace and protect and exploit the lands between the two Walls. In its finished form, with a running barrier of turf equipped with forts, fortlets and platforms for lookout posts, the concept of the new Antonine frontier was exactly the same as that of Hadrian's Wall. When the Antonine Wall was abandoned, the Romans did not adopt an entirely new policy, but reverted to the Hadrianic system and put the Wall back into commission.

The Stanegate

There has always been debate about whether the Stanegate was a true frontier ever since the idea was first proposed in the early twentieth century. Concomitant with this debate is another contested idea, concerning the influence that the Stanegate may have had on Hadrian's choice of frontier, and the form that it took. In Domitian's reign the Stanegate was a road in the hinterland of Roman occupation, guarded by a few forts and watchtowers, and linking the two main north–south routes on the east and the west of the Pennines. In the early years of Trajan, when it became the most northerly occupied line, it seems to some archaeologists to warrant the appellation frontier, in that it probably marked the furthest known limit of Roman government, at a time when huge resources and manpower were being devoted to the Dacian wars and then to Trajan's eastern conquests. Not everyone agrees with the description of the Stanegate as a frontier, the late Brian Dobson, noted Hadrian's Wall scholar, being the most emphatic, denying that there is any evidence to prove that there was a frontier of any description in the period between the withdrawal from Scotland and the establishment of Hadrian's Wall.[19]

Even the full extent of the Stanegate is uncertain, which has a bearing on how its function is interpreted. If it was to serve as a frontier, it surely ought to have stretched from the west to the east coast. It used to be affirmed that the Stanegate did not extend beyond Carlisle in the west or Corbridge in the east. New evidence suggests that the road may have reached the coast in the west, and probably also in the east, but the evidence for the eastern side is weaker. It is not yet proven beyond doubt that the Stanegate divided the northern areas of Britain from the more southerly ones, stretching from sea to sea.[20] Behind the meanings and implications of the term 'frontier' there lies Imperial policy, but this is difficult to discern purely from archaeological evidence, which cannot always elucidate Imperial thought processes. It cannot be known whether Trajan's intention was to convert the Stanegate line into a border, or more pertinently into a frontier dividing the province into Roman and non-Roman sectors. If there is a distinction between the two concepts, a frontier suggests more strongly than a border line that territory beyond it has been given up. Trajan died in 117 without having the chance to crystallize the frontier, if such it was to be. He could have intended to garrison the line more densely, with outposts to give early warning of trouble, and then it could more justifiably be called a frontier. Alternatively Trajan's plans for the future may have included another advance into Scotland to regain what had been given up when the troops were withdrawn, which would have made the Stanegate redundant as a frontier. Without any indication of Trajan's intentions no one can say what his policy was in *c.* 105, or would have been if he had lived. After his death it was left to his successor to decide how to deal with northern England.

Whether or not the Stanegate could have functioned as a frontier depends on the definition of the word itself and on the disposition of the forts and fortlets. There used to be a theory that the siting of the forts and fortlets was governed by regular spacing in terms of a day's or a half-day's march, with alternating large and small forts, but the predicted sites where such forts should appear has not been supported by archaeological findings. This is not such a disaster, because regular spacing is not the most ideal way to protect a frontier. The lie of the land and the potentially vulnerable points can be overlooked in such a rigid scheme. It has been pointed out that in Germany at the same time that the Stanegate was being strengthened as the northernmost occupied line in Britain, frontier forts and fortlets were not spaced at regular distances, according to a neat pattern of alternating small and large installations. Instead the locations and also the dimensions and capacities of the forts and fortlets were dictated by the lie of the land and the potential threat.[21] The military installations of the Stanegate are not located according to a specific pattern on grounds of spacing, but at places where the line crossed rivers or routes which required surveillance. On this basis it could be regarded as a frontier without a running barrier, but still with the capacity to protect the territory behind it from attack.

Accepting the Stanegate as a pre-Hadrianic frontier causes headaches for archaeologists, not simply because the term frontier embraces different shades of meaning and therefore also of function, but also because archaeology is not a sufficiently precise tool to distinguish between Trajanic and Hadrianic building work on the Stanegate line. If it was a frontier at all, which is still debatable, was it Trajan's idea or Hadrian's? An older generation of archaeologists were convinced that the additional forts on the Stanegate line besides Carlisle, Nether Denton, Vindolanda and Corbridge were Hadrianic, and the fortlets at Haltwhistle Burn and Throp were also part of this plan. This would imply that Hadrian originally intended to convert the Stanegate to a new frontier line, but then perhaps after viewing the territory for himself, he decided to build the Wall further north. This dating has now been revised, and new thinking views the additional installations of the Stanegate as Trajanic. This means that they do not represent the first of Hadrian's schemes for the frontier. The implication is that Hadrian inspected what was already there and decided to make the line more permanent and to strengthen it by building the Wall to the north of it. Whatever the dates of the additional Stanegate forts and fortlets, Hadrian's initial plan may have been for the two lines to work together, the Wall with its milecastles and turrets as a running barrier, and the road slightly further south with its forts and fortlets as back up. If so, the scheme was soon changed when the so-called fort-decision was taken and new forts were built, attached to the Wall itself. Hadrian may have intended to put the forts on the Wall from the very beginning, but in view of the fact that parts of the Wall foundations and some turrets were demolished to make room for some of the new forts, it is arguable that the first plan for the Wall was to use the Stanegate forts as the bases for the soldiers, similar to the German frontier, but after a short time this scheme was found inadequate. An alternative view is that since there is a lack of evidence for fortifications on the eastern Stanegate, there were no units to be moved forwards to protect the Wall in this sector, so Hadrian cannot have failed to notice this and therefore he intended to build forts on the line of the Wall from the very beginning.[22]

Some fifty years ago it was thought that when the decision was made to put forts on the Wall itself, all the fort garrisons moved from the Stanegate to the Wall forts, so according to this scheme it would seem certain that the Stanegate was simply a pre-Wall frontier line, altered and improved upon when Hadrian devoted his full attention to Britain.[23] This scenario now has to be amended because not all the forts of the Stanegate were given up when the Wall was built, Carlisle, Corbridge and Vindolanda being still occupied by the military forces while the Wall and its forts were functioning, and it now seems that Kirkbride, Burgh-by-Sands and Nether Denton were still in use after the Wall was built.[24] The jury is still out on the case for the Stanegate as a frontier from *c.* 105 to 122.

Hadrian's Options in Britain

Inheriting the Trajanic scheme for the northern boundary of the island, Hadrian had other options besides building the Wall. He could have moved even further south, renouncing the wild north, or he could have resumed the advance into Scotland and drawn a line there, much as his successor Antoninus Pius did only a few decades after the Wall had been built. The first option was probably never considered, if only because Hadrian was not likely to find a better geographical and topographical location to create a frontier line than in the relatively short Tyne–Solway gap, along the north-facing cliffs of the Whin Sill in the central sector.

The second option, involving the recovery of all that Agricola had achieved in Scotland might have seemed worthwhile to some of the military men, but evidently did not appeal to Hadrian. Despite the fact that the governors of Britain were usually senior officials with considerable experience, the province was not the most important on the Imperial agenda, especially when there was a threat closer to Rome, such as that represented by the Dacians. The original withdrawal from Scotland in the late first century probably caused little heartache, except to the man who had spent some years in conquering it. The fertile areas of Lowland Scotland could have been useful for supplying the army, but the control of the Highlands, while not totally impossible, would have produced little for the Romans to exploit, except perhaps for the slave trade, and there is some doubt that anyone lived in the Highlands anyway.

Trajan and Hadrian had lived through the period of the Agricolan conquest, and the cost in manpower and resources that were involved in annexing and holding Scotland would be known to them. They may even have discussed the matter, aware that there were higher priorities in other parts of the Empire. They would have had access to official reports about the Agricolan campaigns, the tribes, the terrain and the potential yield in agricultural produce, minerals and slaves, and perhaps reasoned that in fiscal terms staying out of Scotland would be ideal because the expense outweighed the profits, and the numbers of soldiers who would be needed to regain and retain the territory could be better employed elsewhere. Although Antoninus Pius did advance into Scotland and take in territory up to the Forth–Clyde line, the occupation was very short-lived. Hadrian probably considered that the resources to be found in Scotland would not provide adequate recompense for the effort of building forts and placing garrisons in them to keep the population under control. Ten centuries later, William I, ruler of Normandy and England, journeyed north to Abernethy to meet the king of Scotland, Malcolm Canmore. A treaty was arranged that probably neither of them intended to keep, but it postponed trouble for the time being. With no remorse William was able to renounce indefinitely any idea of conquering Scotland, most likely because he knew how costly and difficult it would have been, for little gain. The *Anglo-Saxon Chronicle* laconically and dismissively records that William went to Scotland, and there he found nothing that he was any the better for.

When Did the Frontiers Begin?

On the land frontiers of Upper Germany Hadrian erected a palisade from the Rhine to the River Neckar, taking in the northward-facing bulge around the fertile land of the Taunus–Wetterau region. In Raetia the frontier was not constructed all at the same time, nor was it uniformly designed using the same materials. It was marked by a palisade as in Germany, but in parts there was only a timber fence, labelled the Flechtwerkzaun by archaeologists, which sometimes predates the palisade, and in some places appears to replace it. For some years there was a gap at the western end of the Raetian frontier, where it did not join up with the eastern border of Upper Germany, but this was closed after the mid-second century, and at the turn of the second and third centuries the Raetian frontier was rebuilt in stone, on a narrower scale than the Wall in northern England.

Remains of the palisade, not all of Hadrianic date owing to later repairs, have been revealed by archaeological investigation along much of the frontier lines in Germany and Raetia. The ancient sources do not specifically state where Hadrian built this palisade, but the *Historia Augusta* refers to it in a passage explaining that in places where the tribesmen were not held back by rivers, they were checked by running barriers, consisting of high stakes buried deep in the ground and fastened together.[25] The term used is *limes*, plural *limites*, which originally denoted the roads used by the Romans to march into enemy territory, but came to mean the frontiers themselves.

Hadrian's visit to Germany and the creation of the palisade frontier may not have been exactly contemporary. Some of the earliest timbers have been dated by dendrochronology, or tree-ring dating, and the results show that they were felled within a date range from the winter of 119–20 to the summer of 120.[26] This, obviously, is before the accepted date for Hadrian's visit in 121, and has important implications. The evidence will bear the interpretation that Hadrian had begun to conceive of the idea of creating a frontier before he inspected the terrain, though not as far back as 117 when he succeeded Trajan. Since he had served in Germany, he may have already possessed more knowledge of the land and the natives than many of his contemporaries. When he set out on his tour of the provinces he had probably begun to devote some thought to the means of defending the land between the Rhine and the Neckar, and in Raetia. The implication of setting the army to felling trees in 119–20 is that he did not wait for four years or so after his accession to go and see for himself what was necessary and then subsequently plan the route that the frontier was to take and the materials that were to be used to build it. If felling began in 119 as the dating evidence suggests, then Hadrian presumably sent orders to prepare the timbers before he arrived in the German provinces. Felling the timber is not the same as starting to build, so it could be the case that stocks of felled trees were allowed to mature before building began, and then when Hadrian descended on the governor and the troops, he waved the starting flag and set everything in motion. Alternatively, he may have arrived with the purpose of checking on the progress of a frontier that was already under construction. Bearing in mind the ancient authors' description of Hadrian's character, his diligence, his determination to get things done, his tendency to investigate everything personally in infinite detail, his impatience with slow progress, more or less wanting everything completed yesterday or sooner, this may be the more accurate scenario.

After his visit to Germany, with the precedent for frontiers marked by running barriers established, Hadrian crossed to Britain, where the *Historia Augusta* is quite specific about his new frontier, described as a wall (*murus*) built 'to separate the Romans from the barbarians'.[27] Once again the timetable has been questioned. Did building only begin in 122 after Hadrian had inspected the terrain and decided where to build the new frontier? In 1966 C. E. Stevens, without the benefit of the knowledge that the timbers for the German palisade were being felled in 119–20, suggested that work on the Wall in Britain began in 120, under the governor Pompeius Falco.[28] This idea was rejected by Breeze and Dobson in the fourth edition of their book on Hadrian's Wall, but the possibility that Falco began the work was recently revived by Bennett in 2002, on archaeological grounds.[29] In 2012, Graafstal resurrected the discovery by F. J. Haverfield, the renowned Roman scholar, that the ditch to the north of Hadrian's Wall at Chesters contained a sizeable deposit of debris, which suggested that it had been open for a considerable time, and yet this part of the ditch had been filled in to allow for the fort at Chesters to be built across it, projecting to the north of the Wall, probably in 124, or at least not long after the building of the frontier had begun. In order to account for the length of time that may have elapsed between digging the ditch and then demolishing it when the fort was built, it seemed that the ditch belonged to a period before Hadrian arrived in Britain, probably when Pompeius Falco was governor.[30] The possibility that Pompeius Falco was sent from Moesia to Britain as early as 118 has already been mentioned in connection with the probable war in northern Britain at Hadrian's accession. There is only suggestive evidence and no concrete proof either that Falco's appointment was in 118 or that he was sent to Britain in response to an outbreak of trouble, but he was in the province until the middle of July 122, by which time he had granted honourable discharge to some auxiliary soldiers who had completed their twenty-five years of service in thirteen cavalry units and thirty-seven cohorts, but the bestowal of Roman citizenship on the discharged soldiers was completed by

Hadrian's governor Aulus Platorius Nepos.[31] This means that by summer 122 Falco was replaced by Platorius Nepos. The term of service as governor usually lasted three to four years, which would support the suggestion that Falco was in Britain from 118. This does not constitute proof that Falco starting building the Wall or that he had been ordered to begin to find quarries and build up stocks of stone, but Birley says that the suggestion deserves consideration.[32] As with most aspects of the Wall's history this debatable point can only be settled by indisputable evidence, such as an inscription removing all doubt that Falco was the first builder. Such things are not wholly unimaginable. In the last years of the sixteenth century, William Camden surveyed parts of the Wall except for the wild central sector which was unsafe because of the moss troopers who threatened travellers. From Camden's day until the early years of the nineteenth century, it was thought that Septimius Severus built the Wall. This theory derived from the fact that Severus carried out so much repair work on the Wall that it seemed as though the whole work must have been originated by him, but because there was also a literary reference attesting that Hadrian built a frontier, despite the fact that the word that was used unequivocally referred to a wall, the literary evidence was taken to mean that Hadrian was responsible for the Vallum ditch that accompanies the Wall on the south side. Then from the nineteenth century onwards inscriptions were discovered describing building work on the Wall under Platorius Nepos, attested in the literary sources as Hadrian's governor. The Reverend John Hodgson, when he wrote his *History of Northumberland* in 1839, was among the first to realise that the inscriptions that had been found up to his day showed that it must have been Hadrian who built the Wall, so opinions had to be revised, and the name had to be amended from Severus' Wall to Hadrian's Wall.[33] So, reverting to the topic of Pompeius Falco, one fine day evidence may emerge that he started work on quarrying stone and building the Wall. This sentence invites incredulous mutterings about porcine aviation.

4

Building the Wall: AD 122 to *c.* AD 142

Hadrian's Wall in its final version consisted of several component parts. It is important to note that not all of the features described here were established at the exactly the same time.

The Wall did not stand alone as a fortified line running west to east across what is now Northern England. There were forts to the north of it, labelled outpost forts in modern terms, not attached to the Wall but nonetheless part of the whole system. South of the Wall some forts of the Stanegate, such as Vindolanda and Corbridge, continued in occupation, and routes further south in the Pennine hinterland were still guarded, though a map of Roman Britain showing all the known military sites should not be taken to indicate that all the forts were occupied simultaneously. Though the Wall itself did not continue down the western coast of Cumbria, the fortifications did, with forts at Beckfoot, Maryport and Moresby, accompanied by smaller fortlets and towers.

The Hadrianic and later frontier line comprised several features: two ditches, one wall, a road (not a primary feature) to the south, and installations ranging from small towers, small fortlets, and eventually the forts themselves. The western part of the Wall from the River Irthing to the west coast, was originally built in turf, but was rebuilt in stone, probably in two instalments, by the middle of the second century. In Wall terminology, Turf Wall refers to this western sector.

North of the Wall a ditch was dug, except in places where a high crag made such a defence redundant, or as at Limestone Corner west of Chesters fort, where the hard Whinstone bedrock was difficult to cut. The lack of a northern ditch at this point was not a crucial feature since the ground is high enough for defence and observation. Then behind the ditch there was the Wall itself, with fortlets called milecastles in Wall-speak, placed every Roman mile as the name suggests, and two towers known as turrets between them, spaced one third of a mile apart. Then slightly later, the forts were built on the Wall. Whereas the forts are known by their Latin names if these are known and more frequently by their modern names, the milecastles and turrets are numbered from east to west for ease of identification, the two turrets being given the same number as the milecastle to their east, but distinguished from each other by the letters a and b.

South of the Wall there is the larger ditch, roughly twenty Roman feet wide at the top, and accompanied on the north and south sides by mounds of earth running parallel with it. This ditch was labelled the Vallum in the work of the Venerable Bede, and the name has stuck, often with its initial capital letter, to distinguish it from the northern ditch. To the Romans the ditch would have been a *fossa* or *fossatum*, the Latin for a wall was *murus*, but the Romans did use *Vallum* as a term to embrace the whole of the Wall system. On an undated inscription found near Kirksteads farm, between Stanwix and Burgh-by-Sands, the legate of *VI Victrix* dedicated an altar to give thanks for successful activities *trans Vallum*, across the frontier.[1] In the late Roman document known as the *Notitia Dignitatum*, which lists the forts and garrisons in each province, the frontier is denoted by the phrase *per lineam valli*, 'along the line of the Wall'. A more recent discovery bearing the Roman, possibly even the Hadrianic, name of the Wall is the so-called Staffordshire Moorlands pan, found in 2003 near Ilam. The pan or skillet is made of copper alloy, not quite nine centimetres in diameter at the rim, with coloured enamel inlays in abstract Iron Age style round the body of the cup. It once had a handle, which supports its description as a pan. Apart from its decoration it is very similar to two other vessels, the Rudge cup and the Amiens skillet, named for the places where they were found. Like modern saucepans, it is supposed that each of these vessels had a handle, the Amiens version having a broken section in the rim where it was once attached. All three pans have the names of the forts at the western end of the Wall incised around the top, but the Staffordshire pan contains the words *rigore val(l)i Aeli Draconis*, followed by the fort names. The translation is open to two interpretations: the owner of the pan may have been called Aelius Draco, or perhaps more likely the name of the Wall was *Vallum Aelium* after Hadrian's family name Aelius.[2] In other words the Wall was known as the Aelian Wall, not as the Wall of Aelius, much as in modern times the wall built around the city of Rome by Aurelian in the late third century is called in English the Aurelian Wall.

At a later time, a road now called the Military Way was laid down between the Vallum and the forts, sometimes running along the north mound of the Vallum. This was seemingly not part of the original Hadrianic plan, but was built after the Romans had advanced into Scotland in the reign of Antoninus Pius and established another frontier, then withdrawn back to the Hadrianic frontier. The term Military Way was coined by modern archaeologists to distinguish the Roman road from the modern B6318, known as the Military Road, which was built by General Wade a few years after the 1745 rebellion, when considerable difficulty had been experienced in marching an army from Newcastle to Carlisle. The new road facilitated east–west communications, much as the new Military Way assisted the Romans of the later second century. Wade sealed some parts of Hadrian's Wall by utilising some stretches of it as foundation for his road. Between them, the Romans and General Wade provided a predominantly straight road that facilitates modern communications at an average speed of seventy miles per hour.

The Route of the Wall

When the decision had been taken to renounce the hold on Lowland Scotland and the territory even further north, it remained to decide which parts of the province to keep within Roman administration and which parts to let go, and then draw a line between the two. Geographical determinism played an important role in choosing where to draw this line. The land between the River Tyne and the Solway Firth provides the narrowest gap between the eastern and western sides of Northern England, and in the central sector there is the added factor of the crags of the Whin Sill, conveniently

facing north. These features readily assist anyone intending to build
a north-facing frontier and will have been known to the military
commanders and the governors of Britain, who may have been
asked for advice and included in the planning process. It has been
suggested above, but not universally agreed by archaeologists, that
the Wall may have been planned during Pompeius Falco's term as
governor, up to two years in advance of Hadrian's visit in 122.[3] If
this is correct, then the military officers will have had a preponderant
influence in the choice of location, subject to Hadrian's approval
by correspondence, probably with no more delay than is involved
in submitting architect's drawings to the planning department of a
local authority. The extent to which Hadrian was personally and
directly involved in the planning, the design and the smaller details
of his Wall is not known, but the possibility that Hadrian was the
original designer of the Wall has been discussed by David Breeze.[4]

Whether or not the decision had already been taken to build the
frontier before Hadrian arrived, it is hard to resist the scenario of
the Emperor and his entourage riding along the proposed course
of the frontier and inspecting the details. He will have been closely
associated with the military units, and the legionaries who were to
do the building work. When he toured other provinces Hadrian
paid great attention to the soldiers, who most probably put on
displays for him, as they are known to have done in Numidia,
where Hadrian's *Adlocutio* or address to the soldiers was inscribed
at the legionary fortress at Lambaesis.[5] During his tour of Britain,
it has been suggested that Hadrian may have visited Vindolanda, or
even stayed there for a while.[6]

The new frontier would have to cross rivers, notably the Eden
at Carlisle and the Irthing at Willowford in the west, and the
North Tyne at Chesters in the east. Little is known of the bridge
over the Eden where the fort at Stanwix was built, but at Chesters
and Willowford there are visible remains of supporting piers, now
on dry land because the rivers have changed their courses. The
remains visible today are not always of Hadrianic date because
repairs and sometimes alterations were carried out under Severus
and later Emperors. Bridge building was well within the capacity
of military architects and protecting the crossing points was well
within the capacity of the soldiers.[7] The frontier would also have
to take into consideration the protection of the coasts. The frontier

was to run along the southern edge of the Solway Firth as far as Bowness, opposite modern Annan. This was the logical choice, because it would not have been feasible to take in the country to the north of the Solway Firth, into which the rivers Annan, Esk and Eden flow. Control of the northern shore of the estuary would have meant that the frontier could not stop until it reached the Rhinns of Galloway and the coast. At Bowness-on-Solway the Firth is narrow, and since the land mass of southern Scotland extends well to the west of England, it would be possible to cross the water and infiltrate the country behind the frontier. In order to counter this potential threat from the Scottish tribes and possibly from the Irish Sea, fortifications were established along the coast of what is now Cumbria. Some of these may have already been in existence prior to Hadrian's reign. In the east, the frontier was located on the north bank of the Tyne, so the Romans controlled the river traffic. Interested tourists sometimes ask how far did the Wall run to the east, and usually laugh when told it ended at a place called Wallsend, but embedded in the joke is the question of when did the Wall reach this location? Current thinking, with a few dissenting voices, is that the original plan for the Wall was to start at Newcastle upon Tyne, and archaeological excavation work has been interpreted to show that the initial building work ran westwards from there, with the eastern extension to Wallsend being added later.

In recent years, new theories about the original plan have been advanced, for instance Peter Hill suggests that it was intended from the beginning to carry the Wall down to the Tyne at Wallsend, making this sector less of an afterthought and more of a primary plan.[8] It is not necessarily suggested that building work started at Wallsend and worked westwards, but the theory that it began at Newcastle is questioned, an alternative view being that work began on Dere Street, the modern A68, where there was a gateway through the Wall called Portgate, near milecastle 22. According to this theory, the builders started here and worked eastwards to Newcastle.[9] Yet another idea is that one group of builders started off at the North Tyne and worked eastwards, meeting another group working westwards from Newcastle.[10] In discussing the feasibility of these different suggestions for the order of building, Hodgson says that it is conceivable that building work under different gangs began at the same time at Newcastle, Portgate and the North Tyne.[11] More recently the construction order of the Wall has been discussed by Symonds, in connection with the order of building of the milecastles, proposing that some of them were built early in the sequence, the priority being to watch river crossings and valleys.[12] A few years later Graafstal argued that there were identified weak spots along the line of the Wall which required immediate defence, and this determined which sectors would be built first.[13]

Another controversy concerns the borders of Brigantian territory, and whether part of the tribe was cut off when the frontier was created. It used to be thought that some of the Brigantes were isolated, based on the evidence of an inscription found at Birrens, recording a dedication to the goddess Brigantia set up by a soldier called Amandus who describes himself as an *arcitectus* (*sic*).[14] The dedication is dated to the early third century when the Wall had been established for some time, but although Brigantia was a local goddess of the Brigantian tribe, it is not necessarily the case that she was worshipped only within her own territory.[15] It is suggested that Amandus may have been based at York where the worship of Brigantia was encouraged in the third century, as reflected in another dedication to this goddess, dated to 208, at Greetsand.[16] The theory that the Wall cut off some tribesmen from their homeland has been questioned. In the third and fourth editions of *Hadrian's Wall* Breeze and Dobson argued that the number of outposts beyond the Wall in the west may have been necessary to control the disgruntled tribesmen, but in 2005 Breeze suggested that the northern boundary of Brigantian territory did not project beyond the Wall and in fact influenced the siting of the frontier line.[17] On this question there is only speculation and opinion and no solid evidence, so until something definite turns up it is still not known for certain whether the Brigantian border was concurrent with the present line of the Wall.

The Workforce

After deciding upon the route that the Wall was to take and the materials with which it was to be built, officers would have to be appointed to organise the quarrying, the transport of the stone, the allocation of the different types of more detailed work to the relevant specialists and the labouring jobs to gangs of soldiers. The equivalent of the modern project manager was presumably the governor Aulus Platorius Nepos, to whom all except minor queries would probably be addressed, but the overseers on site would have been the *praefecti castrorum* or camp prefects of the three legions in Britain, *II Augusta*, *VI Victrix* and *XX Valeria Victrix*, all of which are attested at work on the Wall by inscriptions.[18] There was only one camp prefect in each legion, and he would have been the most influential and powerful officer after the legionary legate and the *tribunus laticlavius* or broad stripe tribune, who acted as second in command. Unlike these two men, the camp prefect was not originally of senatorial rank, but was usually a soldier of long experience. He may have risen from the ranks and had usually served as centurion, most probably in two or more different legions, before reaching the coveted legionary post of chief centurion, *primus pilus* or first spear. Some camp prefects had held this post more than once, and would have a thorough working knowledge of the legions and the operation of the fortresses and camps. The *praefectus castrorum* of each legion would be responsible for the building operations of his legionaries, answerable perhaps to his legate, who were in turn answerable to the governor. Other than this hierarchy, the procedure for carrying out such a vast operation is not known. It is permissible to envisage Hadrian gathering his officers and explaining the concept, arranging meetings and conferences, copies of maps and plans being made for consultation by the officers on site, and possibly meetings continuing after Hadrian had left, in order to monitor progress and deal with problems. The Romans did use maps, and it is suggested that plans and elevations for building works were drawn on papyrus, carved in stone, or laid out on floors and Walls as the medieval builders did.[19]

The workforce would have to be assembled and groups allocated to individual tasks. In general the legionaries did the building work, and thanks to the sixth-century compilers of a law code, a list of specialists in the legions has been preserved.[20] This list was drawn up in the second century by Taruttienus Paternus, whose name is reported in books as Tarruntienus or Tarrutenius and other variants. The list covers the many tasks that were performed by the *immunes* of a legion. The term *immunes* indicates that these soldiers with special skills were excused ordinary fatigues such as guard duties or the Roman equivalent of potato peeling, though they had to take part in training when necessary, and also fought as legionaries in battles. They were paid at the normal rate, and being an *immunis* was not regarded as a special rank, but each man was given time to carry out his specialist task, possibly fitting in ordinary fatigues if their tasks were not necessary on a continuous basis. Each legion possessed, among other specialists, stone cutters, carpenters, glass workers, plumbers, cartwrights, blacksmiths, coppersmiths, lime-burners and charcoal burners, surveyors and ditchers. There were also several clerical *immunes* who compiled strength reports and kept the legionary records of enlistments and discharges, transfers to other units, expenses for the whole unit and pay records for the men.

Among the most relevant specialists would be the *architecti* who are mentioned in the list of *immunes*. Amandus, the *arcitectus* at Birrens, has been mentioned above, and another military *architectus*, Aelius Verinus, is known from Mainz.[21] Exactly what the work of an *architectus* entailed is not documented, but it can be assumed that all the *architecti* were responsible for the design and planning of a building, and that they would be familiar with plans and elevations, and with supervision of the works. There were also *artifices qui fossam faciunt*, who planned and supervised the digging of ditches.[22] This would have been a highly relevant skill with regard to the final version of Hadrian's Wall, which was equipped with a ditch to the north that was not continuous over the eighty Roman miles of the frontier, and the Vallum to the south, which was, except for the last few miles between Newcastle and Wallsend. There would be a great deal of work for these legionary *artifices*. Even if auxiliaries dug the ditches, the supervisors would probably have been legionaries.

When building was to start on Hadrian's Wall, these men with special skills would be called on to work on the new project. It is possible that more men were trained to work in the relevant spheres on a building project that was so vast and covered a large territorial area. The labour force would consist mainly of legionaries without special skills, but some of them may have been specially trained to do the semi-skilled work as well as transporting stone to the sites and other simple tasks. Peter Hill suggests that non-skilled men could be trained to produce square facing stones in a short space of time, backing up his theory by teaching a group of people who had never worked with stone to produce squared blocks like those used to build the Wall. After only a very short training session, each member of the group could complete a stone block in about five minutes.[23]

Auxiliary soldiers do not seem to have played a predominant role in the actual construction of the Wall, but were involved in the proceedings, building the external walls or internal buildings of some forts. At Carvoran, shortly before Hadrian's death, soldiers of an auxiliary unit under their prefect Flavius Secundus rebuilt the fort which was originally part of the Stanegate system.[24] A detachment (*vexillatio*) of the fleet, the *Classis Britannica*, who set up a building inscription at the entrance to the granary at Benwell. The granaries at Rudchester and Halton Chesters are very similar to those at Benwell so it is thought that the men of the fleet built these as well.[25] The inscription from Benwell is damaged and only the letter C survives after the word *vexillatio*, then there is a gap followed by BRITAN, an abbreviation for *Britannica*. It could be argued that the missing section should read *Cohors*, and the abbreviated BRITAN stands for Britannorum, referring to a cohort of Britons, but the usual form is to abbreviate *Cohors* as *Coh*, which would not fill the whole space, whereas the word *Classis* can be comfortably fitted in using lettering of comparable size to the rest of the line.[26] The sailors of the Roman fleets were considered to be soldiers, and were usually called *milites* in official documents, not *nautae*, which referred to non-military sailors. The members of the fleets were treated as soldiers throughout their careers. They enlisted in the same way as the auxiliaries, were paid regular wages and discharged with the grant of Roman citizenship after a specified length of service, like the auxiliaries.

Between Benwell and Rudchester several building inscriptions were found on the north or south mound of the Vallum, naming a centurion and thereby indicating that the men commanded by this officer had dug a section of the ditch.[27] These could of course be legionary centurions since the inscriptions are comparable to the centurial stones recording legionaries of a particular century in building the Wall, but auxiliary infantry units also had centurions, and one of the stones from the Vallum names the unit as *cohors I Dacorum*, the First Cohort of Dacians, together with the centurion Aelius Dida.[28] Most of the other centurions named in the series of inscriptions from the Vallum probably also belonged to auxiliary units, and Hill suggests that the whole of the Vallum may have been dug by them.[29] Similarly auxiliary units may have been responsible for digging the northern ditch as well, since the work is not specialised, but involves physical fitness and endurance, and the finer details such as dimensions, depth and angle of slope can be supervised by officers, legionary or auxiliary. Transport of the stone from the quarries to the building sites may have been carried out by auxiliaries, who may have provided guards at quarry sites, along routes, and on the line of the Wall while it was being built, much as auxiliaries are depicted on Trajan's Column, standing in the foreground while legionaries build forts behind them. The auxiliaries are shown wearing their helmets and carrying their shields, with their swords very prominent on their right sides, which strongly suggests that they are on guard duty.[30] Auxiliaries may have been involved with convoys supplying food and equipment to the builders at various sites. None of this speculation is supported by any evidence, but somebody had to do it.

The numbers of men in the workforce are hard to estimate because there are too many unknown factors. One important question concerns the number of men in each of the three legions in Britain. The generalisation of 5,000 to 6,000 men per legion is exactly that, a generalisation, because there is no extant ancient source that states unequivocally how many legionaries made up a legion. The figure of *c.* 5,000 to *c.* 6,000 is worked out by counting the typical numbers of barrack blocks in a fortress and multiplying that by the typical numbers of men in each century which would occupy the barracks. This does not take into account the possibility that legions may have differed in size in different parts of the Empire, or varied according to circumstances, for instance in wartime extra men may have been added and in peacetime the complement of men may have been reduced. Even supposing that there was a standard size for all legions at all times, that figure, whatever it was, would hardly ever be representative because there would be times when there was a shortage of men and at others there would have been a surplus. Military reports preserved on papyrus show that auxiliary units were sometimes under strength and sometimes over strength and the same was most likely true of the legions.

Even supposing that the exact strength of all three legions in Britain in 122 could be revealed, the size of the workforce that was available to build the Wall and dig the northern ditch and the Vallum would still only be an estimate because it is not known how many soldiers would have been sent out on special errands, or detailed to remain behind at headquarters for administrative purposes and to look after the fortresses. Caerleon, Chester and York could hardly have been left completely empty with the gates locked and a note saying we reopen in the autumn. Soldiers were usually kept busy at all times, and not just on duty on or near their forts, so even while the Wall was being constructed an unknown number of men would be in different parts of the province, accompanying various officers and officials in a variety of tasks. Some would be at provincial headquarters in the administrative departments, others would be anywhere in the province carrying out police work, guarding markets, ports, roads and other facilities, or overseeing the collection and delivery of food supplies, clothing, fuel, and raw materials, all of which duties and more are attested in the military records from different parts of the Empire. Another unknown factor is whether there was a rota system for building the Wall, with groups of men sent out for a specified term and then swapped over with another group. Such a system would probably only involve the unskilled labourers, not the specialists, though there is no evidence as to whether all the masons, stone workers, metal workers, carpenters and the like from each legion were allocated to Wall duty. Fortresses and forts which had been in existence for some fifty years by the time the Wall was being built would need repairs and the relevant specialist workers to deal with them. Added to these totals of absentees there would be others who may have been subtracted from the workforce building the Wall, including those who were sick or temporarily out of action because of injuries and accidents, and some who had simply gone AWOL.

All these imponderables have to be assessed before estimating the size of the workforce, and it is tempting to say, before moving quickly on, that in the AD 120s there would be more people in the vicinity of Hadrian's Wall than there are in the twenty-first

century, including the tourists. Peter Hill devotes some effort to
this problem, and arrives at a figure of 7,200 legionaries to build
the Wall, made up of 2,400 from each of the three legions.[31] Crow
estimates that the total number of men would be 15,000.[32]

Hill also considers the possibility that gangs of civilians may
have been brought in to help build the Wall. Several inscriptions
have been discovered recording building work by civilians from
different *civitates* or tribal capitals, but Hill acknowledges that
these inscriptions are not dated and possibly belong to a later period
when repair work was being carried out.[33] It has been suggested
that the *civitas* inscriptions probably date from the fourth century
when the province was under more serious threat than it was in
Hadrian's reign, and when civilians could perhaps be more easily
persuaded that it was in their own interests to provide labour for
strengthening the frontier. More recent suggestions connect the
Britons from the *civitates* with the rebuilding of the Turf Wall in
stone, probably in the 160s, or alternatively with the rebuilding
programme of Severus at the beginning of the third century, when
he perhaps requisitioned labour forces from the civilians while the
military forces prepared for and fought the wars against the tribes
of northern Scotland.[34]

While slaves were probably not employed in the building work,
there would have been plenty of them in evidence at the time of
construction, attached to officers and ordinary soldiers and catering
for their needs. More recent armies were accompanied by a number
of servants, and it is known that a whole host of people not engaged
in building work gravitated to the large building projects of the
nineteenth century, to do the laundry and provide the refreshments
and entertainments, as for instance at the shanty town that grew
up at the site of the Ribblehead Viaduct when the Settle to Carlisle
railway was being built. Unless the Romans expressly forbade it,
similar groups of people would gravitate to the camps housing
soldiers with money to spend. There is no evidence for this, except
that human nature has not changed much in twenty centuries. The
slaves and the hypothetical extra people would need to be housed
and fed, but there is no evidence as to where and how. All the
soldiers would have to be housed somewhere near the building
sites, most likely in camps laid out like the forts with an earthen
bank and ditch, and probably four gateways protected by various

styles of earthen bank, the simplest being the *titulus*, a mound lying opposite and parallel to the opening. The men would live in tents, which would be made of leather, or even in temporary wooden buildings. The building seasons would have occupied a period from late spring to early autumn, because at either end of each season there would be a risk of frost damage to the work just completed. The camps would probably not be reoccupied each year because as building progressed their locations would change according to the areas to be worked on. Camps of different shapes and sizes have been revealed along the line of the Wall, several of them south of the Wall between Carvoran and Vindolanda and most especially around Haltwhistle Burn, where one of the smaller forts belonging to the Stanegate was built. On the later Antonine Wall between the Forth and the Clyde, the camps are more definitely associated with the building work, but it is not possible to state with confidence that builders of Hadrian's Wall lived in any of the known camps, because insufficient material has been recovered for dating purposes, and because there was a lot of activity in the late first and early second centuries, possibly dating from the early campaigns under the Flavian governors, or to the withdrawal to the Stanegate and the erection of the fortlets. When the Romans ceased to use a campsite or a fort, they usually demolished everything and tidied up all their accumulated rubbish, stowing it neatly away in the rounded ends of the ditches where they flanked the entrances, and then filled in the ditches and levelled them. Short occupation provides fewer opportunities for pottery to be accidentally broken and an accumulation of rubbish to be buried, or for the soldiers to lose coins and other datable objects while they dig the ditches and erect the turf and earth defences. There would most likely have been camps not only for the builders but also for the quarry workers, and one such camp near Corbridge may have been associated with a quarry.[35]

Wherever the soldiers and possibly some slaves and hangers-on lived during the building work, food supplies would have to be delivered to them, but the procedure would be the same as for armies on campaign. The soldiers could supplement their diets by hunting, fishing, foraging, purchasing from the locals, or sometimes no doubt by theft. If work continued over one or possibly two of the three pay days per year, cash would have to be procured and possibly brought to the men on site, since working for extended periods knowing that cash was safe at headquarters would not satisfy the soldiers because they would have no means of buying whatever was on offer.

The Financial Cost of Building

In the modern world the workforce would be one of the most costly elements in a massive project like building the Wall, most especially because of the current rules and regulations involving Health and Safety and insurance, and the extra costs for overtime, bonuses, and employers' pension contributions. Building the Wall today would cost millions if not billions of pounds. Breeze and Dobson report on an estimate obtained in the nineteenth century from a builder, Robert Rawlinson, who did not have the advantage of modern machinery and was therefore accustomed to organising a labour force of navvies. The estimate took into account the amounts of stone and other materials and the number of days that would be necessary to construct a stone Wall sixty-eight miles long, sixteen feet high and eight feet wide, together with digging the northern and southern ditches. The conclusion was that it would take 240 days in all and cost £1,021,269.[36] Fortunately for the Romans, the provincial and central governments were not bothered by modern considerations and restrictions. The soldiers were being paid anyway, whether they built the Wall or not. Health and Safety regulations had not been invented, so the army relied upon its own medical staff to deal with injuries, and probably no soldier sued his officers or the army over compensation for accidents in the workplace or the development of industrial-related diseases. There was no such thing as overtime payments, since the soldiers worked for as long as their officers directed. Pensions had been provided for legionaries since Augustus' day, and though it is uncertain whether the auxiliaries received pensions, they were encouraged to save part of their salaries and sums could be deducted on each of the three annual pay days and meticulously recorded at headquarters. A modern workforce would bring their own food with them, and in a way the Roman soldiers did the same, except that the army supplied the food and then deducted money for it from the soldiers' pay. None of the Wall-building activities of the soldiers would cost the Roman government anything more than usual. The stone was most likely freely quarried on lands which the Romans administered, though some raw materials such as lead may have come from private firms or contractors who owned and operated lead mines in Britain, with payment negotiated via the provincial governor's office, or that of the procurator dealing with financial affairs.

The Building Work: Surveying

One of the first tasks in building the Wall and its accompanying features would be to survey the line on which it was to run. It is generally agreed that the Romans surveyed the line of the Wall from high-point to high-point, and the army had its own surveyors, called *mensores*, who would be trained in laying out camps and forts and surveying for road-building. An altar was set up at an unknown date by the *mensor evocatus* Attonius Quintianus at Piercebridge, *evocatus* meaning that he had served his full term, but remained in service, perhaps because his skills were still in demand.[37] According to the Greek author Polybius, the Republican Roman army marked out its camps and the internal areas by using flags, so this may have been how the Romans initially marked sections of the Wall and the northern ditch and the Vallum.[38] After outlining the man route the finer details of the topography and the composition of the ground could be dealt with when the builders and diggers arrived on the scene. One important feature of the line of the Wall is that it does not always run on the most advantageous course for observation to the north, so there is a lot of dead ground where supervision could not have been carried out from the Wall itself. When soldiers and officers of a modern military unit came to a seminar at the University of Newcastle upon Tyne, they toured the Wall, and commented that it was not defensible from behind it or on top of it, because of the extent of the dead ground in front of it. This would apply whether there was a wall-walk on top of the Wall, a hotly debated subject, or whether it ended in a flat top or in an inverted V. It would seem therefore that the Roman surveyors and planners were more concerned with following a direct route to form a barrier, rather than making surveillance the main priority and building the Wall in the best locations where unrestricted views could be obtained.

Building Materials: the Turf Wall in the West

The choices of building materials for the Wall were limited to three main commodities: earth and turf, timber, or stone. Everyone who has visited Hadrian's Wall or has seen photographs of it knows that it is built of stone, but in the sector west of the River Irthing the first version of the Wall is known as the Turf Wall, being built with turf blocks with an earth infill. This was the usual method of building forts in the first century. The Roman term for such an earth and turf wall was *murus caespiticus*, or *caespiticius*. Hadrian visited the African provinces in 128, and in his *Adlocutio* to the soldiers in Numidia, he specifically refers to walls built of turf, praising the soldiers for building a wall (*murus*) from rough, heavy stones, which had scarcely taken them much longer than it would have done to build one made of turf (*non multo diutius ... quam caespite*). He goes on to say that turf is easy to cut, to carry, and to handle in construction.[39] The soldiers in Britain probably never got to hear of Hadrian's assessment of turf cutting and carrying, but if they had done so they may have taken issue with his opinion that the work was easy, since they had to cut enough of it to build two faces of a fortified line more than thirty miles long, complete with its turf milecastles.

There was a special tool for cutting the turf, looking exactly like the modern versions of turf cutters available in garden centres, as shown by examples found at Great Casterton and other places in Britain.[40] There was an optimum size for turves, because if the blocks were too small they would not stack so well, and would not be able to form stable outer skins to contain the infilling of earth. If they were too large they would fragment and be difficult to handle. Modern sources give varied measurements, ranging from square blocks with sides one Roman foot long to oblongs one and a half Roman feet by one foot, and half a Roman foot in depth.[41] It is possible that the size may have differed according to the type of earth and grass being dug, some blocks in more friable earth being more likely to break up and accordingly cut to a more compact size and shape, and others made up of more cohesive earth and grass with firmer rooting systems being cut to a larger size. The turves were used like bricks or stone blocks, stacked grass to grass and earth to earth, in two lines built up around a core of earth, which at forts was usually provided by digging a ditch round the defences. On the Turf Wall the earth would have come from the northern ditch.

At forts with ramparts built of turf, the front and rear faces of the walls would be steeply sloped to help the turves to stack properly and to bond together. The gateways of these forts would be constructed in wood and the ramparts would have been wide enough at the top to allow for timber-lined walkways, most probably protected by timber palisades or fencing. If there was a rampart walk around turf and timber forts there would have been timber steps set into the inner face of the turf and earth rampart to enable soldiers to reach the rampart top, and timber interval towers built higher than the fence or palisade. This is how the reconstructions of turf and earth ramparts have been built at the Lunt fort at Baginton near Coventry, and at Vindolanda south of the Wall. These have been standing for some decades now, probably for longer than any Roman fort of the first century would have been in continuous use, and have demonstrated what sort of repair work would have been necessary, and how often it would have to be done in order to maintain them in peak condition.

When work started on the Wall the legionaries would be highly experienced in constructing forts in turf and earth with timber fittings, since until Trajan's reign this is how military installations were built. A large part of a legionary's life would be spent digging, felling trees and building. Many scenes on Trajan's Column show soldiers working in this way during the Dacian Wars, and though the several forts that are depicted look as though they are built of stone, they were probably constructed in turf. Even when not on campaign, or when no new forts were being built, soldiers were kept busy, some of them being sent out to practice building camps with ditches and turf ramparts. Examples of such practice camps have been found in Wales near Castell Collen and Tomen-y-Mur, and at Cawthorn, not to be confused with Cawthorne, in Yorkshire, there are several earthwork enclosures, some of which may have been for practice and some for occupation. It seems that emphasis was laid on perfecting the rounded corners and the protected entrances that would have been necessary in the construction of forts and camps.

The Turf Wall consisted of a bank of earth and turf about twenty feet wide at the base, with a ditch to the north. While the turrets of the Turf Wall were stone-built, the milecastles were built in turf and earth, as were the forts. Turf and earth phases have been found at the forts at Bowness, Drumburgh, Stanwix near Carlisle, Castlesteads and Birdoswald, where more than one turf-built phase preceded the stone fort.[42] In most places it is thought that the turves were laid directly on the ground, but this conclusion is based on an examination of only one section across the Turf Wall by F. G. Simpson and Ian Richmond, reported in 1935.[43] In later investigations it was found that cobbles had been laid as a foundation, at Turf Wall milecastle 72 and at milecastle 53, and at Burgh-by-Sands.[44] Similar cobble foundations have been discovered in sections of the turf-built Antonine Wall between the Forth and the Clyde.[45]

Tradition holds that at an indeterminate date, but probably before Hadrian's death in 138, a section of the Turf Wall running westwards from the River Irthing was replaced in stone, but the remaining Turf Wall was not rebuilt until the 160s. In 2014 David Breeze devoted a chapter to the question of the rebuilding of the Turf Wall.[46] It is usually stated that in the first phase of rebuilding, the Turf Wall was converted into stone from the River Irthing as far as milecastle 54, which lay north-west of Lanercost, but the western terminus of the new stone Wall and its junction with the remaining sector of the Turf Wall has been questioned by Breeze, who points out that milecastle 54 is the furthest point reached by the original investigation in the 1930s, and no further work was done to verify that this milecastle was indeed the terminus of the Hadrianic conversion of the Turf Wall into stone. It is possible that the rebuilding in stone before Hadrian's death extended much further to the west than milecastle 54, though exactly how far to the west is difficult to discern because so little of the Wall survives.[47] The rest of the Turf Wall, from whichever point the stone Wall had reached in the first phase of rebuilding, had to wait until a later date, traditionally in the 160s when the Antonine Wall was abandoned.[48]

The Turf Wall is no longer visible, with the notable exception of a short stretch to the west of Birdoswald, where the stone Wall deviates from the line of the Turf Wall instead of replacing it on exactly the same alignment. This section of the Turf Wall was left in its original state, and can still be seen running along higher ground to the west of the fort, with the stone Wall further north, with the modern road running parallel to it. In the original layout at Birdoswald the turf and timber fort projected to the north of the Turf Wall, as shown by the discovery, under the stone fort, of pits belonging to the earlier fort. These pits, containing leather and military metalwork, were situated north of the line of the Turf Wall, which joined with the southern gate-towers on the long western and eastern sides of the fort.[49]

The reasons why the western sector of the Wall was originally built in turf have been much debated. There is a geological divide between the western sector and those of the eastern and central areas, where the limestone gives way to sandstone at the Red Rock Fault line. This can be demonstrated by the red colour of the stone used to build Carlisle castle and cathedral, compared with the colour of the castle and city Walls of Newcastle upon Tyne, minus the modern pollution-black. The decision to build the Turf Wall in the west was once attributed to the deficiency of limestone for making mortar, but this suggestion was made when it was thought that the preponderant bonding material in the core of the first building phases of the Wall was mortar.[50] This was a reasonable hypothesis considering that the Romans regularly used mortar and concrete in buildings, and they did use mortar in much of the repair work on the Wall in the early third century. Until recently there were only a few known places on the Wall where the Hadrianic builders had used clay instead of mortar, but these examples were considered to be rare exceptions, until more and more excavations were carried out and it was discovered that it is mortar that is the exception, used sparingly for the core and on the outer faces of the Wall. It is significant that the limekiln near Housesteads, in the valley of the Knag Burn immediately to the east of the fort, is the only one known in the area, and as yet no further evidence has been discovered for more lime pits, which if discovered would suggest more widespread use of lime mortar.[51]

Lack of materials to manufacture mortar therefore does not explain why the Turf Wall was built. Although sandstone was

readily available in the west it would not have been considered
suitable for building the Wall, because of its friable nature and
its relatively rapid deterioration after exposure to wind and rain.
Stone from Lowland Scotland or the Pennines was better, and
the eventual rebuilding in stone demonstrates that extraction and
transport of more durable stone was not too much of a problem for
the Romans.[52] There may have been a time factor in the transport
of stone, coupled with a need for rapid building, but shortage of
suitable stone in the immediate area or a delay in transporting it
does not entirely explain why the Romans chose to construct the
Turf Wall. It has been suggested that the whole western area may
have been under greater threat than the central and eastern sectors,
so there may have been a need for speed in erecting the running
barrier in order to foil potential attack or attempts to turn the
frontier and come up behind the soldiers working in other areas.
Shotter considers that the war that broke out at the beginning of
Hadrian's reign concerned the western sector of the country, and
that consequently as soon as it was over, the need for haste in
protecting the area may have led to the building of the Turf Wall
before Hadrian arrived in Britain, probably in 119 when building
in turf was the normal method of construction.[53]

The controversy over the Brigantian border has already been
mentioned, but the erstwhile theory that some of the tribesmen
were to be cut off and excluded by the new frontier is still not
proven. Even if the line of the Wall followed the line of the
Brigantian border, and did not exclude any part of the tribe, this
does not entirely remove the idea that there was a greater threat in
the west, especially since the Hadrianic outpost forts were clustered
on the western side in the area north of the Wall. In addition,
milecastles 47 and 48 in the west were larger than the norm,
and there was also a corresponding disproportionate number of
western Stanegate installations, implying that the western area had
always been a difficult one to control.[54]

Building Materials: the Stone Wall

It would have been possible to build the eastern sector, if not the
whole Wall, in earth and turf as well as the western sector, but

building here was in stone from the beginning. The construction of a timber palisade as in Germany and Raetia was probably not even considered because of the shortage of trees in the northern parts of England compared to the abundance of stone, and also because a timber palisade running across the Whin Sill could not have been easily embedded in the tops of the crags. Therefore stone would have to be found and quarries reopened or new ones started.

During the early occupation of a province, forts that were built in the initial stages of pacification and consolidation were usually occupied only for relatively short periods until the units moved around to new sites, but from the early second century onwards forts in Britain and other provinces became more permanent. In the Trajanic period the Romans were beginning to rebuild earth and timber forts in stone, stripping away the outer face of the rampart, or in some cases the timber revetment that had been put in place, and then building a stone wall in front of the earth rampart, but retaining the rear half of the earthen bank on the inside of the forts. When forts were newly built in stone, they still had an earthen rampart back all round the interior, for added support, and serving other purposes, for instance ovens were built into the turf, so the risk of setting fire to the fort was reduced. There is evidence that the legionary fortresses in Britain were being rebuilt in stone in the last years of Domitian's reign and in the early years of Trajan's. Caerleon was perhaps the earliest, with work being done between 90 and 100. Chester was rebuilt in stone from about 102, and York from about 107–08. These three fortresses remained the headquarters of the legions in Britain from this time onwards.

Hadrian's new frontier was built as a single wall, with squared stone facings on both sides, and had to be wide enough to support itself, without the added reinforcement of an earthen rampart back. Vast quantities of stone would have been necessary to build the curtain wall, the milecastles and turrets, and then shortly afterwards the forts. Several quarries are known to the north and the south of the Wall, but use of them cannot be closely dated, so it is not certain if the original Wall builders used all of them. A soldier of *II Augusta* left an inscription dated to 207 in a quarry site near Brampton, which may represent repair work on the Wall by Severus, who arrived in Britain in the following year, but it is not a certain indication that first-century quarries worked the same site.[55] Work has been done on the geology of the area and the sources and quality of building stone, not all of which was of a uniform standard.[56] It is not known if the stones were cut to the specified size and shape at the quarry, but to do so would reduce the weight to be transported from the quarry to the building sites, and would also mean that space would not be taken up with soldiers performing this task in the same area as the builders were working. Ready-shaped stones could be loaded onto carts and dropped close to the building area, whereas roughly shaped stones would have to be loaded, unloaded near the building site for the stone masons to work on them and then possibly loaded up again to be carried to the parts of the Wall that were being built.

The original plan for the Wall was to build it to a width of ten Roman feet, but before the Wall was completed to the ten foot gauge, it was decided to reduce it in width to about eight Roman feet, and these sections are referred to as the 'Narrow Wall'. In some places the Wall was judged to fit neither of the categories of Broad or Narrow Wall, and so the term 'Intermediate Wall' was coined to distinguish these sectors. However it has been shown that this conclusion about the width of the so-called Intermediate Wall was based primarily on the foundations with little knowledge of the Wall that once stood on top of them, and excavation at sites where the Wall survives has demonstrated that the width of the foundations is not a reliable guide to the width of the Wall.[57] Another complication is that where the Emperor Severus carried out repairs at the beginning of the third century, the Wall is also only about six feet wide, and must not be confused with the Narrow Wall of the Hadrianic building works.

The Broad Wall was, with some exceptions, built westwards from Newcastle for about eighteen to twenty miles, while the eastern sector from Newcastle to Wallsend was built as Narrow Wall.[58] West of the River North Tyne the foundations had been laid for the Broad Wall before the decision to reduce the width had been taken, and in these cases the foundations can still be seen protruding to the south of the Narrow Wall that was built on top of them. In at least one instance, east of milecastle 39, which lies between the modern car park at Steel Rigg and Crag Lough, excavations showed that the Broad Wall foundation layer had been set down, but was never used, and the Narrow Wall was built nearer to the edge of the crags.[59].

The locations of the turrets and milecastles were surveyed and plotted, and building started before the Wall itself, which is clear from the fact that some of these installations had been equipped with wing walls at either side, measuring ten Roman feet wide, ready for the Broad Wall curtain to be attached to them, but in some cases when the builders arrived they constructed the Wall at the Narrow gauge. A good place to observe this is at Willowford, where the wing walls of the turrets protrude from the rest of the curtain wall by about two feet on the south side, so there are two ninety degree angles, one between the Wall and the turret wing wall, and another between the south face of the wing wall and the turret. The exposed corners of the wing walls were properly finished off with large stones. Another example can be seen at Black Carts turret, number 29a, on the Hadrian's Wall path between Chesters fort and Limestone Corner, just off the B6318.

The Wall was built on a foundation layer of cobbles or broken stones rather than on a base of squared stones like those used to build the Wall itself. In some places larger flagstones were used, and in the past it was thought that these were used solely for the Broad Wall, while cobbles formed the base for the Narrow Wall, but Breeze and Hill have shown that this is false. They suggest that the flagstones were used by only one legion, probably *VI Victrix* since they do not appear as a universal feature all along the Wall.[60] In some places the flagstones were used as kerb stones, and at turrets 26a and 26b where Broad Wall foundations had been laid down, the builders placed a layer of flagstones on top to form a level base for the Narrow Wall.[61] The foundations were sometimes set into a shallow trench and bonded with clay in most places, though earth was also used, and in two places in the central sector where the Whin Sill predominates, there was no trench but the foundations were laid onto the rock. Compared to the monumental buildings of the Roman world the foundations of the Wall were almost non-existent. The first-century Roman author Vitruvius, who had been a military architect, recommended that foundations should be dug into the solid ground, if such ground could be reached, or as far as necessary according to the size of the building to be erected, and the foundations should also extend further out than the width of the walls.[62] The foundations of the temple of Jupiter on the Capitoline Hill, all that remains of this once massive building, can be seen in the Capitoline Museum. They are at least five metres in height, dwarfing visitors. For a building such as the temple to the chief god of Rome, the intention was not just to achieve stability but to impress or even overpower. For Hadrian's Wall, foundations on this scale were obviously not thought necessary.

The foundation layer was slightly wider than the Wall, and on top of this first layer one or two courses of offset stone footings were laid down, set back from the edge of the foundation, but also projecting slightly from the rest of the Wall, giving the appearance of small steps from the ground to the face of the Wall. Footings such as these were once used in modern brick buildings, in order to distribute the pressure of the walls over a greater area of the foundations, but concrete is now used instead. Presumably the offset footings of Hadrian's Wall served the same purpose in Roman times, to spread the weight for greater stability. During later building phases, the offsets were not used, as shown by investigations in the region of milecastle 45, west of Great Chesters.[63] It is postulated that separate gangs were detailed for foundation work, while a different set of legionaries built the Wall. It is not clear whether it was the Wall builders or the foundation builders who provided the offset footing courses.[64] The terminology used for stone work, foundations and offsets in excavation reports is not uniform, and Breeze and Hill have appealed for greater standardization, which would lead to greater clarity.[65]

The external faces of the Wall were constructed from two skins of roughly squared stones, with a rubble core infill, bonded with clay or mortar, clay apparently being the favoured bonding material rather than mortar. Clay bonding was not always secure, as demonstrated by a stone tower on the Turf Wall, number 54a, which fell into the ditch, and had to be replaced by another stone tower sited behind the first one, and set back from the Turf Wall, but when the stone Wall was built it was joined to the turret.[66] Where mortar was used in parts of the Narrow Wall it was less durable than the mortar that was used later in repair work, especially the Severan repairs.[67]

No one can say how high the Wall was in its completed state, but as the Wall grew in height, scaffolding would become necessary to enable the builders to construct the two outer skins and fill the gap between the two with rubble and clay. To date, there is no evidence from any part of the Wall for the use of scaffolding, except at the fort of Birdoswald, where there is evidence that it was used in building the granaries.[68] It is not possible to say how the postulated scaffolding was constructed for the Wall, except by analogy with evidence from other parts of the Roman world. A wall painting from the tomb of Trebius Justus on the Via Latina in Rome shows two men laying bricks at the top of a wall, one of them hidden behind the wall and the other standing on planks across the scaffolding at the front of the wall. He wields a modern-looking trowel. The scaffolding is clearly shown, with another man climbing up a ladder which leans against it.[69] Peter Hill devotes a chapter to the probable nature of the Wall scaffolding, pointing out that to try to build the higher levels of the Wall while standing on top of the uneven rubble core would have been impractical.[70]

The different widths of the foundation layers and the Wall itself probably indicate that different gangs of soldiers worked on them, which in turn presupposes that the three legions which did the building work were divided up into groups and each was allocated a stretch of the Wall to complete, with its turrets and milecastles. It has been suggested that five-mile lengths were the norm for each gang.[71] It is reasonable to suppose that each work gang would have been told where to start and where to end their work, but there is no absolute proof that they all constructed five-mile sections. At one time it was thought that the work of individual legions could be detected in the various styles of building work, notably the gateways of the milecastles, which vary in design. Inscriptions show that *II Augusta* was responsible for building work at three milecastles within the same area, numbers 37, 38 and 42, between Housesteads and Great Chesters. Further to the west, work by *XX Valeria* is attested at milecastle 47, which is situated between Gilsland and Carvoran but is not currently visible.[72] On the basis of the epigraphic evidence it seemed clear that the legions were assigned to building stretches of the Wall together with its milecastles and turrets, but this theory has been eroded as more work has been done on the Wall and further variations in style have come to light.[73] The confident allocation of different styles of building work to *II Augusta*, *VI Victrix* and *XX Valeria Victrix* has been modified, and a new convention has been developed, labelling the work as that of legions A, B or C, without trying to name them. It is also recognised that in some cases one legion could have begun the work, and another was detailed to finish it off.[74] The possibility does not seem to have been considered that different work gangs from the same legion could have built in different styles, perhaps depending on who was supervising them.

The Milecastles and Turrets

As mentioned above, it seems that the milecastles and turrets were surveyed and laid out before the Wall was built. The gateways of milecastles were built to at least four different patterns, and the milecastles themselves adopted two different shapes, some of them being attached to the Wall on their longer sides, now labelled short-axis milecastles, as measured north to south, while others were attached by their shorter sides, extending further to the south than the former type, and labelled long-axis milecastles. Whatever their shape, the milecastles enclosed roughly the same area, with exceptions in the west where some of the stone milecastles are larger than those on the rest of the Wall, reflecting the larger size of the turf milefortlets that they replaced. Whether they were short or long-axis the milecastles were joined to the curtain Wall at their northern sides, and had rounded corners on their southern sides. There were two single-portal gateways, one in the north side through the Wall itself, and another directly opposite on the south side. Reconstructions of the milecastles usually show a tower over the gate to the north, probably influenced by the theory that observation to the north was of paramount importance, but since the foundations of both the north and south gates are the same size and shape, whatever their individual design, they could presumably have supported a tower, and it was proposed by the late Charles Daniels that there was also a tower over the south gate, which if correct could be taken to indicate that observation was also necessary to the south. It has to be acknowledged that, since no gateway survives above the first few stones of the arch, it is not certain if there were any towers at all.

Between the two gates there was usually a road through the

milecastle dividing it into two halves, but it is controversial whether these roads led out to the north, and whether it was only military personnel who were allowed to use them. This is discussed further in the chapter on the function of the Wall. On either side of the roadway, early excavations revealed that there were structures interpreted as short barrack blocks, which was once taken to indicate that the two structures could have accommodated perhaps a half century of an auxiliary unit. However, this pattern of accommodation was probably not standard in all the milecastles, and it is now thought that only about eight men manned the milecastles.[75] The nature of the occupation and the purpose of the milecastles is disputed, and probably changed significantly over time. The problem is circular: if the number of men were known in each milecastle it might help to elucidate how the milecastles functioned, and if it were known how they functioned it might help to elucidate the size of the garrison. Some soldiers obviously did remain in the milecastles, rather than coming out to them from the forts each day. Usually there was an oven in one corner of the milecastle, indicating that some soldiers lived there and cooked meals. In the opposite corner there may have been a stairway up to the walls, but only one example has been discovered at Poltross Burn, where the lower portions of such a stair can still be seen. It is not known what the top of the walls would have looked like, despite the reconstructions that often show a rampart walk all round the top of the milecastle, with accompanying crenellations, and a junction with the Wall that continues the crenellated parapet of the milecastle to the parapet of the Wall. In a few examples, there was a ditch around the milecastle, but at present this is rare and cannot be shown to have been a normal defensive feature.

The turrets between the milecastles were usually partially embedded within the Wall itself, rendering the curtain wall, which formed the northern wall of each turret, thinner than the Wall. Turrets protruded a short distance south of the Wall with a doorway in the southern wall, sometimes on the left or sometimes on the right as seen from the south. It is usually assumed that the turrets would be higher than the Wall, but since the height of the Wall is not known it is not possible to say how high the turrets would have been, and therefore it is not known if they had two or even three storeys. Access to the top of the turret may have been by a ladder, or possibly by wooden stairways from the platforms that have been found in some turrets. These platforms are not usually a primary feature of turret design but were added at some later time, and were probably not provided at all turrets. Access to the top of the turret does not automatically imply that there was also access to the top of the Wall, especially as it is very much disputed whether there was a wall-walk on the Wall. Reconstructions of turrets show them with a variety of roof styles, flat with a crenelated parapet, or with pitched roofs covered by thatch or tiles, sometimes with a projecting gallery all around the tower, based on the towers depicted on Trajan's Column. This means that no one really knows what happened at the top levels.[76] A flat roof would allow for enhanced observation, but would have been somewhat cold and uncomfortable, and there would have been drainage problems to overcome in wet weather, while a pitched roof would provide shelter and deflect rainwater, but it would have inhibited observation.[77] Much of the controversy over roof styles is related to the perceived purpose of the turrets, which is in turn related to the perceived purpose of the pre-Hadrianic towers in the vicinity of the Wall, and also that of the examples of free-standing towers depicted on Trajan's Column.

The Northern Ditch

An outer ditch was a normal defensive feature around Roman marching camps or temporary camps, and around forts, fortlets and free-standing towers. Some forts, such as Ardoch in Scotland and Whitley Castle in England had multiple ditches. The ditch or ditches would have impeded access to any military installation, so when the Wall was built the northern ditch served the same purpose. It used to be thought that the ditch was dug to a standard pattern, V-shaped but with a square channel at the bottom, known as an ankle-breaker, for drainage and to assist with cleaning out the debris that would inevitably collect there. As more excavations have taken place it is now known that there was no strict adherence to this alleged pattern. The width and the depth of the ditch vary, the angle of slope varies according to the terrain, and there was not always an ankle-breaker slot at the bottom.[78] The berm, or the space between the Wall and the edge of the ditch, also varied in width. On the Turf Wall the ditch was only about six feet away from the turf rampart, but on the stone Wall it was further away, allowing for a berm of about twenty feet, which Breeze and Dobson suggest was to prevent the weight of the stone Wall from causing the southern edge of the ditch to subside.[79] The earth dug out of the ditch was thrown up onto the northern edge to create a heightened slope on that side.

The northern ditch accompanying the Wall was not continuous. In some places where the Wall ran over elevated ground, such as the Whin Sill, the almost sheer cliff rendered the ditch unnecessary, but in some places there are gaps in the crags which would have been easier to penetrate, so stretches of the ditch were dug to protect the Wall. At Limestone Corner not far from Chesters, the ground is not quite as elevated as that of the central sector, but it is solid rock. The northern ditch was started here but never finished. The accumulated blocks of stone in the dip show that the Romans would have been capable of creating a ditch, but it would have taken a long time, and so they decided that such a feature was not of prime importance to the northern side of the Wall at this location. Immediately to the south of the abandoned ditch at Limestone Corner, the Vallum was dug without a break through the rock, implying that it was of extreme importance to the Hadrianic builders of the Wall, but no one today knows exactly why, so theories continue to multiply. The aborted northern ditch, the line of the Wall represented by the modern road, and the Vallum, are very close together at this point.

A Possible War in the 120s and Changes to the Original Plan for the Wall

The native response to the building of the Wall may have been violent, and trouble may have broken out quite early. There are hints that there was a war in Britain a few years after the alleged unrest in 117–18, probably in the early 120s. Tribes living on either side of the Wall could have harboured grievances about their newly restricted movement, or the clear intention to restrict it, so the unrest could have been south of the Wall among the Brigantes, or in

the north beyond the Wall, or possibly both. Pinpointing an exact
date for a renewed outbreak is not so simple.[80] Not all scholars
agree that there was another war after peace had been made early
in Hadrian's reign, but separate inscriptions attest that two men,
Maenius Agrippa and Pontius Sabinus, took part in a Hadrianic
expeditio Britannica.[81] The contentious point concerns the meaning
of *expeditio*, which normally refers to a military action, but it
has been argued that in the case of Agrippa and Sabinus it simply
refers to Hadrian's visit in 122, somewhat pretentiously labelled.
Sabinus' contribution to the British expedition was to convey
3,000 legionaries from the legions of Upper Germany and Spain.
Unfortunately his career inscription does not furnish archaeologists
with a date for this event, nor a specific purpose, so it leaves
the argument open as to whether he arrived with the Emperor
himself, or at some later time. Without a specific date for the
arrival of the 3,000 troops, it is not possible to discern whether the
reinforcements that Sabinus brought were intended to replace the
military losses in the war of 117–18, or to assist in another war at
some unknown date between *c.* 124 and 130.

Advocates for a second war in Britain have suggested various
dates. Frere placed the probable war in 128–30, linking the fighting
with the arrival of the governor Julius Severus, who may have put
an end to hostilities.[82] After serving in Britain, according to Dio,
Julius Severus was sent to Judaea to quell the Jewish revolt which
broke out in 132, though Birley suggests that Hadrian may have
delayed until *c.* 134 in choosing Severus for this task.[83]

C. E Stevens and D. J. Breeze have linked the postulated fighting
to the disruption in the building work on Hadrian's Wall. Breeze
opts for 124–26, causing a halt in the construction of the forts,
while Stevens thought it took place in a narrower time slot in
125, and that it was responsible not only for the disruption in the
building work but also for the decision to build it to a narrower
width.[84] Studying coin issues from Alexandria, John Casey noted
that whenever there had been significant military conflicts in the
Empire, coins were issued celebrating Nike, the Greek Goddess
of Victory.[85] Large numbers of coins of this type date to the years
between 124 and 126. Nothing is known of a major military action
in other provinces during these years under Hadrian, so the coins
may refer to a victory in Britain, and could possibly imply that

the *expeditio Britannica* of the career inscriptions of Agrippa and Sabinus probably was a military expedition and not just a visit by the Emperor in 122, and could possibly belong to the summer of 124. Casey suggested that the probable war in the early 120s may have triggered the decision to build forts on the Wall itself, and Hodgson also suggests that there was trouble, probably in 123 almost immediately after work on the Wall began, so after the war, instead of relying upon the forts in the rear on the Stanegate system, the decision was made to add forts to the Wall.[86] The number of forts on the Wall would eventually outnumber the forts on the Stanegate, so the fort decision also involved increasing the garrison.

Archaeological evidence points to a hiatus in the building work on the Wall, which probably occurred *c*. 124. In Wall terminology this is called dislocation, when parts of the Wall in different stages of building were left unfinished, preceding a change of plan. In the stretch between milecastle 22 and turret 27a, the Wall was built to different specifications. Some parts of the Wall were on broad foundations with the ten foot Broad Wall started, but in other places the Broad Wall foundations had Narrow Wall built on them. The same mixture of broad foundations and Broad and Narrow Wall are found east of the Irthing.[87] This reveals that the plan for a Wall with a width of ten feet was changed quite suddenly, leaving stretches of Broad Wall half built, and in some places Broad Wall foundation had been laid in some parts, but the Wall had not yet been built up. At least one turret was in progress when the orders arrived to change the specification for the Wall, so it has one wing designed for Broad Wall on one side and the other side the wing wall was designed for the Narrow Wall. Some stretches of the Wall east of the Irthing had been started as Broad Wall, and built up to about five courses, then the Narrow Wall was built on top of this, leaving a protrusion like a step on the south side, indicating that orders had been issued to stop building to the wider gauge and from then onwards to continue the work at the narrower gauge.

The interruption of the work is linked to the decision to put forts on the Wall itself, instead of relying upon the Stanegate forts for protection of the whole line. There is no incontrovertible proof that the fort decision and the reduction in the width of the Wall were related and simultaneous, but since fort building would take some considerable time, the reduction in the width of the Wall would compensate a little, saving not only substantial amounts of infill material, but also man-hours in the quarrying, transporting and building, using reduced quantities. As Crow points out, though a narrower Wall would reduce the amount of infill, it would not reduce the amount of facing stones, unless the original intended height of the Wall was also reduced, a speculation that cannot be proved but might reflect a change in the function of the Wall.[88]

The revised plan required the construction of at least eleven or perhaps twelve forts, at Bowness, possibly Burgh-by-Sands, where the fort labelled Burgh I may be Hadrianic but this is not certain, Stanwix, Castlesteads, Birdoswald, Great Chesters, Housesteads, Chesters, Rudchester, Halton Chesters, Benwell and Wallsend. The dates of the forts at Drumburgh in the west and Newcastle in the east are not established, and Carrawburgh and Carvoran probably did not belong to the original fort decision, being added, or perhaps refurbished in the case of Carvoran, some ten years later. At South Shields on the south of the Tyne, it seems that the first fort was built somewhere near the current site, but the only buildings that have been found up to now belong to a civilian settlement dating to about 125, so the Hadrianic fort which was presumably next to the settlement has still not been found.

When the forts were built on the Wall, some parts of the curtain wall, one milecastle and some turrets, had to be demolished in order to build the forts on the same sites. Not all archaeologists agree with this scenario, a dissenting voice suggesting that on the Stanegate line, which may or may not have extended to the coast, the lack of forts to the east of Corbridge would have made it necessary from the start to put forts on the Wall in this area, because there was no back-up, as there undoubtedly was in the western and central areas.[89] According to this scenario the demolition of work already done can be dismissed as mistakes arising from rigid adherence to the specifications for the turrets and milecastles on the Wall, but it is debatable whether the builders worked within the confines of such an intransigent bureaucratic mindset, or whether the initial plan was drawn up for a Wall without forts.

The establishment of some of the forts involved not only demolition of installations already started, but also filling in some parts of the northern ditch and the Vallum. At the fort at Halton Chesters the fort projected beyond the Wall so that the west and east gates were built over the ditch to the north of the Wall, which was filled in and levelled, but the gate towers had to be supported on massive foundations to prevent them from sinking into the disturbed ground.[90] At Chesters, projecting beyond the Wall like Halton Chesters, the northern ditch accompanying the Wall had been dug, the foundations for the Broad Wall had been laid down, and the turret which would have been 27a had been started. All this had to be demolished, and the Wall ditch had to be filled in, which as at Halton Chesters would have rendered the ground above it prone to subsidence, so the fort builders at Chesters compensated by laying extra deep foundations at the points where the ditch had once been laid out. At Housesteads the Broad Wall running along the crags had already been started together with turret 36b, but this had to be taken down to allow for the building of the fort. The northern wall of the fort extended beyond the original line of the Wall, which had been set further back from the edge of the crag. These features are still visible at the fort. The fort at Great Chesters was built over the site of what would have been milecastle 43, which despite its absence is still retained in the modern east to west numbering scheme. On the Turf Wall, turret 49a together with part of the Wall and the northern ditch were obliterated by the first fort at Birdoswald, which was built of turf and projected beyond the Wall, as did the stone fort that replaced it at some time before 138. The three elements of the building work, consisting of a detectable pause when building ceased, the change from Broad Wall to Narrow Wall, and the demolition of early structures to make way for the forts, cannot be dated with any precision, but all tend towards changes of plan about how the Wall was to function, possibly all made simultaneously.

Roman forts were built to roughly similar plans but not to unchanging uniform designs. Most forts in Hadrian's day were shaped like a playing card with rounded corners, and four double-portal gates, one in each of the long and short sides. The central range was usually occupied by the administrative buildings, the *principia* or headquarters in the middle, flanked by the commander's house on one side and the granaries on the other. In the rear portion or *retentura* which lay behind the centre range, and similarly in the larger front sector, the *praetentura*, there would be barrack blocks and other buildings such as stores, workshops and the hospital. There was no standard position for these latter features in forts and fortresses. As more and more excavations have been carried out, it has been shown that forts were adapted to whatever purpose they served, or whatever location they were built in, and the expected rectangular shape with the internal three-part division is not always found. It might seem logical that when building a new stone fort the Romans would also construct all the internal buildings in stone as well, but it has been pointed out that in excavations of a fort with stone defences, internal buildings also built of stone may not represent the first phase or phases of the internal layout, because the headquarters, barracks and other buildings of the early stone forts might have been constructed in timber, only being replaced in stone at a later date.[91]

When the forts were built on the frontier line, several of them projected beyond the Wall with about one third of their total area to the north. In projecting forts the Wall usually connected with the southernmost tower of the dual-portal gateways in the east and west sides, and there would usually be a single-portal gate in these two walls, lying to the south of the Wall, totalling six gates in all rather than the usual four. This arrangement would enable the soldiers to exit more quickly to the north and reach potential trouble spots.[92] The projection was clearly of importance, judging from the amount of work that had to be done at Halton Chesters and Chesters to fill in the Wall ditch and then build elaborate foundations for the gate towers that sat over the infilled sections.

It has been stated that originally all the forts were designed to project beyond the Wall, with three of the gates on the northern side. It would have been much easier to align the northern walls of all the forts with the Wall itself, but the theory goes that it was only in places where the topography made projection to the north impossible that the forts were lined up with the Wall, with only one of the gates allowing access to and from the north. At Housesteads for instance, the northern wall of the fort, its longer side, is joined to the Wall, so the north gate is situated on the edge of a crag, and in Roman times a ramp was constructed to enable soldiers to deploy to the north. The theory that all forts were designed to project to the north of the Wall has been questioned by Austen, who examined why some forts were planned to sit astride the Wall and others were not.[93] The scheme for three gates to the north was soon amended, and Breeze and Dobson suggest that the Romans realised that they had over-provisioned the forts with access points.[94] The west gate at Halton Chesters had not been completed when it was decided to block it up, and at Housesteads the north gate was reduced to only the western portal, while its companion roadway in the eastern portal was blocked. The topography at the fort at Great Chesters would have allowed the fort to project beyond the Wall, but it was not built to this plan. It was the last fort to be constructed and by the time it was built it could be argued that the need for three gates beyond the line of the Wall had become obsolete. Similarly the fort at Carrawburgh, added later still, did not project to the north. It is suggested that the forts which did project were part of a design conceived at some distance from the frontier, where theories did not match reality.[95]

Although the Alexandrian coin issues of 124 and 125, described above, hint at a war in the 120s and have been linked to a hiatus in building work followed by the fort decision, in archaeological terms the starting date for the building of the forts is not certain, except that plans were probably revised early in Hadrian's reign, not very long after his visit to Britain. Inscriptions found at the forts at Benwell and Halton Chesters attest building work under the governor Platorius Nepos, so the governor who began the building of the Wall also began the construction of forts.[96] This can be dated to some point before the summer of 127, by which time Nepos had been replaced as governor by Lucius Trebius Germanus, who may even have arrived in the province by September 126.[97] There is always the possibility that Nepos served for the usual term of about three years as governor, leaving Britain *c*. 125, and the next governor arrived and departed without leaving a trace of his presence before Trebius Germanus became governor, but at present it can only be said that building at Benwell and Halton Chesters was in progress if not completed at some date before 126 or 127.

The forts were spaced at intervals averaging just over seven miles, variable according to the lie of the land.[98] The distance between Halton Chesters and Chesters is only six miles, and that between Chesters and Housesteads is just over nine miles, but the fort at Chesters had to be placed on the River North Tyne and would not have been able to guard the river crossing if rigid adherence to spacing had been observed. The later fort at Carrawburgh, built over the original line of the Vallum which was simply filled in and not re-dug around the fort, plugged the nine-mile gap between Chesters and Housesteads, and Great Chesters was built roughly half way between Housesteads and Birdoswald.[99]

The Vallum

The southern ditch labelled the Vallum which accompanies the Wall to the south stretched the whole distance from the western end of the Wall as far as Newcastle, but so far it has not been traced east of Newcastle to Wallsend. As mentioned above, at Limestone Corner where the digging of the northern ditch through solid rock was abandoned, the Vallum was continued without a break regardless of the difficulties of constructing it. Common sense suggests that the Romans would not dig the deep ditch of the Vallum until all the building work on the Wall and the forts was nearing completion, because it would hinder transport of the stone and other building materials to the site of the Wall. Support for this theory is derived from the fact that the Vallum diverts to pass round the southern defences of some of the forts, for instance at Birdoswald and Halton Chesters, and opposite the forts a part of the Vallum was never dug out, leaving a causeway to provide access across it, to and from each fort. The first causeway to be discovered was at Birdoswald, and the only one visible today is at Benwell, where it was clear that there had also been a gate on the north side of the Vallum.[100] The implication is that the forts were already built or being built when the Vallum was created, or better still, that the forts and the Vallum were planned as a unified entity, but built consecutively.

As with all neat theories, a niggling problem arose at an excavation in the 1950s at the Limestone Corner sector of the Vallum and Wall, which produced contradictory evidence for the supposed chronology of Wall first and Vallum last. The excavation by Brenda Heywood, or Swinbank as she then was, yielded indications that the Vallum had been dug *before* the foundations for the Broad Wall had been laid down.[101] This is a strong hint that received opinion, based on theories which are in turn based on a few excavations, is not established fact, and until every inch of the Wall and the Vallum have been explored, an open mind must be maintained in formulating ideas and then applying them uniformly from Bowness-on-Solway to Wallsend. It has been recognised in more recent times that forts, milecastles and turrets may have individual histories and discoveries at one of them or even a few of them, and do not necessarily imply a policy for all the frontier installations.

The Vallum was more of a zone than a line, covering a wide area of about 120 Roman feet, to allow for the two mounds of earth, one on the northern and one on southern side, each measuring about twenty feet at the base. The mounds were set back to allow for a gap or berm of about thirty feet between each mound and the edges of the ditch, and the ditch itself at twenty feet wide. The sides of the ditch were sloped for greater stability of the earth, and the bottom of the ditch was flat. In all it was a considerable obstacle to free movement, except at designated crossing points opposite the Wall forts. The causeways across the ditch probably all had stone-built gates with wooden doors, as discovered at Benwell, and these were presumably operated and guarded by soldiers from each fort, to prevent unauthorised personnel from entering the area between the Vallum and the Wall without supervision.

Another feature of the Vallum is the existence of metalling, mostly found on the northern berm between the mound and the ditch, and occasionally on the south berm, which may have formed a trackway.[102] It is suggested that there was a track along the south berm near milecastle 50 on the Turf Wall.[103] New theories have evolved to explain the metalling of the berm of the Vallum. Breeze and Dobson suggest that civilians would be allowed to use the causeways across the Vallum opposite the forts, then pass along the northern berm as far as the nearest milecastle, and thence through the Wall.[104] Since the metalling cannot yet be shown to have been laid down all along the whole length of the berm on one or both sides of the Vallum, it cannot be said that this was a major element in communications in either direction between east and west.[105] One problem concerns ingress and egress to and from the metalled tracks, which would have been enclosed between the mound on one side and the ditch on the other. In the past it was assumed that there would have been access to each milecastle via a causeway across the Vallum, with concomitant gaps in the north mound, but this theory is controversial. While causeways were provided at forts, the evidence was not so clear that there were causeways at milecastles. It had always been maintained that there was a causeway at milecastle 50, and there are gaps in the north mound of the Vallum opposite milecastles 20, 30 and 42, but no proof of a causeway at these locations.[106] Investigations at several milecastles were undertaken by Humphrey Welfare, who found evidence that causeways had once existed at at least sixteen milecastles, and at four milecastles a mound had been built across the northern end of the causeway. He concluded that the Romans had assessed each milecastle with regard to the need for passage through the Wall and provided causeways where they were necessary, and then in the later second century when gateways at milecastles were narrowed and access was restricted, the causeways were removed.[107] Wilmott concluded that where causeways had been placed opposite milecastles, they were secondary, provided after there had been some slippage and erosion down the slope and in some places growth of vegetation. He suggested that when the move north to the Antonine Wall was made and the Vallum was slighted, the causeways were created by using the earth from the gaps that were deliberately cut into the mounds of the Vallum.

At present it is only possible to say that there was probably access to some milecastles where the Romans thought there was a need for it. The question of civilian access, routes through the milecastles, together with the various theories concerning the purpose of the Vallum and how it may have worked are discussed in the chapter on the function of the Wall.

The Outpost Forts

Since it is not possible to demonstrate with any precision when it was decided to build the outpost forts on the western side of the country beyond Hadrian's Wall, it is not certain whether they belonged to the same planning process as the so-called fort decision described above, or whether they were planned to accompany the first version of the Wall guarded by milecastles and turrets on the line of the Wall backed up by the forts on the Stanegate. The outpost forts at Birrens, Netherby and Bewcastle have been dated to Hadrian's reign, Birrens on the basis of pottery associated with the defences, generally dated to sometime before 128, and Netherby and Bewcastle are each dated from only one inscription from each site, seen and recorded before the early eighteenth century, but since lost. At Netherby an inscription was first noticed in 1601 built into a sixteenth-century house near the fort, and the text recording building work by *II Augusta* under Hadrian exists only in a description and a manuscript illustration. Only one inscription from this fort mentions Hadrian, the rest are all third century.[108] At Bewcastle an inscription mentions building work under Hadrian by *II Augusta* and *XX Valeria Victrix*. It was found while a grave was being dug in the churchyard, and was visible there when John Horsley saw it and included a discussion of it in his *Britannia Romana* which was published in 1732. Unfortunately it is now lost.[109] Despite the lack of extant epigraphic proof that Bewcastle was part of the original Hadrianic scheme, it would seem that it was planned to build the fort during the earliest phase of the Wall, since a road runs north towards the outpost from milecastle 50 on the Turf Wall. The road cannot be shown to go as far as Bewcastle, but it is unlikely that it would have been laid out in isolation, terminating at an unknown destination north of the Wall, and if the sole purpose of a road leading to the north was to provide a crossing point through the Wall, then a better place would have been at Birdoswald.[110] It follows that if Bewcastle was Hadrianic, then Birrens and Netherby would also have been part of the scheme. Breeze and Dobson suggest that the outposts were completed by about 130.

It has been pointed out that on the eastern section of the Wall the views to the north are unimpeded, while on the western side the terrain conceals movement from the north towards the Wall, which serves in part to explain the necessity for the outposts. After Hadrian's reign, outpost forts were added in the east, at Risingham and High Rochester. Both these forts lie on the north–south route approximating to the modern A68, which runs dead straight for much of its length, over several steep east–west ridges with blind summits at the top. Marching north from the Wall would not have been as easy as it looks on a modern road map.

The Cloud of Unknowing

Hadrian's Wall has been studied and investigated for at least five centuries, but despite all the labour and thought, there are still many questions about it for which there are no ready answers. There was a setback in the study of the Wall in the 1930s because it was considered that the problems had been solved, and as Breeze points out this was damaging, because the statement was taken at face value, especially by people in charge of the cash for grants to carry out excavations and further studies.[111] But the sheer volume of subsequent publications, debating, arguing, questioning and theorising, demonstrates that there are more things that are *not* known about the Wall than things that are understood. There has been a staggering amount of excavation and publication since the 1930s, and knowledge has increased by several hundred percent, and as more knowledge is accrued, it prompts contemplation and questioning. Regarding the many problems of Hadrian's Wall, it is probably fair to say that the only certainty is *where* it is, but other questions, beginning with *how*, *when* and more importantly *why*, are still being debated, which testifies to the enduring fascination of the Wall for people from all walks of life, from mildly interested tourists to serious and intense academics.

The question of how long it took to build the Wall and when the building work ended is only partly understood. Once again unequivocal dating evidence is lacking. It is known that building work was still going on towards the end of Hadrian's reign. The last fort to be built on the Wall was at Great Chesters. A dedicatory inscription from the fort names Hadrian with the initials PP, representing his title *Pater Patriae*, Father of the Fatherland, which was awarded to him in 128, but without any other dating evidence on the inscription of the building work that it commemorates cannot be dated more closely than to the decade between 128, when the honorary title was awarded, and Hadrian's death in138. Inscriptions found at Carvoran have been interpreted to show that building work was carried out in 136–37 to convert the fort defences from turf and earth to stone. Part of a dedication slab found reused in a field wall names Hadrian as the Emperor, and other inscriptions, one an altar and two recording building work, name Titus Flavius Secundus, prefect of *cohors I Hamiorum sagittariorum*.[112] Secundus is known to have commanded this unit of archers for some years between 135 and 139, and the altar that he dedicated was set up for the welfare of Lucius Aelius Caesar, who was adopted by Hadrian in 136 and died in 138. The building inscriptions are noteworthy, firstly because they denote building work by an auxiliary unit, and secondly because of the use of the term *vallavit*, a laconic one-word means of expressing that a particular century had built a length of wall, in this case measured in feet (*pedes*) and not paces (*passus*). Carvoran was not strictly a Wall fort. It belonged to the Stanegate and therefore predates the Wall, but it is not certain if it was abandoned and left empty for a while, or fully or partly occupied throughout the pre-Wall period and also during the construction work on the Wall. It was never attached to the Wall but actually excluded from it by the Vallum which makes a detour around its northern edge.

By the time of Hadrian's death in 138 the forts on the Wall had been completed and work had started to convert the Turf Wall to stone. In one sense a terminal date for building on the Wall can never be provided, except in an artificial, academic sense, because alterations were continually being made, so it was an evolutionary process rather than a finite building period. Breeze and Dobson provide a draft chronological table of building work, based on the evidence so far discovered and therefore subject to alteration if future discoveries add to or amend current thinking.[113]

How high was the Wall? Since there is no part of the Wall that survives to its original height, this question is impossible to answer, but estimates usually settle for about fifteen feet.[114] This is the height of a fort wall at Wörth in Germany, which keeled over intact into the fort ditch. The tallest section of Hadrian's Wall so far discovered is at Hare Hill, a short distance east of the now vanished milecastle 53. This short section of the Wall stands sixteen courses high. Unfortunately there is no clue at this remarkable site as to how the Wall was finished off at the top. It is even possible that the Wall was never built to an absolute standard height all along its length.[115]

Was there a wall-walk at the top of the Wall? This is a problem that will probably never be resolved because the Wall does not survive to its full height, and since the existence or otherwise of a wall-walk is related to the way in which the Wall was intended to function, the discussion of the various points is reserved for the chapter on how the Wall worked. Bidwell has presented a good case for a wall-walk, and a brief summary of the arguments for and against such a feature are presented by David Breeze in the fourteenth edition of the *Handbook to the Roman Wall*.[116]

In relation to the wall-walk question it is permissible to assume that hostiles would not normally have been allowed to penetrate close enough to the Wall to attack it, and this is borne out by discoveries made in recent years at Wallsend, at Byker, and also between Throckley and Heddon-on-the-Wall. At all three places, on the berm between the outer face of the Wall and the northern ditch, rectangular pits with straight sides were found, set in offset rows so that the gaps between them were covered. At first these were interpreted as *lilia*, pits containing an upright sharpened stake, often concealed from view by branches and leaves so that unwary attackers would fall into them and be impaled. Examples of these are known from forts, for instance Rough Castle on the Antonine Wall. But these newly discovered rectangular features are not the same shape as the *lilia* and are now thought to have contained a series of closely entwined stacked branches, which have been labelled obstacles on the berm. The effectiveness of such obstacles in keeping unauthorised people away from the Wall can be demonstrated by the fact that the British Army used branches in the same way to protect their camps when they laagered for the night or for a few days. A laager was defended by a circuit formed from wagons and pack-saddles, whereas a defensive circuit was formed from stacked thorny branches or scrub and the like was called a zeriba. Such defences were frequently used in the Sudan, made predominantly from mimosa bushes, and in the campaigns in Somaliland in 1903–04. Some camps of this type were supplemented by trenches serving the same purpose as Roman ditches, and could be converted into fortified posts.[117] On Hadrian's Wall, accompanying the obstacles on the berm in some places there was also a raised bank on the southern edge of the ditch, which may have served to prevent anyone who had managed to cross the ditch from coming up close to the lower portions of the stacked branches, possibly to uproot them or set fire to them.[118] Further work on these features by Paul Bidwell showed that the berm in straight stretches of the Wall is generally wider than the berm opposite the turrets, and at the site of turret 11b at Heddon-on-the-Wall, it was observed that the northern ditch and the obstacles curved inwards opposite the turret, which would afford the soldiers a clear view to the front and sides of their tower.[119] The areas where the obstacles were found are marked on the revised edition of the English Heritage/Ordnance Survey map of Hadrian's Wall published in 2014. It cannot yet be shown that the obstacles on the berm extended along the whole northern frontage of the Wall, but it is considered likely that it did, except perhaps on the crags, and that furthermore there may have been similar obstacles further out in the territory beyond the northern ditch. Whether these features were part of the original Hadrianic plan is not known. The fact that the ditch and the line of the obstacles turned inwards at one of the turrets is not proof that the pattern was repeated at other turrets, but even with only one example it would seem that the obstacles belong to the periods when the turrets were operational, and after 180 or thereabouts many of the turrets went out of use, and some were demolished. A Hadrianic date is not out of the question, but it is feasible that the obstacles belong to a later period when repairs were being carried out, as for instance in the early third century under Severus, or under Caracalla when, after his father's death at York in 211, he made peace with the northern Britons and returned to Rome. To interrupt the narrative, it should be pointed out that Caracalla is a Roman nickname, derived from the Gallic tunic that he habitually wore. He started out as Septimius Bassianus, and when his father became Emperor, claiming descent from Marcus Aurelius and Antoninus Pius, Caracalla became Marcus Aurelius Antoninus, by which name he is known on official records; no inscription bears the name Caracalla, but use of this name in English avoids confusion with Antoninus Pius. One reason why the peace that Caracalla arranged lasted for a long time may have derived from a thorough strengthening of the Wall defences, making it well-nigh impossible to get anywhere near it without being seen. All this is conjecture, but the known features will bear that interpretation.

With regard to the relevance of the obstacles on the berm to the hypothetical wall-walk, two diametrically opposed suggestions can be made, one that the obstacles alone would not be sufficient to protect the Wall, unless someone was watching, and observation from the turrets may have involved coming out at Wall-top level and patrolling, and on the other hand it could be argued that because there was no wall-walk, the obstacles were intended to keep people away from the stretches of the Wall between the turrets, and the curvature inwards towards the turrets may mean that this was where the watching was done, not from the Wall itself.

Was the Wall plastered and/or whitewashed? There has been considerable debate about this since the discovery of whitewash on a chamfered slab from Peel Gap, which immediately polarised opinion, opponents maintaining that it simply meant that mortar had run down and stained the block, and supporters maintaining that such decoration was normal.[120] But it is possible that the Wall may have been plastered over, in part at least, if not along the whole of its length. At Denton, wall plaster was found which had fallen from the south face of the Wall.[121] Plasterwork and whitewash would serve to protect the Wall from wear and tear in a climate that is not kind to buildings. Another point is that modern authors have commented on the poor and even shoddy techniques used in building the Wall, but if it was to be covered in plaster or even just a thick coat of whitewash the stone work would not have been visible, so the construction methods would not matter as long as the Wall remained standing.[122] It is known that some fort walls and probably the internal buildings were plastered and whitewashed, sometimes with red lines painted on to give the appearance of large blocks of stone, and this is how artists now depict reconstructions of Roman forts. At the Wallsend Roman site a wall has been decorated with a succession of panels in the known styles to show how the fort may have looked in Roman times.[123] An analogy from more recent times is the fact that most castles, which we now see in unadulterated stone, were once whitewashed, the alternative name of the Tower of London, once known as the White Tower, being a prime example. Records exist of payments to certain individuals for doing the whitewashing of castles, and in France, the famous Book of Hours of the Duc de Berry depicts major castles in gleaming white. It would not have been an entirely impossible task to apply such treatment to both sides of the Wall, given the military manpower that the Romans could call upon, and the task would have kept the soldiers occupied and out of mischief. It's just that in the mind's eye, the conversion of the Wall as we see it today to an image of a long white frontier, with fake large stones outlined in red paint, is more difficult for some than others.

5

Antonine Interlude: *c*. AD 142 to *c*. AD 165

Warfare or at least military action seems to have been a regular feature in the northern areas of Britain, mentioned too many times in the sources for all instances of trouble to be dismissed in their entirety as *topoi*. Having renounced control of Lowland Scotland and the areas further north in the late first century and withdrawn the troops, the Romans more or less gave free rein to the tribes beyond the Stanegate to fight each other, or to invade the territory of the more settled pro-Roman tribes, or to direct their energies against the Roman forces. Hadrian's Wall provided a means of controlling movement into the province and would contribute to supervision of the areas further north, but unless the Romans could fully pacify the tribes on both sides of the new frontier, there would likely always be a restive element, probably composed of young warriors seeking to prove themselves according to their own traditions. It does not require an enormous band of such men to cause chaos.

The alleged wars of 117–18 at the start of Hadrian's reign, and the outbreak of war *c*. 124–25, are not firmly established facts, but it is nonetheless quite possible that the native tribes objected strongly to the building of the Wall. Whatever action had been taken to pacify the tribes north of Hadrian's Wall it was probably not effective enough for the Romans to feel that they could control the population via diplomatic means alone, and there may have been some disturbances. This may be one of the reasons behind the war conducted by Antoninus Pius through his governor Lollius Urbicus, which ended *c*. 142, and was followed by the construction of a new frontier further north.

The Advance to the North

The building work on Hadrian's Wall may have only just been completed, or was possibly still going on, when orders arrived to leave off the proceedings and march north. There has been much speculation as to Antoninus Pius' motives in moving north. Military action and adding territory to the Empire was always a popular move with the people and senators of the Roman world, so it has been suggested that Antoninus may have regarded action in Britain as a means of gaining prestige. Antoninus was not a military man, and so like Claudius almost a century earlier in 43, he required some military success in order to win over the ambitious senators who could potentially agitate against him. An advance in Britain, far away from Rome, would not endanger the Empire, but would provide an outlet for frustrated military men who wanted to see some action after all the years of peace under Hadrian.

Prestige and support in the early years of his reign would bolster Antoninus' reputation and offset his initial insecurity as Emperor. He was patently not Hadrian's preferred choice of successor. The designated heir Lucius Aelius Caesar died in January 138, then there was a gap of about two months before Hadrian announced the adoption of Antoninus, suggesting that Hadrian was uncertain of the suitability of his chosen candidate, but he chose him anyway because he realised that there was no one else. Antoninus was almost in the same tenuous position as Hadrian had been when Trajan died, because like Hadrian, he had not been unequivocally marked out for the succession during his predecessor's early reign. If there had been no doubt that Antoninus was second in command to Hadrian and was definitely going to succeed him, the transition would have been easier. But his adoption had come almost at the last moment of Hadrian's life, though at least there was no room for suspicion of subterfuge as there had been when Hadrian succeeded Trajan. Antoninus' succession was public and legal. He had been adopted on the proviso that he also secured the future succession by adopting his nephew by marriage, Marcus Aurelius, and Lucius Verus, the son of the late Lucius Aelius Caesar. The main problem was that Hadrian was almost universally detested, so some of the distrust rubbed off on Antoninus. He had some initial trouble with the Senate, because the senators refused at first to deify Hadrian, and moreover wanted to annul all his acts, so it had to be pointed out to them that a blanket rejection of all Hadrian's legal proceedings would mean that many officials and military commanders all over the Empire would no longer be legitimate, including the new Emperor himself. The acts were approved, Hadrian became a god, and Antoninus earned the name Pius.

The military action in Britain may have been welcomed by Antoninus as support for his regime, but this may only have been an added bonus. He may not have been primarily concerned with his military reputation, but perhaps responded to disturbances which have escaped documentation. Events in Roman Britain did not affect the rest of the Empire to any great extent, and consequently they are not generally explained in full in the literary sources. Epigraphic sources within Britain are usually only incidental to what was happening, representing personal actions or rebuilding after peace had been re-established, so speculation is always necessary on the part of historians and archaeologists. This is sometimes related to Imperial policy or events elsewhere in the Empire, such as the first withdrawal from Scotland which more than likely was due to the Dacian wars and the need for troops. On occasion, Roman actions in Britain may not have been instigated as part of Imperial policy or occurrences elsewhere, but may represent responses to events confined to Britain. The Antonine advance may be one of these occasions. The sources indicate that warfare was involved, and that the aggressive action was not initiated by the Romans. Of course the Romans always claimed that they were not the aggressors and their wars were justified, but Antoninus was probably faced with troubles which cannot now be estimated or located. Whatever the causes of the war, he had choices. He could allow the northern Britons free rein to attack each other or eventually the Roman frontier, while he kept the army safe behind the new Wall and waited for the hostiles to turn up. The Wall had not yet been tested in such circumstances, nor had any other running barrier, and the new frontiers may not have been intended for this purpose in the first place. Alternatively Antoninus could go out and meet the troublesome elements head on in the field, which is how most historians and archaeologists maintain that the Romans operated, rather than defending the Wall as if it were a castle. It has been stated that the Hadrianic frontier was a tactical success in controlling or preventing movement, but it has been labelled a strategic failure, because it was in the wrong place to facilitate control of the tribes of the far north, who were free to make war on each other or combine against Rome. But any frontier in Britain could be dubbed a strategic failure, because the only way to achieve complete success would have been to conquer the whole island. When Hadrian and then Antoninus created their running barriers they indicated quite plainly that they were not prepared even to attempt subjugation of the northern tribes and to hold the entire island of Britain. Did they build frontiers in complete ignorance of the fact that that these military installations could not effectively control the tribes of the far north, or were they aware of this and were instead intent on protecting what lay behind the barriers, fully prepared to march beyond the frontiers as and when necessary? In similar fashion, with regard to the two German provinces, and Raetia, and the Pannonian and Moesian provinces, the river frontiers and the running barriers were not in the right place to control any of the tribes further north, and were no more effective for this purpose than Hadrian's Wall was in Britain.

If the threat in Antonine times originated in Lowland Scotland between the Forth–Clyde line and Hadrian's Wall, friendly tribes may have required greater protection than could be afforded simply by the presence of the Wall, but the frontier would support military action in the regions beyond it and contain any attempts to move southwards. If the threat came from beyond the Forth–Clyde, then Hadrian's Wall was not in the right place unless an army was assembled to march north, as the modern strategists insist, just as it was not in the right place for the campaigns of Septimius Severus in the early third century. The only difference is that after the conclusion of the war, Antoninus decided to enclose and occupy the Lowlands of Scotland between his new Wall and that of his predecessor, while Severus and Caracalla chose to repair Hadrian's Wall and the outposts.

In his *Description of Greece* the author Pausanias sums up Antoninus Pius' reign as mostly peaceful, because Antoninus never willingly made war, but did so when necessary. He describes how Antoninus deprived the Brigantes in Britain of much of their territory because they had invaded the Genounian district, where the people were subject to Rome.[1] This is puzzling, for several reasons.

Pausanias provides no dating evidence, so some scholars prefer to see this passage as a reference to warfare in Britain in the mid-150s, nothing to do with the advance into Scotland. Another difficulty is that the Brigantes, or at least the majority of them, were already in the province and therefore subject to Roman administration, so they could hardly be deprived of their lands.[2] Salway prefers to date Pausanias' description of trouble with the Brigantes to the later period of *c.* 155, but he suggested that one way of depriving existing provincials of lands would be to confiscate them in order to create Imperial estates directly owned and administered by the emperors, and this is as valid for the 140s as it would have been for a later decade.[3]

More puzzling is the Genounian district, hitherto unknown in Britain, so the location of the events that Pausanias describes is not clear. It has been suggested that the passage does not concern Britain at all, but the province of Raetia, where a tribe called the Brigantii lived next to another tribe called the Genauni.[4] This sounds more plausible, but requires some explanation. Pausanias worked in the 170s, not too long after the events at the very outset of the reign of Antoninus Pius. He cannot have failed to hear of the northern campaigns of Antoninus' governor of Britain, Lollius Urbicus, which took place only about three decades before Pausanias wrote his book, and yet in the extant work he makes no mention of this governor by name. He may have conflated a war in Britain with a less serious problem in Raetia, coming across the tribal name Brigantes in whatever source he used, and automatically connecting them with Britain, but Britain was not the only place in the Empire where Brigantes were known. Apart from the group in Raetia, there were also Brigantes in Spain. It has been suggested that at some point, probably at a considerably later time after Pausanias wrote the original, a copy of his work was altered, and the words 'in Britain' were inserted after Brigantes.[5] This implies that a scribe trying to make sense of defective manuscript amended the work using the limited knowledge available to him. Perhaps a line had been omitted by a previous copyist, not impossible, as all typists know who have converted handwritten documents into tidy typeface. In turn, a line missed out of one of the early copies could mean that Pausanias perhaps did originally describe the revolt of the Moors, the trouble in Raetia, and also the wars in Britain under Lollius Urbicus, but this war was omitted and lost forever. Apart from the evidence of inscriptions, it is known that Lollius was Antoninus' legate from a historical work produced much later than Pausanias' book. In the biographies of the emperors known as the *Historia Augusta*, it is stated that Antoninus waged war through his legates, and the author makes particular mention of Lollius Urbicus, through whom the Emperor won the war against the Britons and built a wall of turf (*murus caespiticius*) across the island.[6] The modern name for this frontier is the Antonine Wall.

The British situation in 138, whatever it was, occupied Antoninus' immediate attention after he became Emperor. Apart from the scant literary references, there is further support for a serious war in Britain in the 140s. Antoninus accepted a salutation as Imperator, or victorious general, for the second time, at some point in or before 142. The date is provided by an inscription showing this title along with his third consulship and his annually renewed tribunician power for the fifth time.[7] From Augustus' time onwards, from the end of the first century BC, when a general was victorious in war, the title Imperator was bestowed on the emperors, and sometimes the generals received the prestigious reward of *ornamenta triumphalia*, insignia of a triumph without actually parading through Rome with the booty and captives, as they would have been entitled to do during the Republic. Antoninus readily adopted the title Imperator for the British victories, but not for other notable achievements. He advanced the Hadrianic frontier in Germany about twenty-five miles to the east at its furthest point, and a revolt in Mauretania was quelled in the 140s. Breeze acknowledged that Antoninus accepted the acclamation for actions in Britain but not for any other achievements, but he considered that the title Imperator in this instance was related to the special significance of the northern advance in Britain without a specific military victory or skirmishes in Lowland Scotland.[8] However, opinion now swings to acceptance of a war fought by Lollius Urbicus. In the fourth edition of *Hadrian's Wall* Breeze and Dobson locate the fighting in the area between Hadrian's Wall and Strathmore.[9] Birley also accepts that there was a war, a defeat of the Britons, and a military victory under Lollius Urbicus.[10]

Antoninus probably did not wait for several months to despatch Lollius Urbicus to Britain. The new governor could have arrived in 138. It is attested that building work was being done under his command at Corbridge by 139, when an inscription from this site, bearing his name, was set up to record the building of stone granaries by *II Augusta* during Antoninus' second consulship. Another inscription, dated to Antoninus' third consulship in 149 shows that building work was still going on at Corbridge.[11] Urbicus is also named on an inscription recording building work by *cohors I Lingonum* at High Rochester, on the main eastern route to the north.[12] When the Antonine Wall was begun, he was responsible for building work at the fort at Balmuildy.[13]

The fact that Lollius Urbicus was made governor of Britain soon after Antoninus' accession shows that the decision to advance into Lowland Scotland and possibly beyond was made very quickly, suggesting actual or potential trouble which required a rapid response. A possible factor in the outbreak of warfare is that tribes made treaties with individual leaders, not states, and when the leader was removed or when they died, the arrangements made with him were considered null and void. There is no evidence that any tribes north of Hadrian's Wall had made treaties with the Emperor Hadrian when the Wall was being planned and built, but it is not impossible. The tribesmen would not be as isolated or out of touch as might be imagined, and they would know of Hadrian's death probably as soon as the Romans did. If they had agreed not to make war on their neighbours, now was the time to do so, or if they had made promises not to attack the Romans, but objected to the Wall, Hadrian's death meant that they would not technically be breaking their promises. Honour would be saved all round. The reasons for the advance into Scotland may be as simple as an outbreak of war which escalated out of control. One of the problems inherent in the history of Roman Britain, as presented in the ancient sources, is that there seems to have been trouble at the beginning of the reigns of so many emperors that it strains the credulity of modern archaeologists and historians. But it may all be true. Just because trouble at t'mill became a well-worn concept in northern England in the nineteenth century, it should not be taken to imply that all t'mills were always well-ordered and peaceful.

This postulated war conducted by Lollius Urbicus is more than usually devoid of historical evidence. It is not known why the

Romans engaged in military activity just as Hadrian's Wall was being completed, unless its very presence had provoked it, or as suggested above, the death of the Emperor rendered any treaties invalid. No tribes are named in the sources as the adversaries of the Romans. Nobody knows whether the war was a highly localised affair somewhere in Lowland Scotland, or whether it had originated in the far north and become more widespread. There are no marching camps among the series of such camps in Scotland that have been identified as Antonine in date, so the progress of Lollius Urbicus and his army between High Rochester and Balmuildy cannot be mapped. Did all three legions, or parts of them, take part in the fighting? How many auxiliary units were involved, and which ones? There is no information about the conclusion of the war, or about possible peace treaties with a tribe or tribes, except that the author of the *Historia Augusta* notes that some of them were driven back, or more correctly led away to distant parts (*summotis barbaris ducto*), but with no further clues as to what that really means.[14] The author may have read Tacitus's biography of his father-in-law Agricola, who campaigned in the same regions, and drove back the Britons as if they were in another island: *summotis barbaris velut in aliam insulam*.[15]

This statement in the *Historia Augusta* concerning removal of 'the barbarians' could be happily linked by previous generations of scholars with the appearance of the *numeri Brittonum* in Germany, because the earliest dated inscriptions attesting these units at several of the forts of the German frontier belong to the reign of Antoninus Pius.[16] The *numeri* were thought to have been irregular units, not attached to the army, and possibly living with their families, just as some units did in the later Empire, but this theory had to be revised in the 1960s when Dietwulf Baatz excavated the *numerus* fort at Hesselbach, on the Hadrianic frontier running through the Odenwald.[17] The excavations revealed a headquarters building, indicating that the small unit which occupied it was organised like any other regular unit, except that it contained fewer men than an auxiliary cohort. There is no proof that the occupying unit at Hesselbach was called a *numerus* or that it contained Britons, but the small forts of the Odenwald frontier were all very similar in size and shape, and *numeri* are attested at some of them, particularly the *Brittones Triputiensium*, which left several inscriptions at watchtowers along the frontier and was based at the small fort at Schlossau, just south of Hesselbach and very similar to it in plan.[18] The excavations also showed that the fort had been occupied since 90–100, beginning with a turf and timber fort which was rebuilt in drystone Walling *c.* 115, and rebuilt again, this time with mortared stone defences *c.* 140. This implies that the formation of the *numeri* began under Trajan, or perhaps even under Domitian, and the units were maintained until the reign of Antoninus Pius and later. By the time the war in Britain was concluded by Lollius Urbicus, the units of Britons on the German frontier could have been reconstituted at least twice, keeping their names even though perhaps not all the replacements were Britons. The other auxiliary units besides the *numeri* retained their ethnic names even though the army recruited some of their replacements from the local area, but the theory that local recruitment was the favoured method of keeping units up to strength has been questioned. It is known that replacements for the units of archers from Syria and the eastern provinces, whose special skills were learned almost from birth, were usually brought in from the same ethnic groups, and more recently it has been suggested that the Spanish troops also retained connections with their homelands.[19] The length of service of soldiers of the *numeri* is not known, but apart from losses via formal discharge procedures, there would have been wastage from accidents, disease and possibly desertion. It is not impossible that some of the defeated tribesmen of northern Britain were removed by Lollius and sent to Germany to fill gaps or even to constitute new units of *numeri* for the German frontier. This need not involve the deportation of entire tribes with their families, which was probably never undertaken.[20] There is no evidence of widespread depopulation in Scotland after the campaigns of the early 140s, but recruitment of soldiers from among the Britons need not have involved huge numbers of men, probably nothing like the 5,500 Sarmatians that Marcus Aurelius removed from the Danube and converted into Roman soldiers in Britain. The removal of some of the warriors of northern Britain would not be detectable in archaeological investigations, and would not necessarily have impacted on the British tribes too severely in terms of population figures, but it would have served as a warning to potential warmongers, and perhaps contributed to settling the tumultuous elements at least for a while. Removal of the troublemakers, rather than wholesale execution or deportation of entire populations, was employed again at the beginning of the seventeenth century, when James VI of Scotland, by now also James I of England, sent some of the men of the raiding clans, or surnames as they were known, from the Borders to join the English army in the Low Countries, and then when most of them deserted and filtered back home, he deported them to the colonies in America, which was as *summotis ducto* as was possible at the time, Australia not having been discovered.

The Antonine Wall

Antoninus' new frontier was an almost identical copy of Hadrian's Wall, except that it was built of turf, not stone. The concept of the frontier as devised by Hadrian had been accepted, and presumably the purpose and function was the same as that of the more southerly Wall, but it seemed necessary to move the entire frontier further north. The most persistent opposition to the Roman government of Britain is seen as emanating from the Highland zones, despite the fact that some scholars deny that there was any sizable population living there, and given that this area was probably the main source of trouble, Hadrian's Wall lies too far south to deal with this effectively, as mentioned above, so building another frontier on similar lines would protect Lowland Scotland from attack and help to keep the peace internally.[21]

It has been suggested that Antoninus Pius' original plan was in fact to conquer the whole island, as Agricola had done.[22] This would have taken the situation back to the reigns of the Flavian Emperors, and would have solved the problem of frontiers altogether, because none would be needed. Instead of drawing lines and fortifying them, the Romans would guard estuaries and harbours, river crossings and potentially restive tribes. But is equally likely that Antoninus had no intention of trying to achieve total conquest, and it is not even certain that at first he intended to move the frontier to the Forth–Clyde line when he authorised Lollius Urbicus to advance beyond Hadrian's Wall. It is just possible that he limited his initial plan to fighting a war, and only decided to build another wall after the final victory and an investigation into the best method of controlling the tribes without trying to garrison the entire country. It is significant that although wars were fought beyond Hadrian's Wall in the third and fourth centuries, none of the emperors after Pius fought to win and hold the far north, relying instead on the Hadrianic frontier and its outposts to keep the peace. According to Dio, when Septimius Severus came to Britain in 208, he too planned to conquer the whole island.[23] Severus and his son Caracalla may have reached the northernmost limit of Scotland in their campaigns from 208–10/11, but even though they could claim that they had succeeded in vanquishing the tribes, they did not garrison the territory. If Severus had survived, he may have attempted to garrison and hold Scotland, but if he entertained such plans, they did not come to fruition. Caracalla quickly made peace, and went back to Rome as fast as possible after his father died at York in February 211. At the beginning of the fourth century Constantius I campaigned in Scotland but did not hold it, and he too died in Britain, in 306. The indications are that from the Roman point of view there was no profit in holding the far north. As Hanson points out the exploitation of resources was a high priority for the Romans, usually involving metals, as well as slaves, recruits for the army and taxation.[24] If there had been gold or silver deposits in any part of Scotland the Romans would have been eager to conquer and more than capable of taking over the country and combatting the disadvantages of hostile terrain or equally hostile tribes. If that had been the case, Agricola's conquests would never have been abandoned, and the history of Roman Britain would probably have been much simpler.

Unlike Hadrian's Wall, which has furnished epigraphic evidence that Aulus Platorius Nepos was the governor of Britain when the Wall was begun, there is no evidence to show which governor was responsible for building the new frontier. Lollius Urbicus was still in command when the fort at Balmuildy was built in stone, with wing walls like the milecastles and turrets of the Hadrianic frontier, but he probably left Britain in 142 or possibly 143. His successor is not known. A milestone from Ingliston, datable to somewhere between 140 and 145, once had a governor's name inscribed on it but the carving was deleted, possibly because the unknown man had conspired against Antoninus.[25] In 146, a diploma recording the honourable discharge of auxiliary soldiers attests Gnaeus Papirius Aelianus as governor, and then nothing is known until Gnaeus Julius Verus is attested in 158.

The building of the stone-built fort at Balmuildy *c.* 142–43 implies that the Antonine Wall was also begun or at least planned at the same time as the fort, and the fact that this fort was equipped with wing walls suggests that the original plan for the new frontier was to build all of it in stone. It is, after all, only half the length of the completed stone version of Hadrian's Wall, and it was perhaps originally intended to build about six forts along the length of the frontier, so the task would not have been overwhelming.[26] One factor which may have influenced the decision to build the new wall from turf instead of stone may have been that some soldiers would still be required to guard Hadrian's Wall and its hinterland, and some men would perhaps have been allocated to building and occupying new forts in the Lowlands, so the workforce that would have been available to build a frontier half the length of Hadrian's Wall may have been only half as large as the Hadrianic workforce. Nonetheless, Nic Fields estimates that 7,000 men would have been working on the new frontier, which is similar to the estimate made by Peter Hill for the number of soldiers who built Hadrian's Wall.[27] Since the ancient sources have not furnished statistics illustrating the size of the workforce, these modern estimates must remain theoretical, but this still does not alter the fact that building in turf ought to have been accomplished more rapidly than quarrying, transporting and shaping stone, building with it and finding and transporting clay or making mortar to bind the stones.

Inscriptions show that the builders of the Antonine Wall included all of *II Augusta*, detachments of *VI Victrix* and *XX Valeria Victrix*, and some auxiliary units.[28] There was no absolute uniformity in dimensions and building styles along the Antonine Wall, which may represent the work of different groups of soldiers, possibly even the work of different gangs from the same legion supervised by different centurions. On Hadrian's Wall it is difficult to identify construction camps because such camps could belong to building works for the Stanegate forts or other activities predating the Wall, but on the Antonine Wall, where there is not such a mixture of different periods, construction camps have been detected. The gangs of builders would be allocated their sections for building the Wall in turf and digging the northern ditch. On the Wall, archaeologists perceive three main categories of building sections, at three Roman miles, three and two thirds, and four and two thirds Roman miles. This explains in part why the camps so far discovered vary in size, because the numbers of soldiers needing to use them will also have varied. At both ends of each allocated sector inscriptions with relief sculptures were set up recording which troops had built the particular stretch of the Wall. These are known as distance slabs, the majority of them discovered in the west, but it is assumed that they were erected all along the Wall. The distance slabs are very well preserved, and the example from Bridgeness in the east is particularly fine. The good state of preservation is due to the fact that they were deliberately buried when the Romans withdrew from the Antonine Wall, and since the occupation of the Wall was quite short, only about twenty years or so, the stones had not been exposed to the elements for very long before their burial. The distance slabs are much larger and more elaborate and pictorial than the crude centurial stones of Hadrian's Wall recording building work by one century. Distance slabs are equipped with figures of deities, soldiers and natives on either side of the text, usually designed to show Romans triumphing over barbarians. In the eastern part of the Antonine Wall, at least in one sector marked by distance slabs, two camps were built at each end of an allocation of four and two thirds Roman miles, totalling four camps in all for one stretch of the frontier. It is suggested that one of the paired camps housed the construction workers while its partner housed the ditch diggers, and the work progressed from both ends and met in the middle.[29] These sectors in the east were measured in paces (*passus*). A stretch of Wall measuring four and two thirds of a mile long would comprise 4,666 *passus*, so the section measuring 4,652 paces recorded on the Bridgeness distance slab is not far short of this allocation.[30] In the west where no construction camps have come to light, the sectors of the last four miles were less than one Roman mile long, and from the fort at Castlehill to the western end of the Wall distances were measured in feet (*pedes*).

The Antonine Wall ran from Old Kilpatrick on the north bank of the Clyde, so that the Romans controlled the estuary, to Carriden on the south side of the Firth of Forth, though this fort stands alone, not attached to the frontier, and the frontier itself has not been shown to extend right down to the coast. All the forts of the Antonine Wall were built of turf except for Balmuildy and Castlecary which were built of stone. The forts do not project beyond the turf rampart but the Wall serves as their northern sides, except for the forts at Bar Hill and Carriden, mentioned above, both of which were built a short distance to the south. With one exception, all the forts face north, their orientation being determined from the way the headquarters building faced. In the more usual plan, the central range of the fort with the granaries, headquarters and commander's residence, was placed across the short axis of the fort to form a right angle with its long sides, and the main gate would be on the long axis leading directly to the headquarters. On the Antonine Wall the plans of the forts were related to the frontier line itself, so the centre range and especially the headquarters building faced north whether the fort was attached to the frontier by its short side or its long side and in the latter instance the internal layout had to be adapted accordingly. According to Breeze and Dobson this represents a significant development for Roman frontiers because the design of the forts was integrated with the Antonine Wall from the beginning.[31] The concept of frontiers was after all quite new, and the Romans were learning empirically how to accept the concept and how to manage and operate it.

The Romans seemed to have learned a few helpful practices while building the Turf Wall and the stone sections of Hadrian's frontier. Probably the first element to be constructed on the Antonine Wall, at least before some of the installations were begun, was a road south of the frontier line, known in modern terms as the Military Way.[32] This useful feature was not added to Hadrian's Wall until after the withdrawal from Scotland *c*. 158, and is also called the Military Way by archaeologists. Communications and transport may have been catered for when Hadrian's Wall was being built, and the metalled track found south of the Wall at Denton, laid down and then resurfaced twice, may have been intended for transport and also patrolling, but so far no other example has been discovered.[33] There seems to have been no road like the Military Way on the Hadrianic frontier until after the withdrawal from the Antonine Wall. The Romans made sophisticated arrangements for the Military Way at the Antonine Wall forts, where the road heads straight for the fort gates on the east and west sides, sometime forming the *via principalis* across the front of the headquarters building, but a second branch skirts the fort to the south to allow for traffic to bypass the fort if that is not the destination, thus preventing congestion inside the fort with convoys meandering along the main road.[34]

Some Turf Wall installations on Hadrian's frontier had been founded on a layer of cobbles, but this foundation was seemingly not used for the whole line of the Turf Wall. The Antonine Wall on the other hand was built on a foundation of heavy stone cobbles about fifteen feet wide, held in place by stone kerbs. This not only stabilised the turf wall built on top of it, but also allowed for better drainage, because the stone foundations made it easier to incorporate culverts at the start of the building process, placed at intervals in the stone work.[35] On Hadrian's Wall, water that collected behind the Turf Wall could not be let out, and it would not have been an easy task to bore drainage channels through the width of the turf once the Wall had already been built. Learning empirically, the Romans installed drains on Hadrian's Wall when the Turf Wall was replaced in stone.[36]

The Antonine Wall was built to a narrower specification than the Turf Wall, which would save time and effort in digging out enough earth to fill the gaps between the two skins of turves. It may have been about three metres or ten feet high, but like Hadrian's Wall it is not known for certain if there was a wall-walk. At no point can the Wall have survived to its full original height, so the top levels have most likely been eroded and consequently there is no archaeological evidence of posts sunk into the Wall to provide a firm support for a sturdy fence. It seems eminently logical to suppose that there was a wall-walk, so it has been suggested without firm evidence that a timber platform would have been laid down at the flattened top level and possibly a breastwork of wattles erected to protect the soldiers, most likely made of willow, hazel or ash, because these provide pliable young branches that can be conveniently woven round upright stakes to create a wattle fence. The only hints that there may have been such a breastwork derives from the remains of burnt wattles, the majority of them willow, found outside the eastern rampart of the fort at Bearsden.[37]

As on Hadrian's Wall, there was a northern ditch accompanying the Antonine Wall. This was much wider at the top than the

Hadrian's Wall ditch, and the berm between the turf rampart of the Wall and the inner lip of the ditch was also much wider. The greater distance between the Wall and the outer edge of the ditch would have kept unauthorised people away and made it more difficult to throw missiles at the military installations. On the northern lip of the ditch, soil was thrown up to form a mound on this edge, which served to lengthen the depth of the ditch from top to bottom on this side.

On the Antonine frontier there was no Vallum to the south, but instead the forts had annexes attached to one side of the fort and defended by a turf rampart and external ditch. At Rough Castle the fort defences were extended to include the annexe. Probably carts and other items belonging to the forts which could not be accommodated inside them were placed inside the annexes. Animals may have been kept there, since even wholly infantry units would need riding horses for the officers, draught animals, and probably sheep and cattle for food. Excavations reveal that at least some annexes had timber buildings inside them, and it is not impossible that they all contained buildings, possibly store rooms or workshops, but until more extensive and detailed excavations can be conducted the purpose of the timber buildings remains unknown. In some cases the fort bathhouse was built in the annexe, or in some instances inside the fort, a departure from the normal arrangement where bathhouses were usually outside the forts, one reason being the avoidance of the hazard presented by the constant need to light fires under the floors of the baths to heat the rooms and to keep stoking the furnaces that heated the water. The suggestion that civilians were accommodated inside the annexes derives from slender and sparse evidence, but is not generally accepted. Future excavation could possibly show that on occasions civilians were present, possibly on a transitory basis for trading purposes, but not as residents.

It has been mentioned above that the original scheme for the new frontier may have been to build only six forts, not more than nine miles apart, with fortlets spaced at one mile intervals between them. This theory was first put forward by John Gillam, and nothing has yet come to light which disproves it.[38] These primary forts, judging from their sizes and their distances from each other, are considered to be Carriden, Mumrills, Castlecary,

Bar Hill or less probably Auchendavy not far from Bar Hill, Balmuildy and Old Kilpatrick. The fort at Mumrills is the largest at six and a half acres, and the others range from three and a half acres to just over four acres, so at least five of them could hold a complete auxiliary unit of a nominal strength of five hundred men. It seems that the decision to add more forts was made quite soon, while the turf rampart of the frontier was still being built. The new secondary forts were built at Duntocher, where a fortlet was incorporated into the new structure, and at Castlehill, Bearsden, Cadder, Kirkintilloch, Auchendavy if Bar Hill is considered to belong to the primary forts, Croy Hill, Westerwood and Rough Castle. These forts are certain, but it is probable that the full complement of forts is not known. Falkirk and Inveravon on either side of Mumrills are confidently placed on maps because the theoretical spacing and the likely siting seems to demand a fort in each of these locations. In general the fortlets are smaller than the six primary forts listed above, all of them being under three acres in size. These could not hold a complete auxiliary unit, while all except one of the larger forts could do so. One problem is that where evidence exists of which units were in occupation at some of the forts, including the larger ones, the whole unit could not have always been accommodated, for instance inscriptions attest two different and presumably successive cohorts at Castlecary, each with a nominal strength of one thousand men, which would normally have required a larger fort. The obvious solution, a theory rather than a proven fact, is that Castlecary was the headquarters fort for the whole unit, but some men were posted to other locations, either permanently or on a rotational basis, and the absence of a headquarters building at Bearsden and the small fort at Duntocher supports the idea that detachments rather than whole units garrisoned these two forts and most probably some of the others.[39]

There are also fortlets on the Antonine Wall, similar in size and shape to the milecastles of Hadrian's Wall, but unlike the milecastles they are surrounded by one or two ditches. On Hadrian's Wall the Vallum to the south would obviate the need for defensive ditches around the milecastles, though some ditches have been found. The similarity to the milecastles suggests that the overall plan allowed for a fortlet every Roman mile, so there should be about thirty-five to forty of them in total, but so far only a few have been found, and excavations at places where it was thought that a fortlet should have been built, on grounds of spacing, have failed to find any extra ones. It is acknowledged that the spacing could not be quite as regular as the spacing of the milecastles of Hadrian's Wall, because on this Wall the original plan was to leave the forts in the hinterland on the Stanegate, and build the Wall with regularly spaced milecastles and turrets. On the Antonine Wall, the primary forts seem to have been planned as one with the Wall, without regard to spacing of the fortlets at one mile apart. Nevertheless, although the majority of the known fortlets were built in the intermediate sections between forts, three of them are very close to forts, for instance at Croy Hill the new fort was laid out only about fifty metres away from the fortlet. Investigations have been made at the fortlets at Cleddans in the west and at Seabegs Wood and Kinneil in the east.[40]

Two other features have been discovered on the Antonine Wall, with no clear evidence as to their function. These have been termed enclosures and expansions. Three examples of enclosures have been found around the fortlet at Wilderness Plantation. The enclosures were very small, lightly defended by a rampart and ditch, and nothing inside the ones that have been excavated has so far shown what their purpose was.[41] The six so-called expansions are almost as much of a mystery. West of Rough Castle one of these was excavated, consisting of a square stone base about eighteen by eighteen feet that was perhaps built separately from the Wall foundations, but the expansion itself was turf-built and integrated with the Wall as an extension on the south side. The expansions come in pairs, two west of Croy Hill and two on each side of Rough Castle, but it cannot be demonstrated that this arrangement pertained all along the length of the Wall. Their purpose is not known. They could have fulfilled the same function as the turrets of Hadrian's Wall, especially as nothing that compares with the turrets has come to light on the Antonine Wall, and like turrets the expansions seem to be grouped in pairs, but since the way in which the turrets worked is not fully understood it would be difficult to pontificate about how the expansions worked, though it is permissible to theorise.[42] The presence of burnt material around the base of the excavated expansion near Rough Castle gave rise to a theory that they were watchtowers or signalling towers with beacons lit on top of the turf, perhaps to give warning of attack, but in the absence of any corroborative information, the theory that the expansion acted as watchtowers or signalling towers must remain as speculation.[43]

The close spacing of the installations of the Antonine Wall makes it the most densely defended frontier in the Roman Empire. The forts and fortlets were never more than about two miles apart, far less than the more usual distance of a day's or half day's march that seems to apply to the Stanegate or Hadrian's Wall. As mentioned above only a few of the forts were large enough for a whole auxiliary unit, so some men were presumably stationed in the smaller forts, and some forts contained detachments of legionaries. It is notable that there were fewer mounted units on the Antonine Wall than on Hadrian's Wall, only one *ala* or wholly mounted unit being known at Mumrills, the largest fort in the whole system, and a few part-mounted units, consisting of infantry and cavalry together, attested or surmised at other forts. Castlecary was the headquarters fort for 1000-strong, part-mounted cohort, a 500-strong, part-mounted unit is known at Castlehill, and there were possibly some cavalrymen at Bearsden. The use of cavalry may have been restricted by the terrain, which was much more wet and boggy than it is now.[44] Travelling through Scotland in modern times, it is difficult to appreciate just how much drainage work has been done, and that until relatively recent times the routes were dictated by the presence of bogs. The castle at Stirling for instance controlled the main north–south route on the eastern side of the country, unless travellers were willing to risk struggling through the boggy lands.

As on Hadrian's Wall the defences of the Antonine Wall were heaviest on the western side, which faced more hazardous terrain to the north where approaching enemies could conceal themselves, and also like Hadrian's Wall there were outpost forts on the western side, but on the Antonine Wall they were grouped on the eastern side, shadowing the Agricolan and Flavian defences around the western edge of the Fife peninsula. Just north of the Wall, a fort was built at Camelon, and new forts were planted at Ardoch, Strageath and probably Bertha. No fort has been discovered between Camelon and Ardoch, but an Antonine establishment may be lurking undetected to guard the Forth, especially since the other forts were most probably associated with river crossings and defence of the routes, Camelon on the River Carron, Ardoch and Strageath guarding the River Earn and the postulated fort at Bertha guarding the Tay. There is no sign of any installations to mirror the Gask Ridge towers, which may mean that the function of these outpost forts had changed from that fulfilled by the installations of the Flavian so-called frontier line, rendering watchtowers obsolete.

The Antonine forts and fortlets were not extended down the coasts of Scotland, emulating the Hadrianic frontier around the western edge of Cumbria and the south bank of the Tyne. A fort was built on the south side of the Clyde at Bishopton, and there were two smaller forts, one further west at Whitemoss, and another on the west coast at Outerwards. There may be more forts or fortlets to be discovered. On the east coast, one of the main functions of the forts at Cramond and Inveresk was probably to protect harbours. In the hinterland of the Antonine Wall the Lowlands were more closely guarded than ever before or afterwards. The dispositions were similar to the Agricolan pattern of forts, but not a slavish copy of it. In the Flavian era there had been large forts at Milton, Dalswinton and Glenlochar, but only the last of these was reutilized. This fort, and the one at the important site of Newstead, were the only large forts in the Lowlands during the Antonine reoccupation. Instead of placing large concentrations of troops at certain sites, the military planners favoured a greater number of smaller installations, so there were more fortified bases than in the previous occupation, which had been less dense.

Hadrian's Wall and Its Hinterland in the Antonine Period

The troops that were necessary to fill all the new forts, fortlets and other installations presumably came from Hadrian's Wall and from forts in the Pennines and probably Wales. It is not possible to draw up a complete list of which units garrisoned all the new forts on the new Wall and in Lowland Scotland. Breeze and Dobson have tabulated the forts of the Antonine Wall and their attested units, together with the types of unit which may have occupied the forts with no attested garrison.[45] There is not enough information to pinpoint all the forts south of Hadrian's Wall which were either abandoned or shuffled units around to provide troops for the new frontier, but likely candidates are forts in Durham, Yorkshire and Lancashire, and the Pennines as far as Derbyshire. Binchester and Ebchester were probably evacuated, with Lanchester replacing them. Lancaster and Watercrook probably provided troops for the Antonine Wall.[46]

Hadrian's Wall itself does not appear to have been left entirely devoid of troops, but its defensive capabilities were much reduced. There is no evidence to show that the curtain wall was deliberately damaged or slighted, but the Vallum was. The mounds on either side of the southern ditch were cut through at more or less regular intervals of about 135 feet or forty-one metres, and the earth was knocked into the ditch to form causeways, which were left without any sign of fortified gateways to stop people from crossing. In some milecastles there is evidence that the gates were taken out, not an easy task without knocking the whole gateway down because the gates had projections at the top and bottom which slotted into holes in the lintel and base, acting as hinges on which each gate swung open and shut. In order to wrench them out the soldiers had to damage the stones and the pivot slots. It is not known if every single milecastle was treated in the same way, but if they were not manned, leaving the gates in place would have allowed hostile elements to use the milecastle as a fortified base. On present evidence it seems that the Hadrianic frontier was deliberately opened up to traffic. This does not mean that there was no military presence on the Wall, though evidence of occupation is sparse. At Chesters a diploma recording the discharge of time served to soldiers was discovered dating to 146, and a fragmentary diploma of the same date was found at Vindolanda.[47] From this evidence it cannot be determined whether a complete auxiliary unit was present at Chesters on the Wall fort or at Vindolanda on the Stanegate, but there was clearly some activity suggesting that these two sites were not completely abandoned. The Stanegate forts at Carlisle and Corbridge, as well as Vindolanda, seem to have been retained, and the Wall fort at Birdoswald may have continued in occupation, judging from the pottery and coins found there.[48] Housesteads may have had a holding garrison of legionaries, but there is no firm dating evidence for the two inscriptions attesting soldiers of

II Augusta at this site. Both inscriptions were found outside the fort, one in the Mithraic temple to the south, and the other near milecastle 37 to the west of the fort.[49] The presence of legionaries in the area of the fort would not necessarily imply that that they were garrisoned there, but on one of the inscriptions, the soldiers of *II Augusta* are described as *agentes in praesidio*, meaning that they were definitely in charge of the fort as an acting garrison. If only the soldiers had included the names of the two consuls of the year on their dedications to Jupiter and other deities, then all doubt would have been removed as to the date. As it stands, all that can be said is that the period when the Antonine Wall was being built and garrisoned would be a likely slot for legionaries to be posted to Housesteads.

Another War in the 150s?

There are certain indications in the archaeological record which have led to the suggestion that there was a war somewhere in Britain in the mid-150s. Except for the passage from Pausanias' *Description of Greece* referring to recalcitrant Brigantes, there is no direct literary evidence that describes a war in Britain at this time. The troublesome Brigantes have been mentioned above in connection with the campaigns of Lollius Urbicus, but since the passage has no specific date and could therefore belong to any time during the reign of Antoninus Pius, some scholars have interpreted it as supporting evidence for a war that must have taken place *c.* 153 or 154, the Roman victory being celebrated by a coin of 154/55, most probably minted in Britain. No mention is made on the coin of a victory over the Britons, such as the legend *Britannia devicta* or similar phrases, but the reverse seems to show the personification of Britannia in subdued mode.[50] There is also an undated inscription from Newcastle referring to troop movements involving detachments of all three legions of Britain in the later 150s, and the fort at Birrens was reconstructed in 158 after being destroyed and burnt.

Opinion is divided about the significance of these disparate pieces of information. Taken together, such snippets of evidence can be viewed as pieces of a jigsaw that implies disturbances among the tribes, but as usual with archaeological evidence no one has the picture on the box lid, the majority of jigsaw pieces are missing, and there is room for suspicion that the extant pieces do not even belong to the same jigsaw. It is possible to lump all these separate items together to produce a scenario of hostile action on the part of the Britons, but it is also possible to interpret them as unrelated and not nearly so dramatic. The depiction of Britannia subdued on the coin of 155 depends on opinion. To some historians she appears no more dejected than she does on other coins. The troop movements recorded on the Newcastle inscription are ambiguous and the destruction of Birrens need not be the result of hostile action, but instead might be a sign of deliberate levelling by the Romans before the new fort was built.

Apart from the Britannia coin, the other indications of some disturbances in Britain all belong to the period when Julius Verus was governor, but the date when he arrived is not known. He was in office when a diploma from Ravenglass was issued in February 158, so Verus was most likely in Britain by the end of 157, but Birley suggests that he may have arrived even earlier.[51] Even so, since he was in Lower Germany up to about 154, his arrival in Britain was probably at least one or two years after the alleged war of *c.* 153/54 that was celebrated on the coin of 154/55, so he could be viewed as the governor who cleared everything up after his predecessor had fought the war.

The Newcastle inscription recording troop movements was found in the Tyne in 1903 during operations to dredge the north channel of the swing bridge.[52] It concerns a dedication to Antoninus Pius when Julius Verus was governor. The text of the inscription refers to vexillations of *II Augusta*, *VI Victrix* and *XX Valeria Victrix*, contributed to, or from, the army of the Upper and Lower provinces of Germany (*contributi ex Germaniis duobus*). Its wording is subject to different interpretations. According to one version, under the governor Julius Verus reinforcements were being contributed from the two German provinces to all three legions of Britain, indicating that there had been some trouble and lots of casualties from the probable outbreak of hostilities *c.* 153, so the soldiers were needed to fill gaps in the ranks. An alternative has it that troops had been sent *from* Britain *to* Germany, which means that the province of Britain was calm and peaceful and troops could be sent out of the island without risk.[53] In this case, the inscription most likely records the return from the two Germanies (*ex Germaniis duobus*) of soldiers who had been contributed (*contributi*) from the three legions. Julius Verus had been governor of Lower Germany *c.* 154, and it is feasible that when he came to Britain he brought back with him the legionaries who had been sent to Germany, not to fight battles but perhaps to help to build the new Antonine frontier which had been advanced a few miles to the east in the Odenwald.[54] If this theory is correct, the relevance of this inscription to the probable turmoil of the 150s is possibly the need for the return of the legionary soldiers *c.* 158 because there had been some losses and there would be repair work to be done at some forts.

At Birrens, the inscription bearing a dedication to Antoninus Pius is dated to 158 via the Emperor's twenty-first year of tribunician power, and specifically mentions Julius Verus as governor.[55] Although it does not record building work as such, it may indicate refurbishment of the fort. The inscription mentions *cohors II Tungrorum milliaria equitata c. L.* which may have been in occupation after the fort had been rebuilt or was in course of rebuilding. This 1000-strong, part-mounted unit was once thought from its initials to have been rewarded with Latin citizenship status, *civium Latinorum*, considered a first step towards full Roman citizenship, but this award is now discounted, and it is suggested that the initials stand for *coram laudata*, which taken literally means personally praised, presumably by an Emperor. There is also some evidence that legionaries from *VI Victrix* and *XX Valeria Victrix* were engaged in building work at Birrens, though without proof of dates when they were at this fort it cannot be said that they were involved in the repair and reoccupation. At Brough-on-Noe in Derbyshire building work was being carried out by *cohors I Aquitanorum*, under the prefect Capitonius Priscus, during Verus' term of office, but the inscription bears no precise date.[56] These inscriptions and the Britannia coin comprise the sum total of the evidence for a war in the 150s. The possibility that a war was fought somewhere in Britain at this time is discussed below in the context of the withdrawal from the Antonine Wall.

Two other inscriptions found in the eighteenth century and recorded in drawings, but now lost, have shown that while Julius

Verus was governor, building work was being carried out by soldiers from *VI Victrix* somewhere on the eastern part of Hadrian's Wall a few miles west of Newcastle.[57] There is no mention of Verus by name, but one of the two inscriptions is dated to the consulship of Tertullus and Sacerdos, which the two men held in 158, and has the abbreviation 'ref' for *refecit*.[58] The wording on the second inscription can also be interpreted as *refecit*, but it is not as clear in the eighteenth-century drawing and may be *perfecit*.[59] At any rate, something was being rebuilt, not built from scratch, so these inscriptions are not like the centurial stones of the first building phase. The compilers of *Roman Inscriptions in Britain*, dealing with drawings of inscriptions recorded two centuries earlier but no longer extant, had little to go on and assumed that the find-spot was at or near Heddon-on-the-Wall, which does not rule out the possibility that the stones could have been brought there from the nearby Hadrian's Wall fort at Rudchester, so it could have been the fort that was being repaired in 158. This would not have been of tremendous significance while the Antonine Wall was in operation, because some of the forts of Hadrian's Wall were still occupied and possibly required repairs. A re-examination of the archive concerning these inscriptions by Nick Hodgson has shown that the find-spot given as Heddon-on-the-Wall is incorrect. The stones were found at some point near the Wall about four to six miles from Newcastle city centre, probably in the area of Newburn. In this case, the stones were not in close proximity to a fort, and it is certain that they came from the Wall itself.[60] In other words the frontier was being repaired, and this has great relevance for the alleged war in the 150s, the abandonment of the Antonine Wall, and the reoccupation of Hadrian's Wall.

The End of the Antonine Frontier and the Return to Hadrian's Wall

Utilizing the information that was at hand, previous generations of scholars proposed that there had been three phases of occupation of the Antonine Wall, each divided by a period of abandonment. On the basis of finds from a few sites it seemed that the third occupation had lasted until the 180s, but this was shown to be false. Opinion then settled on only two occupations labelled Antonine Wall Periods I and II, which were punctuated by a brief withdrawal, followed by a brief reoccupation. It was thought that the first phase ended in *c.* 155 or at the latest by 158, and this is supported by coin evidence from Mumrills. At this fort a coin of 154/55 was discovered in the outermost west ditch. This is the latest stratified coin on the Antonine Wall, as opposed to unstratified coins of later periods, which cannot be used to indicate occupation of the sites where they were found, because there is no certainty as to how they arrived there.[61] The coin of 154/55 supported the assumption that there had been a war, probably in the territory of the Brigantes, as potentially indicated by the various pieces of evidence cited above from the mid-150s, and it was thought that this war had been serious enough to warrant a withdrawal from the Antonine Wall in order to fight the tribes of the Pennines. It seemed that when the first Antonine phase ended, there was to all appearances a brief and rather sketchy attempt to put Hadrian's Wall back into commission under the governor Julius Verus. It was not envisaged that the two Walls could have been held simultaneously, so a withdrawal from the more northerly frontier was postulated. The break in occupation of the Antonine Wall between Period I and Period II could only have been for a short time, especially as the building activity on Hadrian's Wall datable to 158 seemed to be curiously incomplete, even allowing for the possibility that Verus' work may have been more extensive and there may be more building inscriptions which have escaped detection. Thus the building programme under Verus was seen as an abortive attempt to bring troops out of Scotland, with the implicit allegation that the army had suffered at the hands of a determined but unknown British tribe or perhaps a federation of tribes. Some authors pointed out that if the Britannia coin really signified a victory in 154/55, Verus could not have arrived until after the war was concluded, but it was assumed that the rebellion must have caused so much disruption that he had started to withdraw from the north, probably on his own authority without waiting for imperial sanction from Antoninus Pius. It was thought that the Emperor must have reacted badly and immediately ordered the return to the Antonine Wall and its subsequent refurbishment. The theory gains support from the fact that Verus is not known to have occupied any post until the early years of the reign of Marcus

Aurelius, so it could be assumed that he was in disgrace and never regained Antoninus Pius' trust, and had to start again under the new Emperor in 161 after the death of Pius.[62] The few known facts would bear that interpretation, even if it stretches credulity. Roman governors of Britain were usually experienced men and would surely have some resourcefulness in clearing up after a war or holding out until hostilities were over, and they would all know very well that a momentous decision to abandon a frontier without waiting for Imperial authority could only result in opprobrium and no further appointments.

Since the Romans were obviously still present on the Antonine Wall after 158, it was reasonable to suppose that after a couple of years of neglect, the second phase of occupation involved some reconstruction, which seemed to be the best way of explaining why there was more than one construction phase at some forts, where rebuilding was sometimes preceded by destruction and accompanied by a change of garrison. It may simply mean that the Romans cleared the sites for new building, but for some authors the rebuilding signified troop movements and fighting against the British tribes from Brigantia up to the far north in the 150s. The so-called second phase was thought to have lasted until 163 or 164, the terminal date being unequivocal, attested by pottery studies of both the imported red samian wares and locally made coarse vessels, both of which types disappear from military sites in Antonine Scotland after the mid-160s, though coarse ware is found on civilian sites after that date. Coin evidence supports this date for the withdrawal, as does the absence of inscriptions in Scotland after the reign of Antoninus Pius. This scenario of a withdrawal in 163–64 fitted nicely with the activity of the governor Calpurnius Agricola from about 161 to 163. He is attested in the Hadrian's Wall area, and may even have been present in person. At Corbridge while he was governor two dedications were set up, to Marcus Aurelius and Lucius Verus, and to the Unconquered Sun. At Vindolanda a broken inscription was found bearing nothing except Calpurnius' name, and at Carvoran a dedication was made to the Syrian goddess, appropriate for the Syrian archers who were based there. On another inscription from this fort the text has not survived, but something was achieved during Calpurnius Agricola's term of office. Inscriptions also mention him at Ribchester in

Lancashire and Hardknott in Cumbria. There is nothing to prove that Calpurnius was organising repairs or building work, but the inscriptions indicate that building had been done, and at the very least they show that the forts that have produced them were occupied.[63]

The abandonment of the Antonine frontier is now focussed more sharply on the governor Julius Verus and the rebuilding work that was going on in 158. This can no longer be regarded as an aberration and an unwarranted interruption in the occupation of the Antonine Wall, but instead is seen as part of the preliminary stages of the final withdrawal. This follows a seminal article by Nick Hodgson proposing that there was only one occupation of the Antonine Wall, from *c.* 142 to *c.* 164, never interrupted by any withdrawal and return.[64] This new scenario envisages that some of the secondary building phases at some Antonine Wall forts may belong to the changes of plan when it was decided to add smaller forts to the original six, probably necessitating changes of garrison and therefore accommodation, while other building phases and changes of garrison may belong to a gradual winding down of installations on the frontier and in Lowland Scotland from about 158 onwards. The phased withdrawal process would involve resettlement of some units on Hadrian's Wall and in the Pennines, and a consequent reshuffling of troops on the Antonine Wall, which was still held after 158, but not in such great strength. Units were generally smaller, as for instance at Ardoch, and Bearsden fort was deliberately destroyed by the Romans and not reoccupied.

It can be construed that the most telling evidence against a phased reduction in the occupation of the Antonine Wall and Lowland Scotland and the gradual refurbishment of Hadrian's Wall, derives from the important pottery study by Brian Hartley, who concluded that the supplies of imported samian ware to the Antonine Wall and to Hadrian's Wall were mutually exclusive, and therefore the two Walls were not being supplied at the same time and could not have been held in strength simultaneously.[65] But as pointed out by Hodgson, the study was made at a time when it was thought that the Antonine Wall had three occupation phases, the final one extending into the 180s. But Hartley did suggest that if the two Walls were held at the same time, it could only have been for a very brief period. In archaeological terms the length of time from the refurbishment of Hadrian's Wall in 158 to the last phase of the withdrawal from Scotland *c.* 164 qualifies as a very brief period, and it is feasible that the two Walls could have been held simultaneously while one was wound down and the other recommissioned.[66]

A rapid withdrawal would have resulted in the dislocation and homelessness of many of the units before their new accommodation had been prepared. While auxiliary units were capable of building or repairing their own forts, the strain on transport and logistics, combined with keeping the province in order, may have been considered too great to attempt to withdraw from Scotland and reorganise Hadrian's Wall and the hinterland all at once. The forts of Hadrian's Wall and its outposts could not have accommodated all the units being brought out of Scotland, but some of them could have been accommodated in the Pennines and possibly Cumbria. Therefore there was probably a selection process to determine where to recommission old forts or to build new forts if necessary, and which units would be best suited to which locations. When their recommissioned forts became available, units could be moved south, and the vacated Antonine forts on the Wall or in the Lowlands could be taken over by other units or part units.

The occupation of Lowland Scotland south of the Antonine Wall was similarly reduced before the final withdrawal in the mid-160s. The forts and fortlets of the Lowlands were thinned out and the distances between occupied installations was lengthened so that they were now about a day's march apart, which was, after all, the more usual spacing for a network of forts. The south-western area was more or less abandoned. On the evidence of pottery studies the military presence in the Lowlands ended in the mid-160s, with the exception of the outpost forts belonging to Hadrian's Wall. Birrens was occupied after 158 by *cohors II Tungrorum milliaria equitata*, and the unit remained there until the mid-180s.[67] Newstead was also held in considerable strength until the 180s. High Rochester was retained, probably occupied by *cohors I Lingonum equitata*, and Risingham may have been held under Pius but the only certain evidence of occupation dates to Marcus Aurelius when *cohors IV Gallorum equitata* was stationed there. A vexillation of this unit is also known to have been at High Rochester.

The maverick fort is Castlecary on the Antonine Wall, miles

to the north, where a Roman presence is attested by finds of late Antonine samian ware and an altar set up by soldiers of *VI Victrix*, for which Breeze and Dobson propose a broad date range of 165 to 190, but prefer a later date, long after the withdrawal from the Antonine Wall. It is suggested that the Romans sent out patrols as far as, and possibly beyond, the Forth.[68] It is possible that other Antonine forts besides Castlecary were used for patrols sent out from bases further south.[69] Such long-distance patrolling seems to be indicated on other frontiers, especially in Africa, where evidence of Roman activity is found over 200 miles away from the nearest base.

The reasons for the withdrawal from the Antonine Wall are not given in any source. Speculative causes have been adduced for the beginning of the demise of the Antonine Wall under Pius. It could be argued that by 158 the Antonine Wall had served its purpose, because military glory had accrued to the non-military Emperor Antoninus Pius, and the gradual thinning of the garrison in Scotland for the last few years of the occupation could indicate that the Romans had gained the upper hand and all was peaceful on the northern front. Alternatively it could mean that the hinterland of Hadrian's Wall was not as pacified as the Romans had imagined and they needed a greater concentration of troops in the north of England than they could afford, unless they brought units out of Scotland. There is no proof for these theories.

Hodgson's proposal, that there was only one occupation of the Antonine Wall and a phased withdrawal started *c.* 158, rejected the idea of the Brigantian revolt in the 150s, which was supposed to have been the main reason why the Romans left the Antonine Wall, came back south to put the rebellion down, then returned to the north and reoccupied the Wall.[70] In 2009, following up the ideas proposed in 1995, Hodgson suggested that there could still have been a war, not in northern England, which is suggested solely on the authority of Pausanias and his undated and aggravating reference to the Brigantes, but in south-west Scotland.[71]

The tribes of northern Britain never fully accepted Romanization, though some of them were more amenable than others. In the south of Britain some of the tribes had been acclimatised to Roman culture and had been receiving Roman imports for some time before the invasion in 43, so converting to a Roman way of life was not such a difficult transition. The Britons adapted to town life, and in the country, villas and small-scale industrial establishments sprang up. It seemed that there was a dearth of villas in the north, but this reflected lack of excavation rather than lack of Roman-style houses, and villas are now known to have been built much further north than previously thought. But still the majority of the native people of the north continued to live in Iron Age style houses even if they received and used Roman goods within them. The Roman army was once seen as the prime agent in the Romanization process, but as Martin Millett pointed out, the army was distributed predominantly in the northern parts of Britain, which were also the least Romanized throughout the occupation.[72]

Understanding of native society during the Roman occupation is hampered by the lack of records, which makes the study of Roman Britain very one-sided, more Roman than British. Compared to the Romans the tribes have no voice to allow insights into their attitudes and the principles by which they conducted their lives, except through the artefacts that they left behind. A telling factor is the amount of Roman goods found on native sites, which may be an indication that the owners of these goods were not opposed to dealing with the Romans and were willing to absorb at least part of their culture. One tribe in southern Scotland which remained impervious to Romanization were the Novantae in Galloway. Their name is noted in Greek in Ptolemy's *Geography* and there is mention of *Novantarum peninsula* and *Novantarum promontorium*, peninsula and promontory of the Novantae, which makes it fairly certain that Galloway was the homeland of this tribe.[73] In Annandale and Nithsdale there is a marked absence of evidence of Romanization. Finds of Roman artefacts are very sparse in this whole area in comparison with other tribal lands of Scotland, probably indicating a conscious rejection of Romanization if not outright hostility. The study of a range of native Iron Age sites in Scotland supports this argument. The lack of Roman finds on native sites in Dumfriesshire led to the conclusion that the tribes living there were at best totally unconcerned with Romanization or at worst were actually hostile.[74] Another study showed that the tribes of Lowland Scotland varied in their use of Roman goods, with the south-west being the least interested in acquiring such material.[75] This suggests that very few traders, if any, from other parts of

Britain or indeed the Empire successfully penetrated the tribes of south-west Scotland, nor did Roman diplomacy in the form of gifts and subsidies succeed in winning the hearts and minds of the tribal leaders, at least in this period. On a map showing Roman coin hoards from the late second to the fourth century, which may indicate diplomatic activity and the payment of subsidies to tribal chiefs, the majority of finds are in the north-eastern area of Lowland Scotland, and on the east coast further north. Most of the south-west area yielded nothing except for hoards discovered at Stranraer, a possible centre of the Novantae according to Ptolemy, and at Stoneykirk, Corsock and Langholm, all in Dumfries and Galloway, but they are probably late Roman, the Stoneykirk hoard containing coins of Constantine I and his successors, dated 306 to 353.[76] If subsidies had been given to the tribes of the south-west in the mid-second century, or trading activities had taken hold, it is to be expected that the chiefs courted by Rome would then distribute their gifts to their supporters, and archaeologists would surely have found some evidence of this in native settlements. It has been pointed out that trade between the Romans and the natives in northern Britain seems to have flourished only during periods of Roman occupation, but the Antonine Wall was held for about twenty years, and if trading activities had taken hold during that short period, there ought to have been at least some evidence of it.[77] Indifference to Roman blandishments can be interpreted as not quite passive resistance that would flare up if provocation went too far, and provocation may have arisen from attempts to levy taxes and to demand recruits for the Roman army to be sent away to other provinces.[78]

It has to be admitted that modern knowledge of the attitudes and dispositions of the native British tribes is non-existent, and in order to elucidate these concepts clues have to be gleaned from the archaeological remains of both native sites and Roman forts, and the artefacts found in or near them. Breeze has pointed out the inadequacies of this state of affairs, arguing that a dense Roman occupation usually leads to the conclusion that the natives were restless, but geographical determinism also had its part to play besides political and military reasons for the placement of forts, which had to be located according to topographical demands, to watch routes and rivers, and forts are not entirely absent from the territories of tribes considered to be friendly.[79] Nevertheless the distribution of Roman forts in south-west Scotland still suggests that the Romans needed to watch the area very closely.[80] The large fort at Glenlochar has been tentatively equated with the place name Lucopibia in Ptolemy's *Geography*, which he lists as one of the centres of the Novantae.[81] If this is correct the fort was well placed to keep watch not only on routes but also on the tribesmen, much as the fort at Newstead on the eastern side was placed next to the Eildon Hills to watch over the north–south route and also the Selgovae, who were neighbours of the Novantae, and tradition maintains that these tribesmen were also hostile to the Romans. It is significant that there is a preponderance of Roman forts and fortlets at the western end of the Stanegate and similarly at the western area of Hadrian's Wall, supported by the Hadrianic outpost forts north of the Wall at Birrens, Netherby and Bewcastle. These forts, accompanied by the fortification of the coast on the western side, but not emulated on the eastern side, suggests that there was a need for greater vigilance and manpower to guard against threats from the natives of south-west Scotland.[82] A question has been raised concerning the years after the abandonment of the Antonine Wall and the return to the Hadrianic frontier, why were the turrets and milecastles of the Cumberland coast abandoned in the later second century, if the Novantae were such a considerable threat?[83] The answer is that no one knows, except possibly the tribesmen had been successively decimated, perhaps by Lollius Urbicus, and/ or during the postulated war in the 150s, and finally by Ulpius Marcellus under Commodus in the war of the 180s. The Romans were capable of such horrific measures. The Eburones of Gaul gave Julius Caesar little trouble after he had finished with them because he despoiled their lands, invited rival tribes to join in the pillage, and eventually wiped them out. After a war in North Africa, the Emperor Domitian boasted that he had 'forbidden the Nasamones to exist'. According to Dio, the Emperor Marcus Aurelius, dealing with the Sarmatian Iazyges, had wished to exterminate them utterly.[84]

It is not impossible that the perceived warlike spirit of the Novantae is not simply all smoke and mirrors, and they may have taken to the warpath in the 150s. The destruction and burning of the fort at Birrens, previously dismissed as deliberate Roman levelling of the site before rebuilding, now comes into sharper focus, together with the Roman siege works around the old Iron Age hill fort at Burnswark. At Birrens the signs of destruction by burning were not limited to one area of the fort, which would have been expected if the Romans were clearing the site and bringing all the unwanted material to a bonfire. Instead the signs of burning were discovered in different locations and were described as haphazard, and this is not the usual method that the Romans employed when they were clearing and levelling a site prior to rebuilding. The possibility that Birrens went up in flames during a native revolt must now be considered.[85]

The siege works at Burnswark are undoubtedly there and still visible, one Roman camp to the north-west of the hill fort and labelled the North Camp, and the other to the south-east, labelled the South Camp, placed on the lower slopes of the hill fort. This camp has three breaks in the north-western earth rampart facing the hill fort, fronted by three round mounds of earth which were labelled artillery platforms, but this was questioned by Campbell, who considered that they were designed to deflect objects rolled down from the hill fort above, not to support siege engines.[86] In the northern corner there is a small fort, surrounded by a ditch. No evidence of timber buildings was found inside it, but there was some Roman pottery which formed a high percentage of all the pottery found on the whole site.[87] The dating of the fortlet has been problematic. It was once considered to be a native site, but more recently it has been suggested that it is Roman and belongs to the Antonine period. Lead sling bullets were found inside the hill fort, indicating that missiles had been fired, which as Keppie points out would have been used to pin down the enemy to prevent them from appearing on the ramparts while the Romans prepared for an assault on the hill fort.[88] Focused around one of the hill fort entrances, there were tanged arrowheads, suggesting that the Romans had concentrated on that area. When these discoveries were originally made, the evidence was immediately accepted as a genuine sign of warfare, with the Britons gathered in the hill fort and facing a Roman army which eventually defeated them. Then it was pointed out that occupation of the hill fort had ceased long before the Romans arrived, and the ramparts were badly decayed when the sling bullets were fired at them. Consequently the siege works were then interpreted as Roman practice camps, where soldiers learned to use artillery.[89] The fact that arrowheads were found near the entrance to the hill fort could simply mean that the soldiers were being trained in target practice. This sounded quite reasonable, since the hill fort was in a remote area where there would be little damage to military or civil buildings, except that only the soldiers from the fort at Birrens would have benefited from the practice camp, and others would have to cover a considerable mileage to get there and back, in preference to using an artillery range closer to their forts.

More recently the idea of a genuine siege at Burnswark has been resurrected.[90] Even though the hill fort had been abandoned a long time ago, it could have been hastily reoccupied in the Antonine period by Britons who had raised revolt, and despite the dilapidated defences it could still have afforded some protection. The Burnswark camps have been recently been related to the events of the 150s.[91] There may have been a dramatic last stand here, and the fort at Birrens may have been one of the first targets in an uprising *c.* 153.

The Antonine Wall was given up by 164 or 165 at the latest, as both pottery and coin evidence attest, so the final stages of the withdrawal were carried out under the Emperor Marcus Aurelius, but the main question is who made the decision to abandon the northern Wall and return to Hadrian's frontier? Some scholars cannot accept that the withdrawal began in 158, with the governor Julius Verus starting proceedings to put Hadrian's Wall back into commission, because it seems incredible that Antoninus Pius would abandon his own conquests. It seems to some scholars that after making so much effort to take in Lowland Scotland and build a new frontier, the reversal of his forward policy would cause irreparable damage to Antoninus' reputation.[92] It seems much more realistic to assign the decision to withdraw from Scotland to Marcus Aurelius. According to the *Historia Augusta*, Marcus faced warfare in Britain, and also in the eastern provinces when the Parthians began to test Roman strength.[93] No date is provided for the alleged war in Britain, and the location is also unknown. The *Historia Augusta* equates the British problem with the Parthian war, which broke out shortly after Marcus' accession, so it may mean that there was trouble in Britain immediately after the death of Antoninus

Pius. If this is correct, the withdrawal from the Antonine Wall could be attributed to Marcus Aurelius as part of a reduction of commitment on the British frontier in favour of devoting resources to the eastern campaign.

The awkward fact remains that repair works on the Hadrianic frontier began when the Antonine Wall was still occupied. Reluctance to attribute this decision to Pius himself persuaded some authors that the governor Julius Verus must have started to withdraw from the Antonine Wall and Pius reversed the process, involving a very brief return to the northernmost frontier. This seems highly unlikely and does great disservice to Julius Verus. In 2009 Hodgson reiterated and augmented his arguments, originally made in 1995, that the withdrawal began under Pius, pointing out that there is not enough evidence to disprove either of the current theories that on the one hand the abandonment of the Antonine Wall was begun under Antoninus Pius in 158, or on the other that the two Walls were held in tandem, with changes taking place on both of them until the decision was made to evacuate the northernmost Wall a few years after the accession of Marcus Aurelius and Lucius Verus.[94]

There are other factors towards the end of the reign of Antoninus Pius which may have influenced the Emperor to start proceedings to withdraw to Hadrian's Wall. According to the *Historia Augusta*, when Pius was close to death, in his delirium he spoke of nothing except the state (*res publica*) and certain kings with whom he was angry.[95] As Birley points out, this can only mean the Parthian king and other rulers of states on Rome's eastern borders.[96] There were signs of trouble in the east during Antoninus' reign. As usual the main point of contention between the Romans and the Parthians concerned the rulers of Armenia, where pro-Roman and pro-Parthian kings were installed and uninstalled with monotonous regularity. Coins dated to 143 celebrate the fact that Antoninus installed a king in Armenia. The legend on the reverse says *Rex Armeniis Datus*, a king given to the Armenians, and Pius is shown standing on the left placing a crown on the head of the new king of Armenia.[97] According to the *Historia Augusta*, he settled the disputes and pleas of several kings – this occurs in a passage concerned with the eastern kingdoms. He reinstalled Abgarus, king of Osroene, who had seemingly been exiled, and this he achieved solely by personal influence (*sola auctoritate*).[98]

There had been civil war among Parthian rulers leading to periods of internal weakness, but when Vologaeses II became king the Royal House became stronger. Towards the end of Hadrian's reign, probably in 134 Vologaeses was able to buy off the Alani when they erupted into a war instigated by Pharasmanes, king of a smaller state, causing damage in Albania and Media, then endangering Armenia and Cappadocia, though Dio says that the Alani were stopped because they were afraid of the governor, Flavius Arrianus.[99] Arrianus, or Arrian, writing in Greek, produced, among other works, a pamphlet outlining his preparations for war against the Alani called in English *Order of Battle Against the Alans*. Eastern affairs were smoothed over when Vologaeses sent envoys to Rome to complain of Pharasmanes and his behaviour, and the latter agreed to a peace settlement. In the extant version of Dio, this episode is assigned to Hadrian, but the editor of the Loeb edition says it seems out of place and could belong to the reign of Antoninus Pius. Relations between Rome and Parthia degenerated under the next king, Vologaeses III, son of Vologaeses II, who came to power in 148. It may have been this king, rather than his father, who asked for the return of the Parthian throne, which had been seized and taken to Rome by Trajan. Antoninus refused, probably starting a sort of Cold War punctuated by niggling hostilities.[100] Two passages in the *Historia Augusta* indicate that Vologaeses started to prepare for an invasion of Armenia. In the biography of Pius, it is said that the king was dissuaded from this action when Antoninus simply sent him a letter, and in the life of Marcus Aurelius, the beginning of the Parthian war is prefaced by the statement that Vologaeses had planned the war under Pius.[101] But Antoninus did not limit his activity to sending a letter to Vologaeses. He sent troops to the east, attested on an inscription recording the career of Lucius Neratius Proculus, who was sent to Syria as leader of the vexillations (plural) for a Parthian war: *misso ab Imperator Antonino Augusto Pio ad deducendas vexillationes in Syriam ob bellum Parthicum*.[102] As another precaution Pius left in post the governor of Syria, Lucius Attidius Cornelianus who had almost completed the usual term of three years or so. Cornelianus was probably kept in office in order to deny the Parthians the opportunity of exploiting the changeover when a new governor arrived, who might not have been properly acquainted with the current problems.[103]

War broke out very soon after Marcus Aurelius and Lucius Verus succeeded Antoninus Pius in 161. Vologaeses invaded Armenia and placed on the throne Pacorus, a member of the Arsacid clan, the ruling house of the Parthians. The governor of Cappadocia, Marcus Sedatius Severianus, reacted swiftly, marched out of his province, and was immediately surrounded by the Parthians at Elegeia, where he and his entire legion were wiped out.[104] The legion is not named, but it was possibly *IX Hispana*, last heard of in 108 building a gate at York.[105] It may have been stationed at Nijmegen in Lower Germany, and then gone to the east.[106] The Parthian war was begun in earnest in summer 162 under Lucius Verus.

These events in the east may be relevant to the withdrawal from the Antonine Wall. Antoninus Pius knew that sooner or later there would be a war if Vologaeses III was not checked, but he probably did not wish to open hostilities himself. It was better to wait for Vologaeses to make the first move as the aggressor, then the Romans could be seen as the victims and Pius could declare war in a just cause, not wasting Roman lives in a struggle that he as Emperor had begun without provocation. He prepared for trouble by sending vexillations to Syria, and leaving the experienced governor in command. Concerning Britain at the other end of the Empire, he probably reflected that he had fought a war in the early 140s, and had gone to elaborate lengths to retain the conquests and maintain the peace thereby creating another frontier and garrisoning the land between it and Hadrian's Wall. Then about ten years later, if the postulated trouble in the 150s really did occur in south-west Scotland, he had to fight another war in the same territory, so the effort in garrisoning it was probably never going to ensure that the land was peaceful and exploitable. With the threat of further trouble looming in the east, where the wars were on a larger scale against the most powerful and organised enemy that the Romans faced, Antoninus Pius may have reflected that the northern areas of Britain were not vital to the survival of the Empire, but Syria and the eastern provinces were, and danger in that area was potentially more damaging to Rome than any events in Britain. From the point of view of trading links alone, it was worth any amount of effort to retain the whole area of Syria and the eastern provinces through which trade routes extended as far as India and China, whereas Britain did not yield the same potential profit, and never could do so. Moreover there was a large number of troops in Britain, most of whom had recent experience of marching, fighting, organising supplies and building forts, and they might be needed at some time in the not too distant future in the east.

It may be that after 155 Antoninus Pius had the foresight to discern that the end of the frontier in Scotland was approaching because the pacification of the most resistant tribes was taking too long, absorbing resources and manpower for little gain, and it was clear that he would probably need those resources and manpower for the east, so pragmatically he set in motion a project to relinquish his conquests and abandon the frontier, but he did so carefully, reducing the strength of the northernmost frontier while increasing the strength of Hadrian's Wall, to enable the Roman army to protect the territory from attack until the Hadrianic frontier could take on the task on its own. The elaborate distance slabs recording the building work were carefully buried in prepared pits, which Hodgson sees as a ritual of closure, signifying the end of an era and no intention to return.[107] Antoninus Pius was just over seventy years old in 158, and he died before the process of withdrawal from Scotland was completed. He bequeathed the final stages of the withdrawal to his successors.

Whatever their reasons, Antoninus Pius and Marcus Aurelius placed the frontier of Roman Britain back on the line that Hadrian had chosen. If ever there were doubts in the Imperial government that the frontiers were not performing as they should, this was the moment when the entire concept could have been changed. Antoninus Pius, or Marcus Aurelius, or indeed any of the emperors who came after them, could have organised a reversal to the previous method of control, dispensing with the running barrier that Hadrian had installed, and placing forts near to centres of population and to guard routes and river crossings. No such retrograde movement was made, and Hadrian's Wall was retained. The emperors of the later centuries, when the frontiers and the troops manning them had become much more static, have been accused by John Mann of suffering from a crippling inertia, unable to see any other solution to protect the Empire.[108] But energetic emperors such as Severus,

Constantius I and Theodosius all repaired frontier works in Britain, as did Diocletian and Valentinian on the Rhine and Danube, and a new frontier was built in the lands between these two rivers when the Romans had been forced to move southwards in the late Empire. If the frontiers were not working as the Romans desired, then surely someone would have noticed and applied some thought to the matter. Were all the emperors from Hadrian to Honorius afflicted with Mann's inertia?

After the Antonine interlude, Hadrian's Wall was repaired, the forts were put back into working order for the same types and sizes of units that had occupied them in the first phase, the milecastles received new gates and were reoccupied, the turrets were repaired, the fortifications of the Cumberland coast were reduced but the system was retained, outpost forts protected the Wall on the west and now also on the east, and the Pennine forts were recommissioned. With changes in the details but not in the concept, this is how the north of Britain was defended, or as Breeze points out, perhaps a better choice of terminology would be protected, until the end of the Roman occupation in the fifth century.[109] Perhaps Hadrian's shade looked on, saying 'I told you so'.

6

Hadrian's Wall from Marcus Aurelius to Severus: AD 161 to AD 211

The division of continuous history into manageable portions, each with a beginning and an end, always has a connotation of abrupt changes which do not reflect reality because life goes on before the changes and continues after them, but the title of this chapter is not entirely artificial. During the early years of the reign of Marcus Aurelius the return to Hadrian's Wall was completed, and after the death of Severus in 211 there were administrative, legal and social changes that affected the whole Empire, and some which affected Hadrian's Wall, so both these turning points, if such they were, seem appropriate for the beginning and end of a section of the narrative.

Antoninus Pius died in 161 and was succeeded by Marcus Aurelius, who took as colleague and joint Emperor Lucius Verus, the son of Hadrian's first choice of successor. At the time of the accession of the two new Emperors, the move southwards from the Antonine Wall and the refurbishing of Hadrian's Wall was still progressing. The governor Julius Verus had departed by 160, to be replaced for a short time by Pisibanus Lepidus, whose name appears in fragmentary form on a diploma recording the discharge of soldiers from auxiliary units in Britain, probably in 160.[1] As usual, according to the *Historia Augusta*, war was threatening in Britain (*imminebat ... Britannicum bellum*) but there is no clue as to why there was trouble or where the potentially hostile tribes were located.[2] In the summer of 161 Marcus Aurelius and Lucius Verus chose Marcus Statius Priscus as the new governor, and then shortly afterwards they appointed Sextus Calpurnius Agricola. The *Historia Augusta* specifically states that this governor was sent against the Britons, but there is no evidence as to what he achieved or where he operated, and it is not certain if there was any fighting or anything approaching a war.[3] Although his arrival in summer 161 is fairly certain, the terminal date of his office is not known, except that by 168 he was on the Lower Danube.[4]

Sextus Calpurnius Agricola is attested on several inscriptions in Britain, all of them dedications to deities or the Emperors and not explicitly mentioning building work, though they are usually interpreted as such, because while attached to a new building or a repaired structure it would be obvious that work had been carried out. Repairs and reconstruction work would be necessary while Calpurnius Agricola was governor to accommodate units coming south from the Antonine Wall.

At Ribchester in Lancashire a detachment of cavalry from Upper Germany set up a dedication to the two Emperors Marcus and Lucius Verus, also naming the governor.[5] There is no indication that the cavalrymen from Germany were needed because the threatened war mentioned in the *Historia Augusta* had broken out in the north-west, but the inscription does indicate that the fort was occupied in the 160s. A fragment of an inscription, now lost, was found near the south gate of Hardknott fort, bearing the letters GRIC, which is reasonably restored as Agricola, but which Agricola is not certain; it could be the first-century Gnaeus Julius Agricola, earliest conqueror of Scotland.[6] Calpurnius Agricola is also attested at Carvoran and Vindolanda, though he was not necessarily active at these sites. The Carvoran inscriptions are dedications to deities set up while he was governor, and the Vindolanda inscription is too fragmentary to be certain what it represents.[7] At Corbridge an inscription shows that a vexillation of *VI Victrix* was based there under Calpurnius Agricola, and another inscription which does not name him attests building work by soldiers of *XX Valeria Victrix*.[8] It seems likely that the fort at Corbridge was being transformed into a base for vexillations of these two legions.[9]

Under Calpurnius Agricola and possibly later governors the forts on Hadrian's Wall were being reoccupied. At some time after the withdrawal from the Antonine Wall a new fort was built at Newcastle upon Tyne. At first it was dated to the mid-Antonine period but it probably belongs to the later second century or the early years of the third century.[10] It seems to have been a new build, because the main features of the levels beneath the fort are associated with agricultural use. The fort was not built to the usual playing card shape, but followed the contours of the land above the River Tyne, rather like the fort at Whitley Castle, which was lozenge shaped to fit the lie of the land, and the third-century fort at Bewcastle, which also assumed an irregular shape to fit comfortably into the terrain on which it lies.

Little is known of the auxiliary units in Scotland and the north of England in the early years of the joint reigns of Marcus Aurelius and Lucius Verus, and the situation is potentially complicated because some units or parts of units may have been taken out of the province when the Parthian wars began. It is not possible to produce a complete list of the units occupying the Wall in the later second century, though the type of unit, if not the actual names, can sometimes be discerned from the size and layout of the forts where excavation has been extensive enough. After the withdrawal from the Antonine Wall and Lowland Scotland some forts of Hadrian's Wall held mixed garrisons of auxiliaries and legionaries. At Corbridge, as mentioned above, vexillations of two legions were stationed. At Benwell, epigraphic evidence shows that at least some soldiers of the 1000-strong, part mounted *cohors I Vangionum equitata milliaria* were in occupation at an unknown date. The suggestion that only part of this unit was present derives from the fact that its commander was a prefect, whereas a commander of a thousand-strong unit ought to have been a tribune, therefore perhaps only half of the unit was present under a lower-ranking prefect while the tribune was absent with the rest of the troops.[11] If this was the case there would have been room for detachments of legionaries. Two inscriptions from Benwell record legionary centurions, one from *XX Valeria Victrix* under Antoninus Pius and the other from *II Augusta* under Marcus Aurelius and Lucius Verus.[12] Opinion is divided as to whether there were legionary vexillations at Benwell. It is pointed out that the presence of centurions does not prove that they commanded detachments at this fort.[13] There is no mention on the inscriptions of *vexillationes*, or of ordinary soldiers from the century commanded by each of the centurions, who could simply have been passing through or staying at the fort on some unknown military business without legionaries in tow. Nonetheless it remains a possibility that legionaries were stationed in this fort.[14]

After the withdrawal from the Antonine Wall more forts on Hadrian's Wall may have contained a mixture of troops, but hardly anything is known of the units in garrison at this time. It is not until the third century that sufficient information is available to list the unit names and their locations, and from then on individual units were permanently associated with their forts. Although most of the evidence points to this as a third-century development, the process may have begun in the 180s.[15] When Hadrian's Wall was reoccupied, at some of the forts there was little or no change in the layout or design, implying that a similar type of unit, if not the same unit, was to be installed. At Wallsend the timber barracks were replaced in stone with no alterations to the original plan. It is thought that a 500-strong, part-mounted unit, a *cohors quingenaria equitata*, was stationed there in both the first and second phases, but it is not known whether the same unit, or a different one, was installed after the withdrawal from the north. The date when the *ala II Asturum* arrived at Chesters is not known. It may have been at this fort in the late 160s, but the first known record of it dates to the late 170s, when it is recorded there under Ulpius Marcellus, who was governor from *c.* 177.[16] Marcellus may also have installed *ala I Asturum* at Benwell, though the only hint is an inscription recording a cavalry prefect at this fort, but his unit is not named, and no inscription survives which mentions both the *ala I Asturum* and Ulpius Marcellus together.[17] At Housesteads the thousand-strong *cohors I Tungrorum* was stationed there at an unknown date after it left its headquarters fort at Castlecary on the Antonine Wall. It has been suggested that it arrived at Housesteads possibly as early as 158.[18] The fort at Great Chesters may have been occupied under Hadrian by *cohors VI Nerviorum*, but the unit did not return to this fort. By 166 under Marcus Aurelius a *cohors Raetorum* was in garrison at Great Chesters, but the unit number is not certain. By the reign of Severus Alexander in the third century *cohors II Asturum* was at Great Chesters, rebuilding the granary that had fallen down through old age.[19] The unit of Hamian archers from Syria, *cohors I Hamiorum sagittariorum*, was stationed at Carvoran under Hadrian, and returned to the same fort when it was withdrawn from Scotland. It was already at Carvoran under the governor Calpurnius Agricola, when the commanding officer, the prefect Licinius Clemens, set up two inscriptions, one of them dedicated to the Syrian goddess.[20] This is the only securely attested example of a unit returning from the Antonine Wall to its original location in the Hadrianic system.[21] The fort at Stanwix was extended in the Antonine period probably at some time after 160.[22] Without benefit of secure evidence it is assumed that the only thousand-strong cavalry unit in Britain, *ala Augusta Gallorum Petriana milliaria civium Romanorum*, must have been stationed at this fort because no other would have been large enough to accommodate the numbers of soldiers and horses.[23] Whether or not it had been there under Hadrian is not certain. At Burgh-by-Sands, where three forts are known, at least two of them with more than one phase, the chronology and occupation of the forts are the least known of all the Wall forts. The first fort labelled Burgh I lay to the south of the Turf Wall instead of being attached to it, and another fort was located to the west of this fort, labelled Burgh III. There may have been a major change associated with the reoccupation of the Wall from *c.* 158 onwards, and the rebuilding of the Turf Wall in stone. Burgh II lies over the line of the Turf Wall, projecting beyond it, but the excavators did not think that the fort belonged to the Turf Wall phase. A ditch presumed to be the northern ditch of the Wall was filled in and the fort laid out over it. The Wall deviated to join the northern edge of the fort, as it did at Birdoswald when the Turf Wall was replaced in stone, and it may even be the case that the stone Wall and Burgh II were built at the same time. It is suggested from pottery evidence that the Burgh I is Hadrianic, not attached to the Wall, Burgh II belongs to the rebuilding of the Turf Wall in stone, and Burgh III could be a pre-Hadrianic fort or possibly a camp,[24] but few statements about Burgh II can be taken as gospel truth until more excavation has been done.

The milecastles and turrets along the Wall were put back into operation during the 160s. It is assumed that the gates that had been taken out of the milecastles were replaced. Actual evidence for this is harder to detect than the disruption caused when the gates were taken out, but wherever the milecastles have been investigated it seems that they were reoccupied in the 160s, which strongly suggests that the soldiers inside them did not eschew the safety that gates would provide. At milecastle 35, named after the farm at Sewingshields, the excavators detected several phases in the internal buildings, but in the 160s only slight alterations seem to have been made to the original Hadrianic layout. The pottery evidence shows that the milecastle was occupied until the later second century.[25] The turrets of the Wall were probably repaired or rebuilt, but without excavation at all of them, it cannot be stated unequivocally that all of the turrets were recommissioned in the 160s. Where investigations have been carried out it seems that the turrets were occupied from the 160s until the end of the second century, and sometime after that some of them were demolished, but specific dates for this demolition work are not certain. Turrets 33b at Coesike and 35a on Sewingshields Crag were occupied until the end of the second century and demolished later, after which the Narrow Wall was built up over the recesses where the turrets had been built into the Wall, thus permanently renouncing the use of the turrets on at least that part of the frontier.

South of the Wall, the gaps that had been deliberately cut into the mounds on either side of the Vallum were not repaired and the causeways created by the infill were not all removed. It was usually stated that the Vallum ditch was cleaned out and the soil placed on the south berm, creating an extra mound dubbed by archaeologists as the marginal mound, to distinguish it from the other two. This was a reasonable assumption, because some erosion might be expected during the few years that the Wall was not fully manned, but the creation of the marginal mound from material from the bottom of the ditch has been questioned by Tony Wilmott. If the ditch had been cleaned out, there ought to be silt and organic material in the soil used for the marginal mound, but excavation at Black Carts showed that the marginal mound there was composed of the same clean material as the south mound of the Vallum, and therefore ought to have been contemporary with it. Wilmott points out that Charles Daniels, in the thirteenth edition of the *Handbook to the Wall*, favoured an early date for the marginal mound.[26] Unfortunately the results from other investigations are mixed, and in some places dirty soil was found in the marginal mound. As with many facets of Hadrian's Wall, what is found at one or two sites does not necessarily mean that the results can be applied to the entire Wall. Wilmott says 'we still cannot generalise'.[27]

It is thought that the western end of the Turf Wall was replaced in stone at this time, though as mentioned in the chapter on building Hadrian's Wall, the traditional view that the Hadrianic rebuild in stone had reached only as far as milecastle 54 has been questioned by Breeze.[28] It is not an established fact that the rebuilding of the rest of the Turf Wall belongs to the refurbishment of the 160s, but when investigations were made of the Turf Wall levels at milecastle 79 and turret 54a, that is at both ends of the stretch from the notorious milecastle 54 to the last milecastle in the west, the pottery that was discovered contained nothing later than mid-Antonine.[29] This overturns the suggestion that it was Severus who replaced the Turf Wall in stone during his extensive programme of repairs.[30] The theory is based on passages in the works of two late Roman authors who worked in the second half of the fourth century, Aurelius Victor, who produced *de Caesaribus*, (*On the Caesars*), and Eutropius, who wrote a history of Rome known as the *Breviarum ab urbe condita*.[31] Both authors say that Severus built a Wall thirty-two miles long, which fits so well with the length of the Turf Wall from milecastle 49 on the spur above the west bank of the River Irthing to milecastle 79, plus the remaining distance to Bowness-on-Solway. But this means that the Turf Wall would have been standing for about eighty years, and it has been questioned whether it could have survived for so long without repairs.[32] On the other hand, next to nothing of the Turf Wall is known in detail, so there could be evidence of repair work lurking under the stone Wall. Give or take another four decades or so, it will be seen how the reconstructed turf ramparts at Baginton and Vindolanda have fared, and if a turf wall could have survived from the reign of Hadrian to that of Severus.

There is less doubt about the Military Way, which probably does belong to this phase of refurbishment. Occasionally the new road runs along the north mound of the Vallum, which means that the road obviously post-dates the construction of this southern ditch and its two mounds. On the Antonine Wall a road to the south of the frontier was laid down almost immediately, while some of the forts were still being built or even in anticipation of the establishment of forts, but it is not clear whether it was empirical experience of building Hadrian's Wall without a communications route that prompted the establishment of the road on the Antonine Wall, or whether it was an innovation on the more northerly frontier that was later emulated on Hadrian's Wall. In other words, it is not known who thought of it and when. The use of the Military Way has been questioned after a survey of part of it near milecastles 40 and 41 east of Great Chesters fort. In other sections of the Military Way, roads branching off it have been found heading towards some of the turrets and milecastles, but the transport capabilities of the road would seem to be compromised by the fact that in some places it is very steep with gradients of 1 in 4 or 1 in 3, and in other places it is very narrow, about two metres wide, as compared with the more usual four or five metres. Doubts were once expressed in the nineteenth century by Collingwood Bruce as to whether wheeled traffic could pass along it, and these doubts are reiterated by the surveyor of the relevant stretch of the Military Way.[33] Bidwell stresses the continuing importance of the Stanegate as the main communications route, and suggests a general overhaul of the transport system along with the establishment of the Military Way, because it has been revealed that the road bridge at Chesters which replaced the Wall bridge is not the work of Severus, as once thought, but the pottery from the tower at the west end, previously unknown, is mid-Antonine in date. Furthermore, the details of the construction of the bridge at Corbridge are exactly the same as those at Chesters, suggesting that the two are contemporary and Antonine in date.[34]

The outpost forts to the north were retained when the Wall was recommissioned. Birrens and Netherby were reoccupied in the 160s, and presumably if they were occupied so was the third outpost on the western side at Bewcastle, though firm evidence is lacking, save for an inscription which was discovered in 1977 in the north-west corner of the fort.[35] It records building work by *VI Victrix*, which has been attributed to the Antonine reoccupation of the fort on the grounds that *II Augusta* and *XX Valeria Victrix* were associated with the building of the Hadrianic fort.[36] On the east side of the country Newstead was rebuilt in the 160s, and since it probably did not stand alone on Dere Street leading to the north, the small fort at Cappuck, and the two forts south of Newstead at High Rochester and Risingham were also probably occupied. What was happening at High Rochester is not certain, but a 500-strong, part-mounted unit, *cohors IV Gallorum equitata*, was stationed at Risingham probably in the joint reigns of Marcus Aurelius and Lucius Verus.[37]

The fortifications of the Cumberland coast were much reduced when Hadrian's Wall was put back into commission. With one or two exceptions most of the turrets were abandoned, and only some of the milefortlets were repaired and reoccupied, though excavations have not been carried out at every single one. The forts were retained, however. Moresby was occupied until the fourth century and at Maryport the garrison under Marcus Aurelius was *cohors I Baetasiorum civium Romanorum*, a unit which had distinguished itself and been awarded Roman citizenship.[38] The fort seems to have been occupied till at least the third century, as was Beckfoot.

On the east coast, a new fort was built at South Shields *c.* 160. This is the first phase of the multi-period fort that is partially visible today, and its plan was similar to that of Wallsend. It lies on a different site from the Hadrianic fort which is not yet located, but an early fort dating to about 125 is attested by finds from the civil settlement that was probably established close by the postulated fort. Further south, pottery evidence and three inscriptions show that forts were occupied in the 160s and 170s at Ambleside and Old Penrith in Cumbria, at Binchester, Ebchester, Lanchester and Chester-le-Street in Durham, at Bainbridge, Ilkley, and Templeborough in Yorkshire, at Ribchester, Lancaster and Manchester in Lancashire, and at Brough-on-Noe in Derbyshire where building work was going on in 158 under the governor Julius Verus.[39] The forts that are known to have been occupied in the 160s reveal only a part of the whole picture in the Pennines at that time, so in drawing up a map to illustrate the network of military installations along routes and river crossings, archaeologists are obliged to speculate that if a particular fort provides evidence of occupation then it is fairly certain that other forts along the same route would presumably have been garrisoned as well.

The dense occupation of the Pennines, compared to the pattern of occupation while the Antonine Wall was in use, need not necessarily indicate that the natives had recently become more hostile and required close supervision. The units evacuated from

Scotland would need to be housed somewhere, and it would do no harm to use them to protect the routes through the Pennine Valleys and the two main arteries to and from the north of England and the Wall, though it must also be emphasized that Roman soldiers were by no means limited to these functions. They undertook duties that in modern times would be allocated to a variety of officials such as policemen, customs guards, and security guards for the governor and the procurator or provincial finance officer. Papyrus records show that many soldiers were engaged in the administration of their own units, gathering and transporting food, fuel and clothing supplies, and the Vindolanda writing tablets make it clear that soldiers were delegated to these and other duties for much of their time. Some units may have been responsible for law and order and the administration of the regions around them, as attested by two different third-century legionary centurions at Ribchester who both describe themselves as *praepositus*, usually meaning a temporary commander, of the unit and the region.[40]

Some of the forts in the Pennines and elsewhere may have been occupied by the cavalry of the Iazyges, a branch of the Sarmatians by which name they are better known. About a decade after the abandonment of the Antonine Wall, Marcus Aurelius sent 5,500 of them to Britain.[41] This large number of men would have been sufficient to form over eleven cavalry units, but there is little trace of the Sarmatians, except that some of them are eventually attested at Ribchester.[42] Some of the Sarmatians may have been incorporated into the existing *alae* or *cohortes equitatae*, the part-mounted units. Although the primary purpose was most likely to remove the tribesmen from their homelands, the fact that the Roman army in Britain could accommodate them may indicate that there was some minor skirmishing that has escaped the chroniclers, towards the end of the reign of Marcus Aurelius, a foretaste of what was to break out not long after the Emperor's death.

War in Britain under Commodus

Commodus had been made his father's colleague as Emperor in 177, and became sole Emperor in 180 when Marcus Aurelius died. Dio is the source for the premature despatch of Marcus Aurelius by Commodus, or by the doctors attending the Emperor, which allows script writers for modern films to have Marcus poisoned by Commodus' ambitious friends or smothered by Commodus himself.[43] After Marcus' death, Commodus made peace with the Danube tribes, demanded the return of prisoners, extracted a large number of recruits for the army and an annual tribute of grain, and returned to Rome.[44]

According to Dio, the most serious war of Commodus' reign was fought in Britain. Writing about forty years after the events he describes, Dio says that the tribes crossed the Wall that separated them from the Roman legions, did much damage and killed a Roman general together with his troops. Commodus became alarmed and sent Ulpius Marcellus against the Britons, and the new governor ruthlessly put down the barbarians.[45] Dio's brief reference to the war merges into a long passage describing the virtues and vices of Ulpius Marcellus.[46] Despite the character sketch, much ink and keyboard skills have been devoted to this governor. As a prelude to the war of the 180s, a Roman general was killed along with his troops. Was it the governor of Britain who was killed, or a legionary legate? Dio uses the Greek *strategos* for the general who was killed, which ought to indicate that the officer was legate of a legion, but as Birley points out, Dio sometimes uses the same word to describe the governor if he is writing in a military context.[47] If it was the governor who was killed in the war, which is considered to have broken out *c.* 182 or 183, this complicates the term of office of Ulpius Marcellus, because it seems that he was already in post as governor of Britain from about 178 and was still in office until 184 when he won the final victory.

Marcellus is named as governor on diplomas securely dated to March 178, and an inscription from Benwell names him as governor under 'our best and greatest Emperors' in the plural, which refers to the joint Emperors Marcus Aurelius and Commodus, indicating that Marcellus was governor in the years before Marcus' death in 180.[48] He was still governor in the early 180s, when an inscription was set up at Chesters fort, naming him as *leg. Aug. pr.pr.* which stands for propraetorian legate of the Emperor.[49] The abbreviation *Aug.* indicates that there was only one emperor at the time when the inscription was carved, the convention being to use the abbreviation *Augg.* with two Gs to indicate two emperors. The sole emperor in this case can only be Commodus after his father had died in 180.

The difficulty that is presented if it was a governor who was killed when the tribes crossed the Wall gave rise to different theories in the past, before the discovery of the diplomas of 178. The text of the Benwell inscription makes it clear that when the inscription was set up under Ulpius Marcellus as governor, two Emperors reigned jointly, but no names are provided to identify them. Dio's assertion that Commodus sent Marcellus against the Britons implies that this must have been in *c.* 182 or 183, and if this is true, then Ulpius Marcellus ought not to have been in Britain under Marcus and Commodus, which in turn means that the governor who had been killed must have been an unknown senator, replaced as quickly as possible by Marcellus after the disaster had occurred. On this premise the two Emperors of the Benwell inscription were thought to have been Caracalla and Geta, the sons of Septimius Severus who reigned together for a short time after Severus' death in 211. If the Benwell inscription really did belong to the early third century, this meant that there must have been another Ulpius Marcellus, possibly the son of the first one under Commodus. Alternatively, if the Benwell inscription referred to the same Ulpius Marcellus as the governor sent by Commodus, it was suggested that he had been governor for a couple of years under Marcus and Commodus as joint Emperors, and had been replaced by an unknown governor who was killed, then Commodus sent him back to Britain to deal with the crisis, so he served for two terms of office as governor.

The difficulties can be resolved by interpreting Dio's statements in a new light. If the man who was killed was not the governor, but a legionary legate, then there is no problem with the dates when Ulpius Marcellus was governor, from about 178 to 184, except insofar as this is twice as long as the more usual appointments lasting three years or so. Perhaps Marcellus was about to be recalled *c.* 181 or 182 when signs of an impending war became apparent and Commodus decided to leave him in post. It is probable that when Dio said that Ulpius Marcellus was sent against the Britons, he simply meant that the Emperor authorised the governor who was already in post to make war on the Britons, not that Marcellus was in another province and Commodus appointed him as governor of Britain in 182 or 183.

Apart from Dio's statement, virtually nothing is known of this serious war in Britain except that it was concluded by 184 when Commodus received his seventh acclamation as Imperator, and took the title Britannicus Maximus.[50] Dio's few words contain several difficulties besides those concerning Marcellus. Which Wall was crossed, the abandoned Antonine frontier or Hadrian's Wall? When Dio wrote his history, the Antonine Wall had been relinquished about sixty years earlier, and Dio presumably knew this, so this implies that Hadrian's Wall was crossed. Much depends on subtly different modern interpretations of what Dio actually says. Some translations have it that the Wall, whichever it was, separated the Britons from the Roman forts, and others say the Wall separated them from the Roman legions. Breeze and Dobson, preferring a separation from forts, consider that Dio must have meant that the Antonine Wall, now unoccupied but not yet obliterated and forgotten. However if Dio intended to convey the idea that the Wall separated the Britons from the legions, and if he is to be taken absolutely literally, it can be taken to imply that Hadrian's Wall is indicated much closer to the legions which were based at Chester and York in the north and at Caerleon further south. But then, ancient Greek phraseology from eighteen centuries ago, copied several times, is probably not a firm basis for any theories.

There is some supporting archaeological evidence for the possibility that it was Hadrian's Wall that was crossed. On the eastern side, at Halton Chesters and Rudchester on the Wall, and at Corbridge south of it, excavation revealed considerable destruction layers, which may be the result of enemy action rather than deliberate Roman demolition and levelling before rebuilding. At Corbridge, the huge rectangular structure still visible on the site, labelled Site XI, was probably begun in the mid-160s as part of a restructuring of the fort, but it was never finished. There was a serious fire which was probably not accidental, and may belong to the war under Commodus.[51] Significantly these forts are close together, and all of them are on or near Dere Street, which runs more or less on the line of the modern A68 and would have been the principal route from the north which the Britons may have used to cross the Wall that separated them from the Roman legions.[52] There is further potential support for disturbances in the vicinity of Corbridge in the form of a fragmentary inscription that may have originated there.[53] It was found in 1725 built into the crypt at Hexham Abbey, and drawn by John Horsley, but it has since been lost. The text does not furnish any clues as to date, and the inscription could therefore belong to any other episode besides the war in the 180s. It records the actions of a prefect of cavalry, Quintus Calpurnius Concessinius, who slaughtered a group of Britons called the Corionototae, an otherwise unknown group or tribe. Attempts have been made to relate this name to the Pictish Cruithentuatha, but Picts are not yet attested in the late second century.[54] Rivet and Smith suggest that the Corionototae may be a small group of people incorporated into one of the larger tribes.[55] This is not impossible, as larger tribes sometimes absorbed smaller ones; by the early third century, according to Dio, most tribes in the north had been merged with the two main ones, the Maeatae and the Caledonii.[56] All that can be said is that an officer, probably from Corbridge, killed some tribesmen, probably in the immediate area, perhaps during the war in the reign of Commodus.

In the central sectors and on the western side of the Wall, there are as yet no signs of destruction to match the archaeological evidence from the east, but there is at least some attested, if undated, Roman activity in the west. At Kirksteads Farm, a few miles north-west of Carlisle, an altar was discovered, with an inscribed text recording the legate of *VI Victrix*, Lucius Junius Victorinus Flavius Caelianus, who gave thanks for a successful operation across the frontier, *ob res trans Vallum prospere gestas*.[57] There is no dating evidence and the reigning emperor is not named, but only one emperor is in question, indicated by the abbreviation *Aug.* with only one letter G. The actions beyond the *Vallum*, meaning the frontier, could possibly belong to the troubles of the 150s when it is thought that the Novantae may have started a war *c.* 153 that resulted in the destruction of the fort at Birrens, but at that time Hadrian's Wall was not manned in strength, even though the label *Vallum* may have still been in use to describe it while the Antonine Wall was occupied. On the other hand, at present it cannot be disproved that it was Commodus who reigned when Caelianus and his troops were successful in an action during the 180s beyond Hadrian's Wall.[58] Another inscription from Carlisle, on the surviving left half of an arch, records how a cavalry prefect, Publius Sextianus and his fellow soldiers (*commilitones*) slaughtered a band of barbarians. This was possibly in the 180s, but no dates are provided.[59]

The information derived from some fragmentary inscriptions and from destruction layers at three sites on the eastern side of Hadrian's Wall are taken as indications of the war attested by Dio under Commodus. The evidence strongly suggests that Hadrian's Wall was crossed and some forts damaged on the eastern side, and some fighting occurred on the western side but there was probably no damage to forts. As usual it is not known who the enemy was, what they wanted, what caused the war, or how it ended. There may have been punitive expeditions north of the Wall, a peace treaty, maybe even a promise of subsidies on the part of the Romans, and on the part of the Britons, delivery of hostages and recruits for the armies in other provinces. On the Wall, the army will have had to clear up and repair or rebuild, and also replace men or shuffle units around, and perhaps reassess their dispositions on the Wall and to the north and south of it. There are indications that this did happen in the 180s. But what happened almost immediately after the war was a mutiny.

For reasons which are not clear the soldiers in Britain tried to declare for the legionary legate Priscus as Emperor, but Priscus had more sense than to accept the honour.[60] The role of Marcellus in this strange episode is not stated directly, except that he was threatened with execution by Commodus, but was pardoned.[61] He was presumably recalled from Britain somewhat precipitately, possibly because Commodus suspected him of instigating the mutiny. Marcellus may have been too harsh for the soldiers' liking, but this is not stated in the ancient sources. The legions were probably more disaffected than the auxiliaries, because according to the *Historia Augusta* Commodus' favourite Perennis, who had been made Praetorian Prefect and had accrued immense powers in the process, replaced the senatorial officers of the army in Britain by appointing equestrians, men from the non-senatorial middle class, which probably means that the legionary legates had been removed.[62] Dio does not mention this, but picks up the story with the officers in Britain being rebuked for insubordination, and then deciding to send 1,500 soldiers to Rome, where they met Commodus and accused Perennis of harbouring intentions to make his son Emperor. Dio points out that Commodus had many more men at his disposal than the 1,500 soldiers from Britain, but nonetheless he sacrificed Perennis to the soldiers, who killed him and all his family.[63]

During the rest of the year 184 and into 185, the soldiers were restless, and without a newly appointed governor to keep them in order. In the meantime the province was governed by Marcus Antius Crescens Calpurnianus, a senator who had been *iuridicus*, or legal official, in Britain while Marcellus was occupied with the war in the north. After Marcellus' departure and the removal of the legionary legates, Calpurnianus would be the only senatorial official in the province, and would be acting governor until a replacement arrived.[64] Publius Helvius Pertinax was appointed governor in 185, by means of a letter from Commodus.[65] He squashed the mutiny, but almost got himself killed in a riot while doing so, probably because the soldiers wanted anybody but Commodus as Emperor, and Pertinax refused to fill the role. He asked to be recalled, but his successor is not known. Ironically he was made Emperor for a short time after the assassination of Commodus on the last day of 192.

Changes on the Wall

The mutiny probably left the soldiers and officers of Hadrian's Wall largely unaffected, but it is likely that during this time there were changes to the Wall, the northern outposts and the Cumberland coast, not closely datable except within the broad range of somewhere in the 180s. On Dere Street leading to the north beyond the Wall some or possibly all the forts seem to have been given up. Pottery evidence shows that Newstead was occupied until the 180s but in the intervening years before the expedition of Severus in the first decade of the third century. The small fort to the south of Newstead at Cappuck was probably also given up at the same time. There is no certain evidence that High Rochester was abandoned, but it is possible that Risingham may have been deserted. Certainly the unit changed at an unknown date. The 500-strong, part-mounted *cohors IV Gallorum equitata*, based at Risingham in the joint reigns of Marcus Aurelius and Lucius Verus, or possibly Marcus and Commodus, was at Vindolanda by 213.[66] The Risingham garrison at the beginning of the third century was the 1000-strong, part-mounted *cohors I Vangionum milliaria equitata*.[67] The inscription attesting the presence of this unit provides the only indication that there may have been a period when the fort was abandoned, because extensive rebuilding work took place under the governor Lucius Alfenus Senecio, who was in post *c.* 205 to 208. The south gate and a stretch of wall were being repaired because they had fallen down through old age – *portam cum muris vetustate dilapsis*. This implies that no one had been in occupation for a long time, because it goes against modern sensibilities to imagine that the Romans remained in a fort that had a gate tower and part of an external wall in such a state of disrepair. But it may be that Risingham was in fact still occupied. As Breeze and Dobson point out, an inscription dated to 221 from Corbridge, which had definitely not been abandoned, bears more or less the same text as the Risingham inscription documenting rebuilding work.[68] Perhaps modern perception of the Roman military needs revising. The tacit assumption, never elaborately expressed, is that all units contained super-efficient, well-disciplined soldiers based in spick and span forts in perpetual good repair, which may be wide of the mark. Apart from the Corbridge example of an occupied fort needing extensive repairs, in the second century the legionary fortress at Chester was found to be neglected and dilapidated. From Flavian times, just after it was founded, there were empty spaces that were never built upon, but from the building of Hadrian's Wall to the arrival of Severus in Britain, a large proportion of the legionaries of *XX Valeria Victrix* were absent, and although the fortress was not entirely abandoned it was in a bad state, not just with empty areas in the interior, but with newly built stone barracks left to decay, timber barracks half converted into stone and then just left derelict, and other timber barracks collapsed. Some of these were used as rubbish dumps, and one even had cremation burials inserted into the accumulated debris. In the 160s there was some reconstruction and barracks were reoccupied but it is not known by whom. Neglect on this scale is not what would be expected, but the archaeology cannot be ignored.[69] There are similar signs of dilapidation at Birdoswald in the later third century. An inscription explains that the headquarters building and the baths were rebuilt during the joint reign of Diocletian and Maximian, and the commander's house was reconstructed because it had fallen down and earth had accumulated over it (*quod erat humo copertum et in labem conlapsum*).[70] Probably at an earlier date the western ditch had silted up and flooded the berm, blocking the drains from the fort. Despite the neglect, it seems that *cohors I Dacorum* was in occupation throughout the whole period, since it is attested at the fort in the early third century and it was still there in the late Roman era when the *Notitia Dignitatum*, the list of forts and units of the Empire, was compiled.[71] On the other hand, it was thought that during the late third and early fourth centuries at Halton Chesters and Rudchester, soil had accumulated over collapsed buildings before they were rebuilt, indicating a long lapse of time between decay and reconstruction. But the evidence has been re-examined and reinterpreted to suggest that in this case the different phases of the late third to late forth centuries were not clearly distinguished, and the site was simply being cleared and levelled to prepare for late third-century building work.[72]

With regard to Risingham, it is still possible that the dilapidated state of the fort at the beginning of the third century may have been somewhat exaggerated on the inscription, or alternatively the wording could be perfectly honest, but the essential point is that although the fort may have been falling to bits it does not constitute proof that it had been deserted. More evidence is required before it can be stated with confidence that the fort had been abandoned in the 180s.

On the western side, Birrens probably went out of use *c.* 184. At Netherby and Bewcastle the evidence for their fate after the reoccupation of the 160s is less certain. The installations of the Cumbrian coast had already been thinned out when Hadrian's Wall was refurbished in the 160s, when some but not all of the milefortlets were reoccupied, but many of the towers seem to have been relinquished. In the 180s the milefortlets probably went out of use altogether. On Hadrian's Wall, probably in the 180s or at least before the opening of the third century the turrets went out of use, some of them having their doors blocked up, then perhaps shortly afterwards at least some of the turrets were destroyed, and the recesses where they had been keyed into the Wall were built up to the width of the Wall on either side.[73] All the turrets from 41b east of Great Chesters to 33b west of Carrawburgh were not necessarily destroyed but went out of use, probably because views to the north were easily obtainable from the crags, though this is to presume, reasonably enough, that observation was one of the main functions of the towers. It is significant that turret 44b roughly half way between Great Chesters and Carvoran, was still in use, most likely because it was in a good position for observation and signalling.[74]

The use of the milecastles in the 180s is not fully understood, but at least one, milecastle 27 east of Chesters fort on the opposite side of the River North Tyne, was abandoned. Access through some of the milecastles was restricted. At two of them, milecastle 22 between Halton Chesters and Portgate on Dere Street, and milecastle 35 east of Housesteads, the north gates were blocked up, though in the latter case there may have never been a north gate because it was built on top of a crag. At others the north gates were narrowed to only allow people on foot to pass through, though at a few of them it was the south gate that was restricted.[75]

At the forts on the Wall, the governor Ulpius Marcellus may have changed some of the units during the time of the war under Commodus, possibly but not certainly installing the units which have long-term associations with some of the forts. The *ala II Asturum* is recorded under Marcellus at Chesters, though he may not have been responsible for locating the unit at this fort, since it is suggested that the *ala* may have already been in garrison in the 160s. At Birdoswald *cohors I Aelia Dacorum* may have been located there by Marcellus, though the earliest dated record of it at this fort belongs to the early third century, when the cohort was building a granary under the governor Lucius Alfenus Senecio, who arrived in Britain probably in 205 and left *c.* 207.[76] Similarly the *ala I Asturum* is first recorded at Benwell under the governor Alfenus Senecio.[77] The possibility that this unit may have arrived at Benwell in the late 170s or early 180s is supported by an altar dedicated to the god Antenociticus by Tineius Longus, a prefect of cavalry, while Ulpius Marcellus was governor.[78] It is unfortunate that Tineius Longus did not include the name of his cavalry unit on his inscription.

The previous unit at Benwell was a mixed cohort containing both infantry and cavalry, and at Chesters, though the Hadrianic garrison was an *ala*, the unit preceding the *ala II Asturum* may have been infantry. Some alterations would most likely have

Right: 1. Modern copy of a statue of Hadrian in the park behind his mausoleum, now Castel Sant'Angelo.

Below: 2. The Wall running south-west to north-east up to the top of the crags at Walltown, otherwise known as the Nine Nicks of ThirlWall, named after the gaps of lower-lying land between the heights. Some of the Nicks are no longer visible because the Greenhead quarry to the west obliterated some of the Wall and turret 54b. The photo shows the conserved version of the Wall, with its rubble core and two outer skins of squared stones, only a few courses high, because many were robbed to build more recent farms and houses.

Left: 3. This short section of the Wall at Hare Hill is about four miles west of Birdoswald, and near the now vanished milecastle 53. The first version of Hadrian's Wall here was the Turf Wall which ran from the River Irthing to Bowness-on-Solway, and an excavation in 2004 showed that this sector of the stone Wall was built on top of the remains of the earlier turf-built frontier. It is the highest extant stretch of the Wall, sixteen courses high, but although the core stood to this height the facing stones had been robbed, and were replaced in the nineteenth century. Despite its height, there is still no clue as to what happened at the top: did it slope inwards, was it flat, or was there a wall-walk and parapet?

Below: 4. When the Turf Wall was replaced in stone, a short stretch of the turf-built frontier was left intact to the west of Birdoswald fort, while the stone frontier lies further to the north, with the modern road running parallel to it. This photo was taken looking towards the west, from the top of the remains of the Turf Wall with the southern ditch called the Vallum on the left. As a photo it is somewhat unprepossessing, but after nearly nineteen centuries it is amazing that the first Hadrianic running barrier, the predecessor of the stone Wall, is still so clearly visible in the landscape. The Turf Wall in this sector runs along a ridge with good views to the south as well as to the north, but the builders of the stone Wall that replaced it presumably did not require the higher elevation and the southward views.

5. The first plan for Hadrian's Wall was to build it to a width of ten Roman feet. In some places building was begun at this width, while in others only the foundations were laid, before the plans changed to build the Wall to a width of only about eight Roman feet instead. The terms 'Broad Wall' and 'Narrow Wall' were coined to describe the two, but dimensions of neither the Broad nor Narrow Wall were rigidly standardized. This photo, taken at Willowford looking west, shows broad foundation with Narrow Wall built on top.

6. As part of the first plan the Wall towers, called turrets in Wall parlance, were built every third of a Roman mile, bonded with the Wall. Since the turrets were built before the curtain wall, they usually had wing walls, springing from the east and west sides, as at this turret, number 45a at Willowford. The wing walls are quite long here and were obviously intended to join with the Broad Wall, but when the Wall was finally built it was to the narrow gauge, so the projecting sections of the wing walls had to be properly finished off at the corners. It is not known how high the turrets would have been, and there are several suggestions as to the design of the roof.

7. Free-standing towers for watching and probably for signalling were commonly used by the Romans before Hadrian invented frontiers consisting of running barriers. This is a depiction of a tower used in Trajan's Dacian wars of the early second century, from Trajan's Column in Rome. The tower is surrounded by a timber palisade and has a gallery round the top storey, with a lighted torch protruding from the top window. This is usually interpreted as a means of signalling, but might just as easily have been to enable the soldiers to see what was happening in the dark. This design may have no bearing on the turrets on Hadrian's Wall, but the Trajanic towers have influenced the reconstructions of frontier installations in Germany and Britain.

8. In addition to the turrets, the first plan for the Wall included larger installations, attached to the Wall and spaced one Roman mile apart, hence the modern name 'milecastle'. The spacing was not always rigidly applied, and on occasion a milecastle would be sited to the west or the east of the proper position, according to the topography and the possible need for better sight lines. This milecastle, number 42 at Cawfields, is an example of this, because on strict spacing grounds it ought to be situated several yards further to the east. The milecastle is attached to the Wall by its longer northern side, and is therefore known as a short-axis milecastle. Some milecastles are attached by their shorter sides, and these are known as long-axis milecastles. Whether they were short- or long-axis, the internal area of most milecastles was about the same size.

9. This is the eastern side of the south gate at Cawfields milecastle. The gates of milecastles were built according to different designs, originally labelled I, II and III, which could be allocated to one of the three legions, *II Augusta*, *VI Victrix* and *XX Valeria Victrix*, which built the Wall and its installations. More recently a fourth design has been discovered, a variant on type II, so it is no longer possible to assert that a particular gate type belonged to a particular legion. This gate is type I, built entirely in large stones, whereas type III is very similar but usually has large stones in the piers and small ones in the walls of the passageway. Reconstructions of milecastles usually show a tower over the north gate, but since the foundations of both gates are the same, it is possible that there were towers over both of them.

10. Milecastle number 48 at Poltross Burn is a long-axis milecastle, with its rear wall facing due north, but the Wall on its eastern side runs north-east to south-west and joins the north-eastern corner at an angle. Excavations in the early twentieth century revealed the base of the stairway in the north-east corner, as shown in this photo. The stair is so far unique, but there are many milecastles which have not been excavated so there may be others awaiting discovery. The stair obviously leads to the eastern wall of the milecastle, but nothing survives to explain what happened after that. Was the stairway simply a means of access into the postulated tower over the northern gate, did it lead to a wall-walk around the milecastle, or most controversial of all, did it lead to a wall-walk along the Wall itself?

11. The Wall was accompanied by a ditch on its north side, except where the high crags made such a feature unnecessary, and for a short stretch at Limestone Corner, as shown in this photo looking east. The Wall turns to the south-east at this point to head for the crossing of the River North Tyne near Chesters fort. The land is fairly elevated here, though not giving onto a sheer drop like the crags further to the west. A northern ditch would have added some protection, but the Romans stopped trying to cut through the rock and abandoned their work.

12. As well as the northern ditch, the Wall was protected on its south side by an even larger ditch called the Vallum, which in modern terms refers only to this ditch but to the Romans the *Vallum* referred to the entire frontier system. The Vallum was flanked on the north and south sides by mounds of earth, which do not appear complete today because gaps were cut into them by the Romans when they advanced into Scotland and built the Antonine Wall in the 140s. Unlike the northern ditch at Limestone Corner, the Vallum was cut through the rock, and runs all along the Wall, except for the last few miles from Newcastle upon Tyne to Wallsend. This photo shows the Vallum running eastwards, south of Cawfields milecastle.

13. A hitherto unknown feature of the Wall was discovered in the 1990s, consisting of three rows of holes on the berm between the north side of the Wall and the northern ditch at Wallsend. It was thought that these were associated with the defended annexe attached to the fort, but later similar features between the Wall and the northern ditch were found at Byker, as shown here, and between Throckely and Heddon-on-the-Wall. First interpreted as pits containing sharpened stakes, called *lilia* because they resembled lilies, these rectangular pits are now known as obstacles on the berm. It is thought that they contained stacks of forked branches to form a three-line barrier, each stack offset so as to leave no gaps. It is not yet known if the obstacles extended all the way along the Wall or were confined to its eastern sections. (Photo by Dr. D. J. Smith)

14. When plans were changed to reduce the width of the Wall, perhaps at the same time or shortly afterwards it was decided to put forts on the frontier instead of relying on the forts further south on the road now known as the Stanegate. The building of the forts necessitated the destruction of some features that had already been built, as depicted in this photo of the northern fort wall at Housesteads. The fort wall extended further towards the edge of the crag than the frontier Wall, and turret 36b was demolished. In the third century a building was erected against the rampart back, so the visible remains at this point are of several periods.

15. Where the frontier met rivers, bridges had to be built carrying a footpath or a road across the water. This is the east abutment of the bridge at Willowford, exposed because the river Irthing now runs further north, steadily eroding the cliff around Birdoswald fort. The remains are mostly third century, but there were at least two earlier building phases because flooding damaged the structure. The photo shows part of the pier and the flood-relief channels of the last version of the bridge. A modern footbridge now takes walkers across the river to Harrow's Scar milecastle, number 49, east of Birdoswald fort.

16. The remains of the bridge abutment on the east bank of the North Tyne, opposite Chesters fort, which lies on the western side of the river. The river has moved further to the west since Roman times. The Hadrianic bridge carried the Wall across the river on eight hexagonal piers, the easternmost of which was incorporated into the later abutment shown here. The second bridge was thought to belong to the reign of Severus, but excavations in the early 1990s revealed that it was probably earlier, belonging to the mid-Antonine period. Ramps from the eastern and western sides led up to the road, which was carried across the river on only three piers, larger than the Hadrianic versions. The western and eastern ends of the bridge were guarded by square towers, and the remains of the eastern one can be seen in the photo. Most of the large stones in this photo have a rectangular slot cut into them, parallel to their long sides; these are Lewis holes, cut inwards in a triangular shape so that the base of the slot is wider than the opening. Triangular pieces of metal were inserted, separated by a spacer slotted in between them, and all three would be clamped between both sides of a U-shaped metal hook, with a horizontal bar inserted through holes in each piece to hold them all together, so the stone block could be lifted by crane. (Photo by David Reid)

17. Roman soldiers of the first two centuries AD would spend a lot of their time digging ditches and building various installations. This photo of a scene on Trajan's Column shows the legionaries building a fort, carrying timber and blocks of wood or stone, digging, probably hammering a stake which may have originally been represented on the sculpture, and carrying a basket perhaps containing earth. Though arms and armour are stylized to portray different kinds of troops, it can be assumed that legionaries did the work and the auxiliaries, two of whom are shown in the foreground, stood guard. The soldiers were working in a war zone, and according to these scenes they wore their body armour, with shields and helmets stacked close by. The soldiers who built Hadrian's Wall may or may not have worked in the same way, but there is no information about the conditions they had to contend with.

18. Shortly after building on the Hadrianic frontier began, forts were added to the Wall. Most of them were built to the standard playing-card shape, with rounded corners, twin-portal gateways on each side and corner towers and interval towers along the defences. The Hadrianic fort at South Shields on the south side of the River Tyne has not been found, and the extant fort dates to about 160, but the reconstructed west gate at this site gives the best idea of what a Roman twin-portal gateway may have looked like. A modern inscription attributes the building of the gate with towers to the governor Calpurnius Agricola c.161, but it is based on other inscriptions of different dates, including one from Vindolanda. Most of the features are attested from other Roman sites, such as the round-headed window arches and the stones of the projecting string course. The height of the towers, their roof shapes, and the flat roof over the two gates are conjectural, but look perfectly acceptable.

19. This is what remains of the east gate at Birdoswald, the best gate on the whole Wall. On the right of the photo, the first stone of the arch over the northern passageway can be seen. In the third century the north gate tower had a kiln built inside it for the manufacture of tiles, but it eventually collapsed and a floor was laid over the remains. Then in the later third or early fourth century the whole tower was rebuilt and probably at the same time the northern passageway was blocked and converted into an extra room, with the lower courses of its rear wall still visible. On the left is the southern passageway through the gate, which remained open.

20. At the outpost fort of High Rochester the west gate had only a single portal, deeply recessed and flanked by large towers, built from massive masonry known as *opus quadratum*, as in this photo showing the base of the northern tower. It is not known if the masonry of the towers was of this size and quality all the way to the top. The decorated springer of the arch over the entrance is still in situ. The stonework blocking the gate is modern.

21. At Chesters two barrack blocks facing each other have been conserved, oriented west to east in the northern section of the fort, though the ends of each block still remain buried. Each block has a larger house for the officer at the top end, and there would have been a veranda on either side of the central gutter. Fragments of the pillars which supported the roof of each veranda can still be seen. It is probable that an earlier set of barracks preceded the conserved versions laid out here. The individual rooms were most likely divided into two by means of timber partitions, but the complete number of rooms is not known for certain. Five are exposed in the northern block and it is thought that five more lie under the earthen bank to the west. This would make a total of ten rooms, normally associated with an infantry century of eighty soldiers, with eight men in each room, but barracks do not always fit the tidy patterns expected of them. From the second half of the second century the fort was occupied by a cavalry regiment or *ala*, and it is now known that horses and soldiers were accommodated together, horses in one room and soldiers in the other.

22. This photo, taken at Great Chesters in the 1980s, shows individual buildings each separated by an alley too narrow for anyone to pass along. This block is partially exposed in the south-west sector of the fort. These rooms are thought to belong to the so-called chalet-type barracks of the later Roman period, when some barrack blocks were replaced by lines of separate individual houses – a process which may have begun in the first decades of the third century.

23. The so-called chalet barracks in the north eastern corner of the fort at Housesteads, where two blocks have been conserved for visitors to view. The chalets probably date to the late third century, replacing the more conventional barracks built as a continuous block. Although these individual barracks are separated from each other by very narrow alleyways, they share a continuous rear wall on the south side, and are open-ended on their north sides, where perhaps wooden shutters were used to close them off, and then at a later period walls were built at one or two of them. The idea that they were quarters for married couples has been dismissed, but it is thought that the group dwelling in each house was responsible for its upkeep.

24. Most forts possessed a headquarters building called the *principia*, unless the forts were temporary bases or designed to hold only a detachment. All the business of the fort would be done in this building, including the record-keeping and all the clerical work, and the chapel of the standards and the strongroom, usually underground, were housed in the offices at the rear. The *principia* at Chesters does not survive to a great height but the complete plan is visible. This photo is taken from outside the north-west corner of the building looking towards the remains of the offices in the basilica or hall, probably of two storeys, forming the rear of the building. Some of the paving of the open courtyard can be seen, with the circular well appearing as a dark smudge in the stones. There would have been a roofed colonnade round three sides, running along what is now the grassed area between the outer wall and the paving.

25. The underground strongroom at Chesters fort, situated at the rear of the *principia*. All the fort's money would be kept here, for its incidental purchases and expenses, though there would probably not be enough for the soldiers' paydays, which occurred three times per annum, so cash would have had to be requisitioned from the procurator's office. The Emperor Domitian set a limit on how much cash could be stored at a fort, because the usurper Saturninus seized much of the money from the military bases in his province of Upper Germany to finance his attempted coup. When the Chesters strongroom was discovered the wooden door was still intact, but conservation techniques were not so advanced and it crumbled shortly after contact with the air. The arched roof of the strongroom is supported on three parallel ribs, the gaps between which are covered with large slabs. The remains of another arched roof like the Chesters example can be seen at Great Chesters fort.

26. The Romans paid much attention to the food supply, and granaries for storing food were an important feature in forts. This photo shows one of the granaries at Corbridge, with a stone floor supported on stone sleeper walls with gaps between them to allow for circulation of air, assisted by the vents in the lower walls connecting with the spaces under the floors. The Housesteads granaries had floors laid on individual stones, but sleeper walls were more common and can also be seen at South Shields, where many granaries were built in the early third century. Granaries usually had a distinctive ground plan with stone buttresses all around the walls. It is not known how grain and other foodstuffs were stored, and there may have been upper floors for increased capacity.

27. The famous latrine in the south-eastern corner of the fort at Housesteads, where the ground slopes downwards and a whole series of drainage channels can still be seen. Surface rainwater and all the drains from other parts of the fort were directed to this corner to flush out the sewer through an outlet in the curved south-east corner of the fort. Since there was no water supply at the fort and the land was too high to bring in water from the north as at Great Chesters and Chesters, stone cisterns were made, using lead to seal the gaps between the stones, and strategically placed to collect rainwater from roofs. A particularly large tank stands outside the latrine. There were no private toilet cubicles for soldiers to use, but a series of wooden seats would be provided over both sewer channels, and the smaller channels and the trough in the centre would contain water for washing sponges on sticks that substituted for toilet paper.

28. The baths for the soldiers were usually outside the fort, most probably to avoid the risk of fire from the underfloor heating system. This photo shows the entrance and changing room to the baths at Chesters fort, which were built on the slope between the fort and the River North Tyne, and were consequently well preserved when the earth gradually covered the building. The niches in the wall may have contained statues, rather than being used as cupboards for soldiers' clothes, especially as there are only seven and many more soldiers would be using the baths at any one time. The Chesters baths were in use for a long time and underwent several changes. Generally the bathers went through a series of hot rooms to induce sweating and ended in the cold plunge, but in the late phase of the baths there was a range of alternatives comprising hot baths and steam treatments or warm rooms and cold baths. The commanding officer had his own smaller bath suite which can be seen in the house inside the fort.

29. The construction of temples outside the forts was usually left to private enterprise, and inscriptions often record who paid for them. Several gods and goddesses were worshipped by the soldiers on the Wall. This is the Mithraeum at Carrawburgh, west of the fort. It lies close to the spring and shrine of the native goddess Coventina, which was once contained within walls and properly drained, but the ground is now boggy and the temple is prone to slight flooding. The cult of Mithras, imported from the east, was popular among soldiers, flourishing especially when the commanders took an interest in promoting it, as seems to be the case at Carrawburgh. Flanking the central aisle there would have been benches where soldiers reclined for communal meals, and above the replica altars at the end of the room there would have been a portrait of Mithras killing the bull, from whose blood all life sprang. Mithras was a god of light, often equated with Sol, the sun god.

30. Medical services for the soldiers were quite advanced for the time, largely based on Greek practice and improved empirically as the Romans gained more experience. This scene from Trajan's Column shows emergency treatment during the Dacian wars. Hospitals have been identified in some forts, though archaeologists are cautious in labelling them because the workshops in forts were often built to the same plan. However, given that some hospitals have produced finds of medical instruments closely resembling modern versions, the identification is fairly certain. At Housesteads the remains of the hospital or *valetudinarium* are visible, and an inscription records a medical officer, Anicius Ingenius.

31. These buildings just outside the south gate of the fort at Housesteads formed part of the *vicus* or civil settlement, of which twenty-six buildings have been discovered, but only a few buildings have been conserved. These two buildings were probably shops, with their open ends, where slots for wooden shutters can be seen, facing the road into the fort. There may have been upper storeys, probably timber framed above the stone walls, but none of this is certain. The two buildings are situated in front of the eastern portal of the south gate, which was blocked up early in the fort's history. Further south is the building number VIII, called the Murder House, where at the east end two skeletons were discovered under a second floor that had been laid out on top of them.

32. The two granaries shown here at Birdoswald were built in the early third century, and although the fort was occupied in earlier years it is not known where the food stores would have been. The two granary buildings lie between the headquarters and the west wall, on an alignment with the south tower of the west gate, though the south portal was later blocked up. The granaries are oriented west to east, and they both lack the characteristic buttresses on their north sides. The north granary, on the left in the photo, fell into disrepair in the fourth century and the roof collapsed. It was left unoccupied, but towards the end of the fourth century a timber hall was built over the site, the first of two halls, the position of the latest version marked out by the timber posts seen in the photo.

been necessary at both forts to convert the barracks for the 500-strong *alae* now located in each, as it is now known that cavalry barracks differed from infantry versions because the horses were accommodated alongside the men. No epigraphic proof has yet come to light recording such rebuilding work at either fort, but at Chesters the soldiers of *ala II Asturum* were carrying out work under Ulpius Marcellus to improve the water supply. This has great relevance for a unit that had probably more than 500 horses, including the soldiers' and the officers' mounts as well as the animals used for transport, and kept at least a number of them in the fort, even if most of the horses could be taken to the River North Tyne to drink.[79]

The changes to the Wall as listed above cannot be closely dated and may not all be contemporary, so it cannot be said that the war under Commodus must have resulted in a shortage of manpower and a consequent reduction in the number of installations that could conceivably be held. Nor can it be surmised that the mutiny of the soldiers and the period when the province was without a governor had much bearing on the reorganisation of the frontier, where the arrangements do not seem to have been a response to a short interval of anarchy, but instead were long-lasting.

To go well ahead of the evidence, the possible implication is that someone, most likely one of the governors rather than the Emperor Commodus, who was not noted for avid interest in the affairs of Britain, or an enterprising officer under the command of one of the governors, had given some thought to the Wall and considered which units would be best suited to the various fort locations, assessed the value of each turret and milecastle, retaining the ones which were the most useful, and deciding the fate of the Cumbrian coast and the outpost forts. It is possible that Ulpius Marcellus began this hypothetical process, before he was involved in the war from *c.* 182/83 to 184. The governor who succeeded him was performing as a substitute in an acting capacity, and both he and the next governor Helvius Pertinax would have had their hands full with the mutiny of the soldiers. From about 187 to 192 the governor, or possibly governors, are not known, so as always, when an energetic governor is known from literature and inscriptions, it is tempting to attribute to him slightly more work than is attested.

The replacement of a mixed cohort of infantry and cavalry by a wholly cavalry unit or *ala* at Benwell, and the replacement of an infantry unit by an *ala* at Chesters, makes sense in that the country on the east side is suitable for cavalry operations and for keeping and feeding horses. An *ala* was present at Halton Chesters by the third century, whereas a 500-strong mixed unit is assumed to have been there under Hadrian. It seems that the main onslaught of the Britons in the war of *c.* 182/83 was in the east, and the increase in the numbers of horsemen after the troubles, on either side of Dere Street, may have been intended to improve scouting and patrolling to the north of the Wall, and for rapid response if an invasion ever occurred again.

The abandonment of some milecastles and turrets is considered to have stemmed from a realisation that most of them had already been made redundant from the time when the forts were placed in the Wall itself. The original plan for the frontier with milecastles every mile and two turrets in between probably looked good on paper, but with the forts on the Wall in addition to these, Breeze and Dobson have labelled it as overprovision of gates through the Wall.[80] The number of milecastles and towers may also have been interpreted by the Romans as an overprovision of installations to be manned. The main problem is that it is not known what the milecastles, and especially the turrets, were designed to do. What was it that the turrets did that could not be performed somewhere else, or by some other agency, or dispensed with altogether in the 180s? It is not known if the original function of milecastles and turrets had changed by the later years of the second century.

The Severan Era

At the end of the second century, after the assassination of the Emperor Commodus, a civil war broke out which involved the governor of Britain, and at the beginning of the third century the natives were restless yet again, bringing Septimius Severus, the victor in the civil wars, to Britain.

Commodus was killed on the last day of 192, and Publius Helvius Pertinax, the governor of Britain who had almost been killed when he suppressed the mutiny, was made Emperor, but only for a short time, eighty-seven days to be exact. He upset the Praetorians and paid the price with his life. Then two senators bargained for the Empire, offering cash to the Praetorian Guardsmen. Didius Julianus made the best offer and was accepted as Emperor. Watching on the frontiers were Septimius Severus on the Danube, Pescennius Niger in Syria, and Clodius Albinus in Britain, who was in post by 192 or even earlier.[81] According to Dio, all three harboured plans to be Emperor.[82] The situation could only be resolved by warfare. Severus was probably the first to be declared Emperor by his troops in April 193, with Niger a close second before the end of May. The governor and the army in Britain would have to decide whether to stand on the sidelines and await the result, or to join in the contest. Early in the proceedings, probably in April, Severus offered Albinus the title Caesar, which by this time designated the chosen successor of the Emperor, and assured by this, according to Dio and Herodian, Albinus remained in Britain.[83] In the meantime, Severus arrived in Rome, disbanded the Praetorians and created a different Guard. He persuaded the Senate that he was somehow related to the family of Marcus Aurelius, which entailed deifying Commodus for the purposes of seamless continuity of succession as Emperor. Then he turned to the east to declare war on Pescennius Niger. Albinus was made consul for the second time with Severus as colleague in 194, so he perhaps thought that he really was the favoured successor. Alternatively he may not have trusted Severus at all and used the intervening time to gather his troops. In 195 or 196 he embarked with his army, crossed the Channel and was declared Emperor in Gaul. He captured Lugdunum (Lyons), also defeating an army under Virius Lupus, who may have been governor of Lower Germany, and who was appointed as the next governor of Britain. The final battle was fought at Lugdunum, in February 197, and Albinus was killed. His supporters were hunted down and executed, which may have involved the elimination of some military officers and administrative officials who had been left in Britain to keep order.[84]

The situation in Britain in general and Hadrian's Wall in particular is not clear. In the past it was assumed that when Albinus left the province for Gaul, he must have stripped the Wall of its troops to provide a large proportion of his army, and either then or after his defeat at the battle of Lugdunum in 197, the Wall must have suffered at the hands of the natives. This became the accepted orthodoxy, viewing 197 as a horizon dividing one Wall period from another. Breeze and Dobson point out that there is no hint in the surviving ancient literature that Albinus took troops from the Wall.[85] Though the majority of the soldiers in Britain supported him, he probably did not take all three legions and a large proportion of the auxiliaries. It is sometimes pointed out that the auxiliary units in Britain before Severus were not the same as those in the forts after his expedition, but as Salway points out there is not enough information about auxiliary units in the decades from the 180s onwards to be able to pinpoint when the changes occurred.[86] The only hints that there may have been some trouble derive from inscriptions recording rebuilding at some forts by governors of the province after 197, of which more detail below. In 1972 Birley resurrected and restructured the idea that there had been a disaster in 197; Salway said that the argument was presented with 'great cogency' but it was not entirely convincing.[87] In general the 197 disaster theory is dismissed on the grounds that the building and repair work may have been routine, not remedial work that had been necessitated because of destruction by the Britons, either by the Brigantes in the south or the Caledonians or Maeatae attacking from the north.

Rather than leaving the Wall denuded of troops, Albinus may have made arrangements with the tribes on the other side of the frontier, extracting promises of good behaviour and non-aggression from them, possibly shored up with gifts and subsidies. Did he make treaties with the northern tribes, or renew whatever arrangements that Marcellus may have made in 184? According to Dio, promises of some sort had obviously been made by the northern tribes before Virius Lupus arrived as governor, because the Caledonians broke them and started to prepare to help the Maeatae.[88] Dio does not explain to whom the promises had been made, but some sort of arrangement could have been made with Albinus, who possibly shored up the terms that he laid down with gifts and subsidies. At the time Albinus was probably already Caesar, not simply the governor of the province, and there was a possibility during the years 193 to 197 that he might one day become Emperor, and authorise even better subsidies and gifts. When he was killed in 197, the promises that the Caledonians and the Maeatae had made would be invalid, so perhaps they started to prepare for war, or at least make a show if it, when the new governor, Virius Lupus, arrived. Dio says that Lupus was forced to buy peace from these tribes, because Severus was occupied in a war, by which Dio probably means that he was still in Gaul, attending to the aftermath of the civil war. Buying peace instead of fighting for it might have seemed shameful to the Romans, but it seems to have worked, and some prisoners were returned. Money and gifts may have been what the tribes wanted all along. They calmed down for a while, probably nearly a decade. Severus did not arrive hot foot in Britain with extra troops when Lupus paid the price of peace, but embarked on the Parthian war in 198. Or was it the case that the Emperor started to formulate plans that at some time in the future, when an opportunity presented itself, he would sort out those pesky Britons once and for all?

The Division of Britain into Two Provinces

Instead of an end of an erstwhile Wall period caused by death and destruction in 197, there was a horizon of an administrative kind, probably erroneously dated by Herodian to this year.[89] Herodian says that Severus decided to divide Britain after defeating Clodius Albinus in Gaul, and in fact it would have been a form of insurance for Severus and his regime if he could place a separate governor in each half of the province because Albinus as a single governor had been able to draw on the military establishment of the whole province and create an army that enabled him to claim supreme power. There are problems with this dating, but the division is discussed in the context of 197, because some authors accept that this was when Britain was divided into two provinces, called Britannia Superior and Britannia Inferior. The labels Superior and Inferior are not value judgements, but usually the Superior provinces were closer to Rome and the Inferior ones further away. Breeze and Dobson accept Herodian's statement that Severus settled affairs in Britain after the victory over Albinus and divided it into two provinces.[90] This was part of a general policy under the Severans concerning provinces with three or more legions. It was by dint of their command of armies that Clodius Albinus and Pescennius

Niger had been able to challenge Severus, who had also relied on his armies to become Emperor in the first place and remain in the post thereafter. He had been proclaimed by his troops at Carnuntum on the Danube, and subsequently he would not have been able to defeat Pescennius Niger and Clodius Albinus if his armies had not continued to support him. Splitting the larger and better armed provinces involved not only a territorial division but also a division of the armies, so that no commander would have access to more than two legions, which in turn meant that no one could easily emulate what Severus had done, except by collaborating with another governor who would have to be content to pay second fiddle to the main claimant. It was not purely a selfish or jealous gesture on the part of Severus, because after all civil wars damage the economy and the population, and waste trained soldiers.

The example for dividing provinces had been set under Trajan, when Dacia was annexed. Pannonia was divided into Pannonia Superior or Upper Pannonia in the west, with a consular governor who would guard the new province against the German tribes across the Danube, and Pannonia Inferior or lower Pannonia in the east with a praetorian governor instead of the higher-ranking consular, watching the Sarmatians. This arrangement survived until the early third century, during the reign of Severus' son Caracalla. Somewhere between 212 and 217 Caracalla placed consular governors in command of both the Pannonian provinces, and adjusted the boundaries between them, because the earlier division had left one province with three legions and the other with only one. The boundary change meant that *II Adiutrix*, which had been in Upper Pannonia, was now in Lower Pannonia, ensuring that neither province contained more than two legions.[91] In Syria, Severus himself created two provinces, Syria Coele in the north with two legions, and Syria Phoenice in the south with one legion.

The date when Britain was divided into Britannia Superior in the south and Britannia Inferior in the north is not certain, and Herodian's statement that Severus divided the province in 197 entails some problems. Severus may well have formed the intention to divide the province at that time, but it seems that nothing happened immediately to put this policy into operation, though there may have been some preliminary stages which are not documented, since the division and all the administrative arrangements that would be necessary could not have been accomplished overnight. In the final version, epigraphic sources supported by Dio show that sometime after the beginning of the third century, the northern half of Britain, with *VI Victrix* at York, was in Britannia Inferior or Lower Britain, with the legionary legate as the praetorian governor, and *XX Valeria Victrix* and *II Augusta* were in Britannia Superior, with a consular governor in command.[92] The boundary between the two new provinces is not known, except that Chester, where *XX Valeria Victrix* was based, belonged to Britannia Superior and Lincoln was in Inferior, as shown by an inscription from Bordeaux set up by a man who served as a *sevir Augustalis*, an overseer of the cult of Rome and Augustus, at York and Lincoln, which, he helpfully adds in the text, were both in Britannia Inferior.[93]

The main problem with Herodian's date is that the governors for some time after 197 were all consular, and the governors of Lower Britain ought to have been of praetorian status. The absence of praetorian governors is not necessarily due to a lack of epigraphic evidence, because there appears to have been only one governor at a time, whose remit was to operate in the north as well as the south. Virius Lupus, Gaius Valerius Pudens and Lucius Alfenus Senecio, the three attested governors who followed Albinus, were all consulars and they were active in the north, engaged in building or repairing forts. The probable date for the division is *c.* 216 or at the latest by 220, but the several theories about how and when the final division may have come about are relegated to the footnotes, in preference to cluttering up the main narrative in trying to work out how Hadrian's Wall was governed until the time when it is firmly attested in the Lower province, governed by the legate of *VI Victrix*, by the beginning of the second decade of the third century.[94]

Preparations for the Severan Expedition

The campaigns of Severus and Caracalla began in 208, but the extensive programme of repair and rebuilding in northern England, and on both sides of the Wall, in the decade before the northern wars could be construed not only as putting the house in order in Britain, but also as preparation for Severus' expedition. The work began under Virius Lupus, who was probably appointed governor as soon as possible after the defeat of Clodius Albinus in 197. It is not known how long he was in Britain, and it is possible that an unknown governor was appointed between his term of office and that of the next attested governor, Gaius Valerius Pudens, who was in post by 205. Pudens was replaced in the same year, or perhaps in 206, by Lucius Alfenus Senecio. The important point is that the building and repair work was continued by all three governors, and hints at Imperial policy rather than purely provincial planning. Two inscriptions from Bowes attest building work in the later second century by Virius Lupus and by Alfenus Senecio between 197 and *c.* 207 when Senecio probably left the province.[95] One of the inscriptions at Bowes concerns the rebuilding of the bathhouse (*balineum*), which had burnt down. This has been interpreted as the result of an attack, possibly by the Brigantes. If it was the fort baths that were being rebuilt and not the baths in the commanders' house, the building would have been outside the fort and more vulnerable to attack, but of all the buildings in and around a fort, the baths, with fires lit under the floors probably every day, would have been the most likely to have gone up in flames accidentally.

Virius Lupus was also responsible for repair work at Ilkley, though what was being restored is not named. At Bainbridge three inscriptions where the names of the governors are included concern building work; a barrack was being built *c.* 205 under Valerius Pudens.[96] This work was followed by the construction of a wall and a branch of it probably belonging to an annexe wall (*murum cum bracchio caementicum*) under Senecio *c.* 205 to *c.* 207. Another building, not named, was constructed under Senecio at Bainbridge. The inscriptions recording work under Pudens and Senecio are very similar in their wording, which suggest a continuous policy of repair and rebuilding.[97] Under Pudens, the aqueduct channels which had collapsed through age were rebuilt at Segontium near modern Caernarvon, and a dedication to Severus, Caracalla and Geta was set up at Ribchester.

The complete rebuilding of the gate and part of a wall at Risingham under Alfenus Senecio is sometimes used to suggest that the fort may have been damaged in the 180s, and possibly abandoned, but it also comes into play in the disaster theory of 197. The text of the inscription, declaring that the south gate and part of the wall had collapsed though old age, was interpreted as a blatant cover-up for destruction by the enemy, which the Romans were loath to admit.[98] But it is also possible that the Romans were telling the brutal truth, that the fort had been neglected, which need not involve destruction either in the war of the 180s under Commodus, nor as a result of an attack in 197. A fragmentary inscription reveals that another part of the fort at Risingham was rebuilt from the ground up (*a solo restituit*) in the early third century.[99] What was being rebuilt is not known, but it was probably not just the south gate that had collapsed at Risingham.

On Hadrian's Wall there are few if any signs of destruction that can be assigned to 197, nor has any indication of substantial repairs come to light that may have been necessitated by damage at this time. At Halton Chesters, Rudchester and Corbridge, destruction layers have been found which were once thought to have constituted good evidence for the proposed 197 invasion, but this was a case where theoretical events moulded the interpretation of the archaeology instead of the other way round. The destruction layers have been assigned to the war under Commodus, for which there is literary evidence, albeit without any corroborative details. No signs of destruction at the end of the second century have come to light at Housesteads so it appears that 197 passed quite peacefully at this fort. A fragmentary inscription that was found in the commander's house, or *praetorium*, at Housesteads attests that this building was repaired by *cohors I Tungrorum*, which was in garrison at this fort from *c.* 160 to the last phases of the Wall. The work was carried out probably under Severus, though the Emperor's name is missing and there is only a hint that Geta, with the rank of Caesar, is mentioned. The governor's name is also missing, but it could have been Alfenus Senecio.[100] Alfenus Senecio is attested at Greta Bridge in County Durham, where he supervised the setting up of a dedication to Severus and Caracalla, both Augusti and Geta as Caesar.[101] At Benwell the *ala I Asturum* set up a dedication for the victory of the Emperors when Senecio was governor.[102] Senecio is also attested at Chesters, where fragments of an incomplete inscription reveal that unspecified building work was done at this fort, and a granary was built at Birdoswald during Senecio's term of office.[103]

At Corbridge the left-hand section of a broken inscription shows

that a vexillation of *VI Victrix* carried out some unspecified work
under Virius Lupus, the letters LU and part of the letter P certifying
his identity.[104] It is thought that Corbridge had been converted into
a base for detachments of *VI Victrix* and *XX Valeria Victrix* in
the 160s, during or after the withdrawal from the Antonine Wall,
so the builders on this inscription were probably in residence in
one of the military compounds that were built at the site. Another
inscription found at Hexham, but most likely from Corbridge,
records the building of a granary by a detachment of a legion when
Severus was Emperor and his two sons had the rank of Caesar. The
inscription lacks its lower section so the governor is uncertain; Birley
opts for Lupus who was already building at Corbridge.[105] A third
inscription from Corbridge is a broken altar set up by a man whose
name ends in norus, who was an officer in charge of the granaries
at the time of an expedition to Britain – *praepositus curam agens
horreorum tempore expeditionis felicissimae Brittannicae* (sic).[106]
The plural for the granaries is assumed from the surviving letters
ORR, because it would be expected that if a special officer was put
in charge of stores, there would be more than just one granary for
him to look after. There is no dating evidence for this inscription,
and the editors of *Roman Inscriptions in Britain* noted that the
expedition could have been under Ulpius Marcellus in Commodus'
reign, but the exact phrase *expeditio felicissima Britannica* was
used by Severus and Caracalla, so this inscription can be assigned
to the early third century.

The building work at the Pennine forts, on the Wall and at
Risingham differs from other repair work in that the governors
from 197 onwards take charge of the work in several cases. Usually
building inscriptions from forts give the names of the emperors,
the title of the unit doing the building work, the name of officer
in charge of the proceedings, and sometimes but not always the
text of the inscription specifies what was being built, but if the
stone was to be set up on the new or refurbished building then
this information would have been considered superfluous. At the
end of the inscription, the name of the governor is included, and,
if archaeologists are really lucky, the names of the consuls for the
year are given, but this is frustratingly rare. It is usually stated
that the work was carried out under (*sub*) a particular governor,
meaning that he was in office at the time, but not necessarily

directly involved in the work, which was usually carried out by the prefect or tribune commanding the unit stationed in the fort, or sometimes a legionary centurion would take charge. The formula indicating that the named individual supervised the work is *sub cura*, followed by his name and rank. On the inscriptions attesting much of the activity of the governors in the late second and early third century this formula is attached to their names, suggesting that the work was carried out under the charge of (*sub cura* or *curante*) the governor, indicating that at several forts Virius Lupus, Valerius Pudens and Alfenus Senecio were on site for at least part of the time and took a personal interest in what was to be done and how it was to be done. Lupus took charge of the work at Ilkley, Bowes and Corbridge, and Pudens took charge at Bainbridge, but not necessarily at Ribchester or Caernarvon. Alfenus Senecio, for whom there are more building inscriptions than any other governor, took charge of the work at Bainbridge, with the prefect of the unit as supervisor, and he oversaw the setup of the dedication at Greta Bridge. Some of the work was done by order (*iussu*) of Senecio, as at Bowes and Risingham, and at the latter fort, the procurator Oclatinius Adventus took charge. At Chesters, the building work was done under the charge of (*curante*) Senecio, and the procurator Adventus supervised it (*instante* – which has a sense of urgency about it if taken literally).

The procurator was the financial official, a non-senator of middle class or equestrian origin, and he would not normally have included the supervision of building work in his list of responsibilities. Dio says that Oclatinius Adventus' earlier career included a post as *speculator*, or military police, and he had been a centurion in the *frumentarii*, usually interpreted in English as secret police.[107] The functions of a *frumentarius* included a variety of special tasks, often on the direct orders of the Emperor. Adventus had eventually become commander of the *frumentarii* and Severus will have known him and trusted him. The Emperor may have sent him to Britain for the purpose of intelligence gathering, and Birley suggests that Adventus was responsible for reporting on the situation on the north of Britain.[108] Working at Chesters and at Risingham will have furnished him with the opportunities to gather intelligence. Rankov has examined Adventus' career and takes his possible connection with northern Britain a stage further, suggesting that Adventus may have been responsible for recruiting scouts and training them for operations north of Hadrian's Wall. There may be a link between the procurator's presence at Risingham *c.* 205–07, where he supervised building work, and the scouts called the *exploratores Habitancensium*, who are attested at Risingham (Habitancum) by 213, though they could have arrived there a few years earlier.[109] Austen and Rankov point out that Severus had suffered from a lack of military intelligence during the Parthian wars, and having learned from this experience he may have recruited Adventus to prepare the ground rather better for his expedition to Britain.[110]

The governors who carried out the repair and building work in the Pennines and on the Wall were probably all known to Severus, as Adventus was, and had been specially chosen to refurbish the military establishments of northern Britain. Birley examines their origins and their loyalties.[111] Virius Lupus had tried to stop Clodius Albinus in Gaul, and was obviously a partisan of the Emperor. Valerius Pudens had been governor of Lower Pannonia in 193, and was probably included in Severus' circle from the very beginning when he made his bid for Empire. Alfenus Senecio was of African origin like Severus himself, and had been governor of Syria Coele while Severus was in the east. All these governors were personally involved in much of the building work that was done in the north from 197 onwards. It may be significant that only two governors before the reign of Severus took charge of work, and both were at Corbridge, Lollius Urbicus supervising unspecified building work in 139 and 140, just before the advance into Scotland to fight against the northern tribes, and Calpurnius Agricola not directly engaged in building but overseeing dedications to Sol Invictus, the unconquered sun, and to Marcus Aurelius and Lucius Verus, which may imply that building was being carried out.[112] Whatever was being done at Corbridge by Lollius Urbicus and Calpurnius Agricola, the work demanded their personal attention and was seemingly more important than what was going on at other forts, where some repairs were carried out during their terms of office but not supervised by them.[113] The fort at Corbridge was an important site for an army going north on Dere Street, before and after Hadrian's Wall was built, and would have particular relevance for Urbicus marching into Scotland. Risingham too was an important post on Dere Street, an outpost for Hadrian's

Wall but also a staging post in the rear of the army operating in Scotland.

The repairs and rebuilding of stretches of the Wall itself are usually considered to belong to Severus' programme of refurbishment, but the work is hard to date because so far there is no epigraphic evidence for who was responsible or when the repairs were carried out, but in some places late second-century pottery has been found in association with the repair work.[114] This could mean that the governors who repaired the forts had also been ordered to inspect the Wall and put it to rights. Breeze suggests that there was probably a thorough rebuild because the Wall was eighty years old, and the original building work had not been of the highest quality.[115] In places the foundations had collapsed and the Wall had subsided. The rebuilding is best observed in the central sector. At the western end of Crag Lough near turret 38b there is a stretch of Broad Wall foundation with Narrow Wall built on it, with mortar holding the stones of each outer face, but with no mortar binding the core. On top of this there are a few courses of an even narrower Wall, varying in width from not quite seven feet wide to only five and a half feet. This is distinguished by its bonding material of hard white mortar.[116] This white mortar is considered to be the hallmark of the Severan rebuild, and its use would be essential if the very narrow version of the Wall was to remain standing and resist the climate for any length of time.

There is one feature of the Severan campaigns in Britain that defies classification except in so far as it, or rather they, are found inside a fort, namely Vindolanda. These are the round structures or circular stone-built huts first discovered in 1934. On plan they resemble Iron Age roundhouses, laid out in rows of ten huts divided into two sections of five huts facing a second row of five, with a road between them. This is native style subject to Roman regimentation. The first of these structures were originally found underneath the north wall of the second stone fort, and presumably replaced the first stone fort at Vindolanda. It is estimated that there are about two or three hundred of them in total, stretching across the fort from the north gate to the south gate. Each hut had one door, and many of them had floors of clay, or occasionally flagstones. Hearths and remains of ovens were discovered in some of them. Finds have not been abundant but suggest a Severan date.[117] Various suggestions as to their purpose have been put forward, that the roundhouses accommodated hostages taken by Severus, mainly women and children, or perhaps prisoners of war were sent to Vindolanda under guard. Alternatively the occupants of the huts may have been refugees who lived north of the Wall and had become caught in the crossfire between the Romans and the rebels. John Mann thought that the huts may have housed levies of natives from North Africa who brought their families with them.[118] Bidwell has linked the round structures with conscripted labour from the southern parts of Britain, attested on inscriptions recording labour from the *civitates* of the south. These inscriptions were formerly dated to the late Roman period, when it was thought that the civilians would be helping to repair the Wall and forts, at a time when defence of the frontier was in the interests of the entire population. The later dating is not proven, and the inscriptions could just as well be dated to the Severan era.[119] There is, so far, nothing like these structures inside a Roman fort, but similar buildings have been found outside villas.[120] The buildings were probably deliberately destroyed, as indicated by a layer of ash found covering a few of the excavated remains, but it is not known why or when this happened.

Severus prepared well for the *expeditio felicissima Britannica*, in the hinterland of the Wall, on the Wall itself and to the north of it. The repair work in the Pennine forts in Durham, Yorkshire and Lancashire may be indicative of restlessness and raiding by the Brigantes, and attention to these forts was probably concerned with keeping routes open and protected. Greta Bridge, where Alfenus Senecio supervised setting up a dedication, and Bowes, where Virius Lupus rebuilt the baths and Senecio gave orders to build something which is not named, are both close to the modern A66, which approximates to the Roman road between Carlisle and York, where armies marched from Flavian times under Petillius Cerialis and probably ever since. Bowes, or Lavatrae to the Romans, is listed between Brough (Verteris) and Catterick (Cataractonium) on the journey between Carlisle and York, in the fifth route (*Iter V*) of the Antonine Itinerary, which actually starts far to the south at Chelmsford and runs through Lincoln to York and then on to Carlisle. The date of this compilation of major routes in the Empire is disputed, but it may belong to the reign of Caracalla.[121] At Ribchester a dedication was set up to Severus and Caracalla as Augusti, and Geta as Caesar, under the governor Valerius Pudens, and at Ilkley, Virius Lupus supervised some building work. Both these forts are on the route from Lancashire to York.[122] Bainbridge, where Valerius Pudens and Alfenus Senecio supervised building work, is on the next major east–west road through the Pennines south of the A66. This road connects the main north–south routes on the western and eastern sides of the Pennines, in modern terms the A6 and the A1, and where the route across the Pennies through Bainbridge meets the A1, you turn left for Catterick and right for York. If it sounds as though all roads led to York under Severus, it would not be surprising because York is where he set up his headquarters, and the protection of routes, whether or not the natives were restless, would facilitate transport and communications.

The outpost forts were included in the Severan rebuilding and repair programme. To recap, Corbridge received attention under Virius Lupus, and Risingham was repaired by Alfenus Senecio. It can be assumed that High Rochester was occupied at the time of the expedition because there was activity there under Caracalla, including the rebuilding in *c.* 213 of some part of the fort from the ground upwards.[123] It would make sense to occupy High Rochester as a staging post on Dere Street during the expedition, rather than delaying attention to it until the campaigns were over, and though the only evidence that has come to light shows that rebuilding work was being done after the campaigns, repair work may have begun before the army marched north, as at Risingham where repairs were initiated before the expedition set off, and yet further rebuilding was also carried out after the expedition.[124] Without proof, it is assumed that the important site at Newstead, used in previous advances to the north, was reoccupied under Severus, after being given up in the 180s. On the western side, Netherby had probably never been given up, and it can be assumed that it was utilised during the Severan expedition because it was occupied under Caracalla and Severus Alexander. A dedication to Julia Domna and Caracalla was set up probably in 213, and a considerable amount of repair and building work was carried out there in the first decades of the third century, including the completion of a cavalry exercise hall which had been started long before.[125] The fort at Bewcastle had most likely been retained after the 180s but here the evidence is uncertain.

Gathering, storing and enabling the transport of supplies was an important part of planning a campaign. The work done by Virius Lupus and the attention to the granaries at Corbridge can be construed as preparations for an expedition north of the Wall.[126] The overland route northwards from Corbridge could be supplemented by a sea route along the east coast. The new fort built at South Shields in the 160s was converted into a supply base in Severus' reign, when the fort was enlarged and extended to the south, redesigned and divided into two halves. Four short barrack blocks housed the soldiers, who had their own granaries, and in the northern section thirteen granaries were built. Later the fort was altered again, and extra granaries were provided, bringing the total to twenty-two.[127] It was once thought that the supply base had been built earlier than the reign of Severus, but the foundation date was clarified in 2000, when lead sealings of Severus, Caracalla and Geta were found in construction layers, the total haul eventually forming the largest collection of lead seals in Britain.[128] Lead seals were used as a form of protection for goods in transit, which were usually bound with cords or with wire and the seals were clamped onto them, and stamped while still hot, somewhat like sealing wax on letters. A number of the seals found in Roman Britain retain an impression of the cords, and sometimes the seals look like coins, with designs and lettering around the edges, while others bear lettering alone. This useful practice enabled archaeologists to date the seals from South Shields to Severus' reign; one of the seals was stamped *Augg* for the two Emperors Severus and Caracalla, providing dating evidence between 198, when Caracalla was elevated to the rank of Augustus, and 209 when the younger son Geta was also made Augustus. Another seal depicts Severus, curly haired and bearded, in the centre, flanked by Caracalla and Geta.[129]

The seals on merchandise protected goods from pillaging, unless someone stole the entire package, but it is likely that there would be an inventory to be checked off when the merchandise or provisions reached their destination, and then the people who handled the transport could be questioned. Goods could not be opened without breaking the seals, therefore only designated officials had the right to break them, and anyone trying to liberate the contents of a sealed package could be prevented from doing so, or at least discouraged. It would be particularly important at the multiple granaries at South Shields that an officer and his staff, such as the *praepositus* in charge of the granaries at Corbridge, could oversee and inspect everything that went into the stores, instead of into a soldier's pack while no one was looking, or indeed to anyone's pack between parcelling up, loading, transporting and unloading. He would also inspect everything that went out of the stores, and probably nothing was allowed out without the proper written authorisation; at least that was how the supply system worked in the later Empire, when supplies had to be rigorously controlled, and the bureaucracy that developed in the fourth century was probably based on practices current in the third. Acrimonious correspondence is attested in a law issued in 357, when the military commander in Africa had tried to bypass the regulations, taking supplies from a storehouse on his own authority, only to receive a letter from the offices of the Praetorian Prefect, rebuking him for not going through the proper channels, first writing to the *vicarius*, the deputy of the Prefect, to inform him of the number of allowances that were required and to whom they should be issued, and waiting to receive written authorisation to draw the rations.[130]

The building of the multiple granaries at South Shields and the work that was done at Corbridge represented only a part of the preparations for Severus' expedition to Britain. The planning for the war cannot have been done on a whim and accomplished in a couple of weeks, but presumably began in 207 or even earlier, but no one knows when orders went out to the governors of Britain to prepare the granaries.[131] Severus arrived in Britain in 208, together with his family, his entourage, the administrative staff who would carry on the government of the Empire from Britain and the army that he had gathered, but there is no firm dating evidence to say precisely when this influx of people occurred. The granaries would have to be up and running and preferably fully stocked before Severus set foot in Britain, and if this happened in the early summer of 208, the harvest for that year would not yet have been gathered, so it is at least possible that in order to feed the personnel and troops that Severus brought with him, the harvest of 207 would have to be gathered, transported and stowed away, and arrangements would have to be put in place to keep on supplying and filling the granaries while Severus and his army were on campaign, and in winter quarters. Supplies would probably be requisitioned from Britain itself, and perhaps from the German provinces, and sea transport would be provided by the *Classis Britannica* and by ships from the Rhine and Danube fleets. An inscription records an officer in Severus' expedition who was placed in command of the fleets of Britain, Germany, Pannonia and Moesia.[132] Unfortunately his name is missing, but whoever he was he may have played part in bringing supplies from the Continent and from Britain to South Shields, and once the campaigns started he would probably be involved in shipping the supplies up to the depots that were built at Cramond on the south of the Forth, and Carpow on the Tay. It is to be expected that South Shields and Corbridge would be busy places at least a year before Severus arrived.

The Severan Campaigns in Scotland

The impact of the Severan campaigns on Hadrian's Wall cannot be assessed except from the archaeological point of view and the repairs that were made to the forts and to the Wall. The Emperor probably took some troops with him from the Wall. It is not possible to list them, especially since it is unlikely that whole units would be removed, but numbers of soldiers may have been contributed from some or all of the auxiliary units in the Wall forts.

The cause of the war is not spelled out clearly in the ancient sources. The damage done under Commodus would still be fresh in the Emperor's memory, and although the hypothetical disaster of 197 is now questionable if not discredited, when Virius Lupus bought off the tribesmen some prisoners were returned as part of the deal, which implies that the time that had elapsed between the death of Clodius Albinus and the arrival of the new governor may have been turbulent. There may also have been some fighting in the year before the war began in earnest in 209, since Dio mentions that Severus complained about winning wars through the agency of other men in Britain, while he himself could not defeat a notorious bandit in Italy.[133] This was Bulla Felix, not quite the new Spartacus, whose band of allegedly 600 men probably included runaway slaves and, according to Dio, some imperial freedmen who had probably run away from estates in Italy.[134] No names are given for the men who were winning wars in Britain. Lupus presumably avoided hostilities by giving the tribesmen a lot of money, but Pudens was governor for only a short time and Alfenus Senecio may have been the general winning victories in Britain. The dedication to the victory of the Emperors from Benwell set up while Senecio was governor may represent some such action, though it could just as easily be a celebration in 198 of the tenth anniversary of the Parthian victory.[135] According to Herodian, the governor of Britain, not named, wrote to Severus to ask for more troops, and preferably the presence of the Emperor, because the barbarians were laying waste to the land and carrying off booty.[136] It has been suggested that this was all staged by Severus to provide the excuse for going to war. There was a precedent of sorts under Claudius during the invasion in AD 43, when Aulus Plautius was allegedly instructed to halt the campaign and call for the Emperor to come to Britain. Claudius duly arrived, accompanied by some elephants, so that he could be seen to partake in the campaign and acquire military glory. Severus had already acquired military glory, but Herodian says that his appetite for it had not diminished.[137] If Herodian's story is true, the governor who wrote to the Emperor may have been Alfenus Senecio, but the whole episode may be fictitious, and there may have been no letter to summon Severus at all. The scenario depicted by this story implies that going to war was a sudden decision and was executed post-haste, whereas the intention to engage in war probably started some years before, though Birley says that even during Senecio's governorship there may have been no intention of moving back into Scotland.[138]

Both Dio and Herodian affirm that Severus was alarmed by the behaviour of his two sons and wanted to get them away from the temptations of Rome, and Herodian says that this was more important than gaining military glory in Britain.[139] But waging war as a means of reforming the characters of his sons and heirs could hardly be the main reason why Severus came to Britain. Dio says that the Emperor intended to subdue the whole island, and Birley suggests that Severus may have wished to reverse the withdrawal from the Antonine Wall, which could have been construed as a retreat.[140] This was not part of Severus' mentality. He was *propagator imperii* after all, extending the Empire, especially in Africa where the epithet was applied to him. No one knows the Emperor's intentions when he set off for Scotland with Caracalla in 209.

The troops that he brought with him probably included a contingent of the newly constituted Praetorian Guard and some or all of the new legion, *II Parthica*, one of three that he had raised in the east. *II Parthica* had notoriously been stationed not too far from Rome at Albano, and could be viewed as blatant support and protection for his regime in Italy, or more innocently as a reserve army to be taken to trouble spots on the frontiers, a precursor of the much later mobile armies of the fourth century. He probably gave orders to assemble troops from the Rhine as he journeyed to Britain; Whittaker, the editor of the Loeb edition of Herodian, draws attention to an inscription from Germany recording soldiers who went to Britain, *euntes [ad] expeditionem Britanicam (sic)*.[141] When he arrived in Britain Severus levied more troops and mustered his whole army.[142]

Having gone to so much trouble Severus was clearly intent on war regardless of the fact that the Britons became alarmed and tried to negotiate. They sent embassies asking for peace, but Severus refused their requests.[143] From the Roman point of view the track record of the Britons in honouring treaties was not good. Both Dio and Herodian delight in telling their audiences about the dreadful terrain, the horrendous climate and the barbarity of the northern British tribes, the Maeatae who lived near the Wall dividing the island into two, which presumably means the Antonine Wall and the Caledonians beyond them.[144] These groups were confederations of smaller tribes which had been merged with them, not an unusual feature among the tribes of Britain and beyond the Rhine and Danube, where new names sometimes appear in the historical record as though new tribes have arrived on the scene, but frequently they are the same people as before, but amalgamated into a larger group. According to Dio the Maeatae and Caledonians did not live in towns and did not cultivate fields, but lived by hunting and gathering, wearing hardly any clothes and using no armour except a shield, and armed themselves with spears and daggers. They rode into battle in chariots, rode small swift horses and stood their ground tenaciously.[145] Herodian echoes most of this, adding that they used swords, decorated themselves with iron ornaments and tattooed their bodies.[146] Fighting against people such as these and their cold, damp and gloomy habitat, Severus and Caracalla would seem all the more heroic.

The Emperor set off with his elder son Caracalla from York in 209, leaving the younger son Geta in the city, nominally in charge of the government of the Empire with a group of senior advisers, who presumably did all the work and made all the decisions, rather than the young Caesar himself, who was elevated to Augustus and equal status with his brother in the autumn of 209. The progress of the army up the eastern side of Britain is probably traceable via a series of marching camps of different sizes, very large ones of about 165 acres, going part of the way north, starting from Newstead. This is probably where the various strands of the army were mustered for the start of the campaign, which would account for the fact that very large camps have not been traced on the route coming up from the south to Newstead. Further north there are two series of camps, one of about 120 to 130 acres, and another about half this size, sixty-three acres.[147] Much ink has been spilled on the subject of these camps, and trying to assign them to the two specific campaigns in 209 and 210 and the movements of the army during both of them would fill the rest of this chapter and not provide much information about Hadrian's Wall, so moving quickly on with a modicum of relief, suffice it to say that the campaign was thorough, involving marches through difficult country, filling swamps and negotiating marshes by means of pontoons, and a crossing of something important celebrated on the bronze coinage of 209 with the legend TRAIECTUS.[148] It was probably a bridge of boats across the Tay, where the fort at Carpow was built on the south bank.[149]

The sources are coy about the details of the campaign, though Dio says that Severus lost 50,000 men, and the Romans used to kill their wounded to prevent them from being captured. The numbers of men are probably exaggerated, but the horrors of the campaign probably are close to the truth. It cannot have been easy fighting tribesmen who were used to the harsh conditions and knew the terrain intimately, using it to their advantage to lay ambushes and carry out what is now termed guerrilla warfare.[150]

Severus approached the end of the island, where he observed the lengths of the days and nights in summer and winter.[151] In the middle of the summer the sun hardly sets in the far north, and the Romans will have known this from Gnaeus Julius Agricola's campaigns, but to see it for the first time was probably quite surprising for the Roman troops. In the Shetland Islands during the Second World War, at the RAF station where my father was stationed, the announcement over the tannoy in the summer evenings was something like 'Black out will be from 01.00 hours to 01.15'.

Peace was made eventually and the Britons had to cede part of their territory.[152] Does this mean that the Romans occupied part of it? The fortress at Carpow on the Tay was built in stone within a polygonal enclosure, and it was very large, covering about twenty-four acres and could have accommodated a vexillation on a legion, or perhaps parts of two legions. *II Augusta* and *XX Valeria Victrix* are recorded as the builders, and the fort had a substantially built headquarters building, or *principia*, and a *praetorium*, or commander's house, and a bathhouse. Birley says that this indicates that the occupation was meant to be permanent.[153]

If Severus intended to occupy and hold Scotland, why did he repair Hadrian's Wall so extensively? The work done on the forts north of the Wall, on the Wall and to the south could be taken as signs that the Hadrianic line was always to be the frontier, perhaps even if the Romans took in the areas to the north and held them. The repair work on the curtain of the Wall as opposed to the forts cannot be closely dated, so it would be interesting to know if it was part of the plan before the campaigns in Scotland began, or afterward when the war was over. If Severus had planned to hold Scotland, events did not work out that way. In 210 the tribes of the north rebelled and it was alleged that Severus was so angry that he quoted Agamemnon's words, as supplied by Homer, about destroying the Trojans utterly.[154] This was what Severus desired to bring upon the Britons, but he was not able to oversee their utter destruction himself. He had been carried in a litter into Scotland, and his age, his infirmity and disappointment with the behaviour of Caracalla perhaps wore him down. In 209 when he and Caracalla were both riding to meet the Caledonians to arrange the treaty and disarm the tribesmen, Caracalla had drawn his sword and made as if to strike his father. The campaign of 210 was conducted by Caracalla alone. There had been omens that Severus would not return to Rome from Britain, and the Emperor had been fully aware of them before he set out.[155]

Severus died on 4 February 211, at York.[156] Caracalla arranged the funeral of his father, and made peace with the tribes. According to Dio he relinquished the territory that the Britons had been forced to cede to the Romans, and withdrew from the forts.[157] It has been suggested that there may not have been a complete withdrawal in 211. Dio says that just before Severus died he was preparing for another campaign, which would imply that Caracalla had not been successful in quelling the tribes in the previous year. There is no indication in the literary sources that there was a further war in 211, but coins were issued in that year for Caracalla with the title Britannicus, celebrating a victory, or victories in Britain.[158] It was also thought that the fortress at Carpow was occupied for a short time after 211, but this depends on the interpretation of a fragmentary inscription bearing the emblems of *II Augusta*, found near one of the gates. There are only a few surviving carved letters, which may have belonged to the titles of Caracalla, and the inscription has been dated on these grounds to Caracalla's sole reign beginning in 212. But as Birley points out, the mention of Caracalla does not prove that he was sole Emperor. The inscription may belong to his time as co-Emperor with his father, and there may well have been other inscriptions mentioning Severus and Geta.[159] Besides, if Carpow was occupied after Caracalla had arranged peace with the tribes, then other forts ought to have been occupied as well, and so far there is nothing to show prolonged occupation north of the outposts of Hadrian's Wall.

Dio says that Severus wished to subdue the whole island of Britain.[160] But conquering a people is not the same as annexing and administering the territory that has been won. Did Severus actually say that he intended to conquer and hold Scotland, or did Dio invent the story? Alternatively did Severus announce his intentions purely as propaganda, because it seemed that the Romans had been forced to retreat from the Antonine Wall about fifty years earlier, and the expedition would compensate for this? Did he really intend to hold all of Britain, but then changed his mind? And if he did intend to take in all the land up to the far north why did he make extensive repairs to the forts in the Pennines and on the Wall, and also the curtain wall? Did he consider that it would be necessary to maintain Hadrian's Wall even if he did conquer the whole island? The repairs to the curtain Wall cannot be dated so closely as repairs to the forts, but the work is considered to be Severan, and repairs were so extensive that antiquarians of previous eras considered that Severus had built the Wall. In this they were following the ancient authors, many of whom stated that this Emperor had built the Wall after the wars in the north, but they gave widely varying details about its length. Aurelius Victor says that Severus drove out the enemy and fortified the country by building a wall across the island, giving no dimensions, while Eutropius gives the length as 133 miles from sea to sea.[161] Orosius knew more about the Wall, describing how Severus fought great battles, put down the rebellion and divided the unconquered parts of the island from the territory that he had recovered by a great ditch and a strong wall fortified with frequent towers.[162] The *Historia Augusta* converts the Wall into the greatest glory of Severus' reign (*maximum eius imperii decus est*) and this may have stemmed from propaganda issued by Severus himself, or possibly by Caracalla, who did not follow up the war in Scotland by incorporating the allegedly conquered territory into the province. Since he could not claim significant success in Britain, except in so far as a rebellion had been put down, the failure to acquire more territory and extend the Empire required some explanation. After the campaigns were over, the restoration of Hadrian's Wall could be converted into a major victory, possibly even the main aim of the expedition in the first place.[163] If Caracalla chose to represent it in this light, not one voice would contradict him.

After Severus, Hadrian's Wall was the permanent northern frontier of Britain, no matter how many forays were made into the lands further north. The Wall was also the extreme north-western frontier of the Empire, surviving through the third and fourth centuries and into the fifth, until the Empire had ceased to exist.

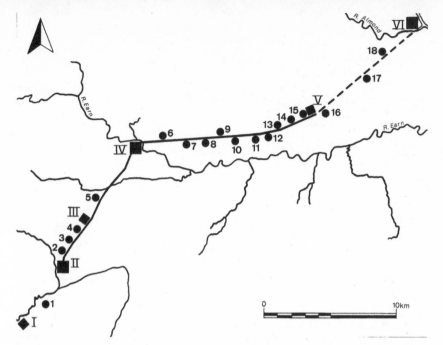

33. Map showing the first-century Roman installations around the eastern edge of Fife, named after the Gask Ridge, where a string of watchtowers has been discovered. The forts and towers are considered to belong to the advance to the north under Gnaeus Julius Agricola, but were probably occupied until the AD 90s, some years after the withdrawal from the more northerly forts. The purpose of the Gask system is disputed, not least its designation as a frontier and whether it was a forerunner of Hadrian's Wall.
Roman numerals indicate fortlets and forts: I Glenbank fortlet; II Ardoch fort; III Kaims Castle fortlet; IV Strageath fort; V Midgate fortlet (also called Thorny Hill); VI Bertha fort. The towers: 1 Greenloaning; 2 Blackhill Wood; 3 Shielhill south; 4 Shielhill north; 5 Westerton; 6 Parkneuk; 7 Raith; 8 Ardunie; 9 Roundlaw; 10 Kirkhill; 11 Muir O'Fauld; 12 Gask House; 13 Witch Knowe; 14 Moss Side; 15 Midgate, close to the fortlet; 16 Westmuir; 17 Peel (possibly); 18 Huntingtower. Drawn by Graeme Stobbs after D. J. Woolliscroft.

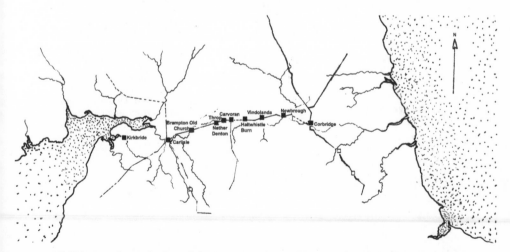

34. This map shows the line of the Stanegate, the road lying to the south of the Hadrian's Wall and its known forts. The road has not been traced west of Carlisle or east of Corbridge, and the postulated fort at Washing Wells in the east is not shown because it has not been attested by excavation. Dere Street, approximating to the modern A68 is shown running through Corbridge to the north, with a branch road running north-east. Like the Gask system, the role of the Stanegate as a forerunner of Hadrian's Wall, and its relationship to the Hadrianic frontier, are hotly debated. Drawn by Susan Veitch from Johnson 1989.

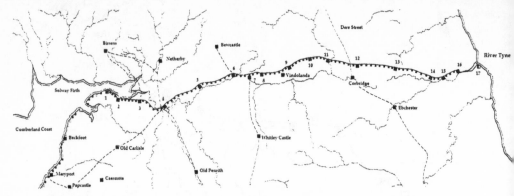

35. Map of Hadrian's Wall including the three outpost forts in the east, at Birrens (*Blatobulgium*), Netherby (*Castra Exploratorum*) and Bewcastle (*Fanum Cocidii*). It is important to note that any map of known forts does not mean that they were all occupied at the same time; that the Hadrianic fort at South Shields has not yet been located, and the site visible today dates from the 160s; the fort at Newcastle was probably not built until the late second century; Vindolanda and Corbridge predate the Wall and are not attached to it. 1 Bowness (*Maia*); 2 Drumburgh (*Congavata*); 3 Burgh-by-Sands (*Aballava*); 4 Stanwix (*Uxellodunum*); 5 Castlesteads (*Camboglanna*); 6 Birdoswald (*Banna*); 7 Carvoran (*Magnis*); 8 Great Chesters (*Aesica*); 9 Houseseteads (*Vercovicium*); 10 Carrawburgh (*Brocolitia*); 11 Chesters (*Cilurnum*); 12 Halton Chesters (*Onnum*); 13 Rudchester (*Vindovala*); 14 Benwell (*Condercum*); 15 Newcastle (*Pons Aelius*); 16 Wallsend (*Segedunum*); 17 South Shields (*Arbeia*). Drawn by Susan Veitch adapted from an original in Jones and Mattingly, *Atlas of Roman Britain*.

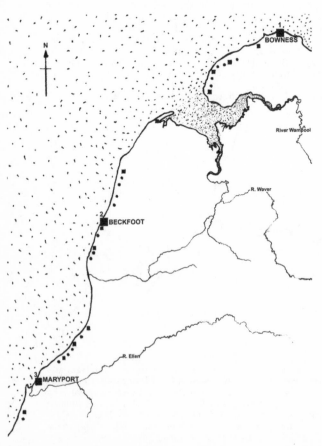

36. Map of the Cumberland coast system. The Wall was not carried southwards after Bowness-on-Solway, but forts, fortlets corresponding to the milecastles, and towers corresponding to turrets on the Wall, were built along the coastline. These are respectively represented on this map by large squares, smaller squares and dots. It is presumed that there would have been towers and milefortlets in the gaps where nothing has yet been discovered. Drawn by Susan Veitch from Johnson 1989.

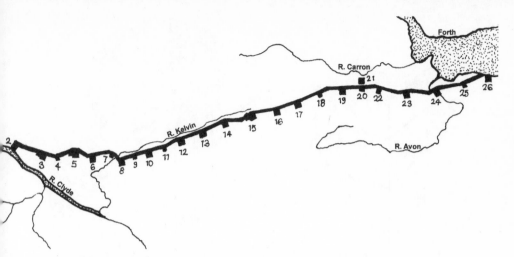

37. Map showing the Antonine Wall, built of turf between the Forth and Clyde, with its forts and fortlets. This frontier was built only a few years after Hadrian's death by his successor Antoninus Pius, perhaps in response to an outbreak of hostilities in the north in the early 140s. Hadrian's Wall may not have been completed when the new frontier was established, but it was not entirely abandoned. The Antonine Wall was held for only a short time from the 140s to the 160s, and it was more or less a copy of the Hadrianic scheme. It is not known if the fortlets were built according to strict regular spacing between the forts, because only a few have been found, and it should be noted that the forts are not all of the same size. The fortlets: 4 Cleddans, 7 Summerston, 9 Wilderness Plantation, 11 Glasgow Bridge, 15 Croy Hill fifty metres west of the fort,18 Seabegs, 20 Watling Lodge, 25 Kinneil. The forts: 1 Bishopton, 2 Old Kilpatrick, 3 Duntocher, 5 Castlehill, 6 Bearsden, 8 Balmuildy, 10 Cadder, 12 Kirkintilloch, 13 Auchendavy, 14 Bar Hill, 15 Croy Hill, 16 Westerwood, 17 Castlecary, 19 Rough Castle, 21 Camelon, 22 Falkirk, not certain, 23 Mumrills, 24 Inveravon, 26 Carriden. Drawn by Susan Veitch from various sources.

38. Early antiquarians attributed the building of the Wall to Septimius Severus because of the extensive repair work that this Emperor carried out at the beginning of the third century, but as more archaeological discoveries came to light, epigraphic evidence made it clear that the work was Hadrianic. These two inscriptions were found on the line of the Wall between Housesteads and Great Chesters, recording building work by *II Augusta* under Aulus Platorius Nepos, recorded as Hadrian's governor of Britain between 122 and 126. Drawn by Susan Veitch from *Roman Inscriptions in Britain*, volume I.

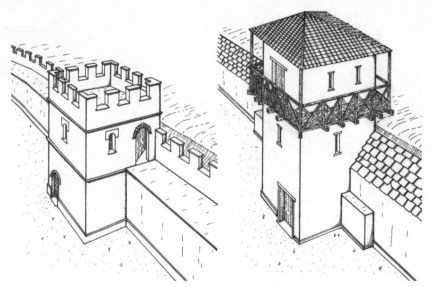

39. In the first scheme for Hadrian's Wall there were no forts attached to it, but there were small fortlets or milecastles every Roman mile and in between them two towers, labelled turrets, the smallest installations along the Wall. These two drawings show different hypothetical reconstructions of the turrets on the Wall. The full height of the Wall and the way in which it was finished off at the top are not known. There may have been a wall-walk all along the top of the Wall, with or without crenellations or a protective barrier, or the Wall may have sloped inwards, finished off with stones or tiles. Several other possibilities have been suggested. No turret survives to its full height, so it is not certain whether there was a projecting gallery near the top, with a pitched roof, like the examples on Trajan's Column in Rome. A flat roof, possibly with crenellations, would allow for all-round vision, but would be inhospitable and would require drainage facilities, while a sloping roof projecting on all four sides would protect the building and shed rain water, but impede surveillance. Note the different suggestions for the doors and windows. There are several unanswered questions: were the upper sections of the turrets built to a uniform style? Were they intended to act as watchtowers with a capacity for signalling, and if so how were signals made and to whom? Did the top floor lead out onto the hypothetical wall-walk along Hadrian's Wall? Drawn by Graeme Stobbs after M. Moore and other sources.

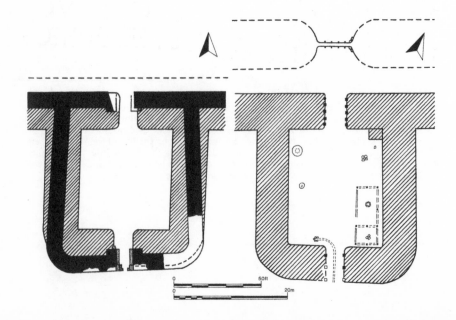

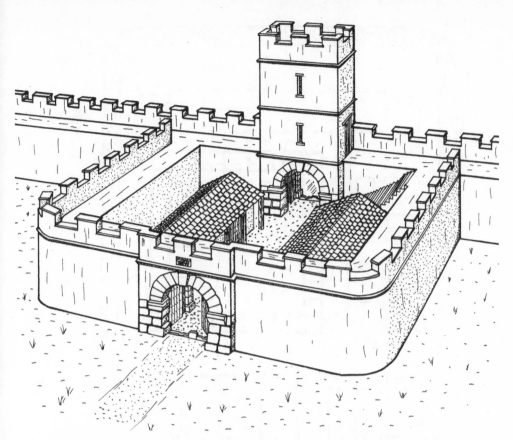

41. Reconstruction of a stone milecastle, showing two buildings flanking the central road and a tower over the north gate. It is not absolutely certain that towers existed, nor is it known how high they would have been if they did exist, but greater height provides greater vision. Both the north and south gates of milecastles were built to the same plan, and both could have supported a tower. This is controversial, as is the hypothetical wall-walk all around the milecastle and the way in which it may have given access to the top of the Wall itself. The stairway in this reconstruction is based on the evidence from Poltross Burn milecastle 48, where the first few steps are still visible in the north east corner. Drawn by Graeme Stobbs adapted from various sources.

Opposite: 40. Plans of two milecastles: (a) Harrow's Scar milecastle, number 49, east of Birdoswald fort, and (b) High House milecastle 50, west of Birdoswald. Milecastles were attached to the Wall and spaced one Roman mile apart except when they had to accommodate variations in topography. Short axis milecastles are attached to the Wall by their long sides, and long axis milecastles by their short sides, but the internal area of both types was roughly the same, except for some larger examples in the west. From the river Irthing to the west coast, the Wall, and also its milecastles, were built of turf, whereas all the other milecastles were of stone. The turf milecastles were eventually rebuilt in stone, as at Harrow's Scar, where the plan shows the turf phase underlying the stone version. Milecastles had two gates, one in the north side and one in the south, and the stone version of milecastle 49 respects the original passageways. The north gateway of the turf milecastle 50 has more postholes than the south gate, most likely to support a tower. This milecastle was occupied for only a short time, and was not replaced in situ by a stone milecastle, because when the Turf Wall was rebuilt in stone the new line ran further north for about two miles, and a new stone milecastle was built on this line. The turf milecastle 50 was demolished, and rubbish was buried in the two pits indicated by the circular features on the western side. Among this rubbish was a fragment of a wooden dedication tablet recording the building work, very similar to the stone dedication slabs set up at forts. Drawn by Graeme Stobbs, adapted from Daniels 1978.

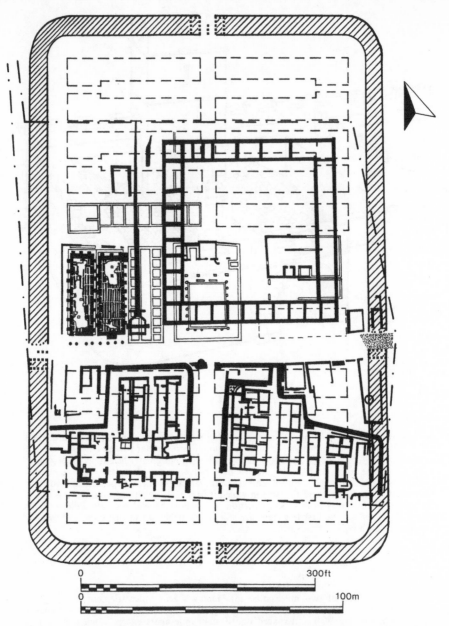

0   300ft

0   100m

42. Plan of Corbridge, which belonged to the Stanegate, and predates the Wall. The earliest fort built under Agricola was further to the west at Red House, but this site was abandoned and a new fort built with turf ramparts and timber internal buildings on the present site. This plan shows superimposed phases within the hatched lines representing the turf rampart of an earlier version of the fort, which was rebuilt at least three times. The black lines represent the features that can still be seen today, and the dotted lines represent the layout of an earlier version of the fort. Probably in the 160s Corbridge ceased to be a regular fort and more alterations took place. The large square building with rooms surrounding the courtyard was never finished. It is known as site XI, and was usually described as a storehouse built to support Severus' campaigns into Scotland, but it is also possible that it was intended to serve as a marketplace. It overlies the headquarters building and some of the barracks of the last phase of the regular fort. In the southern half of the site, the two irregularly shaped Walled areas are known as the west and east military compounds, which may have accommodated soldiers and officers, probably legionaries, and workshops. A military presence was maintained at Corbridge, but the arrangements, activities and accommodation were vastly different from the Wall forts. Drawn by Graeme Stobbs, adapted from various sources.

43. Plan of the fort and vicus at Vindolanda. This fort predates the Wall and strictly belongs to the Stanegate, like Corbridge, but it remained in occupation after the Wall and its forts were built. Excavation over many years has shown that this fort was rebuilt several times, sometimes on a different orientation. The fort had three turf and timber phases, the first dating to the mid-80s in the reign of the Emperor Domitian, followed by two more phases before the first stone fort was built *c*. 163, around the time when the Antonine Wall was abandoned. This plan shows the third-century stone fort which was occupied by *cohors IV Gallorum*. Drawn by Susan Veitch from R. Birley in Hodgson 2009a.

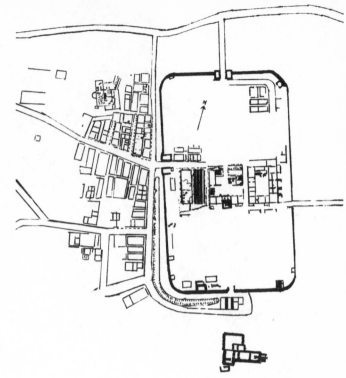

44. The fort at South Shields, south of the river Tyne, is considered to be part of the Hadrianic frontier scheme, even though it is separated from the Wall by the river. The earliest fort on the current site dates from about 160. The Hadrianic fort has not been discovered but finds of Hadrianic date indicate that a fort existed on a different site. The fort was surrounded by ditches, not shown on this plan, three on the west side and two round the other walls. The plan of the mid-second-century fort closely resembles that of Wallsend, barracks in the fort shown here were originally built in timber, but were later replaced in stone, as on this plan, and the four barracks in the south-eastern section accommodated horses as well as the soldiers of a part-mounted cavalry unit. The fort was extended in the early third century and converted into a supply base for the Severan campaigns in Scotland. Drawn by Susan Veitch from Bidwell in Hodgson 2009a.

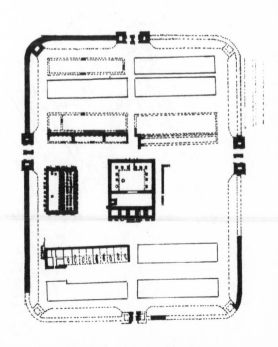

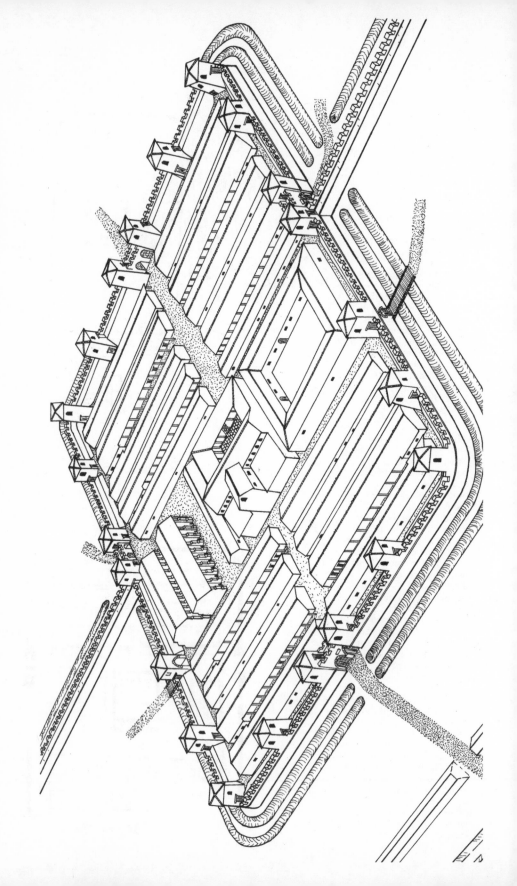

Opposite: 45. A representative reconstruction of a fort on Hadrian's Wall, designed to project beyond the Wall, though not all the Wall forts did project. At the bottom, the drawing shows the road leading to the fort from the south, through the gap in the south mound of the Vallum, the ditch that accompanied the Wall on its southern side, then through the gate guarding the causeway, and through the gap in the north mound. A break in the two ditches surrounding the fort allows access to the twin-portal south gateway, flanked by two guard towers. No one can say if this form of roof construction of the gate towers or the interval towers is correct because generally only the ground plan and a few courses of stone survive. The four main gates of the forts usually had twin-portal entrances, but in some cases one of the gates would be blocked fairly early, and only one passageway would be used. In projecting forts, Hadrian's Wall joined with the south tower, and there were usually extra single-portal gates in the eastern and western sides, shown here with bridges to cross the uninterrupted ditches. Inside the fort, there were usually three divisions, with barracks in the front and rear sections. In the centre range, the granaries, recognisable by their stone buttresses, the headquarters building where the unit standards were housed, the records were kept and the administrative work was done, and the commander's house, a Mediterranean-style courtyard building. Most forts accommodated workshops and stores buildings, or perhaps a hospital as identified at Housesteads. Forts were not built to a rigidly standardised plan, and they changed over time, being rebuilt in whole or in part to cater for changed requirements, so there is no such thing as a typical fort. Drawn by Graeme Stobbs from various sources.

46. Plan of the fort at Benwell. Much of this fort lies buried under modern houses, and the plan of its southern section derives from excavations in the 1920s and 1930s. The northern section, of unknown extent, was irretrievably lost when a reservoir was constructed in the second half of the nineteenth century. The fort projected to the north of the Wall, which probably came up to the south tower of the twin-portal east and west gates, as at other forts which sat astride the Wall, though at Benwell there is no actual trace of the west, north and east gates. Instead of the usual four gates, six gates were usually provided, the extra ones on the west and east sides being single-portal gateways, as on this plan. Probably in the late second century, the occupying unit was the *ala I Asturum*, originally raised in Spain, sister unit to the *ala II Asturum* based at Chesters. Both units may have kept up their association with the Spanish tribes from which they had been recruited. Drawn by Graeme Stobbs.

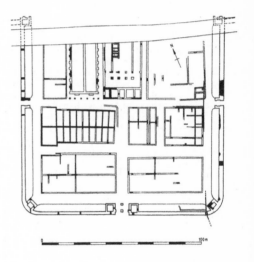

47. At Halton Chesters the Wall had been commenced and the northern ditch had been dug before the decision was made to build the fort, which was planned to project to the north, with the northern towers of its west and east gates built over the filling of the ditch, with the consequent need for extra-deep foundations. The fort has not been extensively excavated, but a reassessment was made of the earlier work by the late John Dore and published in 2009. The only attested garrison, probably from the third and fourth centuries, is the *ala Sabiniana*, originally from Pannonia. If it contained the nominal complement of five hundred soldiers and horses, some of them were probably outposted, since the fort could not have accommodated them all. A notable feature is the bathhouse in the north-west corner, possibly dating to the later Roman period. Bath buildings were usually outside the forts in the early Empire, but from the second half of the third century some of the forts in frontier zones rebuilt the baths inside the forts for greater security, despite the risks of fires. Drawn by Graeme Stobbs.

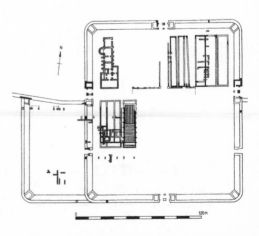

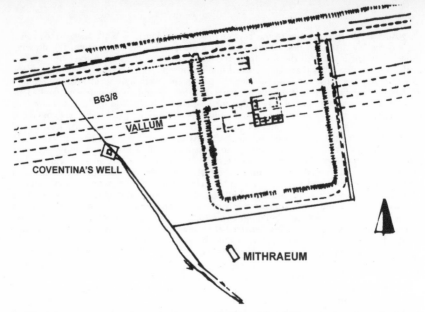

48. The fort at Carrawburgh was built across the line of the Vallum, as shown on this plan, and from the fort platform the line of the Vallum can be clearly seen running westwards, just south of the modern road. The northern wall of the fort was formed by Hadrian's Wall itself and the two may have been built at the same time. This part of the Wall is now under the modern B6318. Limited excavation has been done here, but the outline of the fort and the sites of its gates can be discerned under the turf. To the south-west of the fort the remains of the temple of Mithras have been exposed, but the site of Coventina's Well, marked on this plan, is now overgrown and boggy. The finds and offerings from the Well are housed in the museum at Chesters fort. Drawn by Susan Veitch from Daniels 1978.

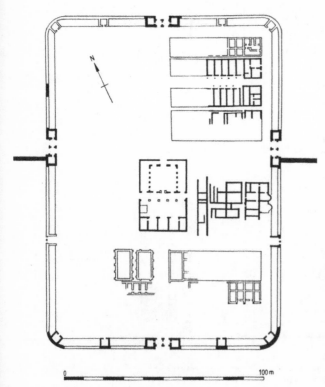

49. The fort at Chesters projected beyond the Wall, and its construction involved the demolition of turret 27a, part of the Wall and the infilling of the northern ditch. As at Benwell, the east and west gates were built over the site of the ditch, and there were four twin-portal gateways and two single-portal gates on the east and west sides. Although inscriptions attest infantry soldiers, if not whole units at the fort, it was probably designed from the outset for a 500-strong cavalry unit, the first attested being the *ala Augusta ob virtutem appellata*, which had received its title Augusta as a reward for an unknown act of bravery. From the late second century to the end of recorded occupation, the garrison was *ala II Asturum*. The site was owned by the Clayton family in the nineteenth century, when private excavations were conducted, better documented than many other excavations of the same period. Only certain areas of the fort have been exposed, all individually fenced off, which make the site less easy to interpret. An aerial view provides a clearer idea of the extent and layout of the fort, which is famous for the remains of its underground strongroom in the headquarters and the baths on the banks of the river. Drawn by Graeme Stobbs.

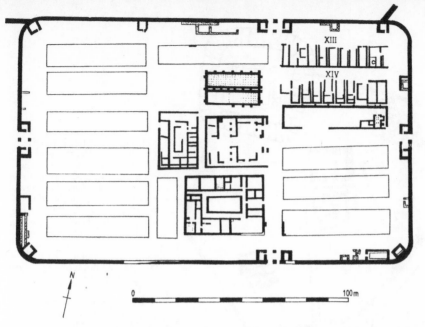

50. Housesteads is probably the best known fort on Hadrian's Wall, set on the heights of the Whin Sill with good views all round, and with a complete circuit of walls and remains of all four gates. The fort accommodated a nominal one thousand infantry soldiers, firmly attested from the third century onwards as *cohors I Tungrorum*, originally from the area around modern Tongres. This unit may have been the occupying force from the earliest times, with an absence of twenty years or so when it was stationed on the Antonine Wall. In the third century Germanic units are attested, the cavalry unit of the *cuneus Frisiorum* and the *numerus Hnaudifridi*, but whether they were supplementary to the garrison, or whether they replaced the Tungrians is not known. When the fort was built, its northern wall extended slightly beyond the original line of the Wall, which had to be demolished along with turret 36b, as seen in the exposed remains. The notable features at Housesteads are the so-called chalet barracks of the late period, in the north-eastern corner of the fort, and in the *vicus* just outside the south gate there are the foundations of the Murder House, where two bodies were found concealed under a false floor laid down in the Roman period. Drawn by Graeme Stobbs.

51. The fort at Great Chesters was the last to be built, between 136 and 138, and it was aligned with the Wall instead of projecting to the north, concealing what would have been milecastle 43 under its foundations. From the early third century until the late period the unit in occupation was *cohors II Asturum*, and although it is listed as *I Asturum* in the late Roman document known as the *Notitia Dignitatum*, it is considered that this is an error for the same unit. The site of the fort is occupied by a modern farm and only small-scale excavation has been conducted, but one of the important finds includes the Aesica Brooch, discovered along with a hoard of some silver and gold jewellery in the late nineteenth century. Notable features include the arched roof of the strongroom, like the version to be seen at Chesters, but not as spectacular, and the late barracks consisting of six discernible individual houses separated by extremely narrow alleys in the south-west corner of the fort. Drawn by Graeme Stobbs.

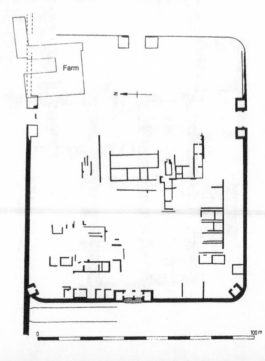

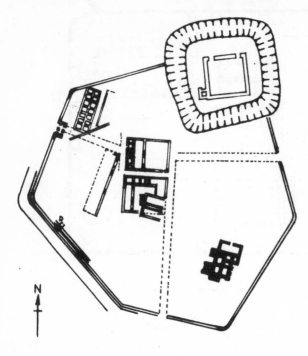

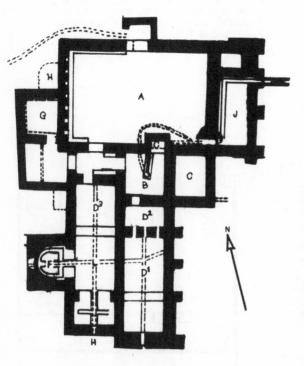

52. Plan of the fort at Bewcastle. On the western side, the Wall was supported by outpost forts to the north at Birrens, Netherby and this fort at Bewcastle. This plan shows the third-century polygonal fort at Bewcastle, its shape adapted to the topography. The Hadrianic fort had turf defences and timber internal buildings, but the gates and the headquarters building were built in stone. The bathhouse shown inside the later fort is of typical Hadrianic plan. The fort lies on a route to and from the north, which explains the presence of the medieval castle in the north-east section, surrounded by its ditch. Drawn by Susan Veitch after Austen in Bidwell 1999.

53. A simplified plan of the baths at Chesters, which have been resurveyed and updated as a preliminary to building the replica baths at Wallsend, and an amended plan has been produced. The baths at the Wall forts were all very similar, fulfilling the same purpose of getting clean and spending some off-duty leisure time. In civilian contexts and especially in the large towns, the baths were more like modern leisure centres, equipped with sports facilities and libraries. Though their military baths were far less elaborate, the soldiers probably played board games and gambled before, during, or after bathing, which accounts for the presence of altars or statues of the goddess Fortuna in some of the baths. At Chesters a soldier of German origin left an altar to Fortuna in fulfilment of a vow he had made to her. The rooms are identified as follows: A Changing room; B Cold room; C Cold bath; D1-3 Warm rooms; E Hot room; F Hot bath with apse, which may have been secondary, the original version probably being rectangular; G Hot dry room with hypocaust underneath; H Stoke hole for hypocaust; J Latrine. Drawn by Susan Veitch from Johnson 1989.

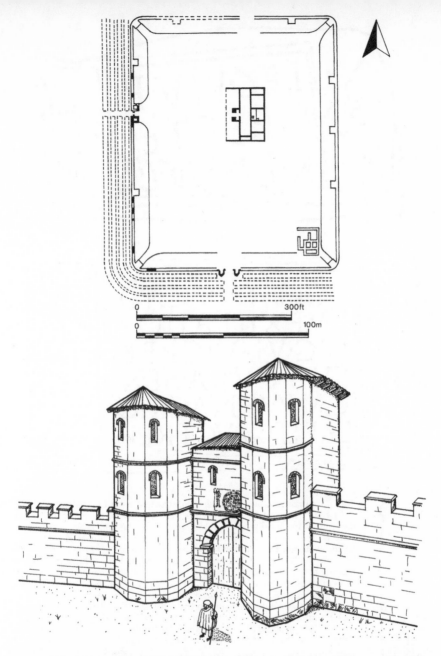

54. Plan of the outpost fort at Risingham and a reconstruction of the south gate. Very little excavation has been carried out at this fort and its original date is not known. An inscription of the early third century records the rebuilding of the south gate and accompanying walls, which had collapsed through old age. As shown on the plan, the south gate was flanked by projecting towers. The fort originally faced south but was restructured, probably in the later third century, to face west. Very few Roman forts have produced epigraphic evidence of their names, but Risingham is one of them. An altar set up by a *beneficiarius*, or official on the staff of the governor, records his first tour of duty at the fort, which was called Habitancum, and this place name can be confidently restored on the missing sections of a monumental dedicatory inscription dating to 213. The garrison was a 1000-strong part-mounted cohort, and extra units of *Raeti Gaesati* and *exploratores* are also recorded. The reconstruction of the south gate at Risingham shows projecting towers each with seven faces, described as finely built. The details shown here are derived from similar twin-towered projecting gateways at other sites in the Empire. The original height of the towers cannot be ascertained, but there is evidence from other places for the windows and the string courses. Plan drawn by Graeme Stobbs from Daniels 1978; gate and towers: an original drawing by Graeme Stobbs based on various sources.

Top: 55. Building stone recording reconstruction work on Hadrian's Wall (*RIB* 1389). Legionaries of *VI Victrix* were responsible for the work, and the stone is specifically dated to 158, when Tertullus and Sacerdos were consuls. This stone was originally assigned to a find-spot near Heddon-on-the-Wall, not far from the fort at Rudchester and could therefore have originally been set up to record routine rebuilding at this fort. More recently the provenance of the stone has been reassessed, with important consequences. It is now thought it came from the Wall about five or six miles west of Newcastle, and that it records rebuilding of Hadrian's Wall itself, prior to the withdrawal from the Antonine Wall. This insignificant looking stone contributes very significantly to the new thinking on the duration of the occupation of the Antonine frontier. Drawn by Graeme Stobbs from *Roman Inscriptions in Britain*, volume I.

Middle: 56. This dedication slab from Corbridge (*RIB* 1137) records building work by a detachment (*vexillatio*) of VI Victrix, the legion based at York, under Sextus Calpurnius Agricola, who was governor of Britain in the early 160s. In this period the Romans were withdrawing from the Antonine Wall, so refurbishment of the base at Corbridge was probably part of the reorganisation. Drawn by Graeme Stobbs from *Roman Inscriptions in Britain*, volume I.

Bottom: 57. This damaged inscription (*RIB* 1143) from Corbridge is not securely dated, but enough of its lettering survives to make it clear that it belongs to an *expeditio felicissima Britannica*, which may be that of Septimius Severus in the early third century. Five lines from the bottom, the broken section could accommodate the letters HORR referring to granaries (*horrea*) under the charge of an officer, most of whose name has been eradicated, and it is a logical conclusion to assign this work to gathering a food supply for Severus' campaigns into Scotland. Drawn by Graeme Stobbs from *Roman Inscriptions in Britain*, volume I.

AQVA·ADDVCTA
ALAE·II·ASTVR·
SVB·VLP·MARCELLO
LEG·AVG·PR·PR

Top: 58. The laconic inscription on this stone (*RIB* 1463) records that at some time in the 180s, under the governor Ulpius Marcellus, a water supply was brought into the fort at Chesters, perhaps at the same time as the cavalry unit of the Asturians, *ala II Asturum*, arrived at the fort, or soon after. The word aqueduct conjures up images of massive arched structures striding across the countryside like those approaching the city of Rome, but water channels feeding the forts do not even need to be piped. At Chesters, a stone channel through the fort wall delivered water into a tank in the north tower of the west gate which projected beyond the Wall, but the inscription was found near the small gate on the east side of the fort, so the text may refer to an alternative supply. Drawn by Graeme Stobbs from *Roman Inscriptions in Britain*, volume I.

Middle: 59. At an unknown date the hunters of Banna, *venatores Banniesses*, set up an altar to Silvanus, god of the countryside and hunting (*RIB* 1905). It is not certain what the *venatores* were. They may have been ordinary soldiers, or a group of soldiers with special skills, of the unit stationed at Banna, who dined well that night. Alternatively they may have had nothing to do with actual hunting, instead constituting an irregular unit with the title of 'Hunters', but the fact that they dedicated an altar to a god who assisted hunters implies that they did actually hunt. An important feature of this stone is that it was found inside the fort at Birdoswald, previously thought to be named Camboglanna. This derived from the evidence of the late Roman document known as the *Notitia Dignitatum* listing the military units and their forts in all the provinces. It is now thought that the copyist of the *Notitia*, listing the garrisons from east to west along Hadrian's Wall, got as far as the *cohors I Aelia Dacorum*, which is well attested at Birdoswald, but then omitted a line and went straight on to the next fort to the west at Castlesteads, and wrote its Latin name after the cohort of Dacians. On the strength of this inscription found at Birdoswald, and the names of the western Wall forts appearing on the enamelled vessel known as the Rudge Cup, Birdoswald is now named as Banna, and Castlesteads as Camboglanna.

Bottom: 60. Civilians as well as soldiers set up inscriptions in the area of the Wall. This is an altar to the god Vulcan, provided by the *vicani Vindolandesses*, inhabitants of the *vicus*, or civil settlement, at the fort of Vindolanda, in honour of the divine household (*domus divina*) of the Emperors. Other inscriptions recording *vicani* show that the villagers possessed a sense of corporate identity within the context of the Roman government of the province. (*RIB* 1700). Drawn by Graeme Stobbs from *Roman Inscriptions in Britain*, volume I.

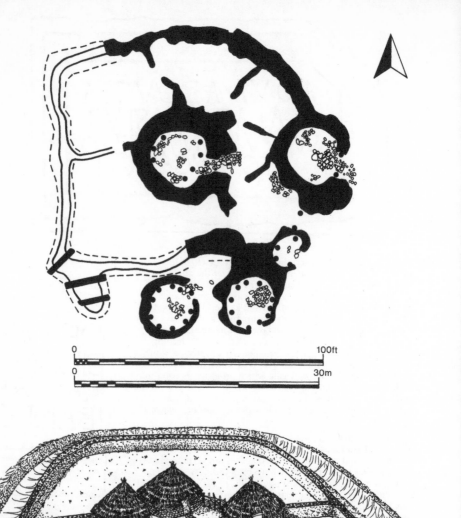

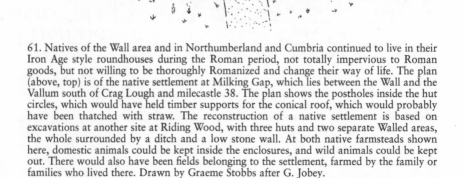

61. Natives of the Wall area and in Northumberland and Cumbria continued to live in their Iron Age style roundhouses during the Roman period, not totally impervious to Roman goods, but not willing to be thoroughly Romanized and change their way of life. The plan (above, top) is of the native settlement at Milking Gap, which lies between the Wall and the Vallum south of Crag Lough and milecastle 38. The plan shows the postholes inside the hut circles, which would have held timber supports for the conical roof, which would probably have been thatched with straw. The reconstruction of a native settlement is based on excavations at another site at Riding Wood, with three huts and two separate Walled areas, the whole surrounded by a ditch and a low stone wall. At both native farmsteads shown here, domestic animals could be kept inside the enclosures, and wild animals could be kept out. There would also have been fields belonging to the settlement, farmed by the family or families who lived there. Drawn by Graeme Stobbs after G. Jobey.

7

Living on the Wall: Soldiers and Civilians

In giving an account of soldiers' daily lives it is sometimes necessary to draw on records from other provinces, even though the Vindolanda records contain so much invaluable information about soldiers in Britain. It should be noted that the armies in different provinces were not exactly alike and their customs sometimes differed. Soldiers were allowed to worship their own gods provided that there was no conflict with Roman interests in each province. During the civil wars of AD 69 which brought Vespasian to power, the legionaries of *III Gallica* who had been brought to Italy from Syria greeted the rising sun at dawn, as they would have done in their own base, and troops accustomed to the cooler climate of the Rhine, also brought to Italy during the civil wars, found the heat too much for them, and many died of disease. Despite the differences among provincial armies, the records on papyrus, preserved in the hot, dry climates, highlight the daily routines and supplement the information for Roman Britain, and are accordingly sometimes cited in this chapter.

Commanders, Officers and Personnel of the Roman Army

The commander of all the armed forces in a province containing troops was the governor, appointed by the reigning emperor, as reflected in his title, *legatus Augusti pro praetore*, literally legate of the emperor with propraetorian power. He was in charge of civil administration and military command of the legions and the auxiliary forces in his province. His usual term of office was about three years, though there are exceptions, such as Gnaeus Julius Agricola who served for seven years. The governor of Britain was a senator who had reached the consulship, and he would have had varied experience of civil administration posts and army commands in different parts of the Empire. He was assisted, or sometimes perhaps frustrated, by the procurator, not a senator but an equestrian from the middle classes, appointed by the emperor. The responsibilities of this official included collecting the taxes and paying the army.

The main military units of the Roman Empire were the legions of Roman citizen status and the non-citizen auxiliaries. The soldiers who manned the Wall forts and those of the hinterland were auxiliaries, while the three legions of the province of Britain were based at fortresses further south, which had been established in the last quarter of the first century. Caerleon in south Wales was the base for *II Augusta*, the fortress at Chester housed *XX Valeria Victrix*, and *VI Victrix*, which arrived with or just after Hadrian in 122, was based at York. This does not mean that the Wall garrisons never saw legionaries, who after all did most of the building work as the frontier was being established, and detachments of legionaries may have occupied some of the Wall forts while the frontier was moved north under Antoninus Pius. Legionaries were also based at Carlisle and Corbridge, and individual legionaries or groups of them would be seen at all times at other places for various reasons, fulfilling various tasks and sometimes just visiting. Legionaries set up inscriptions at Wall forts, such as altars to the gods, and on occasions legionary centurions could command auxiliary units, usually with the title *praepositus*, which normally indicated a temporary command.

The fact that legionaries were Roman citizens does not mean that they all came from Rome, but they were of Roman citizenship status, with the legal privileges and obligations that this entailed. Citizenship could be bestowed on individuals or groups of people in the provinces, and inherited by their descendants. Slaves and freedmen could not join the legions, and were punished if they managed to bypass the investigations of the recruiting officers and were later found out.

Each legion was commanded by the *legatus legionis*, a senator who had served as a military tribune and also had experience of civil posts. Like the governors, legionary legates were appointed by the Emperor and usually commanded a legion for about three years. The legate was in charge of about 5,000 to 6,000 men, but it is important to note that although the Greek historian Polybius provides figures for the Republican legions, no source from any period of Roman history states how many men served in an Imperial legion. There may not have been a standard size for the legions all over the Empire.

Promotion prospects for a legionary legate were reasonable if he retained the favour of the emperor. He could look forward to a post as governor of an unarmed province for two or three years, with predominantly civilian administrative duties, then he could hopefully achieve the consulship. The senior officers under the command of the legate included the *tribunus laticlavius* or Broad Stripe tribune, a young man of the senatorial class, and second in command of the legion, usually for one year. There were five more tribunes in a legion, from the equestrian class, with the title *tribunus angusticlavius* or Narrow Stripe tribune. Their duties mostly concerned staff work, but they could take command of detachments of legionaries from time to time. These men were well connected with auxiliary units, since the first tour of duty for young equestrians was usually as a *praefectus* commanding a quingenary or 500-strong auxiliary infantry cohort. The next post for an equestrian tribune was most frequently as *praefectus* of a quingenary auxiliary *ala*, or 500-strong cavalry unit. Another equestrian officer in the legion was the camp prefect, or *praefectus castrorum*, who was third in command after the legate and the senatorial tribune. In rare cases this officer may have risen from the ranks, attaining the post of centurion and thereby acquiring equestrian status, but most often he had been appointed to a legion directly as centurion, usually on someone's recommendation. It was not what you knew, but who you knew, that counted for embarking on a military career.

The legions were divided into ten cohorts, each comprising six centuries of eighty men commanded by a centurion, the century being further subdivided into ten *contubernia* of eight men, who shared a barrack room, or on campaigns, a tent. The six centurions of each cohort were graded in seniority, with titles that reflected the organisation of the Republican army, starting with the most senior and working down the scale: *pilus prior, princeps prior, hastatus prior, pilus posterior, princeps posterior, hastatus posterior*.[1] The terms *hastatus* and *pilus* each initially derived from the names for types of spear. On the Wall, two centurial stones recording the building of an allocated length of curtain wall mention these grades. One comes from the stretch between Chesters and Carrawburgh, where the building was carried out by the century of Nas. Bassus, *hastatus posterior*, but the legion is not named. The other inscription comes from the sector between Stanwix and Burgh-by-Sands, recording building work by the century of the *hastatus prior* from the fourth cohort, but without naming the legion or the centurion.[2]

The first cohort in some legions contained only five centuries instead of the more usual six, but each of the five centuries was double strength with 160 men. The centurions were graded, the most junior being *hastatus posterior*, through *princeps posterior*, to *hastatus*, then *princeps*, then the most senior centurion called *primus pilus*, the most coveted position for centurions. After holding this post, further promotion was likely, some senior centurions finding posts in the Praetorian Guard. There is no evidence from any period of Roman history that attests to a legionary cohort commander, so the centurions are rightly labelled the backbone of the army. The officers below the centurions were called *principales*, on differing pay scales. Some received double pay (*duplicarii*) and others received one and a half times basic pay (*sesquiplicarii*). The *optio* served as second in command to a centurion, and those with hopes of becoming a centurion themselves are indicated in the title *optio ad spem ordinis*. The standard-bearers of the legion were ranked as officers, the most important being the *aquilifer* who carried the eagle standard of the legion. The *imaginifer* carried the image of the Emperor and the *signifer* carried the *signum* of the century. A junior officer called the *tesserarius* attested in the legions and the auxiliary forces, serving in a clerical post, and he was also keeper of the watchword, making sure that all sections of the legion had received it. Junior officers such as the *cornicularius* and *librarius* worked as headquarters staff, keeping unit administrative and financial records and dealing with the clerical work of the unit. Some of the legionaries with special skills for special tasks were *immunes*, meaning that they were excused fatigues, which allowed them time to carry out their tasks, but there was no extra pay for *immunes*, who were not of officer status. These soldiers could be artillery men, blacksmiths, metal workers, stone carvers, carpenters, or clerical workers in the headquarters. Some men were listed as *architecti*, usually translated as engineers, and three are known from the Wall zone, two from Birrens and one from Carrawburgh. The men were probably all legionaries, though none of the inscriptions includes the name of a unit.[3] The list of such *immunes* comprises many more tasks than those mentioned here.

Although legionaries were never entirely absent from the Wall, the troops based in the forts were auxiliary units of different types and sizes. These were the successors of a long line of support troops which accompanied the Roman legions from the beginning of the Republic. When campaigns were fought in Republican times it was usual practice to levy native troops fighting under their own leaders to help the main Roman army, and after the wars were over the native troops went home and the Roman legions did the same. There was no standing army in the Roman world until Octavian, the heir of Julius Caesar, won the war against Antony and Cleopatra and became head of the state, but he would never have described himself as such. Octavian whittled down the sixty legions that he inherited to about twenty-eight, which he kept in being thereafter. As Augustus, he gradually established regular terms of service, pay scales, and provision for time-served veterans. The establishment of the *auxilia* began when the standing army was formed, but its evolution was slower than that of the legions. Some of the native troops were retained with their own leaders, but there is no significant date when troops such as these were transformed into regular auxiliary units, which were still evolving in the reigns of Claudius, Nero and Vespasian.

In the fully evolved *auxilia*, cavalry units were called *alae*, which means wings, the classic position which early Roman and allied cavalry used to take up in the battle line. Infantry units were called cohorts, the same term used for divisions of the legions, and mixed cohorts with a contingent of infantry and cavalry were called *cohortes equitatae*. An auxiliary unit was either 500 strong, called *ala* or *cohors quingenaria*, or 1000 strong, called *ala* or *cohors milliaria*.

Commanders of the auxiliary units were all equestrians. The most junior commander was the *praefectus cohortis peditata*, prefect of a quingenary infantry cohort, divided into six centuries each containing eighty men, giving a total of 480 soldiers. Each century would be commanded by an auxiliary centurion. On Hadrian's Wall in the third century, when there is more information about which units occupied which forts, there was a 500 strong infantry unit at Newcastle, where *cohors I Ulpia Traiana Cugernorum* was based, but by the later fourth century, according to the *Notitia Dignitatum*, it had been replaced by *cohors I Cornoviorum*.[4] Another 500-strong infantry unit was *cohors I Frisiavonum*, probably stationed at Rudchester. It is listed at this fort in the *Notitia Dignitatum* as *cohors I Frixagorum*.[5] *Cohors II Delmatarum quingenaria* was based at Carvoran. A few quingenary infantry units were based in the hinterland forts, *cohors I Aelia Classica* at Ravenglass, *cohors II Nerviorum c.R* at Whitley Castle and *cohors VI Nerviorum* at Bainbridge.

After two or three years in command, the prefect of an auxiliary infantry unit could attain a post as one of the five *tribuni angusticlavii* in a legion, and then some of them could go on to command a 500-strong or quingenary cavalry unit, as *praefectus alae*. The *alae quingenariae* were divided into sixteen *turmae*, not centuries like the infantry, each *turma* being commanded by a decurion. Frequently these officers had risen from the ranks, but some of them were Roman citizens who had served in a legion. It is generally reckoned that the decurion commanded thirty men, making a total of thirty-two for each *turma*, and a total for the whole *ala* of 512 men. This number was probably never standard in each unit, since strength returns preserved on papyrus records show that actual numbers varied considerably.[6] In the third century, quingenary *alae* on the Wall were stationed on the eastern side of the Wall. Benwell was home to *ala I Hispanorum Asturum*, sometimes attested simply as *ala I Asturum* without the acknowledgement that it was Spanish in origin. At Haltonchesters *ala I Pannoniorum Sabiniana* was in garrison, and Chesters was the base for *ala II Asturum*. These forts are all situated in terrain suitable for keeping horses and for cavalry operations. Another quingenary cavalry unit, *ala Augusta ob Virtutem Appellata*, was stationed in the hinterland of the Wall at Old Carlisle.

The most prestigious posts for equestrian officers were as prefects of the 1000-strong infantry cohorts and finally as commanders of the milliary *alae*. The milliary cohorts were fewer in number than other auxiliary units, and since there was never more than one milliary *ala* in any province, the number of commanders who could hope to attain such posts was limited. An equestrian commander might choose to take up civil administrative posts instead of pursuing a military career. The *cohors milliaria* contained ten centuries of eighty men, each commanded by an auxiliary centurion, so the paper strength of 1,000 men was not quite achieved in reality. This command was the fourth rung of the equestrian military career, prestigious enough to be documented as such on inscriptions as *militia quarta*. There were two milliary infantry cohorts on the Wall, *cohors I Aelia Dacorum* at Birdoswald, and *cohors I Tungrorum* at Housesteads, stationed in areas where infantry would be more effective than cavalry.

The commander of a milliary infantry cohort ranked below the commander of an *ala milliaria*, since this command was the most important military post in the auxiliary arm. On Hadrian's Wall, the *ala Petriana*, or to give it its full title *ala Augusta Gallorum Petriana milliaria civium Romanorum*, had started out as a quingenary unit and was raised in strength to a milliary *ala*. It was probably based at the large fort at Stanwix to the north of the fort and town at Luguvalium, the Roman name for Carlisle. It has been suggested that the commander of this *ala*, senior to all other unit commanders on the Wall, was probably the commander of the whole of the frontier, but there is no evidence to show that this was the case.

There were also auxiliary units containing both infantry and cavalry. These were either quingenary or milliary like the infantry cohorts and *alae*. They were distinguished from the purely infantry cohorts by the description *cohors equitata quingenaria*, or *milliaria*. The additional title, abbreviated to *eq.* for a quingenary unit, or *eq. mil.* in the case of a milliary unit, was not always mentioned in documents and inscriptions. The number of infantry and cavalry soldiers in these units is not precisely known. For the infantry contingents, it is more straightforward, with probably six centuries of foot soldiers for the quingenary units giving a total of 480 soldiers, and ten centuries for the milliary units, giving a total of 800 soldiers, each with their officers in addition. The number of horsemen is not established. There may have been four *turmae* in the quingenary units, totalling 128 horsemen including the officers, and eight *turmae* in the milliary units, totalling 256 horsemen, but these figures have not met with universal agreement.

In the third century, the smaller *cohortes quingenariae equitatae* were based on the Wall at five forts. *Cohors II Asturum equitata* was based at Great Chesters (where it is erroneously listed as *I Asturum* in the *Notitia*), *cohors I Batavorum equitata* was at Carrawburgh, *cohors IV Gallorum equitata* at Vindolanda, *cohors IV Lingonum equitata* at Wallsend, and *cohors V Gallorum equitata* at South Shields, but at this fort the *cohors equitata* was replaced by the *numerus barcariorum Tigrisiensium* which is listed in the *Notitia Dignitatum*.[7] The part-mounted units were the most flexible of all the units in the army, serving as messengers, escorts for convoys or visiting dignitaries, reconnaissance duties, patrolling and as pickets and guards when on campaigns. It has been suggested that the cavalry of a part-mounted unit was somehow inferior to the *alae*, but the horsemen of a mixed unit went through the same training exercises, and usually fought alongside the *alae* in battles.

In the frontier zone of Hadrian's Wall in the early third century, there were *cohortes equitatae milliariae* at the outpost forts, but they were not employed there beyond the first two decades of the fourth century, because these forts are thought to have been given up by *c.* 314. *Cohors I Aelia Hispanorum equitata milliaria* was at Netherby, *cohors I Vangionum equitata milliaria* at Risingham and *cohors I Fida Vardullorum equitata milliaria* at High Rochester. On the Wall, *cohors I Nervana Germanorum milliaria equitata* was at Burgh-by-Sands in the third century but by the late fourth century the garrison according to the *Notitia Dignitatum* was the *numerus Maurorum Aurelianorum*. The unit attested at the smaller fort at Castlesteads, *cohors II Tungrorum equitata milliaria c.L.* may not have been at full strength.[8] The multiplicity of inscriptions from Risingham and High Rochester mentioning the unit commanders leaves no room for doubt that the *cohortes milliariae equitatae* were commanded by tribunes.[9]

Soldiers of the Wall Zone

The commanding officers of legions and auxiliary units usually came from the more Romanized parts of the Empire and would have gained experience in different provinces, rarely serving in the same areas more than once. They remained with their units for little more than three years, and there would probably have been something of a cultural and aspirational gap between them and the soldiers whom they commanded. This social distinction was emphasized in the relative living accommodation of commanders and soldiers. The commanders of cohorts and *alae* were housed in the central range of the fort in a Mediterranean-style house with rooms arranged around a courtyard, usually sited next to the unit headquarters building. The house was called the *praetorium*, which was the name for the general's tent in the Republican camp described by Polybius, writing in the second century BC, but in those days the *praetorium* was also the headquarters, so in older books on the Roman army and Hadrian's Wall this label was applied to the building in the centre range identified as the headquarters, but this is now known as the *principia*. The commanders' houses were well appointed, with their own private bath suites, and some of the other rooms heated by hypocausts and probably wall flues. There is evidence that the walls would be plastered and painted, and some floors would have been adorned with mosaics. The commander often brought his family with him for his three or four year command, and there would be several slaves to run the household. Commanders' wives do not feature in the historical record, except very rarely on inscriptions, and more famously in the letters from Vindolanda, one of the many reasons why these records are so important. The commander of the *cohors IX Batavorum* at this fort in the late first century AD, before Hadrian built the Wall, was the prefect Flavius Cerialis. His wife, Sulpicia Lepidina, was famously invited to the birthday party of Claudia Severa, who is revealed in another letter as the wife of Aelius Brocchus. Lepidina is mentioned in other letters from Vindolanda.[10]

In contrast to the commanders, the centurions of infantry centuries and decurions of the *turmae* lived at the end of each barrack block in much smaller houses, but they were still much better accommodated than the soldiers. Their houses had several rooms adorned with painted plaster, and some of them had heating and en suite facilities. The soldiers of an infantry unit lived in far less attractive accommodation. Eight infantry soldiers of one tent group or *contubernium* lived in a pair of rooms in a barrack block for their century, one room for living in and probably the rear room for sleeping, but sleeping arrangements are not clear. Bunk beds may have been used, but there is no evidence for this. Space would be limited inside these paired rooms, which taken together were slotted into an area measuring roughly four to five meters wide and seven to eight metres long, though there were variations in size in the cubicles in barracks. Glass has been discovered outside barracks, implying that at least some of them perhaps had windows facing onto the veranda running along the length of the barrack block. Walls may have been plastered and painted white, which would reflect light, but even so, the interiors of each double room would have been dark and probably cold. There would have been little room for personal possessions. The ideal number of cubicles for infantry centuries would be ten, housing ten groups of eight men to give the century total of eighty, but as more forts have been excavated eleven or even twelve cubicles have sometimes been found. Extra rooms may have been needed for storing equipment, or possibly the junior officers lived in these rooms, allowing them to avoid the cramped conditions of the ordinary soldiers. No one can confidently say why the Romans did not conform to the tidy arrangements that were expected of them by archaeologists and historians before evidence had been accumulated from several different forts. Cavalry barracks retained the two room arrangement, but it is now known that one of the pair was for soldiers, and the other accommodated horses. One of the earliest forts where this was discovered is at Dormagen, between Cologne and Neuss on the Rhine.[11] Stables had been tentatively identified during excavations at several forts, but it now seems that there were probably no separate building for horses, unless some part of a fort housing cavalry or a part-mounted unit had a space reserved for sick horses that need the attention of the veterinarians, called *mulomedici*. The Dormagen barracks were divided longitudinally, and had hearths in the rooms on one side, clearly for the cavalrymen, and soakaway pits in the rooms on the other, for the horses. Cavalry barracks-cum-stables have been found at Wallsend in the Hadrianic fort when the barracks and internal buildings were constructed in timber, replaced in stone in the second century on the same plan. The same system of accommodating men and horses together was found at South Shields in the fourth-period fort of the late second century. In both these forts, the barracks consisted of eight double cubicles, each housing the stables and the living accommodation for the men, with the decurion's house at one end of the block and an extra room at the other end, possibly for storage.[12] Significantly these forts have been intensively excavated over protracted periods of time. It is to be expected that at other forts garrisoned by a mixed unit with a cavalry contingent, or an *ala*, similar arrangements would have been made, but only excavation can prove this.

The rank structure in auxiliary units is not as well documented as in the legions. The infantry cohorts were divided into centuries of eighty men, like the legions, commanded by a centurion, and in cavalry units, a decurion commanded each *turma*. The second in command to each centurion was the *optio*, sometimes with the title *optio ad spem ordinis* if the soldier hoped for promotion to centurion. An *optio* of *cohors I Frixagorum* is attested at Carrawburgh.[13] Second in command to the decurion may have been the *curator*, attested in the Vindolanda records, perhaps with responsibility for the horses and their equipment, since these men are recorded as checking such items and reporting that they were in good condition.[14] On the other hand *curator* could be a special function, not denoting officer status.[15] The tombstone of Aventinus from Chesters records that he was *curator* of *ala II Asturum*, and had served for fifteen years. He had appointed as his heir the decurion Aelius Camellus, so Aventinus was probably *curator turmae*.[16]

In auxiliary units as well as in the legions, the junior officers were called *principales*, and there were different pay scales for different posts, some soldiers being *duplicarii*, or men on double pay, and others being *sesquiplicarii*, on one and a half times pay. Some soldiers felt it necessary to mention their pay scales on inscriptions. Messorius Magnus, *duplicarius* of *ala Sabiniana*, set up a tombstone for his brother at Haltonchesters, and at Mumrills on the Antonine Wall, Valerius Nigrinus, *duplicarius* of the *ala Tungrorum*, dedicated an altar to Hercules Magusanus.[17] The *duplicarii* of the *exploratores Bremeniensium* at High Rochester clubbed together to set up an altar to the goddess Roma, under the tribune Caepio Charitinus, who presumably commanded *cohors I Fida Vardullorum c.R. equitata milliaria* which was also stationed at the fort.

The titles of several junior officers are attested in military units, but the terms do not always convey any idea of what their duties would have been, and another problem is that during the long history of the Roman army, some of the titles attested in the records may well be synonyms or substitutes for the same post described under other headings at different times. There may not have been complete standardization of junior officer titles all across the Empire, and there is no universal agreement among modern scholars as to the grades of seniority. A junior officer called the *tesserarius*, whose title and functions derived from the Republican legions, is attested in the Imperial legions and in the auxiliary forces. He was responsible for giving the watchword, and probably for other clerical duties. His status may be higher than this vague description indicates, since at Vindolanda he seems to have been third in command in an infantry century or a cavalry *turma*.[18] Each unit would have a standard-bearer of officer status, and each century would probably have had its own standard, called a *signum*, carried by the *signifer* who was also responsible for keeping records for his own century. The standard-bearers were probably on double pay. Probably the best known standard-bearer from the Wall zone is Flavinus, whose tombstone is now in Hexham Abbey. He was *signifer* of the *turma* of Candidus in the *ala Petriana*. He served for seven years and died aged twenty-five, probably at Corbridge, some two decades before the Wall was built.[19] Other *signiferi* are known from the Wall zone. Julius Victor died at Risingham aged fifty-five, but it is only recorded that he was a *signifer* without naming his unit.[20] At Carrawburgh a damaged tombstone records the *signifer* of *cohors I Batavorum*. It lacks the personal name of the soldier but he is recorded as the son of Milanus.[21] An inscription from Maryport simply records the single word *signifer*.[22] Another standard-bearer was called a *vexillarius* who was responsible for carrying the *vexillum* or standard of a detachment or *vexillatio*. The *vexillum* was a square of red or purple cloth with a fringe at the bottom, attached to the top of a lance by a cross bar. There is some controversy over the *vexillarius* Barathes the Palmyrene, who died aged sixty-eight at Corbridge. There is no mention on his tombstone of service in an auxiliary unit, so it is suggested that he may have been a manufacturer of these standards rather than a soldier.[23] His wife was a British lady called Regina from the tribe of the Catuvellauni. She died aged thirty, and the same Barathes set up a tombstone for her at South Shields with a text in Latin and Palmyrene script.[24] Another standard was the portrait (*imago*) of the reigning emperor, carried by the *imaginifer*. Julius Pastor was the *imaginifer* of *cohors II Dalmatarum* at Carvoran, and at Kirkby Thore a soldier called Crescens, *imaginifer* of an unnamed unit, set up a tombstone with a floral banqueting scene for his daughter, whose name is lost.[25]

There were several other soldiers in the auxiliary units with special responsibilities. A *custos armorum* is attested at Housesteads, recorded on a badly damaged inscription, but the shape of the stone and enough of the text survives to attest that it was an altar, dedicated to Mars and the goddess Victory, appropriate deities for a guardian of the armoury to worship.[26] Some soldiers from legions and auxiliary units could be chosen for special tasks and given the title *beneficiarius*. These men could serve the governor of a province, or a legionary legate, or the commander of an auxiliary unit, and they ranked in seniority according to the rank of the officer they served. Several *beneficiarii consularis* working for the consular, meaning the provincial governor, are recorded at forts in the Wall zone, but they were probably not stationed permanently at the forts where they are attested, and they were probably legionaries. At Housesteads a tombstone found in the early eighteenth century, drawn and recorded before it was lost, attests Hurmius, son of Leubasnus, a soldier in *cohors I Tungrorum*, who may have been a *beneficiarius* of the *praefectus*, but the interpretation depends on the accuracy of the eighteenth-century drawing and the letters BE at the beginning of the sixth line. The name Leubasnus is well attested in the Rhineland and in the province of Belgica, so this soldier was probably of Tungrian origin.[27]

Musicians playing different kinds of trumpets were necessary in all units. The three main trumpets commonly used in the Roman army were the *tuba*, *cornu* and *bucina*. The *tuba* was a straight trumpet, played by the *tubicen*, while the *cornu*, played by the *cornicen*, was an almost circular instrument that wrapped around the player's arm and shoulder, with a bar across the middle for grip. Very little is known about the *bucina*, but it was probably used in ceremonials and to give signals in camp, played by the *bucinator*. From literary sources it is known that the Romans used these instruments to sound reveille or cockcrow, and for the changing of the guard when in camps or forts. In the Wall zone, a *cornicen* is attested at Vindolanda, and a soldier called Longinus, *bucinator* of *cohors I Batavorum* at Carrawburgh, is known from his tombstone.[28]

The Roman army was a bureaucratic organisation, and paperwork was large-scale and highly sophisticated, as attested by the records found at Vindolanda and Carlisle in the Wall zone, and by collections of papyri from hot, dry places such as Syria and Egypt. A soldier with a good standard of literacy would soon find employment in the clerical headquarters, and therefore be able to avoid the heavy work that the ordinary soldiers had to endure. Some soldiers probably spent most of their military service in writing reports and filing records, but they trained and campaigned with the other soldiers when necessary. Perhaps they were subject to jokes about ink-stained fingers when training with their colleagues.

The clerical work which constituted such a large part of military life was supervised by *cornicularii* who are attested in all kinds of units, and in the offices of the provincial governors. The title is derived from the *cornu*, or small horn, which used to be attached to their helmets. These men would be in charge of the clerical staff working in the headquarters, attending to all the records of their unit, including financial accounts, unit records such as strength reports and duty rosters, and all correspondence. A *cornicularius* called Severus is attested in the Vindolanda tablets, in a letter concerning the price of food for the celebration of the Saturnalia, which was held 17 to 23 December.[29] Clerks called *librarii* are attested in military units, probably of differing grades according to their functions. The *librarius horreorum* kept a tally of the grain and other food stocks received into the granaries, and the amounts that were distributed from them, together with their recipients. A detailed list from Vindolanda is devoted entirely to the amounts of wheat issued from the stores, but there is no mention of a *librarius horreorum* or any other person. The list is arranged by date and then by recipients, followed by the amounts of wheat, recorded as numbers of *modii*.[30] The *modius* was the standard measure for grain, perhaps doled out in metal vessels such as the one found at Carvoran, with a marker incised round the top, somewhat similar to modern pint glasses in pubs. Another clerical officer was the *librarius depositorum*, who kept the accounts of the soldiers' savings, which they were encouraged to deduct from their pay, and it seems that the men could take money out from time to time, so strict recording of all these transactions would be vital, or fisticuffs could ensue. There were other *librarii* in all military units, and it is known from an inscription from Italy that they were *immunes*, excused from normal fatigues, since Septimius Licinius, a soldier of *II Parthica* at Albano, is specifically listed as *immunis librarius* on the tombstone that he set up for his son, who died aged three years, four months and twenty-four days.[31] In the Wall zone, Titus Tertinius was a *librarius* who dedicated an altar to the goddess Minerva at Corbridge, but he does not record the unit he served in, or whether he belonged to the staff of an official.[32] In the later second century a new clerical official appears, called an *actarius*, sometimes rendered as *actuarius*, who was responsible for keeping the records of the corn supply, and may have superceded the *librarius horreorum*, or the two posts could have existed side by side with slightly different responsibilities. The *actarius* may have kept the daily service records for the men, as well as those concerning the corn supply. An *actarius* of *XX Valeria Victrix*, Gaius Valerius Justus, is commemorated at Chester on a tombstone erected by his wife, Cocceia Irene, and an auxiliary soldier called Julius Gr...nus was *actarius* of *cohors I Breucorum* at Ebchester.[33]

The military records compiled and filed by the clerical staff show that soldiers were usually kept busy on many different tasks, many of them concerned with record-keeping in the fort, but one of the most revealing aspects is the fact that many of the men did not spend all their time inside their forts. Papyrus records from the east attest to short- and long-term absences from various units, and the Vindolanda tablets also show that a large proportion of the men, up to one third of the total complement, were away from the fort at times. In a strength report of *cohors I Tungrorum* five centurions and 456 soldiers were listed as absent, 337 of whom were at Coria, generally agreed to be the name for Corbridge, rather than the previous name of Corstopitum. Six men and a centurion were outside the province, but it is not specified where, and nine soldiers and a centurion had been sent to Gaul. Eleven soldiers and perhaps a centurion had gone to an unknown destination, probably York, to collect pay (*stipendium*). Only 296 men out of a total of 752 were present at the fort, and of these, thirty-one men were sick, ten of them suffering from inflammation of the eyes.[34] Eye problems were very common, judging by the number of oculists' stamps that have been found on archaeological sites. These items were usually made of stone, rectangular in shape, with lettering in mirror image round the narrow edges, used for stamping the name of the oculist and details of the particular remedy on sticks or cakes of ointments, usually diluted for use.[35]

Soldiers could be sent away from their forts to man fortlets, or watchtowers where appropriate, to patrol certain areas, or to carry out police work and guard duty, sometimes in civilian contexts, for instance to stand guard at markets. Many of the tasks outside the forts were concerned with administration of the unit, which had to be more or less self-sufficient and efficiently organised, with regard to food, fuel, equipment, clothing and a host of other materials, within the framework of the central administration. Some of these items were obtained not only outside the fort, but outside the province, demonstrating that there was contact with other parts of the Empire. In one instance, nothing to do with Hadrian's Wall but illustrative of how widespread the military contacts were between provinces, in 138, the first year of the reign of Antoninus Pius, the Prefect of Egypt issued strict instructions to the weavers of the village of Philadelphia regarding the manufacture of white tunics, cloaks and blankets of specified dimension and weights, all of which had been ordered for the troops in Cappadocia.[36] The nine men from Vindolanda who were in Gaul may have been sent to collect supplies of some kind, probably clothing, on analogy with a papyrus record of *cohors I Hispanorum Veterana* stationed in Moesia, in which it is stated that an unknown number of soldiers were in Gaul to collect clothing (*in Gallia vestitum*).[37] In the same document an unknown number of men had also been sent to collect grain and horses.[38]

The duty rosters of various units of the Empire show that each day several soldiers would be assigned to duties inside the fort, guarding the gates, in the towers and on the ramparts, and at the headquarters building and probably the granaries. Some men were allocated to street duty, called *strigis* in the records, from *strigae* meaning streets.[39] The main function was probably to keep them clean and free of rubbish, or perhaps to watch for soldiers engaged in nefarious activities behind the barracks, whatever mischief they may have got up to during the day. Baths duty features largely in the daily rosters, without specific indication of what this entailed, but at Dura Europos in Syria, one soldier called Zebidas in the century of Nigrinus in *cohors XX Palmyrenorum equitata* was listed as *missus lig. balnei* indicating that he had been sent to collect wood (*lignum*) for the baths (*balneum*).[40] Staggering amounts of fuel would be needed in a fort for heating the rooms of the soldiers' baths and the commanders' private baths, and for cooking. The Vindolanda tablets record that on one occasion seven *denarii* were spent on the purchase of firewood.[41] Wood must have been stored somewhere, and there is evidence that the Romans used coal, but stores for fuel, either in special buildings or simple shelters to keep it dry, would be hard to identify in the archaeological record unless there were remains of such material. A spread of coal dust was found at Vindolanda near the commander's house of the second-period fort, probably associated with industrial activity.[42] Coal was also found in the blocked-up south passageway of the east gate at Housesteads, probably for the baths of the fourth century in building XV.[43] The use of coal at two forts at different periods implies that perhaps most forts used it as fuel, and that soldiers had to find outcrops, dig the coal out and transport it back to their respective forts. They probably did not mine for it, but would no doubt have appreciated the fort baths when they returned.

Terms and Conditions of Service from Recruitment to Retirement

The auxiliary units of the Wall zone were originally recruited from non-Romans in the various provinces, where people who were not Roman citizens were termed *peregrini*, which literally means foreigners. The provincial *peregrini* and the tribesmen outside the provinces were not allowed to enlist as legionaries, so they were recruited into the auxiliary units, and after serving for twenty-five years they qualified for honourable discharge and the grant of citizenship. If a cohort or an *ala* had performed exceptionally well in battle or on campaign, all the soldiers could be enfranchised, and their unit became a citizen cohort or *ala*, usually denoted on inscriptions by the initials *c.R.*, standing for *civium Romanorum*, expressed in the genitive case to match the ethnic name of the unit. Only the original enfranchised soldiers would be Roman citizens, and when they were discharged their replacements would be non-citizens, though the units retained their distinguished titles, denoting the honorary award. In 212 or 213, the distinction between citizens and non-citizens disappeared because the Emperor Caracalla extended Roman citizenship to all freeborn inhabitants of the Empire in 212, thus changing the face of military recruitment, and also broadening the base of taxpayers liable to contribute to the Imperial coffers.

Unit titles in the *auxilia* reflect the nationality of the original recruits, and if there were several units of the same nationality the title included a distinguishing number, for instance the third-century mixed infantry and cavalry units at Vindolanda and at South Shields, respectively *cohors IV Gallorum* and *cohors V Gallorum*, were obviously the fourth and fifth cohorts to be raised from Gauls. Some units were given additional titles from the family name of the reigning emperor, but Imperial names are not necessarily clues to the date when the units were raised, since the name could be awarded for distinguished conduct to units which had been in existence for some time, for instance units with the additional title *Antoniniana* or *Gordiana* had been rewarded by the emperors from Septimius Severus to Severus Alexander, or by Gordian III, which helps to date the inscriptions where these names are included.

New units were raised from time to time, often by coercion, especially after a war with tribesmen outside the Empire, when the terms of a peace treaty usually included a demand for a contribution of fixed numbers of men, either en masse as a one-off arrangement, or sometimes it was stipulated that troops were to be contributed on an annual basis. Marcus Aurelius famously sent 5,500 Sarmatians to Britain, but it is not known what happened to them. They do not appear to have been formed as regular auxiliary units, but a *numerus equitum Sarmatarum* is attested at Ribchester in the reign of Gordian III, between 238 and 244, and a *cuneus Sarmatarum* is attested at the same fort in the *Notitia*.[44] Conscription could be applied among any of the subject peoples of the Empire, whenever there was a need for soldiers. The procedure was called *dilectus*, the same term which was applied to recruiting the legionaries in the Republic. It derives from the verb *diligo*, meaning I choose or pick out. If the *dilectus* was carried out among the same people too often, it could cause rebellion. The Thracians made trouble in AD 26, not primarily because of the burden of recruitment, but because the young men were split up and sent away to other provinces.[45] The Thracians offered to negotiate, but probably to no avail. The Romans finally learned the hard way to avoid stationing recruits close to their homes, when the Batavians revolted in 69, led by Julius Civilis, a native Batavian leader who had been granted Roman citizenship. Thereafter the provincials or increasingly the tribesmen who were recruited were sent to distant provinces rather than being allowed to serve in the armies near their homes. The Britons who were recruited as *numeri*, probably from the northern regions, were sent to Germany to man the small forts of the frontier.

Large numbers of replacement troops would be needed to fill the gaps in all the legionary and auxiliary units in Roman Britain, but not much is known about the procedure for finding recruits and allocating them to existing units.[46] On a regular basis, men who had completed their twenty-five years of service would be discharged, but this was a factor that could have been prepared for in advance, since unit commanders and the clerical staff would have known how many men were due for retirement, and could apply for new recruits accordingly. Other vacancies would occur unexpectedly, especially when wars were fought and casualties mounted. There would also have been deaths from accidents and diseases. The natural wastage rate would also include desertion, which was not unknown in the army, and sometimes men who had misbehaved could be dishonourably discharged. There may have been arguments among soldiers that escalated into murder. After all, in one of the houses of the *vicus* outside the fort at Housesteads, two skeletons were found lying on the original floor, successfully concealed for centuries under a new floor that had been laid out on top of them. One body was that of a man with the point of a knife in his ribs, and the other skeleton was considered to be that of a female.[47] It is not known if the man was a serving soldier, but if he was, the *signifer* of his century would have to amend his records, and a clerk in the headquarters would have to note on the next strength report that the man had gone AWOL, and probably everyone thought that he had run off with the woman in question. After this anecdotal diversion, it has to be acknowledged that incidents such as these were probably rare and would not involve large losses.

Recruitment of soldiers was probably on a local and also on a wider basis, not restricted to any single area. Local recruitment is still considered to be the source of the majority of recruits, though there were other sources as well. Some natives were recruited to fill gaps in the existing auxiliary units in Britain, and there were Britons in the army of Gnaeus Julius Agricola when he fought the battle of Mons Graupius.[48] An undated tombstone found near Mumrills on the Antonine Wall records a Brigantian tribesman, Nectovelius, son of Vindex, in *cohors II Thracum* which was originally raised in Thrace.[49] Precisely how local recruitment worked is not clear. Conscription could have been applied, which may be what was happening when a census was carried out among the Anavionenses at the turn of the first and second centuries.[50] In cases like this hypothetical one there may have been a round-up of tribesmen to be sent to other provinces. Volunteers may have turned up occasionally at the Wall forts, especially from the established *vici* of the later second and third centuries, where sons of soldiers may have wanted to join the local unit. In this case the soldiers were probably allowed to recommend their sons to the fort commander, but were the commanders entitled to add recruits to their units without first approaching the governor?[51] Was there a central or a regional area where recruits were subjected to *probatio* by specially appointed officers and then sent on to training depots, or could training be carried out at the forts? Were volunteers necessarily assigned to the unit that they wished to join or were they sent to units which had gaps to be filled?

It is generally considered that specialist units such as the archers of the *cohors Hamiorum sagittariorum*, which was based at Carvoran until the third century, continued to recruit from their original homelands, where young men were trained in their specialist skills and arrived as effective archers in their units stationed in other provinces. This saved the time and effort involved in training local recruits in the art of using their bows and arrows. But these specialist units may not have been the only ones which kept up their links with their original homelands. It is possible that in addition to obtaining recruits from among the local population around the forts, some auxiliary units in Britain received replacements from the original recruitment areas. In 2006 an important inscription was found at Vindolanda, which once formed the pediment for a statue, but had been reused, after considerable weathering, as part of a drain. There is no date on the inscription itself but the excavators considered that it belonged to the third century. The text reads *Cives Galli de Gallia concordesque Britanni*, recording native Gauls as well as Britons in the same unit, attesting to local recruitment and also continued recruitment from the homelands of the Gauls, about a century and a half after *cohors IV Gallorum equitata* came to Britain.[52] The units of Astures from Spain may also have maintained contacts with their homes, and at Chesters where *ala II Asturum* was based, the Latin name for the fort, Cilurnum, has been linked with the Spanish tribe of the Cilurgini.[53]

New recruits had to be inspected and trained before they could be sent to their units. The initial inspection of recruits was called the *probatio*. Ideally potential soldiers should be intelligent as well as physically fit. There was usually a height qualification, and naturally all soldiers had to have sound limbs and good eyesight. If a recruit passed these tests, he was sent for training for four months. Much of the information concerning training comes from the late Roman author Vegetius, whose main aim was to explain what should be happening in the army of his own day, so some of what he says was perhaps not always carried out, but his work is at least based on common sense. According to this author, the initial training lasted for four months.[54] Recruits were taught how to handle their weapons and practised arms drill, and how to use their shields to deflect blows and missile weapons by holding them at an angle. Wooden weapons and shields were used in basic infantry training, twice the weight of ordinary weapons, so that the men would develop the muscle power to wield their real weapons to greater effect.[55] Learning how to dig ditches and

erect defences were important skills, and recruits would devote
considerable time and energy to learning the art, as attested by
an inscription from Vindolanda, which had fallen from the fort
wall near the west gate, recording building work by a group of
tirones probati or recruits who had been approved.[56] Cavalrymen
probably trained as infantry at first, and went on to specific
training to learn how to mount and dismount, for which purpose
they practised on wooden horses. After they had learned the basics
using the wooden horses, recruits probably graduated to real
horses which had already been schooled and would not necessarily
be the mounts that would be assigned to them. They were taught
how to leap onto their horses from either side, first without arms
and armour and then fully equipped, and then they were taught
to do so while the horse was running. Vegetius emphasizes that
cavalrymen should always practise these movements, even if they
were long-serving soldiers.

During this four month training period unsuitable candidates
could be weeded out and sent home. In the case of tribesmen
levied en masse after a war and sent to a distant province, this
was probably not an option, so army instructors may have had no
option but to mould them into shape under strict discipline. If a
soldier passed all the preliminary tests and survived the training,
he was accepted into the army. The *sacramentum* or military oath
of loyalty to the emperor was administered before the new soldiers
were assigned to a unit. The wording for exactly what was pledged
has not survived, but on analogy with the oath that Republican
soldiers swore there may have been clauses about obeying the
generals and promising not to desert. Whatever the relevant words
were, they were spoken aloud by one of the soldiers, and though it
is not known for certain, it is likely that all the others said '*idem in
me*', meaning 'the same for me'.

Each new soldier was issued with an identification tag
(*signaculum*), kept in a leather pouch hung around his neck,
containing an inscribed lead tablet, and then he could be sent to
join his unit, with a travel allowance in cash, called the *viaticum*,
usually three gold *aurei*. New recruits, probably travelling together
in small groups, carried a letter of introduction from the governor's
office to the unit commander, testifying to the fact that the new
men had successfully undergone their *probationes*, followed by

a list of their names, their ages and the presence or absence of any distinguishing marks. The receiving clerk, probably the *cornicularius* or one of the staff working under him, would then enter the names and details into the unit records, and he would also file the letters, the procedure being called *in numeros referre*. When this was done, the recruits become soldiers, and they could be assigned to a century or a *turma* where the standard-bearer would probably add their names and details to his records. The new soldiers were now subject to the obligations, rights and privileges that their military service conferred on them.

One of the privileges was that the soldiers who had been entered on the records would be allowed to make a will. Since most of the men would be quite young, many of the recruits would have fathers still living. Technically this meant that all the property of the young man belonged to his father, but as soldiers who had been entered on the records, the men were considered independent, and could bequeath their savings and their property to their families. The existence of a will made it much easier to dispose legally of a soldier's property if he died or was killed.

While serving in the army, the soldiers who could read and write could hope to find a suitable niche in the clerical offices, but if a soldier was illiterate he would spend a lot of his time digging and doing heavy work, or boring work such as guard duty. On the other hand he would be paid three times a year and although money was docked before he even received it for food, clothing and equipment, he would probably have enough to eat and drink, his medical needs would be catered for if he fell ill or had an accident, and if he did not gamble all his pay away he would have some disposable income to spend on his days off.

Diet and Food Supply

Archaeological investigations, ancient literature and military records have provided much information about the food that soldiers ate. It has been claimed that the military presence stimulated provincial agriculture, providing an incentive to grow more crops than would normally have been necessary simply to feed the natives. In northern Britain it has been suggested that the highland zones, more notable today for stock-raising than for agriculture, could have produced more grain than hitherto imagined. Although the army would not have been able to produce enough to provide food for an entire unit all year round, the soldiers may have grown some of the food that they consumed. Legionary fortresses and auxiliary forts were surrounded by clearly demarcated lands that were owned and administered by the army, usually designated by the terms *prata* and *territorium*. Strictly interpreted, *prata* ought to refer to meadows, perhaps for grazing animals and for producing hay. Cavalry units may have let their horses out to graze, possibly on a rotational basis, and probably corralled within temporary fencing that would be hard to detect archaeologically. There were obviously some differences between the two terms *prata* and *territorium* as far as the army was concerned. The main point is that the military authorities owned lands, which they could use as they wished. An unnamed *ala* at Chester-le-Street used the fort *territorium* to bring in a water supply and build a bathhouse.[57] This shows that land owned by the military was not necessarily used for growing crops, though it remains a possibility. Tacitus refers to fields left empty for the use of the soldiers.[58] At Newstead in southern Scotland sickles were found inside the fort. They had been well used and repaired, suggesting that soldiers used them for harvesting crops grown round the fort.

Much of the documentation compiled by the army concerns the collection of food supplies. A papyrus record shows that an unknown number of soldiers from *cohors I Hispanorum Veterana equitata* in Moesia were sent across the Danube 'to defend the crops' (*ad annonam defendendam*), the reference to *annona* indicating that the crops had been requisitioned for the troops. Other soldiers from this unit were accompanied by a decurion at the grain ships, at some unspecified location on the Danube.[59]

Food was stored inside the forts in specially constructed granaries, usually sited next to the *principia* or headquarters building in the central range of the fort. In early forts granaries would usually be built of wood, leaving only a trace of their postholes, but the stone-built granaries are usually immediately recognisable from their ground plans. The Walls were reinforced by evenly spaced buttresses, and the stone-flagged floors were usually raised on pillars to facilitate the circulation of air and to prevent rats and mice from reaching the stores. It is not known whether the grain was stored in bins, or in sacks which could be stacked up on the floor, or laid on shelves. In the Vindolanda tablet dealing with amounts of wheat distributed to various soldiers, there is a reference to a barrel or cask (*cupa*) into which the writer of the document says he has put the wheat (*frumentum*) and he gave out some of the wheat in sacks (*folles*), which may have been made of leather.[60]

In the later Empire, payments to the army were made partly or wholly in rations instead of cash, under a system that is not fully understood, known as the *annona militaris*. Some scholars suggest that this could have begun as early as the reign of Trajan. A large part of the food supply of Rome was levied as a tax in kind administered by an equestrian with the title *Praefectus Annonae*, so it is possible that the system was extended or diverted to feed the army, but this remains hypothetical.

The military diet was diverse and well balanced. Grain was the basic foodstuff, including wheat and barley, but the latter was mostly fed to horses. Soldiers did eat barley bread on occasion, though it was sometimes used as a punishment ration. Fresh or salt pork formed a large part of daily fare, or alternatively ham and bacon, and there is evidence that domestic fowl were eaten. In the past it was believed that soldiers did not eat meat, but this has been disproved by archaeological finds of bones of various animals. An examination of the finds from thirty-three forts showed that the highest proportion of bones came from those of oxen, pig, sheep and red deer, followed by goat, roe deer, boar and hare.[61] Some of these species indicate that the ordinary provisions were supplemented by hunting, which is supported by the altar from Birdoswald set up to the god Silvanus by the hunters of Banna, and another altar to the same god set up by the prefect of the *ala Sebosiana*, giving thanks for having been able to hunt down a wild boar of remarkable fineness, which no one else had managed to bag.[62] There is evidence that the soldiers also ate a variety of vegetables, such as peas, beans, carrots and lentils. Fruit and nuts also featured in their diets. Freshwater and saltwater fish, and all kinds of seafoods could have been supplied by civilians. Some food could be bought on the open market either by individual soldiers or groups, for daily consumption or special events and festivals. A fragmentary letter from Vindolanda concerns the purchase of food in fairly large quantities, perhaps intended for a corporate event, including one hundred apples 'if you can find nice ones' and one or two hundred eggs, if they could be bought at a fair price.[63] A very important part of the diet was salt, from which the modern word salary derives. It would be used for preserving meat as well as flavouring food, and the horses or any other livestock that may have been kept close by the forts would need salt. The soldiers drank sour wine called *acetum* which could be mixed with water to produce a drink called *posca*, and in the northern provinces they also drank Celtic beer called *cervesa*, made from malted grain. Bowman provides a list of the foodstuffs mentioned in the Vindolanda tablets, showing the immense variety of food that was consumed at one single fort over a relatively short period of time.[64] The subtext implied by this list suggests the vast organization that was required to provision one auxiliary unit.

As well as provisioning the men, supplies would be needed for the animals of the unit. Infantry units would have some horses for the officers and draught animals for transport. The possibility that these were put out to graze on military land around the forts has been mentioned above, but hay and straw would be required for cavalry horses all year round. Cavalrymen received an allowance for fodder. Barley and oats were fed to horses, but these foods are fattening, so the amounts provided must be tailored to suit the work that the horse is expected to perform. The staple food was probably oats, remains of which have been found at Castlecary on the Antonine Wall, and at Birrens. Both these forts housed a part-mounted unit.[65] It is suggested that the presence of Roman cavalry stimulated the cultivation of oats, a crop which is suited to the wetter and colder climate of the north of England and Scotland.[66]

Arms, Armour and Clothing

There is no evidence that there was ever a standard military uniform at any period over the whole Empire. Most authors agree that it was the leather belt or *cingulum* more than anything else that proclaimed the wearer as a soldier, though the term is not attested before the third century. Variations include *cingulum militare*, or *cingulum militiae*. The belt was both functional and decorative, in that metal plates were attached to it, and various hooks and frogs to which the dagger and initially the sword would be attached, though later on the sword was worn on a baldric over one shoulder. An important feature was that mail armour was usually hitched up over the belt, thus relieving the wearer's shoulders of the full weight. In the early Empire, soldiers are generally depicted on their tombstones wearing two belts crossed at an angle over the hips, but later the fashion was for only one belt, perhaps because this was more practical and comfortable when segmented armour was introduced.

There are very few archaeological finds of equipment which indisputably belonged to auxiliaries rather than legionaries, so information about auxiliary arms and armour is derived mostly from depictions on tombstones, which would have been painted to show the finer lines that cannot be sculpted. For protection, auxiliary infantry usually carried an oval shield or *scutum*, with a central boss, usually flat or only slightly curved. There are variations in auxiliary shields, but the oval version is the most common representation. On Trajan's column and the column of Marcus Aurelius, auxiliaries are shown with helmets resembling legionary examples. The neck guards tend to be shorter, at least in the artistic representations. Their armour is most commonly shown as mail or scale tunics, with short sleeves, extending at least to the hips. Mail armour, or *lorica hamata*, was made from iron or bronze rings, each passed through two rings above and two rings below. There were variations in ring size, and some mail was made of alternate rows of solid rings and wire with the flattened ends riveted together. Scale armour or *lorica squamata* was made of small plates of iron or bronze, with two holes at the top where it would be stitched to the leather or linen backing, and two holes at each side where the scales were attached to each other. There is some debate about whether or not the auxiliaries wore *lorica segmentata* like the legionaries. This arises because several examples of such armour have been found inside auxiliary forts. The finest example of *lorica segmentata* was found at Corbridge and is on display in the museum, together with a replica. There are no representations of auxiliaries on monuments or tombstones, or any other art form, showing auxiliaries wearing this type of armour.

The main weapon of auxiliary infantry was the spear, in a variety of styles. The soldiers usually carried more than one spear, clutched in the left hand with the shield. The number of spears carried by each man indicates that they were for throwing. The *lancea* was a spear with a leaf-shaped head, sometimes with very elongated points, which presumably enhanced penetration. The translation as lance is tempting but not strictly accurate. Whereas the legionaries armed with the *pilum* would throw their javelins from a distance and then engage in close combat with the sword, the auxiliaries probably used a range of different types of spear in a variety of ways, though they were armed with swords, both the short sword or *gladius*, usually worn on the right, and from the second century they also used the long sword called the *spatha*, worn on the left. There were auxiliary units of archers (*sagittarii*), both infantry and mounted, like the Hamian archers at Carvoran. Bows were elaborate in construction, known as composite bows because they were made of different types of materials glued together and held with bindings. When not in use the bow was unstrung, and to restring it the archer used his leg to bend it until the string could be attached. Bows and bowstrings were particularly susceptible to damp weather, and archers could be put out of action in rain storms. Usually the only surviving evidence in the archaeological record for bows consists of the antler tips, several of which have been found in Britain. Arrowheads were usually made of iron, often triangular in cross section. They were either socketed or tanged and the shafts were most commonly of reeds, pine or hazel. Shafts and fletchings have been preserved only in the eastern provinces where the climate is dry, but some examples of arrowheads with wood still attached have been found at Caerleon, Corbridge and Housesteads, where a large number of tanged, triangular-bladed heads were found in the headquarters building, underneath stone tiles which had fallen from the roof.[67]

The Roman army was equipped with artillery known as *catapultae*, later called *ballistae*, of varying sizes, some of which shot stones and others iron bolts. Early examples were made of wood, with the torsion springs encased in the wooden frame, protruding at the top and bottom of the frame on metal washers. Operators had to aim at the target over the top of the frame and then calculate the elevation. These were replaced by metal frames which did away with the cumbersome wooden ones, though the slider was probably still made of or lined with wood. The torsion springs were moved further apart, with a metal strut joining them at the top with an arch in the centre, positioned over the slider where the bolt was placed. This enabled operators to frame the target and greatly simplified siting. Metal frames had advantages over wood because the metal resists warping in humid conditions, and metal joints have greater shock resistance when shooting. One type of ballista could be mounted on carts drawn by mules, and depictions of these can be seen on Trajan's column. The third-century *ballistaria* at High Rochester may have been intended for lighter machines such as these. Soldiers were also trained to throw stones, which serve very well as missile weapons, so rounded stones on military sites are not always connected with artillery machines.[68]

Cavalrymen used a long sword called a *spatha*, ranging in length from twenty-six inches to thirty-six inches. It was used for slashing, worn on the right side in the early Empire, and on the left from the second century onwards, when the infantry units also started to use the *spatha*, so discoveries of long swords without any other cavalry gear does not automatically indicate the presence of horsemen. Spears for throwing or thrusting were about six feet long, held overarm for throwing or for stabbing downwards, or underarm for use as a shock weapon. An even longer weapon was the *contus*, probably adopted from the Sarmatian tribesmen of the Danube area. This was a much heavier spear about twelve feet long, which had to be held with both hands for use as a shock weapon, which meant that the *contarii* could not use a shield.

Mounted archers probably used bows that were shorter than those of the infantry, who had the advantage of standing still and could therefore use longer bows with heavier arrows. Horse archers had to learn how to fire arrows to the left or the right of the horse, and sometimes to the rear, the famous Parthian shot. Since they had to use both hands to fire arrows they did not usually carry a shield, but probably had a sword. They may have attached the ends of the reins to a strap worn on the ring finger of their right hands, so that after using the bow and arrow they could pick up the reins quickly. Cavalrymen wore mail or scale body armour, usually in the form of a short-sleeved shirt, sometimes with slits to allow the man to sit astride his horse, and they also wore trousers, which reached just below the knee. Helmets are not always shown on cavalry tombstones, but some examples have been found, and archaeologists have detected a gradual evolution giving greater protection to the face. The earlier helmets had a bowl-shaped head piece, with hinged cheek pieces but only a short neck flange and initially no reinforcement across the forehead, which seems to have been adopted by the second century. By the later second century the cheek pieces were larger, extending further round the face leaving only the eyes, nose and mouth visible. Highly elaborate helmets and armour have been discovered, usually described as sports armour, used for ceremonials and tournaments.

A variety of different styles of cavalry shields are depicted in sculptures, including rectangular, hexagonal, round and oval shapes. By the third century it is thought that round shields became more common, even though an oval shield would afford greater protection for the rider from his lower legs to his shoulder. The shields were generally made of wooden strips or planks held together by glue, with binding of metal or hide round the edge. There was a hole in the centre of the shield, with the *umbo* made of metal on the outside to accommodate the soldier's left hand, and the grip on the inside made of wood or metal, sometimes extending a long way across the hole for extra strength.

The most important pieces of equipment for the horses were the bridle and bit and the saddle, to enable the rider to stay on the horse's back and control it with knee and leg movements. The Romans did not use stirrups. The leather sections of the bridle have not survived in the archaeological record, but there are many depictions of horses on tombstones and sculptures which show the details. Where the strap-work joined together on the bridles and other parts of the harness there were usually metal discs called *phalerae*. These are also shown on sculptures, and several examples have survived along with the different styles of bits. The mouthpiece of the bit could be a solid bar or a two-section jointed bar with rings on either end to attach the reins. The Romans used more severe curb bits, allowing for greater control of the horse. These had a U-shaped bar in the horse's mouth, with another bar or chain running under the animal's chin. An example of this kind of bit was found at Newstead in lowland Scotland.

The shape of Roman cavalry saddles has been determined from finds of leather at Vindolanda, and at Valkenberg in the Netherlands. The saddle had two upright horns at the rear to clasp the rider's buttocks, and two angled horns at the front which curved inwards over the rider's thighs. On sculptural representations the horns at the rear are often visible, but at the front the horns are usually obscured by other details. Saddles have been reconstructed using two different methods, one with a wooden frame or tree, and another with the same shape but simply tightly stuffed, with no frame. It is considered more likely that saddles were supported by a wooden frame, and though no conclusive proof of the existence of such a frame has been found, analysis of the leather covers shows that stretch marks exist, indicating where the leather was pulled over the horns. Bronze plates in the shape of the horns were discovered at Newstead, which were initially thought to have been used as templates for the shaping of the horns, but since names were inscribed by lines of punch marks on the insides of the plates, it is now thought that the metal pieces were placed over the wooden tree and then covered by the leather. The identification of the owner of the saddle would help the saddlers who might have to undertake repairs. The saddle was fitted to the rider as far as possible, but not necessarily to the horse, as modern saddles are. There were straps from the saddle to the rear, passing under the horse's tail, and straps extending forwards around the horse's breast. A thick blanket, or a fur or sheepskin protected the horse's back. Protection for the horse also comprised the chamfron, the peytral and armoured barding. The chamfrons covered the horse's face, with ear guards and holes for the eyes. They were usually made of leather, often decorated with studs. Some were made of metal, and it is thought that these items may have been reserved for the tournaments or *hippika gymnasia*, not that there was anything to stop a cavalryman from using these in combat. The peytral made of leather was suspended from the harness around the horse's chest and may have afforded some protection, though its purpose may have been to prevent the metal pendants of the harness from constantly banging against the horse as it moved. Barding was obviously intended to protect the body of the horse, shaped much like modern winter coats draped over the horse's back to hang down at the sides.

Apart from their armour the soldiers obviously required ordinary clothing, such as tunics and cloaks. Tunics were made of wool or linen, formed from two squares or rectangles of cloth sewn together with holes left for the head and arms. They may have been dyed in various colours, but there is hardly any evidence for this, and it was stipulated that the tunics made in the Egyptian workshops for the army in Cappadocia should be white. It is generally agreed that military tunics differed from civilian versions in that they were actually longer but were worn hitched up over the belt and therefore appeared shorter. Some relief sculptures show the tunics hitched up at both sides, forming a curved skirt at the front and presumably the back. Sleeves were mostly worn short, but evidence from some cavalry tombs shows that at least some of the cavalrymen wore long-sleeved tunics, and long sleeves became more common for all soldiers from the third century onwards. Some tunics were worn off one shoulder, with a split down the back and perhaps with the loose material knotted, but this would not be comfortable with armour on top, so it was perhaps just an arrangement that freed up the arms when working, for instance felling trees and chopping wood.

Cloaks fall into three main categories. The *sagum* was a simple square draped around the wearer and fastened with a brooch on the right shoulder, leaving the sword arm free. It was probably made of wool, and could be decorated with a fringe. Another type of cloak was the *paenula*, which was more like a poncho, perhaps oval in shape and put on over the head, with a split down the front joined by toggles or buttons, and sometimes equipped with a hood. This would not be a specifically military garment since its practicality would appeal to everyone who had to work in the open air in inclement weather. Similarly the *byrrus* or *birrus* was not necessarily a purely military item, but at least one soldier is on record asking his relatives to send one. The relief sculpture of the three *Genii Cucullati* at Housesteads gives some idea of what these cloaks looked like, all enveloping, reaching to the ankles, with a hood as an integral part of the garment. In the later third century the *birrus Britannicus* was a valued British export, specifically assigned a maximum price in Diocletian's Edict on Prices in AD 301. Its waterproof qualities perhaps appealed to the soldiers as well as the civilians of the northern provinces, and soldiers were probably allowed to wear clothes that kept them warm and dry even if they were not regulation issue. Military officers wore a more decorative cloak called the *paludamentum*, draped over the left shoulder and wound round the left arm. The portrait of Marcus Favonius Facilis, centurion of *legio XX* at Colchester, shows this type of cloak quite clearly. The *paludamentum* was associated more and more with the emperors after the first century AD.

Soldiers' boots (*caligae*) are almost as distinctive as military belts, as attested by the terminology of the military records, where the number of soldiers present is often listed as *caligati*. There are fortunately enough extant examples to elucidate all the details of how the boots were made. The uppers looked more like modern sandals, being cut away to form the equivalent of straps which could be laced together at the front to fit most sizes of foot. The uppers, the insoles and the outer soles were nailed together with studs arranged in patterns that prefigure modern training shoes, and the studs will have helped to maintain grip in turf and rough terrain. In order to keep warm, the soldiers wore socks (*udones*), which probably had no toes or heels. One of the Vindolanda letters concerns the despatch of *udones*, and also underpants (*subligares*) which were worn under the tunic.[69] At Vindolanda there is good evidence for the supply of clothing for the ordinary soldiers and for the officers, and remains of textiles have been found in a room on the praetorium of the third-period fort.[70]

Medical Services

Roman forts and fortresses usually contained a building identified by archaeologists as a hospital or *valetudinarium*, such as the courtyard building at Housesteads. The hospital at Wallsend was added to the fort about 180, the successor of a timber building that may or may not have been dedicated to the same purpose. The military hospitals were usually courtyard buildings with small light and airy cubicles opening off the open central area, sometimes with a veranda running all round the interior, and both the Housesteads and the Wallsend hospitals had their own latrines.[71] It should be noted that not all the buildings on this courtyard plan are necessarily hospitals. In some cases, buildings inside forts that look like hospitals may actually be workshops (*fabricae*), which had a courtyard in the centre and small rooms arranged all around it to provide light and air for the metalsmiths and woodworkers who used them.

Each unit would have employed a medical team, with staff called *medici*. At the fort at Binchester, an altar to Aesculapius, the god of healing and to Salus, an Italian goddess of health, was dedicated by Marcus Aurelius ... ocomas, for the well-being of *ala Vettonum*. Only the letters ME define him as a *medicus*, but his appropriate choice of deities supports the identification.[72] The tombstone of Anicius Ingenuus, a *medicus ordinarius* who died aged twenty-five, was found near Housesteads.[73] It is not certain whether Anicius as *ordinarius* was an ordinary soldier, or possessed officer status, perhaps equal in rank to a centurion. There seems to have been a distinction between the *miles medicus* and the *medicus ordinarius*, but all *medici* may simply have been *immunes*, soldiers with special skills, except that some *medici* in the fleets were *duplicarii* and therefore officers. Assisting the *medici* there were the *optiones valetudinarii*, who were *immunes* according to Tarrutienus' list in the *Digest*. Other soldiers called *capsarii* may have been responsible for dressing wounds, since the title *capsarius* is derived from the box (*capsa*) that contained bandages, but some authors say that the box was for scrolls and the *capsarii* may have been clerical assistants. The soldier shown on Trajan's Column bandaging the leg of a wounded man is usually interpreted as a *capsarius*. The medical staff went on campaign with their units. In his book on laying out a temporary camp, Hyginus mentions a hospital tent, recommending that it should be placed where convalescent soldiers could find peace and quiet.[74]

The *medici* would probably have learned their skills in civilian contexts and then joined the army, but it is also possible that the army trained its own personnel. There were medical manuals that would aid the teaching process, one of the best known being that of Aulus Cornelius Celsus who wrote his *De Medicina* in the early first century AD, relying heavily on Greek works. He writes about diseases, pharmacology, therapy and surgery. Some of his cures for diseases could only have increased the mortality rate, and it is not certain whether the Romans fully understood contagion and the efficacy of isolation of patients. In dealing with wounds, however, Celsus either had valid experience of his own or had gained knowledge from someone who had seen medical service in the wars. He writes in detail about how to remove various types of missile weapons, with notes about how to stop excessive bleeding of wounds and what to do to prevent inflammation; if all else fails he explains how to amputate limbs. Roman medical and surgical instruments, looking startlingly like modern versions, have been found at several sites, especially in the legionary fortresses. From Neuss there are needles, scalpels, probes and spatulas, and from the fortress at Aquincum in Hungary there are scissors and forceps, leg splints and a lancing fork.

Pharmacology consisted mainly of the use of herbs. Medicinal plants have been found on military sites, and it has been suggested that the courtyards of the military hospitals may have been laid out as gardens where specific herbs could be grown. One of the best ways of securing good health in the army derived from cleanliness. There were elaborate bathing establishments attached to each fort and fortress, and time was clearly allowed for bathing, which probably became a prolonged leisurely affair involving dice games and gambling. Altars to Fortuna are often found in bath houses. Sick and wounded soldiers in the hospitals may have had their own baths, since it is thought that the hospital at the fortress at Inchtuthil in Scotland contained a bathroom. There were also kitchens in the hospitals where perhaps special foods were prepared. Celsus stresses the importance of diet in the treatment of the sick, enumerating those foods which were thought to be the most easily digested. In one of the rooms in the hospital at Neuss excavators found remains of eggs, peas, lentils and shellfish, all of which are on Celsus' list. The importance of allowing sufficient time for convalescence was recognised, and some soldiers in Britain convalesced at the spa and temple complex at Bath in Somerset.

Pay

The rate of pay of the auxiliary troops is a perennial problem for modern historians. It is deduced from Hadrian's address to the troops of Numidia that auxiliary cavalrymen were paid more than the auxiliary infantry, so on this premise elaborate pay scales have been reconstructed that usually show three basic rates, with the auxiliary infantry as the lowest on the scale, followed by the legionaries and the cavalrymen of a *cohors equitata*, and finally at the top of the scale, the cavalry of the *alae*. There are some different permutations of these rates, none of which can be backed up by firm evidence. More recently Alston argued for parity between legionary and auxiliary pay on the premise that when regular pay was instituted for auxiliary troops, only the standard rates for infantry and cavalry would have been applied, cavalrymen being paid more because they had to feed and maintain their horses, so there was no net gain for the use of the soldiers themselves.[75] The junior officers in auxiliary units were paid at double and one and a half times the normal rate, indicated by their respective labels *duplicarii* and *sesquiplicarii*, but the lack of precision as to what exactly *was* the normal rate hampers any calculation of the likely figures represented by these multiples. Pay scales for auxiliary centurions and decurions are not known.

The evidence is irritatingly confusing, especially in the case of two Roman citizen soldiers from Nicopolis in Egypt, Quintus Julius Proculus and Gaius Valerius Germanus, who were paid in Greek *drachmae*, the currency in use at Nicopolis. The records ought to be quite straightforward and uncomplicated, except for the annoying factor that in each of the three instalments on record, Proculus and Germanus were paid less than the seventy-five *denarii* that legionaries would have earned. So were they legionaries?[76] One suggestion is that the men were charged a small amount for converting *denarii* into *drachmae*. Another suggestion is that they were auxiliaries, earning slightly less than legionaries, but the question is, were they auxiliary infantry or cavalry? They were both charged ten *drachmae* for hay in each of the three instalments, contributing to the theory that they had horses to feed. The fascinating detail of the pay of these two soldiers cannot be broadly applied to either the legionary or auxiliary forces until it is certain whether they were ordinary legionaries, legionary cavalry, auxiliary infantry, or auxiliary cavalry. One fine day another papyrus may be discovered, detailing pay and deductions like those for Proculus and Germanus, but this time complete with the name of an auxiliary unit.

Despite the fact that this papyrus cannot solve the problem of differential or equal pay scales between legionaries and auxiliaries, the information is still important because it reveals how the records were kept and how deductions were taken from each man's pay. On each of the three paydays the two soldiers were charged eighty *drachmae* for food (*in victum*), twelve *drachmae* for boots and socks or leggings (*caligas fascias*), and ten *drachmae* for hay (*faenaria*). It has been suggested that the hay should be interpreted as bedding for the men, despite the fact that the Romans were perfectly capable of making stuffed mattresses. It is worth pointing out that the deductions for hay were always listed first, before the food for the soldiers, so at a pinch it could be said that the two food items, for the horse and for the man, were classified together, and therefore the two men were cavalry. The jury is still out on this question. There were other deductions from each of the three instalments, the first one in January being twenty *drachmae* for the camp Saturnalia, possibly a mess bill for the holiday celebrations held in the previous December. From the second instalment, both soldiers paid out four *drachmae* to the standards (*ad signum*), which may have been a contribution to the burial fund which was looked after by the standard-bearers, and on the third payday the two men were charged 145 and a half *drachmae* for clothing. Since there are no comparable records revealing such minute detail, it is impossible to say whether this was typical of all units in all provinces.

As already mentioned, there was a savings bank system where the soldiers could deposit money, though the amounts were probably paper figures rather than actual cash, recorded by the *librarii depositorum*. When the soldiers were due to retire and needed to withdraw their savings, the final totals would be calculated and if there was insufficient money in the fort strongroom to cover the payments, then the sums would be requested from the procurator, who was responsible for military pay. The Roman clerical assistants would keep at least two sets of financial records, since their accounts were sent to the procurator on a regular basis.

After the standard deductions from their wages soldiers still had some disposable cash, some of which might have been lost in gambling, probably at the baths, where altars to Fortuna have commonly been found, and gaming boards with counters.

Alternatively there was the *vicus* outside the fort where there would be taverns and most probably houses of ill repute, to phrase it delicately, where soldiers could have had a good time in their off-duty periods and the residents made a profit. Extra food supplies were probably purchased by soldiers, not necessarily solely from the *vicus*, but from small farmers in native settlements which are attested in the area in the Roman period. The *vici* of the early years of the Wall do not seem to have clustered around the forts, so it is uncertain if civilians settled near to the military establishments, but after the abandonment of the Antonine Wall, the villages grew up close to the forts, surviving until the late third century, when for some of them at least, abandonment came quite rapidly.

Holidays and Periods of Leave

The Romans did not have weekends and statutory periods of annual holiday, but they celebrated a large number of festivals throughout the year, including the most important Roman state festivals and ceremonies. The most detailed evidence concerning festivals derives from the *Feriale Duranum*, the calendar of events concerning one unit, *cohors XX Palmyrenorum* at Dura-Europos in Syria in the early third century AD.[77] The festivals listed in this document were probably celebrated in all the provinces. While worship of local gods was not generally banned, this was probably not included in the annual celebrations, but could be left to personal discretion.

The official Roman state festivals observed by the army included the annual sacrifices and ceremonies in honour of the chief gods, Jupiter, Juno and Minerva, on 3 January. It was customary to sacrifice an ox to Jupiter, a cow to Juno and another cow to Minerva. A series of altars from the parade ground of the fort at Maryport in north-west England may be related to this ceremony. Of the several altars found there, seventeen were dedicated 'to Jupiter Best and Greatest' (in Latin, *Iovi Optimo Maximo*, abbreviated to I.O.M.). Two auxiliary units feature on the altars, *cohors I Baetasiorum c.R.* and *cohors I Hispanorum equitata*, so it cannot be said that the practice was limited to only one occupying unit. The dedicators were usually the commanding officers, acting on behalf of their cohorts, signifying that this was a corporate ceremony, and since there are so many altars of this type, it was probably an annual event. It used to be thought that the previous year's altar was ceremonially buried, and a new one set up, but the truth is much more mundane in that the stones were used as foundations.

The purely military observances included elaborate ceremonies on 7 January, the official day of *honesta missio*, when the time-served veterans were honourably discharged. If this major event in a soldier's life went unmarked, the incentive to serve what was essentially a hard task master would be considerably diminished, so it was in the army's own interest to make much of this festival. On 10 and 31 May the military standards were decorated in a ceremony called *rosaliae signorum*. These ceremonies would serve to enhance unit *esprit de corps*, as well as emphasising *Romanitas* and the sense of belonging to a larger society than the immediate military environment.

Soldiers of the Roman army could arrange with their officers to be released from fatigues and normal duties for a period of leave, usually accompanied by cash payments to influence the officer's decision. The writing tablets from Vindolanda contain a batch of letters requesting leave (*commeatus*), six of the letters being addressed to the same commander, Cerialis. The majority adopt the same formula, expressing the hope that the commander holds the soldier worthy to be granted leave. These are not simply requests to be relieved of duties, but to go away to another place, which in three cases is actually named in the letter.[78]

Religion

In the Roman Empire there was little religious prejudice and soldiers were allowed to worship whichever gods they preferred. The problem with Christians was that they were reluctant to serve in the army, and would not willingly swear the oath of loyalty to the emperors. At the council of bishops held at Arles under Constantine I in 314, the ruling was made that allowed Christians to serve in the army in war or in peace, and soldiers who laid down their arms in peacetime risked excommunication. The Empire under Constantine and his successors was officially Christian so the military oath changed accordingly and by the time of Vegetius the recruits swore by God, Christ and the Holy Spirit, and by the majesty of the emperor, to perform what the emperor commanded, to brave death in the service of the state, and not to desert.

Inscriptions testify to the plethora of gods and goddesses who were worshipped in the Wall zone over the centuries. The religious festivals would dictate that the Roman pantheon should feature largely in the number of dedications made to the gods, the most important being Jupiter Optimus Maximus, Jupiter Best and Greatest, who was worshipped at most forts. The highest number of extant altars to Jupiter belongs to *cohors I Aelia Dacorum* at Birdoswald, with Maryport and Housesteads not far behind. The stimulus probably came from unit commanders who dedicated nearly all of the altars. Other Roman deities were worshipped, such as Minerva at the outposts of High Rochester and Birrens, on the Wall at Benwell, Corbridge, Carrawburgh, Carvoran and Carlisle, and at Whitley Castle and Ebchester. Vulcan, god of metal workers, and Silvanus, god of the countryside, was sometimes thanked for a successful hunting expedition.

The worship of native gods was not forbidden, including those who were imported with units or individual soldiers from other provinces. It was common for native gods to be equated as far as possible with Roman versions, so gods of war could be worshipped as Mars with native names attached, such as Mars Belatucadrus or Mars Cocidius. These would appear to be British gods, and regional in their appeal. The majority of dedications to Mars Cocidius or Cocidius alone are located in the west. Bewcastle has yielded many inscriptions to this god, and altars have been found at several milecastles in the western sector. Inscriptions have also been found at Birdoswald, Housesteads, Vindolanda, Netherby and Risingham. Where names and ranks are included it is mostly auxiliary commanders, prefects and tribunes who set up dedications, and legionaries are also well represented. Belatucadrus is also more or less confined to the west, under a variety of different spellings, at Bewcastle and Netherby north of the Wall, at Bowness-on-Solway, Burgh-by-Sands, Carlisle, Castlesteads, Carvoran and Carrawburgh on the Wall, and at Brougham, Kirkby Thore, Maryport, Old Carlisle and Old Penrith in the hinterland. The goddess Coventina, whose sacred spring is nearby the fort at Carrawburgh is a purely local deity, all the inscriptions in her honour being confined to the vicinity of this fort.

The worship of Mithras, a god of eastern origin, is attested at Carrawburgh, where the remains of the temple are accessible to visitors, with replicas of three altars set up by different commanders of *cohors I Batavorum*.[79] Another Mithraic temple is known at Housesteads, where a stone sculpture was found showing Mithras rising from an egg, with both arms raised, set within an egg-shaped frame bearing symbols of the zodiac. At Rudchester the plan of the Mithraeum is known, with an apse at the end, and several altars were found there. The Mithras cult appealed to soldiers, but the Christians suppressed it.

The German soldiers who began to appear in the Wall units in the third century imported their own cults, and at many sites on the Wall and in the hinterland, but nowhere else in Britain of the Roman Empire, they set up numerous altars to the Veteres, meaning the old gods, under various different spellings, including Hviteres and Votris, which may approximate to the way in which the name was pronounced.[80] It is suggested that the cult may be connected to the Germanic god Loki, but others interpret the cult as a local British one.[81]

This short survey of gods worshipped on the Wall provides a glimpse of the variety of cults which were observed, indicating that soldiers and civilians alike were not restricted in their religious observances, until the whole Empire was converted to Christianity.

Retirement

The auxiliary soldiers were non-citizens who served for twenty-five years, and were rewarded with a grant of Roman citizenship as part of their discharge, or *honesta missio*. Some auxiliaries would never make it to retirement, dying because of diseases, accidents or in battle before they had completed their service. Several tombstones show that this was the case. If they were ill or disabled, soldiers could be discharged on medical grounds, called *causaria missio*, and on occasion soldiers committed some crime or indulged in some other misdemeanours and were dishonourably discharged, the procedure being labelled *ignominiosa missio*.

Honourable discharge was important to soldiers, expressed by the formula *missus honesta missione* on inscriptions set up by veterans, sometimes reduced to the initials MHM. On discharge soldiers received a two-leaved bronze tablet, called a diploma in modern terminology, held together with wire hinges. The Roman name for this is not known. Each diploma bears the name of the soldier being honourably discharged, and a list of all the units in the province which were also discharging time-served men at the same time. This usually occurred in January or February, probably only every two years. It is probable that the retired soldiers had to ask for a diploma, and perhaps even pay for it, but it would be important to have some documentation at hand to show to the Roman authorities when travelling, especially as there were penalties for people who claimed Roman citizenship on false grounds. It used to be thought that retired veterans would settle down in the *vicus* near their forts, where they probably had families, but this is now being revised in the light of diplomas found in other areas, especially in the Danube regions, where it is made clear that soldiers went back to their homes after serving in other provinces. The diploma of 146 found at Vindolanda issued to a soldier of *cohors I Tungrorum* indicates that this soldier would have enlisted twenty-five years earlier in 121, and he probably served in this unit when it was stationed at Vindolanda. He perhaps went with the same unit to the fort at Castlecary on the Antonine Wall until his retirement, when he returned to the *vicus* at the fort where he had started out and where his family probably lived.[82]

It is not known whether auxiliaries received pensions (*praemia*), as the legionaries did from the last years of the reign of Augustus, who had whittled down the number of legions to twenty-eight from the sixty or more that were in existence at the end of the civil wars in 30 BC. The standing army began under Augustus, and he set up a special military treasury (*aerarium militare*) in AD 6, financed by taxes on inheritances and on sales at auctions, to provide pensions for the time-served legionaries. It has been argued that since the auxiliaries formed about half of the army, the discharged soldiers could not have been excluded from the cash pension scheme, but it is not possible to prove whether they did, or did not, receive pensions.

Although legionaries and auxiliaries alike were forbidden to marry, the citizenship grant for auxiliaries extended to their children, acknowledging that associations with local women had been formed, but the women were not given citizenship. The sons of auxiliaries with Roman citizenship could join the legions, so the recruitment base for auxiliary units was reduced. It may be one of the reasons why Antoninus Pius limited the citizenship grant to children born after the discharge of the soldier.

Civilians

In comparison with the amount of information concerning the soldiers of the Wall zone, the available information about civilians is minute. The native Britons have no voice at all, and their lives are only scantily revealed by archaeology. The Vindolanda tablets show that the Romans of the first century had little respect for the Britons, perhaps judged from the point of view of their use as recruits for the army, but there was evidently a clash of cultures that was never resolved in the north by assimilation and acculturation, and British acceptance of Roman lifestyles. Very few Roman artefacts have been found in native settlements, so it does not seem that trade between Britons and Romans played a large role in native life. The settlements seem to have been left alone to develop as the inhabitants wished. It was once thought that the area between the Wall and the Vallum would have been designated a purely military zone, and consequently cleared of native settlements, but this does not seem to have been the case. The Milking Gap roundhouses inside a Walled enclosure to the west of Housesteads are situated between the Vallum and the Wall, and it was thought that this settlement could not have been occupied once the Wall had been built. But the finds suggest that it was contemporary with occupation of the Wall, and more native settlements have been discovered of probably the same date, one of them at Crindledykes, near to the Stanegate, a short distance south of Housesteads. Native settlements contemporary with the Wall have also been found to the north of the frontier, opposite Wallsend, Housesteads and Birdoswald, indicating that there was no wholesale clearance of the area just beyond the frontier. Not much more can be said about the natives. We do not know them by their personal names. They lived as they had always lived, dressed as they always had, worshipped their own deities, probably continued to celebrate their own festivals, spoke their own languages, and probably rendered their tax payments in kind as submissively as Tacitus says the first-century Britons did. Some of the young men were probably recruited into the army, and possibly sent away from their homes. Apart from Nectovelius, the British tribesman mentioned above, serving in *cohors II Thracum*, not many soldiers with British names are known in the units in Britain, largely because they would probably receive Roman names which were easier to pronounce and write into the records, and in any case personal names do not always indicate affiliation with particular tribes.[83] The northern British tribes are anonymous, and perhaps they preferred it that way.

In some provinces there is evidence of bullying and exploitation of the civilians by the soldiers. Most of the evidence comes from the eastern provinces, but this may be due to the fact that records are better preserved in these provinces. The army was allowed to requisition goods, animals and carts if necessary but there were rules about this and in some cases soldiers exceeded the arrangements, being well armed and equipped to persuade civilians to comply. Demands for protection money are recorded, at least one merchant recording in his account payments for the soldiers under the Greek term *diaseismos*, leaving no doubt about the purpose of these payments. The British tribes may have been subject to the same abuses, but they did not record their experiences.

Most forts in the Roman Empire had a civil settlement close by, called a *vicus*. The word can be used for a village or a section of a city or town, and usually denotes a settlement with an independent council.[84] In a military context *vicus* refers to the settlement outside a fort. Since the military *vici* are found all across the Empire it is to be presumed that the military authorities tolerated the development of civil settlements and there was probably an Imperial policy on the matter, perhaps never written down but something that was understood by governors and fort commanders. The Roman army had always been accompanied by camp followers, condoned by most commanders except where generals wanted to improve discipline and move quickly, as Gaius Marius did when fighting the Celtic tribes of the Cimbri and Teutones at the end of the second century BC. He got rid of all the hangers on, but they soon reappeared with other armies.

The civilian settlements that grew up around early forts were probably only temporary because the troops did not stay in their forts for long, though in some cases the village may have remained after the soldiers had left, if it could sustain itself economically. *Vici* could not become permanent fixtures around a fort until the military units stopped their continual movements, ending up mostly on the borders of the Empire. In the early period the building of a fort or fortress was not an indication that the troops inside them were intended to be stationed there permanently or even on a long-term basis. Fort sites were chosen, occupied and abandoned according to circumstances. Sometimes, as at Wroxeter, the old fort sites were handed over to civilian occupation, allowing some of the people attached to the army to settle there, or to move on with the soldiers, according to their wishes. By the time that Hadrian's Wall was built the three legions in Britain had arrived at their permanent bases, and some of the forts established in northern England remained in occupation. After the late second century, movement of units more or less ceased, and especially on the Wall the units remained in their forts for very long periods and became identified with them and their local areas. This coincides with the flourishing development of the *vici* close to the forts. It is not known where the civilians with connections to the army had been living before the withdrawal from the Antonine Wall, but this lack of knowledge stems in large part from two factors that once formed the accepted orthodoxy about *vici*. It was believed that during the first years of the Wall, civilians were excluded from the forts by the Vallum, and at the few places where excavations in the civil settlements were carried out, mostly confined to Housesteads, there was not much interest in dating the earliest timber buildings that preceded the stone versions.[85] Civilians could have been living outside the forts from the very beginning of their occupation, but this cannot yet be proven beyond doubt. What can be demonstrated is that when Hadrian's Wall was recommissioned starting from the late 150s, the *vici* began to flourish and spread out in extent. Geophysical surveys reveal that the *vici* at Halton Chesters, Castlesteads and Birdoswald extended across the Vallum, and at Birdoswald the process is dated to the period after the withdrawal from the Antonine Wall.[86]

The location of the *vici* is known at several forts, but at most of these nothing is fully exposed to view. At South Shields the remains of timber buildings were discovered, belonging to the *vicus* of the second or third centuries, suggesting that underneath the nineteenth- and twentieth-century housing the *vicus* may be preserved.[87] The civil settlement at Chesters, or at least part of it, lies to the south of the fort between it and the River North Tyne, and the Wallsend *vicus* extended round the south and west sides of the fort. Most of the information about *vici* in general in the Wall zone derives from those that have been excavated, primarily Vindolanda and Housesteads, but even though they have been investigated, the full extent of the *vici* at these forts is still not known. Twenty-six buildings have been traced at Housesteads but of these only six are visible. At Vindolanda about two fifths of the whole area remains unexcavated.

Among the limitless questions that can be asked about the *vici* is how do they begin? Did fort commanders wait until likely candidates turned up knocking on the gates, asking for permission to settle, build a house or establish an industrial firm? Or do the commanders or even the governors actively seek out suitable people who could supply the forts with what they need? With reference to the Housesteads *vicus* Crow says that the settlements were probably deliberately created rather than being allowed to grow in fits and starts.[88] In the Wall zone, some forts were clearly more attractive than others, which may account for the apparent lack of a *vicus* outside the fort at Bewcastle, which was probably too remote and insecure to attract settlers. At the outpost fort at High Rochester, a geophysical survey discovered a defended area next to the fort, but its interpretation from the survey alone without excavation is unclear.[89] It was first seen as a pre-Roman Iron Age enclosure, then as a *vicus*, and latterly as a fort annexe. The rejection of the *vicus* theory is based on the small extent of the enclosed area and the regular geometric plan, like the interior of the fort.[90] At the Wall forts civilians presumably felt secure enough to make their homes.

Hardly anything is known about the people of the *vici*, or where they came from, because they have left hardly any records. Their population was probably a cosmopolitan mixture of people from Britain and other provinces. There is not enough evidence to suggest that local Britons regularly settled in the *vici*, though soldiers' wives may have been natives. Some of the tombstones that have been found outside forts presumably belong to the people of the *vicus*, especially those of women and children. It is assumed that families of soldiers settled in the *vicus*, but it is not known if the women and children would be the first inhabitants, or whether the earliest civil community consisted of shopkeepers and owners of workshops producing goods for consumption by soldiers. Another question, posed some years ago, is who built the *vici*? The buildings on display at Housesteads and Vindolanda obviously had stone foundations, probably representing stone walls with timber superstructures, but there is evidence that the earlier buildings were timber built. The stone buildings that superseded them look very similar to the stone buildings inside the forts, and they display some uniformity in building styles and plan, so it is suggested that it was the soldiers who built them, rather than leaving everything to private enterprise. This supports the theory that the *vici* were deliberately founded.

There is some evidence from inscriptions that the inhabitants of a *vicus* developed a corporate identity, calling themselves *vicani* or people of the *vicus*. At the Antonine Wall fort at Carriden, the villagers set up an altar to Jupiter Optimus Maximus, calling themselves *vikani consistentes castell(o) Veluniate*, the people of the *vicus* at the fort of Veluniate or possibly Velunias, and the inscription records that a man called Aelius Mansuetus, presumably a soldier, took care of the proceedings on their behalf.[91] A fragmentary inscription from Housesteads bears part of the name Julius S and the lettering D VICA, interpreted as *decreto vicani*, by decree of the people of the *vicus*.[92] The inhabitants of the *vicus* at Vindolanda dedicated an altar to Vulcan, calling themselves *vicani Vindolandesses*. This was done under the care of (*curam agente*) a man whose name is lost, perhaps a soldier from the fort, as was possibly the case at Carriden.[93] In the reign of Gordian III, between 238 and 244, an altar to Jupiter Optimus Maximus and the god Vulcan was set up at Old Carlisle by the *vicanorum mag* using money contributed by the villagers.[94] The abbreviation *mag* has been interpreted in two completely different ways. It could be the shortened form of the place name Magis, attributed to Old Carlisle, so the inscription was intended to identify the *vicani Mag(enses)*.

Alternatively, as interpreted by the editors of *Roman Inscriptions in Britain*, the abbreviation may stand for *magister* or *magistri*, masters of the *vicani*, but Hassall points out that officials of *vici* in the western provinces are usually called *curatores*.[95]

The *vicani* at Carriden could only have lived at this fort for about twenty years or so, and had therefore developed as a corporate community quite rapidly. It is probable that the population of a *vicus* were corporately organised from the very beginning. It can be assumed that there were some rules and regulations to be followed in a *vicus*, for example the dead were to be buried only in the designated cemeteries outside forts, houses were not to encroach on the roads and traffic was not to be obstructed in any way along the approaches to the fort. At Housesteads the first two buildings closest to the fort do in fact extend over half of the road leading to the south gate, blocking access to the eastern portal, but this had been already blocked up by the soldiers before the *vicus* buildings were erected.[96] Regulations were probably made clear to the first inhabitants and repeated when new people settled. A *curator* or similar official may have been appointed from the very beginning, who could act as intermediary between the population and the fort commander. If there were different nationalities in the *vicus*, it may have been necessary to find interpreters at first, even though the language of administration was Latin. Military interpreters are known on other frontiers, but usually acting in a higher-ranking capacity on the staff of the provincial governor, to interact with the tribes beyond the frontier.[97] But there is nothing to disprove that lower-ranking officers were appointed at forts to deal with locals. It would make it easier for both parties if all complaints, petitions and suggestions from the civilians could be channelled through an individual, instead of the commander or an officer having to deal with each problem separately. Vice versa, any decrees, orders and ideas emanating from the commander's office could be passed on by the spokesman or his colleagues. The existence of *curatores* as officials in charge of the *vici* is not attested in Britain, and the inscriptions attesting *vicani* are devoid of personal names, but evidence from elsewhere strongly suggests that there were individuals or possibly committees who fulfilled the function of the *curatores* in the *vici* of the Wall forts. Although titles may have differed from place to place, someone was most likely placed in charge of each civilian settlement outside forts to ensure their smooth-running. Was this hypothetical individual appointed by the fort commander, or elected from among the villagers?

The *vicani* inscriptions from Carriden and Vindolanda mention that someone assisted them in setting up their altars, named at Carriden as Aelius Mansuetus. The fragmentary inscription from Housesteads also bears the name of Julius S. but without the rest of the inscription it is not clear who this individual was, and what he was responsible for. Is it possible to extrapolate from this that there was a designated liaison officer within the unit in garrison to deal with any problems and ideas that the villagers wished to act upon? Would the hypothetical spokesman and the hypothetical liaison officer be responsible for keeping law and order within the *vicus*? Human nature being what it is, crimes were no doubt committed, as attested by the concealed bodies at Housesteads, where the murderer presumably got away with his crime. Who dealt with cases arising among the *vicani*? Were the inhabitants subject to Roman military law, and like soldiers who had committed crimes, could they be judged only in military courts?

The *vici* were established on the *territorium* of the forts, on land owned by the military, so the inhabitants would presumably be subject to the jurisdiction of the fort commanders. Were the people wishing to settle within the *vicus* vetted by the commander, subject to examination and perhaps requiring letters of recommendation, as with any landlord and tenant? Then after vetting, the first settlers were probably allocated plots and assisted with the building work. What happened to buildings that became vacant for whatever reason? Did the commander allocate them to someone else, rather than allowing a mad scramble to see who could squat there first? Did the *vicani* pay rent for their properties, the money being directed into the fort coffers? This is suggested by Robin Birley, referring to receipts in the Vindolanda tablets.[98] If this is the case, then one of the duties of the *curatores*, if such there were in every British *vicus*, would probably be concerned with keeping records of the houses and the tenants, with changes when people died or moved out and new people moved in, together with debts and arrears and paid up accounts, like any estate office, reporting to the fort commanders on a regular basis. Is it too fanciful to imagine a scenario of *vicani* with rent books and a rent collector coming round every month, occasionally accompanied by a few beefy soldiers to persuade those in arrears to pay up?

The buildings of a *vicus* do not readily lend themselves to an interpretation of their purpose and use on ground plans alone, but there are clues. The altar to Vulcan dedicated by the *vicani* at Vindolanda was found in the western edge of the settlement, where numerous traces of metalworking were found, Vulcan being an appropriate god for such ventures. Up to six separate buildings were found complete with furnaces, and iron slag was also evident, but no traces of residential accommodation were found in the vicinity.[99] At Housesteads there are two buildings close to the fort, with their short ends facing the road along the south fort wall, the most westerly one interpreted as a shop, and the second building containing a furnace. This may have been used for coin manufacture, since a mould for a coin of Julia Domna, wife of Septimius Severus, was found in the alley between these two buildings. It is not known whether this was an illegal enterprise, or a perfectly legitimate and officially approved operation to provide coins of low denomination for use as small change, which was always in short supply.[100]

Most of the buildings in a *vicus* were probably houses, possibly with two storeys, or storage in the roof space. This is yet another question that cannot be answered. Other buildings in the *vici* are interpreted as shops or taverns. At Housesteads, one of the two buildings with their entrances facing the road to the south gate has slots in the stone threshold for shutters, like the broad entrances to the individual cubicles interpreted as shops in Trajan's Markets in Rome. What was on sale at Housesteads is not known, but the prime position next to the gate surely satisfies the modern concept of location, location, location to attract passing trade. At Vindolanda, a building was discovered which contained cooking facilities far larger than those of a purely domestic house.[101] It may have been the Roman equivalent of a fast-food takeaway.

The end of the *vici* in the late third century is not universal, but decline and desertion is attested at Birdoswald, Vindolanda, Housesteads, Halton Chesters, Wallsend and South Shields in the Wall zone, and at Old Penrith, Watercrook, Ribchester and Manchester.[102] There may have been different reasons at different forts for the desertion in the last quarter of the third century. Various businesses may have declined and failed because of a lack of disposable income among the soldiers, who did not receive their entire salaries in cash, but in food, clothing and equipment. To this could be added the possible reduction in the overall number of soldiers in general. Economic reasons may explain why the *vicus* at Malton did not decline at the end of the third century and in fact continued to prosper in the fourth. If the people of a settlement could find a niche in the market by producing something that other people need, then the settlement could probably survive. As Bidwell suggests, the survival of the *vicus* at Malton may be due to the thriving pottery industry in the village, and trading links with the towns at Carlisle, Corbridge and Catterick.[103] It is not known where the inhabitants went when the *vici* were abandoned, but some of them were probably attracted to the towns at the above-mentioned places. From the towns they may have resurfaced in a different guise, since markets have been detected in some of the forts in the fourth century, at Vindolanda, Newcastle and Wallsend.[104] Instead of living close to the forts to ply their trade, some of the people may have trekked to the forts with their wares on appointed days, like the stallholders at medieval and modern markets.

At some time in the third century the *vicus* at Wallsend acquired a circuit of walls, which may have been necessary because the fort on the Tyne was accessible to raids not only from the land, but also from the sea, since the river is tidal for some distance inland.[105] Proximity to a tidal river does not explain the wall that has been traced by a geophysical survey around the *vicus* at Housesteads, but the military presumably felt the need for defence at this site as well.[106] Defensive walls around *vici* have not been traced at other Wall forts where surveys have been conducted, so the erection of defences was not universally applied across the entire frontier, and was presumably left to the decisions of inhabitants of the *vici* in collusion with the fort commanders. Such defences may not have been entirely necessary, given that the presence of the Wall afforded a high degree of protection, but in the hinterland where forts stood alone on routes, defended *vici* were more common.[107] Despite these differences, the general picture of *vici* on the Wall and in the hinterland is one of desertion in the later third century. The two main reasons that force people to move away from their homes are adverse economic circumstances and lack of security, and towards the end of the third century perhaps both these factors applied.

8

The Wall from Caracalla to the Accession of Diocletian: AD 211 to AD 284

After the first few decades of the third century, the sources for the history of Roman Britain and especially the Wall range from very little to nothing at all. In the wider Empire the third century has been labelled a time of crisis, and although this has been played down and narrowed to a dispute about semantics and what crisis actually means, it was a disruptive period on the frontiers and in some provinces. The so-called military anarchy, when the turnover of Emperors raised by the armies was dazzlingly rapid and usurpers abounded, was temporarily checked by Diocletian and his successors, but at the cost of changing the Roman Empire into a different world.

The native peoples on the other side of the northern frontiers also had their problems. They were pressurized by food shortages caused by exhaustion of the land, or on the western coastal areas, by encroachment of the sea. Sometimes tribes were threatened by the aggressive movement of other tribes. To the people who were displaced for whatever reason, the Roman Empire looked increasingly attractive. There were several precedents from Augustus onwards of settlement of large numbers of tribesmen on lands within the Empire, but in the third century there seems to have been an escalation in the numbers of people wanting access to the Empire across the northern frontiers. From the early third century the pressure on the Rhine and Danube frontiers increased.

Some groups of tribesmen did not necessarily want to attack the frontiers, but were looking for food, shelter and somewhere to live, a situation not unlike the current migrant problem of the twenty-first century. Others were merely intent on hit-and-run raids, carrying off portable wealth and sometimes prisoners, and causing destruction on their way in and out of the Roman provinces. Their numbers may not have been large; Whittaker says that only exceptionally did raids like these involve hundreds or thousands of warriors.[1] In the 230s there were serious attacks on the Taunus–Wetterau frontiers of Germany, and destruction at several forts and civilian settlements in this region has been linked to the incursions. Although Britain did not suffer in the same way as the provinces which lay within reach of the northern frontiers, from the second half of the third century there was an increasing threat to the British coastal areas, and there was most likely a knock-on effect in Britain caused by the disruption on the Continent.

In 260 the Emperor Valerian was captured and his army defeated in a disastrous campaign against the new dynasty which had come to power in the east, which had taken over the old Parthian regime, converting the name of Rome's most powerful enemy from Parthians to Persians. Valerian's son and co-Emperor Gallienus was left alone to deal with the situation after 260, but because of pressure on the Danube provinces he was unable to mount another campaign in the east, allowing the ruler of Palmyra, Odenathus, to restore order in the eastern provinces. Increasing insecurity in Germany and Gaul combined with the inability of the central government to assist or protect the provincials, persuaded the army on the Rhine to declare their commander Marcus Cassianius Latinius Postumus as Emperor. Anyone trying to rally the provincials and the soldiers needed authority, and the highest authority was Imperial power, so there was really no alternative except to declare the new leader Emperor. Postumus' provinces of Germany, at least part of Raetia, Gaul, Spain and Britain became known as the Imperium Galliarum, or the Gallic Empire. There may have been no intention of claiming the whole Empire, but even though the main aim was protection, Postumus and his successors were labelled usurpers.

The unfortunate element in studying the third century is that as problems increase the sources decrease. Literary evidence is derived from late sources with all the misunderstandings that this implies,

for instance in the use of some military terms that had changed
their meaning by the time these sources were compiled, leading
to confusion in using them to illustrate earlier periods. The habit
of setting up inscriptions does not disappear altogether, but this
source of evidence declines as the third century progresses. The
archaeological evidence assumes greater importance, but without
dating evidence to accompany stratigraphy and the finds, a lot
of guesswork is required to understand how the disparate pieces
of evidence fit into the overall pattern. The sources for the eras
preceding the third century, and to an extent for the centuries
afterwards, are more abundant, but it is not possible to elucidate
what had been happening in the third century by comparing the
periods before and after, and distilling the differences between the
two. In Britain, the absence of literary and epigraphic evidence
seems to indicate that the third century was relatively peaceful,
though with more archaeological discoveries this perception is
gradually being eroded. The lack of literary or epigraphic sources
means that there is no framework upon which to hang the results
of archaeological investigations, which can be both a good and
a bad thing. Previous studies of the Wall were deeply influenced
by the framework of the Wall periods, based on documented or
sometimes postulated events, so archaeological findings had to
be fitted into the pattern even though they seemed at times to
contradict the established orthodoxy. In the third century, without
a rigid set of designated Wall periods, archaeological findings can
be judged on their own merits, but although general trends in the
Wall zone can be discerned, these trends could only be upgraded
into fact if contemporary excavations could be carried out to the
same standards at every inch of the Wall, and every fort, milecastle,
turret and *vicus*, or civil settlement next to a fort. This is to enter
cloud cuckoo land, not least because at some locations the higher
levels with all the later material have been removed, as at Wallsend,
where the fourth-century levels were destroyed before the twentieth
century, not unexpected in an area of industrial development.[2] The
imbalance of the available evidence between the earlier history
of the Wall and the later centuries results in a corresponding
imbalance in any account of Hadrian's Wall, with a preponderance
of verbiage devoted to planning it, building it and manning it in
the second and early third century followed by far less verbiage

devoted to what can only be quick overviews of the remaining period from the second half of the third century to the fifth, seen only in glimpses here and there.

Britain in the Early Third Century

The peace that Caracalla arranged in 211 seems to have been effective. For many years thereafter no serious trouble is recorded, but this may reflect a lack of source material as much as non-aggression on the part of the natives or the Romans. Caracalla returned to Rome as soon as he could, with his mother Julia Domna and his brother Geta. Once there he murdered Geta on 1 February 212, not by ordering an officer to carry out the deed but allegedly performing it personally, in front of his mother. It was only three days short of the anniversary of Severus' death at York. The sources emphasize how desperately Caracalla had wanted to be sole Emperor, even being suspected of trying to kill Severus.[3] Now, unencumbered with relatives, he at last held sole power. No one could hope to protest about the murder of Geta and survive. The example of the Praetorian Prefect Papinianus illustrates the point. He was unhappy about the fate of Geta, and as a high-ranking officer who could influence others, he was murdered. The soldiers were upset about Geta's removal because they had sworn allegiance to him, and oaths ought to be taken seriously, but a pay rise from Caracalla, not very long after Severus had raised pay, soon helped the soldiers to adjust their consciences about the oath to Geta. The obliteration of Geta extended to chiselling his name off inscriptions all over the Empire, destroying statues and portraits of him, and even going through papyrus records to scratch out his name. This was the procedure for all those subject to the official process called *damnatio memoriae*, permanently damning memory of them.

Certain changes in administration under Caracalla affected the people of Britain and Hadrian's Wall. Probably in 212, though the date is arguable, Caracalla issued the *Constitutio Antoniniana* granting Roman citizenship to all freeborn inhabitants of the Roman world.[4] It had always been possible to bestow Roman citizenship on individuals or groups of people who were not born in Rome and did not live there, and the recipients usually took the family name of the magistrate or official who had given them citizenship. From *c.* 212 onwards it is probably easier to enumerate people who did *not* have Caracalla's family name Aurelius, or Aurelia for women, somewhere in their nomenclature, because the first recipients of the citizenship grant would pass the name down to their descendants. Citizenship was worth having because it bestowed certain legal rights and privileges, but by the reign of Caracalla it had lost some of its status. The levelling effect of the *Constitutio* eventually gave rise to a new distinction between groups. Possession of wealth had always been the yardstick of status in the Roman world, and after 212 there were two main groups, the *honestiores* and *humiliores*. The distinction was a social one at first, but soon crystallized in law, the *honestiores* possessing higher legal privileges than the *humiliores*, who were treated more harshly and could expect more severe punishments for transgressions than the *honestiores*.

For the people living in Britain, all those who were freeborn would now be citizens, subject to Roman law and taxes, particularly inheritance tax. For the auxiliary soldiers, there would be a change in status, because theoretically only non-Romans could serve in the auxiliary units, and only citizens could join the legions, though by the third century this was more fiction than fact. It is likely that if a desperate legionary recruitment officer came upon non-Romans who were willing to serve, or even unwilling but compliant if threatened, the paperwork could be manipulated and the recruits could be given Roman names, no questions asked. The auxiliary soldiers had to serve for twenty-five years and would then receive Roman citizenship as a reward, if they had not died of disease, accidents or in battle, and if they had not done anything disgraceful and been dishonourably discharged before their term of service had expired. After 212 the soldiers would all be citizens anyway, unless they had been part of a group of defeated enemies who had surrendered.

Severus' relaxation of the rule that soldiers were forbidden to marry[5] was merely acknowledged what had been happening all along, in that legionaries and auxiliaries formed associations with local women and had children by them while they were serving in the army. Marriage between Roman citizens and non-Romans was forbidden, so legionaries as citizens, and auxiliaries who became citizens after completing their service, were given the right to marry a non-Roman, mostly making an honest woman of their existing partners. When auxiliaries retired, a bronze two-leaved tablet was issued, called a diploma in modern terms, but its issue may not have been an automatic process and a diploma may only have been issued if a soldier asked for one. This documentation that accompanied the discharge of soldiers recorded the grant of citizenship, which extended to their children already born, until Antoninus Pius restricted the grant to children born after discharge. The soldiers were also granted the right to marry the women with whom they had been associated, so an unofficial liaison with a woman was tolerated, but legal marriage was out of the question until the soldiers had been granted honourable discharge from the army. If the men were unmarried at the time of their discharge they were given the right to marry in the future, but only one woman per soldier was allowed, which does not necessarily imply that soldiers regularly established a harem.

The Government of Roman Britain in the Third Century

Another administrative change concerning Britain was the division into two provinces, Britannia Superior and Britannia Inferior, which has been discussed in the previous chapter because Herodian says that this occurred in 197 after Severus had defeated Clodius Albinus.[6] Even if the division was made in 197, it would probably have taken a year or two for the final arrangements to be put into place to split the government into two sections, one with its headquarters and administrative personnel at London for the consular governor, who took charge of the two legions at Chester and Caerleon, and another with similar offices at York for the praetorian governor who commanded *VI Victrix*. The delay while all this was organised may explain why there seems to have been only one governor of consular status in the island until the reign of Caracalla. The division was probably fully operative by 216, or at the latest by 220.[7]

From about 216 until the later third century, Hadrian's Wall, its military units and its civilian population were in the northernmost sector of Britannia Inferior or Lower Britain. The governors were senators of praetorian status, who had not held a consulship, combining their post as governor with that of commander of *VI Victrix* at York. They ranked below the consular governors of Britannia Superior. On the other hand the praetorian governor in the north commanded more auxiliary units than his higher-ranking colleague in the south. Though inscriptions of the earlier third century are not lacking in general, there is far less epigraphic or literary evidence for the governors, so it is impossible to produce a continuous unbroken list of the governors for either of the two provinces. The situation is compounded by the fact that on the inscriptions which do exist, none of the named individuals give any firm evidence to prove which of the two provinces they governed, so this has to be inferred from the locations where inscriptions are found in Britain, or from other parts of the Roman world recording the careers of a handful of third-century governors.[8] An example of this lack of information from Britain is demonstrated by an inscription from High Rochester naming Tiberius Claudius Paulinus as the governor (*legatus Augusti pro praetore*) in 220. Since the fort is in Britannia Inferior it is to be expected that Paulinus was governor of that province, but this is not actually stated, no doubt because inside the province there would be no need to over-elaborate. It is due to an inscription on marble from Thorigny that it is known that Paulinus governed Lower Britain, because he is described as legate of the Emperor assigned to *VI Victrix*.[9]

Breeze and Dobson note that the governors of Lower Britain were mediocre when compared to the dynamic governors of the undivided province.[10] The praetorian governors based at York would have less military and administrative experience than the previous consular governors of the undivided province, because their contemporary consular colleagues in Britannia Superior would have occupied a greater variety of administrative and military posts. In Britannia Inferior, governors would not be in a position to gain very much experience in the third century because there seems to have been an era of peace in northern Britain, or at least there is no record of large-scale military campaigns, so the governors were responsible for policing and peacekeeping. Largely because the work of Dio and Herodian ceased before the middle of the third century, and because there is no extant account of any other author who picked up from where they left off, there is a lacuna in the literary evidence. There is no mention of wars or great expeditions in the north until the arrival of Constantius I, also known as Constantius Chlorus, in the later third and early fourth centuries. It used to be thought that there was a hint of trouble in the 270s when the Emperor Aurelian took the title Britannicus Maximus, implying that there had been a victory of some kind. Doubts were expressed because the title may simply have been heroic rhetoric after the recovery of the Gallic Empire, comprising the provinces that broke away from the Empire in the 260s, during the reign of Gallienus. However, it seems that there was no such title for Aurelian because the inscription recording it has been misconstrued, which eradicates the suspicion of trouble in Britain in the 270s.[11]

The governors of the two British provinces after *c.* 216 are no longer the high-flyers of the first two centuries of Roman rule. There were no forward-thrusting fire-eating generals because each of the two new provinces covered a smaller extent of territory and there was no longer any need for conquest and annexation, only a need for administration of law and order and protection of the frontiers, and the roads and the coasts and harbours. The early governors were important men with distinguished administrative and military track records behind them. The governors of Britain were comparable only to the governors of Syria, and an appointment to either of these provinces marked a high point in their careers. They left behind them inscriptions in different parts of the Empire, sometimes more than one each, recording their achievements in the military and administrative spheres, so if a governor is not directly attested in Britain in the first two centuries the lack of information from the province can be remedied by consulting the epigraphic and sometimes the literary evidence for the Empire as a whole. After the division of Britain only a handful of the known governors of either province are recorded outside Britain.[12] If they were mediocre, it is because the political, military and administrative climate had changed across the Empire, and Britain as a whole had lost some of its status. The stars in the Roman firmament were the great generals and the soldier-Emperors who ruled the Empire for short periods in rapid succession from 235 onwards, when Severus Alexander was assassinated and the first non-senatorial Emperor, Maximinus

Thrax, came to power. Maximinus and his successors inherited the growing pressure on the frontiers of the Rhine and Danube, and in the east, and the turnover of Emperors and usurpers for the next five decades or so was, with some exceptions, very quick. Being declared Emperor by the armies was often tantamount to a death sentence.

The government of Britain in the later third century is not well documented. It is not out of the question that unrecorded divisions of the two British provinces occurred in the turmoil of the 260s under Gallienus, when the Gallic provinces broke away from the Empire, or in the decade from 286 to 296, when Britain alone enjoyed or endured independence under Carausius and Allectus. During these years it is not certain how Hadrian's Wall fitted into the government of the province. Under the Gallic Empire the government officials and army commanders were appointed by these Emperors and not by the legitimate Emperor Gallienus, who ruled only the central areas between the now independent western provinces and the territories under Zenobia, Queen of Palmyra, and the widow of Odenathus who had protected the eastern provinces after the military disaster of 260. For the Gallic Emperors there would have been a more restricted pool of officers and government officials from which to choose personnel to govern Britain and to command the legions and the auxiliary units. There was an increasing tendency from the reign of Septimius Severus to appoint equestrians to posts which had been previously filled by senators, and the sources state that Gallienus divorced senators from military command, installing equestrians with the title *praeses* (plural *praesides*) as governors of provinces containing troops, and equestrian prefects as legionary commanders. This process probably took some considerable time to bring into full effect, and cannot have happened overnight across the Empire. In any case it was probably not instituted in the western provinces until the Emperor Aurelian reintegrated them into the Empire in 274. Postumus, the first Emperor of the breakaway Gallic state, appointed a senatorial governor to Lower Britain. This was Octavius Sabinus, attested on an inscription from Lancaster, where at some point between 262 and 268 the baths and a basilica were being rebuilt.[13] Sabinus is labelled *vir clarissimus*, most distinguished, which had become the formulaic title for senators, but his title as governor is *praeses*, which is usually applied to the equestrian provincial governors from the reign of Gallienus to that of Diocletian. From *c.* 260 most legions were commanded by equestrian prefects, but in Britain only three legates are known, all of them commanding *II Augusta* in Britannia Superior, all of them predating 260, and all described as legates.[14]

It is not clear how the governors of Britannia Superior and Inferior related to each other, but it seems that the two provinces were not mutually exclusive. In *c.* 219 legionaries of *II Augusta* and *XX Valeria Victrix* from Superior were building or rebuilding a temple at Netherby in Inferior, though the inscription was recut in modern times and therefore the interpretation is slightly dubious, except that the numbers and initials of the two legions are probably correct.[15] If the province had been divided in 216, this is three years after the split, and if the legionaries were needed in Britannia Superior, the building work could have been continued by *VI Victrix*. In the later second century vexillations of *II Augusta* and another legion, possibly *VI Victrix* or *XX Valeria Victrix*, were based at Corbridge in the two military compounds in the civilian settlement, and remained there in the third century, though it is not known for how long. At Carlisle, pottery evidence shows that the fort was rebuilt in stone during the first years of the third century, and was garrisoned by legionary troops. The excavators considered that *VI Victrix* may have carried out the building work, but it seems that the occupying garrison comprised vexillations from *II Augusta* and *XX Valeria Victrix*.[16] Legionary tiles which bore the names and emblems of each of these two legions were found in the third-century fort, and an altar was set up between 213 and 222 by Marcus Aurelius Syrio, tribune of *XX Valeria Victrix*, which strengthens the case for a number of soldiers of this legion based at Carlisle with this officer.[17] Curiously, along with the other tiles, there were also tiles of *IX Hispana*, long since disappeared from Britain, but this was probably a case of waste not, want not, by using stockpiles left behind when *IX Hispana* left York. Carlisle is like Corbridge in that it predates the Wall, and is not attached to it, but whereas the legionaries based at Corbridge in the third century were accommodated in compounds in the civil town, the vexillations at Carlisle were housed in the fort.[18]

There may also have been legionaries at Piercebridge, as attested
by a dedication to Jupiter Dolichenus by a group of soldiers from
a vexillation of *VI Victrix* and from the armies of both Upper and
Lower Germany (*exercitus Germaniae utriusque*), all commanded
by Marcus Lollius Venator, centurion of *II Augusta*.[19] There is no
dating evidence on this inscription, but the style of the lettering
on this stone is very similar to the lettering on another dedication
to Jupiter Dolichenus from the same site, which is specifically
dated to 217 by naming the consuls of that year, Praesens and
Extricatus, who was consul for the second time.[20] The soldiers
may have been stationed in the large fort that is still traceable at
Piercebridge, though this fort is usually dated to the later third
century.[21] It is possible that in 217 the province had not yet been
divided, but even after it had been split into two, some of the
legionaries at Carlisle, Corbridge and Piercebridge were from
Britannia Superior. Vexillations of *XX Valeria Victrix*, were clearly
stationed at Corbridge and at Carlisle at the same time in the early
third century.[22] These three sites accommodating legionaries guard
important routes, Piercebridge and Corbridge on Dere Street, the
main north–south route on the eastern side, and linking with the
Stanegate at Corbridge, and Carlisle on the main north–south route
on the western side and also linking with the Stanegate. Hodgson
points out in connection with Piercebridge that a concentration of
military strength hardly supports the idea that the north in the third
century was 'a quiet backwater'.[23] If the three legionary vexillation
bases operated in coordination, also requiring soldiers from the
two German provinces at Piercebridge as well as the legionaries *VI
Victrix*, this can only upgrade the suspicion that all was not well
in the north.

Further evidence for soldiers or officials from Superior carrying
out their duties in Inferior comes from Greta Bridge in the Pennines,
and from Vindolanda. At Greta Bridge a centurion from *VI Victrix*
reconstructed some building which had fallen down through old
age. The centurion's name is missing, but another name at the end
of the extant part of the inscription is Urbanus, and the third line
from the bottom reads PERIORIS, which may indicate that an
official called Urbanus from Britannia Superior was at work in the
north.[24] Near the same fort an altar was set up by a *beneficiarius
consularis provinciae superioris* but his name is eroded.[25] Marcus

Aurelius Modestus, describing himself as *beneficiarius consularis* from *II Augusta* in the Superior province, set up an altar to the god Silvanus at Vindolanda.[26] The *beneficiarii* were special military officers with a broad range of duties, and could be attached to the governor, or the procurator, or to legates and other officers of legions, their grades and importance being derived from the rank of the officials whom they served, so the *beneficiarii* at Greta Bridge and at Vindolanda were the highest ranking of all because they served the consular governor. It is possible that one of the duties of the *beneficiarii* was intelligence gathering.[27]

The dates of some of the inscriptions quoted above are not secure, and it is not possible to pinpoint the precise year when Britain was divided, so perhaps not all of the officers and government personnel recorded in the north were from Britannia Superior, but in the absence of evidence to the contrary it may be inferred that the consular governor of Britannia Superior could send officers into the province of his colleague in the north, and this may indicate some sort of coordination between the two governors. It appears that, so far as the meagre sources allow, that there were no campaigns either in the Pennines south of Hadrian's Wall, or to the north beyond the frontier, so the potential for coordinated military action was not tested. But if there happened to be trouble in the zone north of the Wall or if there was infiltration across the frontier, could the governor of Britannia Inferior ask for help from the governor of Britannia Superior as a matter of course, because potentially the whole island was threatened, or did he have to write to the Emperor for authorisation and send messages in triplicate to London? Or had the Emperors given some thought to this possibility and outlined the correct protocol to be followed in emergencies? It is pertinent to ask why Caracalla and his successors thought that Britannia Inferior, comprising the most heavily militarized zone where most of the threats had arisen for almost two centuries, could be governed by a man of praetorian rank with only one legion at his disposal, while the predominantly peaceful southern half of the island demanded the attention of a higher-ranking governor with access to two legions. Did Caracalla have complete confidence in the promises, whatever they were, that the tribal leaders made to him when he arranged the peace terms in 211? Or did he rely on the strengthening of the Hadrianic frontier and its outposts to keep the peace ever afterwards, possibly because he had killed virtually everyone living to the north of it?

Hadrian's Wall in the Early Third Century

The governors of the new province of Britannia Inferior, based at York with *VI Victrix*, were responsible for the whole Wall zone and the northern frontier, as demonstrated by inscriptions from the outposts to the north of the Wall, from forts on the Wall, and from forts to the south, recording building, repairs and other activities under successive governors.[28] At the Wall forts, the outposts and in the hinterland, inscriptions and archaeological evidence demonstrate that the process of repairs, reconstruction and improvement of facilities continued from the reign of Caracalla, through the mercifully short reign of Elagabalus, and through the reigns of Severus Alexander, Maximinus Thrax and Gordian III. The highest number of inscriptions recording building work date to the reign of Severus Alexander who reigned from 222 to 235. This may signify, but does not necessarily prove, that during his reign more building and repair work was actually being carried out than in previous reigns.

It is worth going into some detail about the work done on many of the forts in the Wall zone in the early third century, because this was when the last great rebuilding was carried out at so many of them. Though the forts on the Wall and in the north of England would be suffering from old age by the early third century, just as several inscriptions insist, the continuity of the construction and repairs at several forts, through the successive reigns of a series of Emperors, probably indicates ongoing Imperial policy concerning Britannia Inferior. The rebuilding and repair work was so widespread and so extensive at some forts that it has been viewed as a corporate programme starting with Severus and continuing under his successors, and nothing like it was seen again throughout the rest of the Wall's history.[29]

Although Imperial policy could change along with the turnover of Emperors, from the third century onwards the frontier was never advanced beyond Hadrian's Wall. Even though the Romans probably patrolled north of the Wall, and though expeditions may have been planned or even carried out, the Wall remained the northernmost boundary of the administered province, and its military units remained with it. In former days units moved around from fort to fort, wars were fought and won and the pattern of occupation changed, new forts were built as old ones were abandoned, some units or parts of them were taken to other provinces and not all of them came back. But after the beginning of the third century such mobility within Britain tailed off. Units based in the Wall forts became permanent residents, and most of them were still stationed in the same forts in the late Roman period, as listed in the *Notitia Dignitatum*. This document is a list of officials and military commanders in the eastern and western Empires, including the forts and the units stationed in them. The date of the British sections of the *Notitia* is much debated, but since absolute accuracy will probably never be obtained, the options come down to sometime in the late fourth or early fifth century. During the third century the dynamism of the previous two centuries was lost. The new phase has been labelled as a period of stasis, which has a pejorative tone to it, with connotations of degeneracy and decline.

The longevity of the third-century arrangements on the Wall could be taken to imply a continuity in overall organisation if not local detail, but although units with the same names survive in the same forts, the stasis that has been inferred does not extend to unit organisation or to the appearance of the soldiers, or in the layout and use of the forts. After the early third century, at many of the Wall forts there were alterations and repairs on a localised basis, and at some forts like South Shields the changes went on for some time, with the internal buildings being modified, rebuilt and sometimes reorientated or relocated. During the third and fourth centuries, changes were made in the organisation of the units, the appearance of the soldiers and the layout of the forts, and any expectation that everything would remain the same over such a long period can be dispelled by comparing modern armies with their counterparts during the American War of Independence, or the Napoleonic era. Change is inevitable, even among people who had not invented firearms.

The first decades of the third century marked the apogee of the forts and the *vici* or civil settlements attached to them. It is becoming clear that the later years were not as peaceful as they once seemed. Phrased in the vernacular, the early third century was as good as it gets.

The Outpost Forts

Occupation of the outpost forts north of the Wall continued until the first decades of the fourth century. The outposts do not appear in the *Notitia Dignitatum*, of later fourth- or early fifth-century date, and it was thought that the forts remained in use until the later fourth century, but they must have been evacuated before the *Notitia* was compiled. More recently, a study of the coins and pottery evidence from High Rochester and Bewcastle suggests that the outpost forts were abandoned by the second decade of the fourth century, possibly 312 to 314.[30] The outposts do not appear in the *Notitia Dignitatum*, drawn in the late fourth or early fifth century. Inscriptions dating to the early third century from the outposts record repairs and rebuilding, and also the arrival of units of scouts, *exploratores*, which presumably shared the forts with the existing auxiliary units. The use of scouts to patrol the surrounding countryside from the outpost forts enhanced the degree of control and facilitated intelligence gathering. Scouting may have been undertaken by groups of auxiliaries, but from the third century special units were employed.

Continued occupation of the outpost forts is demonstrated by inscriptions. Not long after the murder of Geta, a number of dedications to Caracalla and his mother Julia Domna were set up by the governor Gaius Julius Marcus at several forts, including the outposts at Netherby, High Rochester and Risingham, declaring his own loyalty and that of his troops to Caracalla as sole Emperor, which places them all after February 212 when Geta was killed. Julius Marcus is firmly attested as governor in 213, on a milestone which bears Caracalla's titles, from the Wall near milecastle 17, about four miles east of Chesters fort.[31] Several other dedications by Julius Marcus have been found at forts on Hadrian's Wall and its hinterland, and it is probable that he sent orders to all military commanders to set up loyalty inscriptions at their forts, indicative of the perilous times for all officials under Caracalla.[32] Julius Marcus may have been in post as governor in 211, appointed by

Severus, or by Caracalla and Geta when they left the province.[33] If so, he will have been in Britain when news arrived of Geta's death, a dangerous time for anyone who had shown the slightest support for the murdered co-Emperor in the past. All the dedications are fairly obsequious, but probably nothing surpasses the inscription from High Rochester, declaring that Caracalla reigned 'for the good of the human race'.[34] No inscription was more long-winded, nor longer in physical extent, than the now fragmentary one from Risingham, a dedication to Caracalla and his mother Julia Domna. The text has been fully restored in modern times to include Caracalla's victory titles and his supposed ancestry declaring his relationship to Emperors as far back as Nerva.[35] Despite the protestations of loyalty that Julius Marcus set up, he lost favour, not difficult to achieve under Caracalla, and suffered *damnatio memoriae*, and along with the obliteration of his memory his name was removed from some inscriptions, including the long one from Risingham, where chisel marks are all that is left of him.

Building work continued throughout the first half of the third century at the outpost forts. Inscriptions record considerable attention to the fort at High Rochester in the early third century. In Caracalla's reign something that had been vowed to a deity was built from the foundations at this fort.[36] The inscription does not name the governor Julius Marcus, but it probably dates to *c.* 213, since the text includes the name of the tribune of *cohors I Fida Vardullorum equitata milliaria civium Romanorum*, Lucius Caecilius Optatus, who was responsible for the dedication declaring that Caracalla reigned for the good of the human race.[37] In 216, under Caracalla, something was constructed by the same cohort, but it is not known what was built.[38] In 220 under Elagabalus, the cohort built a *ballistarium* from the ground up, under the charge of (*sub cura*) the governor Tiberius Claudius Paulinus, with the tribune Publius Aelius Erasinus supervising (*instante*).[39] Probably in 235, another *ballistarium* was restored (*a solo restituit*) by the Vardulli under Severus Alexander and Julia Augusta (Julia Mammaea), *sub cura* the governor Claudius Apellinus, supervised (*instante*) by the tribune Aurelius Quintus.[40] Exactly what is entailed in building a *ballistarium* is not certain. Clearly the new building work and the repairs have something to do with artillery, and the best place to put it would be on the walls, so the find-spot of one half of the inscription dating to 220, discovered outside the west wall of the fort, may indicate that this is where one *ballistarium* was located. The type of artillery machine is debatable. An engine like the stone-throwing *onager*, nicknamed after the wild ass for its kick, would need a fairly large, solid base and some anchorage, not the sort of machine that could be mounted on a top of a tower unless the tower was solid. Since there is as yet no evidence for such a tower, various suggestions have been made to explain the *ballistaria*, one that they were shelters for arrow shooters, or that they were workshops or stores for the artillery who would use lighter artillery engines.[41] The Romans used the term *ballista* somewhat loosely to describe different types and sizes of artillery engines, but the portable machines depicted on Trajan's column being transported on mule carts or in action were probably what the soldiers were using at High Rochester, something like large crossbows mounted on a frame, probably firing bolts, the size of the machine dictated by the size of the missiles to be fired. At High Rochester, the most northerly outpost beyond Hadrian's Wall, the Romans presumably felt the need to be able to defend the fort at long range, even if it never came to that with hordes of natives attacking the walls. In the later Empire defence of forts in this way was more usual, and there were units of *ballistarii*, some of them stationed in the bridgehead forts of the Danube.

The third-century unit at High Rochester was the above-mentioned 1000-strong, part-mounted *cohors I Fida Vardullorum equitata milliaria civium Romanorum*, whose full titles do not always appear on inscriptions, but prove that the unit had been faithful to its Emperor and perhaps on a separate occasion had performed well enough, possibly in battle, to receive a block grant of Roman citizenship. Other auxiliary units are attested at this fort, preceding the Vardulli, but the high number of inscriptions of *cohors I Vardullorum* is indicative of their long occupation at High Rochester.[42] From about 213 if not earlier a *numerus exploratorum Bremeniensium* was also based at this fort; the title *numerus* seems to have been an optional addition, and the unit was sometimes simply listed as *exploratores*. Under the tribune Caepio Charitinus, who presumably commanded the auxiliary unit as well as the new unit, the *duplicarii* or soldiers on double pay, of the *exploratores* set up an altar to the goddess Roma on her birthday.[43] This inscription proves that the *exploratores* received pay, and although no one knows whether the rate was the same as or lower than that of the auxiliaries, the receipt of pay means that the units were part of the army. The *exploratores* and other similar units perhaps ought not to be described as irregulars, as though they were somehow divorced from army administration. To split hairs, it can be said that they were part of the army but not the same as the auxiliaries. Alongside the Vardulli, the *exploratores Bremeniensium* are named on an altar dedicated to the standards of both units, the added title Gordiani placing this inscription between the years 238 and 244, in the reign of Gordian III.[44] It is not known where these units were accommodated within the fort, but extra buildings were erected at some time against the rampart on the south wall, where the door to the interval tower had been blocked in the third century, dated by the pottery found in the stonework. This was taken to indicate that the structures against the rampart were built before this door was blocked.[45] Other structures were built against the west wall, south of the west gate, consisting of a row of five *contubernia*, each one built as an individual rectangular house, separated from its neighbour by a very narrow passage. There was one larger house at the south end. These barracks are not dated, but during the reign of Severus Alexander, between 222 and 235, similar barracks were built at Wallsend, where two rows each with five cubicles were constructed back to back, sharing a single rear wall, but each house was separated by a narrow alley. The two back-to-back rows each had a much larger house at the end. At Vindolanda, remains of two back-to-back barracks were found, dated to *c.* 235 and four more are postulated, but these do not appear to share a continuous rear wall. The more famous barracks of this type, labelled chalet barracks, were built at Housesteads, but these are dated to the later third century. The barracks set against the rampart at High Rochester may have provided extra accommodation, and could possibly have housed the *exploratores*, but proof is lacking.

The fort at Risingham had received attention under the governor Alfenus Senecio and the procurator Oclatinius Adventus before the Severan campaigns, when *cohors I Vangionum milliaria equitata* did the building work.[46] This unit is attested on several inscriptions and probably remained at Risingham throughout the third century and until the early years of the fourth century when the outposts appear to have been abandoned.[47] More construction work was carried out at unknown dates. An inscription records building work, naming *cohors I Vangionum* and its tribune Julius Paullus, but it is not known what was built and there is no clue as to the date, and the find-spot which could have helped to identify the building is not known.[48] Another fragmentary inscription refers to some building having fallen down through old age, and presumably rebuilt, but no names or dating evidence have survived.[49] For at least part of the time in the third century *cohors I Vangionum* was accompanied by two other units, probably both of them acting as scouts. *Exploratores* are attested on an inscription recording the restoration of an unknown building from the ground up. The name of the cohort does not appear on the surviving fragment, but what does survive is sufficient to identify a *numerus exploratorum*.[50] Inscriptions also record a vexillation of the *Raeti Gaesati*, taken to mean Raetian Spearmen, from *gaesum*, denoting a long spear. At Risingham the Raeti are recorded under the command of two different tribunes of *cohors I Vangionum*, Aemilius Aemilianus and Julius Victor.[51] On the inscription listing all three units, the name of the RAETI GAE. is visible on one of the fragments of this inscription, but only EXPL survives for the *exploratores*, and the name Habitancenses is restored, on the grounds that there is space for the lettering at the same size as the letters in the rest of the line. Units of *numeri* named after their forts is not uncommon, and the *exploratores* Bremeniensium at High Rochester were clearly named for their fort, Bremenium, so it can be assumed that the Risingham unit was similarly named for Habitancum.

Very little is known about Bewcastle at this period. There may have been a 1000-strong cohort at the fort, but no unit is specifically attested, and the theory rests upon the presence at the fort of two tribunes who set up altars to the god Cocidius who was worshipped there.[52] Both tribunes, Arunceius Felicessemus (*sic*) and Quintus Peltrasius Maximus, celebrated their promotions, which they may have obtained with the help of the god and so they duly thanked him by setting up their altars. These tribunes may have travelled to Bewcastle especially for this purpose, or alternatively they may have commanded the postulated cohort, but neither of the officers includes the name of any unit and there are no clues as to the dates when they set up their altars.

At Netherby improvements to the fort were carried out in the first half of the third century. Something was built from the ground up (*a solo*) under the charge of Julius Marcus, supervised by Maximus, tribune of the 1000-strong, part-mounted *cohors I Aelia Hispanorum milliaria equitata*.[53] After the reign of Caracalla building continued. Vexillations of *II Augusta* and *XX Valeria Victrix*, and *cohors I Aelia Hispanorum milliaria equitata*, built or rebuilt a temple, under the charge of (*sub cura*) the governor Modius Julius, *c.* 219 in the reign of Elagabalus.[54] In 222 under Severus Alexander, the governor Marius Valerianus supervised *cohors I Aelia Hispanorum* in building the exercise hall for cavalry, *baselicam (sic) equestrem exercitatoriam iam pridem a solo coeptam aedificavit consummavitque*, indicating that work on it had started some time ago and now it was completed.[55] Unfortunately the inscription had been reused as a drain cover, so the position of the building that it commemorates cannot be definitely located in the fort. It may have been associated with a forehall attached to the front of the headquarters building, like the forehalls that were built across the headquarters buildings at several forts in Germany. More recently, forehalls have been identified at Wall forts, at Wallsend, where a forehall was added to the headquarters building, blocking the road between it and the granaries, and at Halton Chesters.[56] Forehalls have been associated with training and exercising horses in inclement weather, as recommended by the late Roman author Vegetius.[57] These forehalls were only discovered relatively recently because in earlier excavations it was not expected that buildings would encroach on the main road fronting the headquarters buildings, and also many of the forehalls were built of timber, attached to the stone buildings, but supported on posts, and the traces of the timbers or the postholes were often missed. In infantry forts, the forehalls attached to the headquarters may have been used for training the soldiers in use of weapons, and at forts housing cavalry units or part-mounted units, as at Netherby, cavalry soldiers may have used them, as outlined by Vegetius.[58] It is assumed that *cohors I Aelia Hispanorum*, named on a number of inscriptions, remained in garrison through the third century.[59]

Since the third-century name for the fort at Netherby is Castra Exploratorum, fort of the scouts, it is likely that there may also have been a *numerus exploratorum* stationed there, like the units attested at Risingham and High Rochester. Castra Exploratorum was the current name of the fort in the Antonine Itinerary, which may belong to the reign of Caracalla, so if there was a unit of scouts here, this would suggest that it had been there probably from the late second century to allow for the name to enter into official documents as well as contemporary usage.[60]

The Wall Forts

On Hadrian's Wall there is evidence that rebuilding and repair continued after the campaigns of Severus and into the third and fourth decades of the third century, but most of the evidence comes from those forts which have been more extensively excavated, such as Birdoswald, Housesteads, Vindolanda, Wallsend and South Shields.

The unit at Wallsend in the third and fourth centuries was *cohors I Lingonum quingenaria equitata,* a 500-strong, part-mounted unit.[61] The unit was still there in the latest period of the Wall.[62] In the later second century the timber internal buildings at Wallsend had been rebuilt in stone, though the central range including the headquarters, the commander's house and the granaries were already stone-built. A forehall was added to the headquarters building and extended to the west of it, running across the end walls of the granaries and blocking the road between the two buildings.[63] There may be a connection with the cavalry exercise hall that was built at Netherby. Although there is no evidence as to how the forehall was used at Wallsend it remains a possibility that the horses of *cohors I Lingonum* could be put through their paces without taking them outside in a region which is not noted for long hours of Mediterranean-style sunshine.

A courtyard building was also built in the third century at Wallsend, and has been interpreted as a hospital.[64] An undated fragment of an inscription found in 1998 suggests that a bathhouse was built or rebuilt, which may or may not belong to the third century.[65] There were alterations to the external defences dating to the third century, the two extant ditches on the east side being supplemented by a third one. The south gate was blocked and two of the original three ditches were dug across the whole frontage, blocking off the road that used to lead into and out of the fort.[66] The excavations conducted at this fort over a long period demonstrated that the barracks for the cavalrymen of the unit also housed their horses, from the Hadrianic period through to the latest period, though the barracks themselves underwent considerable changes. All the barracks were demolished in the third century around 225 to 235, and in the south-eastern sector two barrack blocks were replaced by a single building comprising two rows of five double cubicles laid out back-to-back with a single rear wall dividing the two rows. In the south-west area the two rows were similar but not joined together to share a dividing wall. The ground plans of these barracks do not display the usual Roman geometric neatness of earlier versions, which would normally have contained between eight to ten *contubernia*. The reduction in the number of *contubernia* at Wallsend, and also at South Shields and Vindolanda strongly implies that the numbers of men in each century had been reduced.[67] At South Shields the earliest barracks, on a similar pattern but without division into individual chalets, probably belong to the period of the Severan campaigns or later. They were rebuilt in the second quarter of the third century and again towards its end, still without division into individual chalets. What they do share with the barracks at other forts is the reduction in the number of cubicles from the usual eight to ten *contubernia* to only five or six. At Housesteads, where the so-called chalet barracks date to the later third century, there are six or seven individual rooms in the two blocks that have been excavated. It may also be at this time that the civil settlement outside the fort was enclosed by a defensive wall, not closely dated except that it belongs to the third century.[68]

West of Wallsend, the forts at Newcastle, Benwell and Rudchester have not been extensively excavated, the first two because they lie underneath occupied buildings. The castle at Newcastle covers much of the Roman fort there, which was built on the same site overlooking the River Tyne, in the late second or early third century. The fort was adapted to the terrain instead of conforming to the usual playing card shape. The fort was quite small, only just over one and a half acres though this figure is based on an estimate because the entire plan is not known. The headquarters building and the granaries were also on a smaller scale.[69] The early third century governor Julius Marcus, known for a number of dedications of loyalty to the Emperor Caracalla from all over the north of England, set up an inscription here, attesting that the unit occupying the fort was *cohors I Ulpia Traiana Cugernorum civium Romanorum*, which had earned a block grant of Roman citizenship for the whole unit as a reward for some valorous action.[70] The subsequent whereabouts of this unit is not known; it is not mentioned in the *Notitia*, which lists *cohors I Cornoviorum* at Newcastle.[71]

The third century garrison at Benwell was *ala I Asturum* attested by an inscription dated to 205–07/08, when the unit calling itself *felix ala I Astorum* (*sic*) made a dedication to the victory of the Emperors under the governor Alfenus Senecio.[72] About a decade later, the prefect Titus Agrippa made a dedication to the Campestres, mother goddesses of the parade ground, from *campus* for parade ground. This time the unit was styled *ala I Hispanorum Asturum Gordiana*, which dates the inscription to the reign of Gordian III, 238–44.[73] Another fragmentary inscription, now destroyed, also mentions the *ala* which was still at Benwell in the late Roman period.[74]

The unit based at Rudchester in the third and fourth centuries may have been the *cohors I Frisiavonum*, presumably the same unit as the *cohors I Frixagorum* of the *Notitia Dignitatum* and the *cohors I Frixiavonum* attested on an altar to the goddess Coventina, set up at Carrawburgh by an *optio* of the unit.[75] Various alterations to the internal buildings at Rudchester have been revealed by excavation, but these cannot be closely dated. The Mithraeum at this fort may have been built in the early third century, like the Mithraic temple at Carrawburgh.

The fort at Halton Chesters was extended to the south in the early third century, perhaps to accommodate the *ala Sabiniana*, a 500-strong cavalry unit, which would have been too large for the Hadrianic fort. This unit is attested at the fort by a tombstone set up for the brother of Messorius Magnus, a *duplicarius* or soldier on double pay of the *ala*.[76] The same unit is listed at Halton Chesters in the *Notitia Dignitatum*.[77] Probably at the same period that the fort was being extended, the timber building identified as a hospital was rebuilt in stone to a different plan, and a forehall was added to the headquarters building.[78] The new hall was built across the frontage of the building and encroached on the *via principalis* or main street in front of it, as at Wallsend at the same period. The original unit at Halton Chesters may have been a mixed unit of infantry and cavalry, so it is possible that horses had been kept there before, but the connection between the arrival of the *ala Sabiniana* and the appearance of the forehall may indicate that the alterations were made in order to keep the horses in trim in winter or bad weather. In the north-west corner of the fort a bathhouse was built perhaps towards the latter end of the third century, probably large enough for the use of the soldiers, which implies that they were no longer going outside the fort for bathing. In the later third century external baths at some forts in Germany were abandoned and new premises built inside the fort, which reflects growing insecurity, but whether this also applies on Hadrian's Wall is not certain.

At Chesters *ala II Asturum* had been in garrison since the 180s under the governor Ulpius Marcellus, and is attested on several inscriptions.[79] In 221, Septimius Nilus, prefect of the *ala*, supervised repair work to a building which had collapsed from old age.[80] The same prefect also supervised the building of an unnamed structure, which may have been the baths outside the fort, where the inscription was found, but the Romans were given to reusing older inscriptions on other buildings, not related to their original locations.[81] Just south of the baths a late third-century inscription was found belonging to a temple of Jupiter Dolichenus, which may have been built earlier than the third century. On the riverbanks there were also buildings of the civil settlement, which the River North Tyne is wearing away. An early third-century inscription was found in the headquarters building, proclaiming that while the Emperors are safe, *ala II Asturum* Antoniniana is happy (*felix*), the Emperors being Elagabalus and Severus Alexander, who shared power in 221–22. Since Elagabalus' reputation was unsavoury, the epithet Antoniniana was removed, not quite successfully, after his death.[82] The Asturians are listed at Chesters in the *Notitia Dignitatum*.[83]

The long-standing unit at Carrawburgh was *cohors I Batavorum*.[84] The earliest attestation of its presence derives from an inscription on an altar dedicated to Mithras by Lucius Antonius Proculus, the prefect of *cohors I Batavorum*, which is dated by its title Antoniniana to the reign of Caracalla or possibly Elagabalus, between 213 and 222.[85] The Batavians remained in garrison until the late Roman period, when the cohort was listed in the *Notitia Dignitatum*.[86] In 237, the year when Perpetuus and Cornelianus were consuls in the reign of Maximinus Thrax, *cohors I Batavorum* were building something in the fort, but the structure is not named, and the find-spot in the north-east corner of the fort does not help to identify it.[87] The inscription was found in the north-east corner of the fort, so it is perhaps unlikely to relate to the Mithraic temple that was built to the west of the fort in the early third century.[88] Much attention was devoted to religious matters at this period at Carrawburgh. Located just outside the door to the Mithraic temple, there was also a shrine where another prefect of the Batavians, Marcus Hispanius Modestinus, made a dedication to Nymphs and the *Genius loci*, or spirit of the place, probably in the early third century.[89] The native goddess Coventina was also worshipped here, and her sacred spring was enclosed by stone walls with an entrance facing west. The site was excavated, but is now overgrown and boggy, just visible from the Hadrian's Wall Path. Coins show that the cult flourished in the later second and early third century.[90]

The garrison at Housesteads, *cohors I Tungrorum*, was previously based at Vindolanda. It is not definitely attested at Housesteads before 200, but it has been suggested that it moved from Vindolanda quite early and was probably based at Housesteads in the Hadrianic period.[91] On the Antonine Wall it is recorded at Castlecary, or more strictly perhaps only part of it was there because the fort could not accommodate a milliary unit. It may have moved back to Housesteads *c.* 158.[92] The Tungrians remained at Housesteads until the later Roman period.[93] The external walls at Housesteads have revealed evidence of repair work which cannot be dated because nothing has been found in association with the work to provide clues as to when it was done.[94] Since the original stonework would have been about a hundred years old in the early third century the repairs could belong to this period, when the other forts were being repaired, but as Crow points out the defences of the fort very often needed repair or reconstruction, especially at the rounded corners, and on the south and north sides, which were built on sloping ground with the added weight of the earthen rampart bank behind them.[95] Modifications and alterations at several different times have been noted in the headquarters building, the granaries and the courtyard building known as the hospital, but none of the changes can be definitely linked to the third century, save for a fragmentary inscription found reused in the fourth-century kitchens of the commander's house, but this inscription could relate to work on any of the buildings mentioned above.[96] The barracks which have been conserved after excavation and are visible today in the north-east sector of the fort have been labelled chalets because on plan they look like a row of beach huts; they are all individual buildings rather than the usual continuous barrack block consisting of a row of cubicles all joined together under the same roof. These chalet barracks were the first of this type to be discovered and on coin and pottery evidence they have been dated to the late third or early fourth century.[97] Barracks of a similar type to the chalets have been found at Wallsend and Vindolanda, but these have been shown to date to the earlier third century, around 225 to 235, and they comprise only five or six *contubernia*. Of the two visible chalet-type blocks at Housesteads, one contained six and the other seven independent cubicles separated by narrow alleys, and a larger house at the end of each block accommodated the centurion. In some of the houses one of the external walls was formed from the original dividing wall of the older barracks, several of which had been reused in this way. The rear or south walls of both of these barracks were retained, not quite but almost continuous, while the northern ends of each house were open, only a few of them being closed off by a wall, and most of them presumably having wooden shutters.[98] Alterations to the barracks were made subsequently, at different times, but apart from a presumably corporate decision to reduce the length and width of the houses in one of the blocks, it does not appear that there was a corporate approach to the work on the barracks, since each house displays individual characteristics. It is suggested that the upkeep of the houses depended on the group of people who were living in it, though the suggestion that soldiers' families were living in the houses is generally rejected.[99]

Accompanying the Tungrians at Housesteads in the early third-century inscriptions attest the Germans of the *cives Tuihanti* and the *cuneus Frisiorum Vercovicianorum*, two units of Germanic soldiers from the Netherlands, who joined together to dedicate an altar to Mars and the two goddesses Alaisiagae, between 222 and 235, during the reign of Severus Alexander.[100] The Frisians proclaim themselves on this inscription as belonging to

Vercovicium, the Roman name for Housesteads, and their unit title, *cuneus*, is usually taken to denote cavalry. The *cives Tuihanti*, again styling themselves *Germani*, dedicated another altar to Mars Thincsus, the two Alaisiagae and Beda and Filimmene, in accordance with a vow they had made.[101] Another unit at Housesteads, possibly the same as the *cuneus Frisiorum*, was the *numerus Hnaudifridi* usually translated as Notfried's unit, Notfried perhaps being the chief who raised the unit from among his Frisian tribesmen, or the commander at the time when the unit set up an altar to the Alaisiagae, and the goddesses Baudihillia and Friagabis.[102] The Frisian units are associated with the distinctive pottery manufactured at Housesteads, not surprisingly labelled Housesteads Ware, which is also found at Birdoswald. This pottery was once thought to be of native British origin, but it is now known as one of the several forms of pottery made in the Frisian homeland in the Netherlands, a tradition that was continued by the Frisians at Housesteads, who chose to manufacture only one of the forms that were current in their homelands. The *cives Tuihanti* were most probably recruited from the Twente region in Holland, but studies of the pottery in that area reveals that the Frisian ware is not found there, so it would seem that this unit at Housesteads was distinct from the *cuneus Frisiorum*. The bulk of the Frisian pottery at Housesteads was discovered in the civil settlement outside the fort, and it is suggested that the soldiers lived there, rather than inside the fort with the Tungrians. The same situation has been observed at Birdoswald, where the Frisians lived outside the fort.[103] German units and individual Germans in the auxiliary units are well attested at Housesteads and at other forts on the Wall, but the units such as the Frisians and the *cives Tuihanti* are not attested in the late Roman period. The *Notitia Dignitatum* does not mention them, and although units called *numeri* are attested in Britain in this document, the use of the word had changed by the late third century, and it does not necessarily denote a collection of tribesmen.

During the third century the civilian settlement or *vicus* outside Housesteads fort seemed to be flourishing, but it has been discovered that the settlement was enclosed inside a presumably defensive circuit at some time in the same period. Ditches on the east and west side were discovered by a geophysical survey, and the southern boundary was formed by the Vallum. The possibility that this was an annexe to the fort was considered but it is more likely a civil settlement since buildings have been discovered by excavation inside the area enclosed by the ditches, some of which were very poor quality and were described as hovels. The enclosure could suggest that security was threatened in some way.[104]

Around 225, the granary at Great Chesters, which had fallen down through age, was rebuilt from the ground up by *cohors II Asturum*.[105] A few years later *cohors II Asturum* were building again, between 238 and 244, in the reign of Gordian III.[106] It was found in the farmhouse on the site so its location does not help to elucidate what the cohort was building. The Asturians probably remained at Great Chesters until the late Roman period, when the *Notitia Dignitatum* lists *cohors I Asturum*, but this may be a clerical error for *II Asturum*.[107] A *cohors Raetorum* is also recorded at this fort, dated to the reign of Marcus Aurelius, but it is not known if Raetians remained here as *exploratores*, as at the outpost forts.[108] The remains of a barrack block in the south-west area of the fort at Great Chesters could be of early third-century date. Instead of a continuous block divided by timber or stone partitions, these barracks consist of a row of individual buildings separated by a very narrow alley, of a type like the Housesteads chalets, which are usually dated to the fourth century, but as already mentioned, more recently examples of such barracks have been found at Wallsend and Vindolanda, dating from a much earlier period, *c.* 225 to 235.

The fort at Carvoran was originally the base of *cohors I Hamiorum sagittariorum*, Hamian archers from Syria, as attested on several inscriptions.[109] The unit was based on the Antonine Wall, and returned to Carvoran when this frontier was abandoned. It was at Carvoran in the early 160s under the governor Calpurnius Agricola, and probably in the early third century, when the tribune Marcus Caecilius Donatianus set up a long inscription in verse in praise of the Virgin of the Heavens equated with the Syrian goddess, which is really in honour of Julia Domna, wife of Septimius Severus and mother of Caracalla.[110] Donatianus mentions that he has been promoted by the Emperor to this rank from prefect of the unit, presumably the Hamian archers, which would explain the strong Syrian connection. Several deities were honoured here, including not only Roman and Syrian gods but also native gods such as

Belatucadrus and Vitiris, probably a Germanic god, who was worshipped exclusively but extensively in the Wall area and may be associated with the Germanic troops which appeared in the late second or early third century. The Hamian archers are not attested in the *Notitia Dignitatum*, which lists *cohors II Dalmatarum* at Carvoran, but this unit is so far attested on only one inscription from the fort, and it is not possible to say when the Hamian archers left and this unit arrived.[111]

At Birdoswald *cohors I Aelia Dacorum*, the first cohort of Hadrian's Own Dacians, wins the prize for the highest number of inscriptions attesting the presence of a unit at a particular fort.[112] This unit is first attested at the fort in the early third century, and it is listed in the *Notitia Dignitatum*, but although the unit is listed in this document, it is placed at Castlesteads, under the Roman fort name Camboglanna or Amboglanna. For a long time this was thought to be the Roman name for Birdoswald, since there is abundant evidence for *cohors I Aelia Dacorum* at this fort and its location in the *Notitia* was taken as literal truth. In 1976 M. Hassall solved the problem by suggesting that two entries in the *Notitia* had been conflated, so the unit name was written down, and then a copyist had probably moved onto the next fort in the list, Camboglanna, and added this, thereby missing out the name of Birdoswald, Banna, and also the name of *cohors II Tungrorum*, the unit which is attested at Castlesteads. The clerical staff who drew up the document in the central offices of the Empire would not have had intimate knowledge of the forts on Hadrian's Wall, so the conflation of two entries would not have been glaringly obvious.[113]

Excavations between 1997 and 1998 showed that the buildings of the *praetentura*, between the main gate and the headquarters building, were remodelled in the early third century.[114] Under Alfenus Senecio between 205 and 207/8, the granary at Birdoswald was built by *cohors I Tungrorum* with the help of *cohors I Thracum* or Thracians.[115] Building work was carried out by *cohors I Aelia Dacorum* alone, *c.* 219 under the governor Modius Julius. The inscription does not describe what was being built, but it was found outside the east gate, near the wall of the south guard chamber, and may represent repairs to the gate or towers.[116] Some years later in 236, in the reign of Maximinus Thrax, a building was constructed from the ground up, but the text of the inscription does not say what was built, and the exact find-spot is not recorded.[117] Archaeological investigation shows that in the early third century the outer wall of the south tower of the west gate was refaced, the stones and the workmanship being of a higher standard than elsewhere in the fort or indeed on the Wall. Sometime later the southern passageway of this same gate was blocked up and the ditch dug across it, leaving only the northern portal open for traffic. Probably in the third century a kiln was constructed for making tiles in the north tower of the east gate, and was operative until the late third century.[118]

At Castlesteads the entry in the *Notitia Dignitatum*, as mentioned above, gives the erroneous impression that *cohors I Aelia Dacorum* was stationed here, but the unit was at Birdoswald, and the unit that really was at Castlesteads is not listed at all.[119] Although it is not mentioned in the *Notitia Dignitatum* several inscriptions attest *cohors II Tungrorum* as the third-century unit at Castlesteads.[120] Only one of these inscriptions bears dating evidence, naming the consuls for 241, the Emperor Gordian and his colleague Pompeianus.[121] *Cohors II Tungrorum* set up a dedication slab, which was already fragmentary when it was drawn and recorded, and has long since been lost, but part of the text has been restored as *sub cura legati Augusti pro praetore*, though the governor's name is missing. The inscription may record building work in the third century.[122] The cohort was nominally a 1000-strong, part-mounted unit, too large to fit into this fort, which was not attached to the Wall, but lay between it and the Vallum.[123]

It is presumed that the large fort at Stanwix, nearly ten acres in area, was occupied after the withdrawal from the Antonine Wall by the 1000-strong *ala Augusta Gallorum Petriana milliaria civium Romanorum*, or *ala Petriana* for short, because no other Wall fort could accommodate such a large unit. So far there is no secure epigraphic evidence to support this assumption. The fort was occupied by someone in the third century, as attested by the rebuilding of some unknown structure that was carried out between 238 and 244 by *VI Victrix* which included on the inscription its titles *Pia Fidelis* and *Gordiana* or Gordian's Own.[124] There is no dating evidence on another inscription recording building work by *XX Valeria Victrix* but since vexillations from both legions were stationed at Carlisle in the third century, it is feasible that the two legions were also working together at Stanwix, not very far to the north of their base.[125]

The forts in the furthest western sectors of the Wall have not been examined to a great degree, and therefore have not yielded enough evidence to produce a complete history of them in the third century. Nevertheless there is some indication of rebuilding work. Nothing is known of the third-century history of the stone fort at Drumburgh, but it was occupied probably until the late Roman period, and the *Notitia Dignitatum* lists *cohors II Lingonum* as the garrison.[126] The problem is that it is too small to hold a normal size 500-strong auxiliary unit, so it may have held a detachment, and part of *cohors II Lingonum* may have been stationed at some other fort, or alternatively the unit was no longer 500-strong in the late period.

At Burgh-by-Sands pottery of the same type as the locally produced Frisian ware that was used at Birdoswald and Housesteads was found in the civil settlement rather than the fort at Burgh-by-Sands, implying that there may have been a unit of Frisians based here in the third century.[127] At Bowness-on-Solway a long stone building near the west gate, running parallel to the rampart, was rebuilt on a larger scale, probably in the early third century. It may have been a barrack block with timber partitions.[128] The fort may have been occupied until the late fourth century but it is not mentioned in the *Notitia Dignitatum*, so it may have been abandoned before this document was drawn up.

South of the Wall

The unit based at South Shields in the third century was *cohors V Gallorum*.[129] This cohort may have been stationed at the fort from *c.* 209, as suggested by the evidence of lead sealings found in construction layers of the granaries when the fort was enlarged and the new Severan supply base was being constructed.[130] The Gauls were certainly in garrison under the governor Julius Marcus in 213, attested on the surviving section of an inscription discovered in 1984. The last legible line contains the V with a line across the top, indicating the number of the unit and the letters GA for Gallorum. The stone had been reused in the headquarters building of the late third or early fourth century.[131] The text was restored by comparing it with another inscription set up by Julius Marcus at Newcastle.[132] In both inscriptions there are deletions where Julius Marcus' name had been chiselled off. In 222, at the very beginning of the reign of Severus Alexander, the governor Marius Valerianus laid on a water supply for the use of the soldiers (*aquam usibus militum*) of *cohors V Gallorum*.[133]

There were alterations to the fort in rapid succession during the first two or three decades of the third century. The fort was enlarged, being extended to the south, to accommodate the multiple granaries of the Severan supply base. Internally the fort was divided into two parts by a wall, and thirteen granaries were built in the northern section, eight of them in a west to east row in the furthest northern section, and three to the east of the headquarters building, which was reduced in size. The twelfth granary was built behind the headquarters at right angles to the other granaries, and the double granary which had served the fort was retained. The *cohors V Gallorum* was accommodated in the southern half of the fort and two new granaries were built for the soldiers. At least this seems to have been the plan, but the building work had probably not been completed when further changes were made. The dividing wall was removed, the number of granaries increased to twenty-two by building the extra ones in the southern section of the fort, and four new barracks were built, all squeezed into the south-east corner of the fort. The barracks were aligned on the long axis of the fort, running south-east to north-west and they were unusually short, consisting of four *contubernia* with a larger one at their southern ends. There was not sufficient space to allow the building of two long barracks of conventional type, consisting of about nine *contubernia* and a house for the centurion at the end, so the barracks had been constructed in two halves, laid out back-to-back, and two of the four larger rooms would have been for the two centurions and the other two for junior officers.[134] Shortly afterwards the headquarters building was displaced altogether and moved further south where a new one was built with no courtyard. Another granary occupied its former site. The barracks in the south-east corner were rebuilt to the same plan but then were entirely replaced, probably in the reign of Severus Alexander, by five new barracks. These were constructed in the same area, but were orientated at right angles to the previous barracks, running south-west to north-east on the short axis of the fort. The new barracks were arranged back-to-back but were separated by a narrow alley, with five *contubernia* in each block and officers' houses at the ends. There were ovens in the front rooms, and hearths in the rear rooms. This work may be contemporary with the water supply being laid on by the governor Marius Valerianus in 222.[135] In this early third-century layout, the troops and the administrative buildings were separated from the supply base. Since the Severan campaigns were finished, there was no need to supply an army in the far north or a host of Imperial staff, so it is thought that South Shields was now the supply base for Hadrian's Wall.[136]

The whereabouts of *cohors V Gallorum* in the later period is not known. There was a serious fire in the late third or early fourth century, and afterwards the fort layout was radically altered, some of the granaries being retained, while others were converted to barracks. In the *Notitia Dignitatum* the garrison is listed as the *numerus barcariorum Tigrisiensium*, literally the bargemen, or lighter men of the River Tigris.[137] Though the English translation of the name suggests that they ought to have had something to do with loading or unloading ships on the Tyne, the function of this unit was more likely to guard the coast, their duties involving ships or small boats. Perhaps they patrolled the sea and the mouth of the Tyne.

On the Stanegate at Corbridge, building and repairs began before the Severan campaigns, documented on a dedication slab recording building of a granary by legion, not named, under Alfenus Senecio. The inscription is fragmentary, and one part of it is still face down and partly hidden in the roof of the crypt at Hexham Abbey with part of the name Antoninus still visible.[138] All three legions of Britain are recorded building at Corbridge, but dating evidence is lacking. Completion of one of the granaries is recorded on a fragmentary inscription.[139] There was some destruction in the 180s when Dio records that the barbarians crossed the Wall, and after the recovery at the turn of the second and third centuries a pair of granaries, the fountain house and a large courtyard building known as Site XI were constructed, but the latter building was never finished, and there is debate about what it was intended for, possibly a civilian Forum, or a market hall with shops off the courtyard, or a military storehouse, or workshops? East of the granaries, the fountain house was rebuilt under Severus, fed by an aqueduct from the north, leading into an aeration basin, then into a large tank and piped to buildings. Corbridge was eventually converted into a legionary detachment base.[140] Two military compounds, each surrounded by a wall, were established, but they were not planned as strict rectangles because they had to fit into the available space around the buildings that were already there. The compounds were not like regular forts, and it is not known what some of the buildings inside them were used for, except that each military compound had a small headquarters building facing the entrance. The west compound originally contained barracks, but was converted into workshops, probably used for making or mending weapons. Inscriptions show that legionaries from *VI Victrix* and *II Augusta* garrisoned the compounds. Several inscriptions attest to the presence of *VI Victrix*, but not all of them are dates and the find-spots show that stones were looted and reused all over the area, but a dedication to the discipline of the Emperors by *II Augusta* was found in the underground strongroom of the headquarters building of the west compound.[141] It is thought that the soldiers lived in the west compound and the east compound may have housed officers.

The *cohors IV Gallorum*, the unit that was based at Vindolanda in the third century and later, is first recorded on a dedication slab dated to 213. This unit of Gauls remained at the fort until the late period, and was recorded in the *Notitia Dignitatum* at Vindolanda. The inscription that attests them in 213 was reused in a drain at the side of the headquarters. It was one of a series set up by the governor Julius Marcus proclaiming loyalty to the Emperor Caracalla, one of many that are known.[142] Julius Marcus' name has been erased from the bottom of the stone, leaving just enough of the cohort name and number to be certain of its identification, but the number is carved as IIII, which is sometimes used on inscriptions instead of IV. This is just before the period when the first stone fort was about to be replaced by the second stone version, dated to the second decade of the third century. In 223 when the governor Claudius Xenophon was in office, *cohors IV Gallorum* restored a gate with towers (*porta cum turribus*).[143] The inscription is now lost, because it was reused in 1702 as a tombstone for someone who had just died at Beltingham, but the text and decoration was drawn before it was all chiselled off. It was thought that the stone came from the south gate of the new fort, but in the second stone fort this gate does not appear to have had towers, so it was probably the west gate that needed repair 'from the foundations', as the inscription seems to say. This extensive rebuild was carried out only ten years after the fort had been rebuilt, and Birley explains that the west wall and gate were constructed on insecure foundations and had to be rebuilt more than once.[144]

The Cumbrian Coast

The rebuilding and repair work of the first three or four centuries that is attested at so many sites on the Wall and in the forts to the north and south of it is not apparent on the Cumberland coast. There is evidence of activity in the second half of the second century, after the return from the Antonine Wall, but nothing is known of the third-century history of the coastal system, except that the forts were held, then there was a period of rebuilding in the second half of the fourth century, traditionally after the disturbances of 367.

Many if not all of the milefortlets and towers were probably already abandoned by the time that the troops came back from the Antonine Wall, if not before. Pottery finds from milefortlet 21 at Swarthy Hill contained nothing later than the reign of Hadrian and it is thought that it was abandoned in the mid-second century, never to be reoccupied. Milefortlet 1 yielded only one sherd of a later date than Hadrian. On the other hand milefortlet 5 was occupied in the later Roman period.[145]

The forts were still occupied, but very little is known about them, largely because they have not been extensively excavated. Judging from the pottery found at Beckfoot the fort was probably occupied from Hadrian to the late fourth century, coin Constantius II, 337–61. According to an inscription from Beckfoot, now in the Senhouse Museum at Maryport, *cohors II Pannoniorum* garrisoned the fort at some time, but the unit is not attested in the *Notitia Dignitatum*.[146]

At Maryport it was once suspected that there had been a stone-built harbour in Roman times, but a survey showed that the red sandstone was natural bedrock not building blocks.[147] As the occupying force, *cohors I Hispanorum* is attested on the largest number of inscriptions from the site.[148] The unit was part-mounted.[149] Also attested are *cohors I Delmatarum* in the reign of Antoninus Pius, and *cohors I Baetasiorum* which remained in the fort until the 180s.[150] In the third century the unit at Maryport was possibly milliary, which is deduced from an ornate altar dedicated to the spirit of the place and other deities by the tribune Gaius Cornelius Peregrinus, who came from Mauretania Caesariensis in North Africa. He calls himself *tribunus cohortis* without naming the unit, and tribunes usually commanded the 1000-strong cohorts. The possible dating is derived from the decoration, which includes a feature not normally used until the third century.[151] After about 180 it is not known which unit occupied the fort, but the *Notitia Dignitatum* lists the tribune of *cohors III Nerviorum* at Alione.[152] This is equated with Alauna the name of Maryport in the *Ravenna Cosmography*, which was produced in the seventh century, so the sources used for the compilation of the names of British establishments would probably have been at least three hundred years old; nevertheless Alauna has been accepted as the fort name.[153]

Two miles south of Maryport there is milefortlet 25 at Risehow Bank, and two towers, 25a and 25b, which are the most southerly installations known that belong to the Cumbrian coast system. Further south there are forts at Burrow Walls and Moresby. Burrow Walls has not yielded pottery of pre-fourth-century date and it is possibly a fourth-century foundation.[154] But an altar, the only one of a group of five with text, implies occupation in the second or third century.[155]

Moresby was a Hadrianic fort, as shown by an inscription recording building work by *XX Valeria Victrix* which includes Hadrian's title *pater patriae* which he held from 128. It was occupied by *cohors II Lingonum* but the dates are not known.[156] Three inscriptions attest *cohors II Thracum* which was a part-mounted unit.[157] The Thracians are also listed in the *Notitia*.[158]

It has been argued by Woolliscroft that the forts at Burrow Walls and Moresby, south of the milefortlets and the towers, do not belong to the Cumbrian coast system because unlike the other forts they are low-lying and not on headlands.[159] Further south Ravenglass is not considered part of the Cumbrian coast installations, but the *Notitia Dignitatum*, complied after threats to the coast had become much more serious than in the second and early third centuries, includes Ravenglass in the same section as the forts of the Cumbrian coast, under the command of the *Dux Britanniarum*. It was more of a staging post for shipping than a Cumbrian coast fort, and it was occupied continuously until the late fourth century. Ravenglass is now known to be Tunnocelum where the *Notitia* places *cohors I Aelia classica*.[160] This unit is also attested on the diploma of 158 that was found at Ravenglass, and this now makes it certain that the name Glannoventa in the *Notitia* does not apply to Ravenglass, but it is still not certain which fort it refers to.

The Hinterland of the Wall

The refurbishment and repair of forts that had begun in the Severan period also embraced the forts in the hinterland of Hadrian's Wall. Activity in the early third century is attested at forts in Cumbria, Durham and Lancashire and continues until the early years of the Gallic Empire in the 260s. The governor Julius Marcus was responsible for several dedications to Caracalla and Julia Domna, as mentioned above in connection with the outpost forts.[161] In Cumbria at Old Carlisle an altar was set up to Jupiter for the welfare of Gordian III in 242, dated to the consulship of Atticus and Praetextatus, and at Old Penrith an unknown building was enlarged under Severus Alexander, between 222 and 235.[162] An inscription from Bowes attests building work by *cohors I Thracum equitata*, probably in the third century, though nothing is known of what was built.[163] Extensive reconstruction was going on at Lanchester between 238 and 244 under Gordian III, when *cohors I Lingonum*, supervised by the prefect Marcus Aurelius Quirinus, built the baths and basilica from the ground up, and rebuilt the headquarters building and the armouries, which had fallen down.[164] A legionary centurion, Titus Floridius Natalis, commanding the unit at Ribchester and also controlling the region around the fort, restored a temple between 226 and 234, paying for its dedication out of his own funds, under the charge of the governor Valerius

Crescens Fulvianus.[165] The latest recorded building work in the area south of Hadrian's Wall was done at Lancaster between 262 and 266, when the *ala Sebosiana* rebuilt the baths and basilica because they had fallen down through old age. This work was done under the governor Octavius Sabinus who had been appointed by the Gallic Emperor Postumus.[166]

The Third Century: A Time of Change

After the phase of rebuilding in the first decades of the third century there was no further corporate programme of repair at the Wall zone. The lack of a corporate approach, combined with the long-term association of the units with their forts, led to a divergence of building styles and techniques, so a sort of localized vernacular architecture developed.[167] Facilities were improved in some forts, making them more comfortable for the garrison. Water supplies were laid on at Chesters and at South Shields.[168] At South Shields the communal nature of cooking facilities, using bread ovens for each century set into the rampart backs changed to a new system when the new barracks were built, with hearths in the rear rooms and ovens in the front room. It is suggested that responsibility for each of the individual houses of the chalet barracks at Housesteads lay with the group of men who were living in it.[169] This may have applied to the individual houses at other forts. These developments point to a necessity for self-reliance not only for each fort but permeating down to the level of each *contubernia*.

Another development that began in the early third century is the reduction in the sizes of each century, an inevitable deduction from the reduced numbers of *contubernia* in the new-style barracks. At the same time as new styles were adopted, in the forts where detailed excavation has been carried out there were usually only five or six *contubernia* instead of the more usual eight or ten.[170] Unless there was deliberate overcrowding of each individual house, destroying the traditional eight men per *contubernia*, which would have been unnecessarily detrimental to the unit organisation, each century must have contained fewer than the normal eighty men. It is too early to say whether this applied to each and every fort on the Wall, but it has been noted that the same sort of shrinkage occurred in Germany as well, so it is not simply an isolated example limited to Britannia Inferior.[171] How was the transition from normal numbers to reduced numbers put into effect? Was it an Imperial decision? Presumably it was done by natural wastage, unless the Romans invented redundancy with early retirement. Were there difficulties in recruiting enough replacements of the correct calibre? Were the campaigns of Severus and Caracalla as deleterious as Dio says, with tremendous losses which were perhaps never made up, but even if there were losses, this does not apply to the reductions in the forts in Germany. Can it be assumed that the new-style barracks were created when the forts were already half empty, representing an adjustment to new circumstances? In northern Britain before the Severan campaigns, the barracks at South Shields were squeezed into the available space that was left after the construction of the granaries, but they were normal size barracks split into two sections in order to fit them in, and when they were rebuilt shortly afterwards they were in the same pattern. Then, not long after that, the new barracks with a reduced number of *contubernia* were built, probably while Severus Alexander was fighting a war in the east, and then had to mount another campaign on the frontiers of Germany. Did the losses in these two wars affect the numbers of available men in the armies? Was the army costing too much? Shortly after Severus had awarded the soldiers a pay rise, Caracalla had given them another one, so were his successors forced to compensate by reducing the number of soldiers in the armies of the frontier provinces? Did this affect all the units or only selected ones? Only further excavation can answer this and other questions.

In the early third century extra units began to appear in the outpost forts and the Wall forts. These were formed mainly of Germanic soldiers organised as *exploratores*, *numeri* or *cunei* attested on various inscriptions. The trend was probably set by Caracalla. The earliest record of such units, styled irregulars in modern terms because they were clearly separate from the auxiliary units, were at Risingham in 213. These were the *exploratores Habitancenses* and the *Raeti Gaesati*, mentioned as two distinct entities on the inscription recording them.[172] It is impossible to resist the temptation to link these units with Caracalla's Danube campaign of 213, recorded in laudatory and long-winded terms in the acts of the Arval Brethren at Rome in the same year.[173] The inscription states that the Emperor crossed the frontier of Raetia for the purpose of exterminating the barbarians (*per limitem Raetiae ad hostes extirpandos barbarorum introiturus est*). The victory was celebrated in September 213. In the same year *Raeti* and *exploratores* are recorded at Risingham under the governor Julius Marcus. The *Raeti* are also attested without dating evidence at Great Chesters on the Wall and at Cappuck to the north of it, though the inscription attributed to this fort was found reused as a lintel at Jedburgh Abbey.[174] The evidence will bear the interpretation that Caracalla set the trend for fortifying the northern frontier of Britain by sending tribesmen formed into units of scouts to perform specialist tasks, and Severus Alexander and later Emperors followed suit. The *cuneus Frisiorum Vercovicianorum Severiani Alexandriani* was at Housesteads under Severus Alexander, as its name suggests, though this is no reliable guide to when it was raised.[175] The *numerus exploratorum Bremeniensium Gordianorum* at High Rochester clearly belongs to the reign of Gordian, but once again it could have been raised at an earlier time.[176] The *numerus Maurorum Aurelianorum Valeriani Gallienique* is attested at Burgh-by-Sands in the joint reigns of Valerian and Gallienus before 260, but its name derived from Aurelius is reminiscent of Caracalla and his *Constitutio* of *c.* 212 granting citizenship to freeborn inhabitants of the Empire.[177] The date when the *numerus Hnaudifridi* and the *cives Tuihanti* arrived at Housesteads is not known, though it is possible that the *numerus Hnaudifridi* was another name for the *cuneus Frisiorum*.[178]

The Frisians from beyond the Lower Rhine frontier probably brought their families with them, and it is thought that the Frisian units at Housesteads and Birdoswald may have lived outside the fort in the *vicus*. But at Wallsend the insertion of an extra cavalry barrack, possibly one of a pair, is thought to have housed soldiers of an irregular, mounted unit[179] of a number of Germanic soldiers who belong to auxiliary units along the Wall, so the question may be asked, why were the Germans of the *numeri* and the like not incorporated into the regular auxiliary units, especially when these units appear to have been reduced in size? The distinction is probably by function, so that the auxiliary forces could attend to policing and administration in the province, while the probably more expendable Germans attend to patrolling and observing. If they were paid less, and the inscription recording the *duplicarii* of the *exploratores* at High Rochester suggests that there was some form of pay, did the new units represent a cost-effective way of keeping up the duties of the military at a time when Severus and Caracalla between them had made the army more expensive than ever by giving the soldiers two pay rises in rapid succession?[180] Fulford has noted that expenditure on Britain after the cessation of the northern campaigns and the peace settlement of Caracalla was 'at all-time low'.[181] The cutbacks in public expenditure and the reduction in the size of the army in twenty-first century-Britain probably had a third-century precedent.

Another change with third-century origins affected the forts of Hadrian's Wall. At at least two of the forts, the *vici* seem to have been enclosed inside defences. At Wallsend ditches and banks were discovered by excavation.[182] Geophysical surveys at Housesteads and High Rochester revealed ditches and banks which were interpreted either as annexes to the forts or possibly defended civil settlements, but at High Rochester the interior of the annexe contained buildings arranged on a regular geometric plan, and its designation as a defended *vicus* is doubtful.[183] Defence of the *vici* does not seem to have been a process adopted at all forts, since there is no evidence of defended enclosures at Halton Chesters, Chesters, Carvoran, Birdoswald or Castlesteads.[184] To the south of Hadrian's Wall defended settlements are more common.

By the late third century the *vici* of the Wall forts which have been investigated had been abandoned. The creation of defences may not have been carried out at all the *vici*, but at the small sample just listed it suggests insecurity for reasons which are not clear. The reduction in the size of the units in the forts may have reduced the policing of the areas and led to more outbreaks of disorder. At Wallsend there may have been raids prefiguring the later years of the third century when there were attacks on the south and east coasts, but at Housesteads this could hardly apply, unless seaborne raiders were prepared to travel a long way inland. The eventual decline of the *vici* may have been caused by a downturn in economics, fewer soldiers meaning less disposable wealth and a lessening of trade in the settlements, but not all the inhabitants were tavern keepers or the owners of the Roman equivalent of coffee shops and bakeries. The civil settlement at Wallsend had gone out of use by the late third century.[185] At Housesteads the *vicus* may have lasted a little longer, but was abandoned by the second decade of the fourth century.[186] The Vindolanda civil settlement was probably abandoned in the last quarter of the third century, and the absence of fourth-century finds from the settlement shows that it was derelict by then.[187] Excavation of the *vicus* at Burgh-by-Sands shows that it too was abandoned in the late third century. South of the Wall, the vicus at Greta Bridge was abandoned somewhere between 296 and 330.[188] The Piercebridge *vicus* was abandoned around the same time.[189]

Where did the inhabitants of the Wall *vici* go? In the past, when it was noticed by Chares Daniels that the *vicus* at Housesteads was deserted by the beginning of the fourth century and chalet barracks were built inside the fort at the same time, it was a perfectly logical assumption that the civilians had removed to the protection of the fort and soldiers and their families lived in the new-style barracks, consisting of individual houses. But in more recent times it is clear that there is no evidence for women and children in the fort itself. The settlements at Carlisle and Corbridge were not affected by the downturn that finished off the *vici*, but were prosperous and active in the later third century, so this is possibly where the people of the *vici* may have gone. If there were legionaries still stationed in both these locations it would probably make people feel more secure.

It is not known if there was a gradual decline caused by emigration over a long period because it was increasingly difficult to make a living, or whether the *vici* ended suddenly in all cases. It is pertinent or possibly impertinent to ask a question for which the answer will fall somewhere between 'there is no evidence' and 'don't be silly'. Were the inhabitants of the *vici* evicted? The last quarter of the third century was probably a disturbed time, with fewer soldiers in the forts, rendering defence more difficult should there be an attack. There is not much evidence that forts were attacked, and anyway the immediate response will be 'by whom?', but the destruction of parts of the fort at South Shields in the late third century has been attributed to possible enemy action rather than deliberate demolition, because some of the soldiers' personal equipment had not been cleared from the barracks and went up in smoke.[190] Besides, perceived threat is what motivates military policy as much as real threat, and a fort with a lot of houses outside it would provide shelter for anyone intent on approaching clandestinely, leading to house-to-house battles to clear the area, which are expensive in terms of time and manpower. The fort commanders would probably have had complete jurisdiction over the surrounding civil settlements from the very beginning and at all times thereafter, despite the fact that inscriptions recording *vicani* seem to indicate that the inhabitants of a *vicus* had some sense of corporate identity. It could be the case that one or two *vici* were deliberately cleared, perhaps not always for defensive purposes. At South Shields, in the abandoned area where the *vicus* had been, a field system was established.[191] It may have been more important to grow crops than to defend civilians.

Increased self-sufficiency is a feature of the third century for the province as a whole, as imported goods declined. Although it has been argued that east Gaulish samian ware continued to be imported to Britain until the mid-third century, a substantial decline in the total volume of imported pottery has been noted, and imports gradually give way to pottery produced in Britain. Millett admits that it is not easy to decide whether British firms stole the market from importers on the Continent, or whether the impetus for home production was stimulated by an absence of imported wares.[192] In the mid to late third century new production of pottery began in the New Forest and in the already established workshops in Oxfordshire, compensating for lack of imported material.[193]

Food supplies, including grain, wine, oil in amphorae from Spain, and the Roman delicacy, fish sauce, also diminished, which is demonstrated by the disappearance of the vessels in which these items were carried. Even in the late second century there was diminished reliance on imported foodstuffs and a consequent decline in the scale of imports, but this was most marked in the last quarter of the third century. A decline in the military supply system is suspected, but the methods of procurement and distribution are not understood.[194] In Severan times much of the grain delivered to South Shields was from the Netherlands, but after the raids of the 230s and 240s on the coasts of Gallia Belgica and across the Rhine it may have been difficult not only to transport the grain across the sea, but also to gather the harvests, which could have been spoiled or stolen. From then onwards in northern Britain, greater reliance seems to have been placed on local produce. The latest deposit of grain of non-local origin found on the northern frontier comes from South Shields, dating to the late third or early fourth century.[195] The emergence of the Gallic Empire and the isolation of the western provinces, at a time when transport may have been disrupted, may have had an effect on the supplies for Hadrian's Wall. With regard to the Wall in the later third century Millett explains the absence of imported amphorae for oil and wine, and the lack of evidence for other foodstuffs, as a change in local tastes, because the troops mostly from non-Mediterranean backgrounds were not accustomed to such foods and therefore there was limited demand for it. Also the soldiers perhaps did not have enough disposable income to buy luxuries and relied instead on cheaper local produce.[196]

At the same time as imports decreased, troops were moved around in Britain or moved out of the island. In the 250s *II Augusta*, or a large part of it, moved to the south coast, to Richborough, where the newly built fort of the mid-third century was established around the remains of the first-century monument. The legion is last attested at Caerleon *c*. 255–60.[197] The fort at Richborough was only large enough for 1,000 men. The Emperor Gallienus withdrew vexillations of XX *Valeria*, attested at Mainz in 255, and then at Sirmium in Pannonia by 260.[198] The vexillation of XX *Valeria* in Sirmium could not return to Britain once it had become part of the Gallic Empire, so it is possible that they were incorporated into other units in Pannonia.[199]

Troops were shuffled around from the north. *Cohors I Baetasiorum* moved from Maryport, where it is last attested in the late second century, to Reculver. Stamped tiles of this unit have been found at Reculver, probably from roofs, but they have been taken to indicate that the soldiers were involved in building work, though probably not the original foundation. The cohort was still at Reculver in the later period, as the record in the *Notitia Dignitatum* shows, listing the tribune of *cohors I Baetasiorum* at Regulbium.[200] Similarly, stamped tiles of *cohors I Aquitanorum* from Brough-on-Noe have been found at Brancaster.[201] These two forts have everything in common with the forts of the early Empire in size and shape, and have been dated to the early third century, between 220 and 240, but not without debate by scholars who would see them as later installations, possibly belonging to the Gallic Empire. Later, Reculver and Brancaster, along with forts at Burgh Castle, Walton Castle, Bradwell, Richborough, Lympne, Pevensey and Portchester, were known as the forts of Saxon Shore, but this label was not used until the fourth century, when the post of Count of the Saxon Shore was created. To label the south-coast forts as the Saxon Shore in the mid-third century is akin to calling Cape Canaveral a rocket base in 1850; it had always been there but it was not put to this usage until the second half of the twentieth century.

The administration of Britain under Gallic Emperors is not known in detail. Only one governor of Britannia Inferior is known, Octavius Sabinus between 263 and 268. The first Gallic Emperor Postumus may have visited Britain in 261 to secure its allegiance.[202] He was recognised in the north, and two units, *cohors I Aelia Dacorum* at Birdoswald, and *ala Sebosiana* at Lancaster, held the title *Postumiana*.[203] Postumus and his successors probably withdrew troops from both Superior and Inferior. These Emperors probably also commandeered resources of both British provinces. Drinkwater has noted that the several milestones of the Gallic Emperors in Britain are not necessarily associated with attention to the roads, but are located near mining establishments, indicating that the extraction of minerals was a prime concern, and concomitantly, so was attention to transport across the Channel to bring the products to Gaul.[204] Although cross-Channel traffic is considered to have dwindled away to almost nothing in the later third century, British exports may have featured to a greater extent than supposed, and in return coinage from the Gallic Empire flowed in. After the Severan settlement of the north, there had been almost no new money entering Britain, until the 260s and 270s when the Gallic Empire was independent of the central government at Rome.[205] A collection of Gallic Empire coinage was found at Birdoswald in the ditch which had silted up, but thereafter there seems to have been a dearth of coinage at this fort.[206] This is probably indicative of the period after the reunification of the Empire under Aurelian. The Gallic Empire was ended in 274, and the Roman Empire was once again under one Emperor. All should have been well. But it was far from that, the worst incursions across the northern frontiers occupied much of the Emperor's time and efforts, and significantly,

Aurelian built walls around the city of Rome. If Rome itself was not secure, what chance was there for the frontiers?

In Britain there is little information to elucidate the archaeological findings, and the picture from the 270s onwards is one of decline, deserted *vici*, depleted garrisons and at one time it was suspected that some forts had been abandoned.[207] This suspicion derives from Birdoswald, which was either deserted for a while or occupied while in a dilapidated state. Although *cohors I Aelia Dacorum* is attested throughout the third century, maintenance of the interior buildings and the Wall itself had lapsed, so that the fort seemed to be detached from it. Industrial activity seems to have ceased and at the same time the ditch silted up, allowing water to overflow and silt to be deposited against the fort wall. This was dated by the finds of coins of the Gallic Empire, from 260 to 274. After this there is a dearth of coins, but more importantly no evidence of repair and reconstruction until the end of the third century. An inscription dating to the early years of the Tetrarchic era, dedicated to the Augusti Diocletian and Maximian, and the Caesars Constantius and Maximianus, shows that repairs were made to the headquarters building and a bathhouse and the commander's house that had fallen down and become covered with earth.[208] This was possibly due to lack of maintenance of the ditches and the drainage system. The date of the inscription has to be before the two Augusti retired in 305, and it is hard to resist connection with Constantius' expedition to Britain in 296, when he secured control of the two provinces, which had been taken over by Carausius and then his assassin and successor Allectus. The case in point is whether or not the fort had been deserted, probably in the 270s. Excavation at other forts such as Housesteads, Vindolanda, Wallsend and South Shields has not corroborated the desertion detected at Birdoswald, because there is sufficient evidence of occupation and activity in the later third century and there is no gap in the coin series.[209] If *cohors I Aelia Dacorum* had departed from Birdoswald, it is not known where it went. Although it is difficult to believe, perhaps the fort was not totally deserted but the soldiers lived in it while the central range was in complete decay. In Britain as in other provinces there are many examples of inscriptions claiming that buildings had fallen down and had been rebuilt from the ground up, but it is suggested that they are not reliable indications of either the extent of the damage or the completeness of the rebuilding work, in other words they are probably full of hyperbole.[210]

The mystery of what happened to *cohors I Aelia Dacorum* and its fort has not been solved, but despite the evidence for activity at other Wall forts, the 270s may have been a difficult time for many forts in Britannia Inferior. As already mentioned, when Aurelian won back control of the western provinces from the last Gallic Emperor, the situation got worse, not better, with the Alamanni, a federation of Germanic tribes, threatening the Rhine and routes through the Alps, and the Frankish tribes menacing the lower Rhine. The focus was clearly not on Britain during these times, the Rhine and Danube frontiers, the east and civil wars claiming nearly all of the emperors' attention. In 284 a new Emperor emerged at the close of the eastern campaigns, an Illyrian officer called Diocles. Perhaps things would be better. They would certainly be different.

9

The Wall from the Late Third to the Mid-Fifth Century: AD 284 to *c*. AD 450

The date chosen for the ending of the previous chapter and the start of this one marks the beginning of fundamental changes that affected the whole Empire. The Romans did not obligingly progress to New Year's Eve in 299 and start a new era on 1 January 300, and the accession of Diocletian in 284 did not herald instantaneous transformations of the Imperial house, the government and the army, but this was the end result of his reign. Diocletian's work continued for some years and was later completed by Constantine from 306 to 337, and was still evolving under Constantine's successors. It is sometimes difficult to discern where and how the earlier arrangements morphed into the later ones, but it has been rightly said that with Diocletian, we enter a different world.

The Reforms of Diocletian and Constantine

Moving from the general to the specific, it is convenient to describe the reforms of provincial government and the army across the Empire in the late third and early fourth century before dealing with Britain, so that the administrative arrangements and the accompanying terminology will be familiar without having to explain them whenever they occur, and the British provinces can be seen against the background of the wider Roman world.

The form of Imperial rule that Diocletian introduced, known as the Tetrarchy, or rule of four men, was rooted in the precedents of the earlier Empire, whereby the emperors or Augusti appointed their sons or chosen successors as lower-ranking Caesars, attempting to ensure that the succession was a smooth process with a clearly appointed candidate to assume power after the death of the reigning Augustus. It did not always work, because in the mid-third century the Caesars as well as the Augusti were frequently despatched by the soldiers who elevated a candidate of their own. Diocletian took the succession process a stage further, with himself and Maximian as Augusti and Galerius and Constantius as their respective Caesars, groomed for promotion to Augusti, when they would appoint Caesars of their own. This began in 293, probably at slightly different dates for the appointment of Constantius and Galerius within the same year. Recognizing that the Empire was too large for the rule of one man, Diocletian placed himself and his Caesar Galerius in the east, and Maximian and his Caesar Constantius in the west. These territorial divisions were not immediately official, but by the time Aurelius Victor wrote his history of the Caesars, the arrangements had crystallized. There were separate headquarters for each of the four Emperors, at Trier for Constantius, Milan for Maximian, Nicomedia for Diocletian and Thessalonica for Galerius.[1] The Empire was not yet split into the separate Eastern and Western Empires, which came about at the very end of the fourth century, but the history of the two halves began to take different paths.

One of the most far-reaching changes across the Empire was the division of the provinces into smaller areas, which were eventually grouped together into new administrative units called dioceses, with an extra tier of officials in charge of them, called *vicarii*. These diocesan governors were answerable to the Praetorian Prefects, who by this time had lost their original function as commanders of the Guard, and had acquired new responsibilities in the administration of the Empire, including legal affairs. The post of Praetorian Prefect has been compared to that of a prime minister, which conveys some idea of the status, power and importance of the Prefects, eventually with one in the east and one in the west.[2]

The division of the provinces into smaller units probably began in 293, perhaps just after the new Caesars were appointed. The new arrangements could not have been carried out overnight, since new boundaries would have to be established, extra headquarters for the governors in each new province would have to be chosen, and they all presumably had to select and house their own administrative personnel. During the early stage the governors of the provinces were *praesides*, and they were still equestrians probably until the reign of Constantine. They commanded troops if their provinces contained an army, just as the previous governors had done. The equestrian and senatorial career patterns had run parallel to each other. From 30 BC under Octavian as he then was, senators had been forbidden to enter Egypt without permission, and the Prefect of Egypt and the commanders of the legions in the province were equestrians. These posts remained anomalous until the second century. Administrative posts in the central government and in the provinces were gradually acquired by equestrians, and they commanded the auxiliary units. In the third century some of them were appointed as legionary commanders in place of senatorial legates. A select few were able to look forward to reaching the heights of their careers in the four great Prefectures, of the *Annona* or food supply, the *Vigiles* combining fire brigade duties with a sort of police work in Rome, the Praetorian Guard, and the most prestigious post of Prefect of Egypt. Senators embarked on their careers by holding junior posts in the armies and in provincial and central government, some of them going on to command legions, then hopefully obtaining a consulship and finally governing one of the more important provinces. The career patterns changed under Severus, who promoted equestrians at the expense of senators. Later, under Gallienus, many senators, but not all of them, were removed from military commands. The equestrian career reached its apogee under Diocletian, who appointed equestrians to the military posts, including the higher ones, and to most of the administrative offices. When Constantine came to power he reinstated senators in the administrative spheres, extinguishing the equestrian order in civil government. He also finalised the separation of military and civil careers. There had been a growing tendency from Hadrian's time for specialism in either the sphere of civil government or in military command, slightly counter to the established norm where careers usually embraced a combination of civil and military appointments. Gallienus had made a start in separating military and civil commands by divorcing senators as far as possible from the armies, and Constantine completed the separation, making civil administration distinct from military command and instituting career paths in the senatorial and equestrian spheres. In the fourth century under Constantine and his successors, provincial governors of whatever status took charge of administrative, financial and legal affairs in their provinces, responsible to the *vicarius* of the diocese and through them to the Praetorian Prefect and then the Emperor.

The reforms of the army under Diocletian and Constantine are difficult to disentangle, so there is debate about who was responsible for which developments. It is more convenient to treat them together, though this should not imply that there was a logical progression towards a previously defined goal. By the late third century the production of arms, armour and equipment for the soldiers had become more urgent, and local self-sufficiency had been disrupted. Diocletian attended to the problem by establishing state arms factories (*fabricae*) where they were needed, mostly in the urban centres in the frontier provinces or in military establishments, for instance there were factories in Pannonia at the old legionary bases at Lauriacum, Aquincum and Carnuntum.[3] Production of food and many other goods was tightly controlled by the state, as was transport and shipping. Owners of manufacturing establishments were forced to join guilds which were made responsible for production, and control extended to family life, for instance the guilds of bakers and millers were strictly governed, and the men who married the daughters of millers were forced by law to become millers themselves. Occupations were made hereditary, and this law extended to soldiers. Previously sons of soldiers had a choice about following in their fathers' footsteps, but under Diocletian and later emperors they were forced by law to join the army. Army service was less attractive, and recruitment was becoming problematic; new recruits on their way to join the units to which they had been allocated sometimes had to be locked up at night to prevent them from running away.

The late Roman army was divided into two components, one on the frontiers, eventually called *limitanei*, or *ripenses*, which could include legions as well as the older *alae* and cohorts, and the other component being the *comitatenses* or mobile field army. Some ancient authors thought that the predecessor of the mobile army could be discerned in Gallienus' cavalry army, which had its own commander, but the continued existence of this collection of troops from *c.* 260 into the fourth century cannot be demonstrated. Zosimus says that under Diocletian the frontiers were everywhere secured by means of forts and fortresses 'which housed the whole army'.[4] There may be some truth in this but Zosimus' main aim in this passage was to contrast Diocletian's arrangements with those of Constantine, whom he accused of taking the troops away from the frontiers and therefore weakening them, and putting troops into the cities which Zosimus considered did not need them. This relates to the question of who really founded the mobile field armies. If Zosimus is taken literally, Diocletian did not have a central field army, concentrating all the troops on the frontiers, whereas Constantine put troops into cities so as to be able to concentrate them rapidly for response to emergencies. The argument hinges on the development of the *comitatenses*, which may have evolved from Diocletian's *comitatus*, or perhaps more likely was a separate development under Constantine. It is certain that Diocletian had organised a *comitatus* possibly consisting of a mixture of troops, such as the *equites Dalmatae*, and the *equites promoti* or legionary cavalry who were removed from their units but were still on the books at legionary headquarters. There were also infantry units such as the *Ioviani* and the *Herculiani* from the two legions named for Diocletian as Jove or Jupiter, and Maximian as Hercules. But the *comitatus* may simply have been a bodyguard, not a forerunner of the mobile field armies of the *comitatenses*. The origins of the Constantinian field army are not clear. Being mobile, based in cities, and not necessarily in one place for long periods, a field army is not as readily traceable as units housed in forts. The field armies are not attested until 325 in the *Codex Theodosianus*, in a law passed by Constantine concerning military service and discharge of veterans.[5] It is clear from this document that the frontier troops ranked slightly below the *comitatenses* with regard to their veterans' privileges. The mobile armies contained cavalry and infantry sections, but nothing is known of the numbers of men, which more than likely fluctuated according to circumstances. For campaigns, which in the past required the assembly of units from the provincial armies, extra troops were probably brought in to supplement the core field army, and it is known that *limitanei* could serve in the mobile armies if necessary, in units called *pseudo-comitatenses*, which attests to their continuing efficiency as fighting troops. Eventually regional field armies were established to assist the central mobile armies.

New commanders were created to take charge of the cavalry and infantry sections of the mobile field armies. When the Praetorian Prefects were removed from military command and placed in charge of a wide range of administrative affairs, Constantine replaced them with two new military commanders called *magister peditum* and *magister equitum* whose titles denote command of foot soldiers and horsemen. Constantine probably intended that the two officers would be equal in power and influence, acting as a counterbalance to each other. Eventually more than one *magister* could be appointed. Under Valentinian there were two *magistri equitum*.[6] The terminology was not applied consistently, so that one and the same man could be called *magister peditum*, *magister equitum*, or *magister militum*, meaning master of the soldiers. This title and *magister utriusque militum*, literally 'master of the soldiers everywhere', imply an all-embracing command. A strict seniority emerged so that the *magistri* close to the Emperor added *praesentalis* or *in praesenti* to their titles to distinguish them from lesser *magistri* and eventually even the distinction between infantry and cavalry officers disappeared, with the *magister peditum praesentalis* in the ascendant over all other officers. In the west, according to the *Notitia*, the *magister peditum praesentalis* commanded the entire western military establishment.[7] The late Roman generals Arbogast and Stilicho held this office and acquired great influence and power. There were also regional *magistri*, probably not permanent posts, such as the *magistri equitum per Gallias* in Gaul, or the *magister peditum et equitum per Orientem,* and also *per Thracias*, and *per Illyricum*.[8]

Immediately responsible to the *magistri* were the *duces*, from *dux* in the singular, which literally means leader, the origin of Il Duce in Italian. The title had been used in the earlier Empire to denote an officer in a temporary command, who was acting in a capacity above his existing rank. He could be in command of a complete unit for a short period, or he could be assigned to command over collections of troops to lead them to an assembly point. By the fourth century, the *duces* had become regular officers, in command of the armies of a province or more usually of several provinces, with complete responsibility for military affairs. Although he was answerable to the *magister*, it seems that the *dux* could correspond with the Emperor directly.[9] Some commands were limited to one province, and were appropriately titled, such as *dux Africae* or *dux Aegypti*. Other commands ranged over more than one province, and the title reflected the names of the provinces in the plural, as in the case of the *dux Britanniarum* denoting the duke of the Britains, or the provinces in the north, with responsibility for the frontier. Some *duces* were in command of a designated frontier area covering the borders of a number of provinces, and the usual title was *dux limitis*, from *limes* meaning the frontier. These appointments and their titles were not permanent, because priorities could change on the frontiers, involving a reshuffle of the command structure, for instance the equestrian *dux Africae* was replaced *c.* 330 by a higher-ranking senator. Also the division between civil authority and military command was not always strictly observed. *Duces* could govern provinces and in some cases the *praeses* could command troops, though perhaps in some cases only on a temporary basis. The *dux Arabiae* was at one and the same time both *dux* and *praeses* with two distinctive sets of staff.[10]

The *duces* were responsible for all aspects of military command in the areas to which they were assigned, but their commands were confined to the provincial and frontier troops. The *duces* did not command the field armies or *comitatenses*, which were established by Constantine. These troops were under the direct control of the *magistri*. The law codes make it clear what the duties of the *duces* entailed, protection of the frontier being an obvious starter, with maintenance of the frontier works as a priority, and the establishment of fortifications in areas where they were considered necessary. The case of the Frankish Teutomeres, *dux Daciae ripensis* on the Danube, illustrates that the Emperors took these duties very seriously. Valentinian I told Teutomeres in no uncertain terms that if he neglected the upkeep of the frontiers during his term of office he would be forced to complete any necessary repair work at his own expense instead of carrying it out with the aid of the soldiers at public expense.[11] The *duces* were also responsible for collecting and distributing provisions for the troops, which probably included clothing, equipment and perhaps fuel, and the administration of the food supply. The ultimate control of food lay with the Praetorian Prefects, so someone on the staff of the *dux* had to send quarterly returns to the Prefect, presumably accounting for numbers of soldiers, the rations that had been received and probably their future requirements, which would have been gathered from the requisitions put in by the commanders of individual units. Recruitment and allocation of newly enlisted soldiers to their units was entirely within the remit of the *duces*. Constantine insisted that even though batches of recruits had been approved by less senior officers, the *duces* should carry out an additional personal inspection, so as to weed out unsuitable men. Responsibility for law and order among the troops, and judicial functions, also accrued to the *duces*, because any soldiers who had committed crimes had to be tried in military courts.

Very little is known of the *duces* in Britain, except for the entries in the *Notitia*, listing the units and their commanders serving under the *dux*, and his administrative staff, but the duties and responsibilities outlined above will serve to illustrate some of the workload. This lack of knowledge about the *duces Britanniarum* is due to the fact that no *dux* is attested until the later fourth century, when Ammianus records that the *dux* Fullofaudes was surrounded by the enemy, and presumably killed, in the disaster of 367. The full title is not provided by Ammianus, so there is room for doubt that Fullofaudes was actually *dux Britanniarum* or simply a leader of some troops.[12] Ammianus names another *dux* called Dulcitius, who may have been the successor of Fullofaudes, but again it is not certain if the title *dux* is being used in its general sense as leader of troops, or in its specific sense of *dux Britanniarum*, and Ammianus provides no clues to resolve this.[13]

Other officials with military duties, some of whom are attested in Britain, were the *comites*. The titles *comes* originally denoted a companion of the Emperor with no specific rank and no official functions, so it did not imply an appointment of any kind. In the late Empire, under Constantine, the title was used to denote officials in civil government and military affairs. The Roman equivalent of a finance minister was the *comes sacrarum largitionem*, and the *comes domesticorum* commanded the *protectores domestici*. The latter consisted of officers and men in the Emperor's immediate entourage, not strictly a bodyguard, but men who usually went on to commands of their own. *Comes* is usually translated into English as count. If he commanded troops, his title was usually *comes rei militaris*, which was neither a regular post with specific duties, nor a permanent one, but it could cover a wide variety of appointments ranging from control of a collection of frontier troops to an important command equivalent to that of a *magister militum*. In Britain the most famous of these posts is the Count of the Saxon Shore, *comes litoris Saxonicum*, who commanded most of the south, while the *dux*, his counterpart in the north, commanded the frontier and its hinterland. The other famous *comes* is Flavius Theodosius, sent to Britain in 367 after the devastating attacks by different tribes on land and from the sea. Ammianus simply labels him as *dux*, used in the non-specific sense, though it is most probable that Theodosius had been given an official post as *comes rei militaris*, commander of the field army.[14]

The army reforms outlined above did not come into force until the first decades of the fourth century, but not even Diocletian's late third-century administrative measures for the government of the provinces could be applied in Britain in 293, when the other provinces were divided. This is because just after Diocletian's accession until 296, Britain was ruled by the usurper Carausius, and then by his assassin and successor, Allectus.

Carausius and Allectus c. 286–96

Marcus Aurelius Mausaeus/Maesius Carausius had probably started out as an ordinary soldier. He had established a military reputation for himself while fighting against the bandits called the Bagaudae in Gaul. He was serving under Maximian, who may have been appointed as Caesar to Diocletian in 285, then elevated to Augustus and co-Emperor in 286, though this is disputed. After fighting against the Bagaudae, according to Eutropius, Carausius was given a command with the purpose of clearing the seas of Frankish and Saxon raiders.[15] This presumably also involved protection of the coasts of Gaul, including modern Brittany, and Britain. His exact title is not known. He may have been commander of the *Classis Britannica*, but the latest inscription attesting this fleet is dated to the reign of Philip the Arab (244–49), and there is no extant record of it after this date, or in fact of any of the other provincial fleets.[16] The fleet base at Dover seems to have gone out of use in the 270s, as does Boulogne. Aurelius Victor says that Carausius was given the task of preparing a fleet, which may mean that he had to build ships. If this is correct, it was probably absence of the fleet which encouraged the raiders to take to the seas.[17] But there may have been at least a remnant of the fleet based somewhere other than Boulogne or Dover, so that Carausius simply had to collect ships. Boulogne certainly featured in later years whether or not it had ceased to be the fleet base, and Carausius captured it from Maximian probably in 290. He did well in his operations against the pirates, until people began to suspect that although he recovered some of the property stolen by the raiders, he did not return all of it to the rightful owners. The story goes that he fled to Britain under a cloud, and perhaps with an order for his execution from Maximian hanging over him. In Britain he set up his own Empire, which included parts of Gaul. Initially Carausius hoped for official recognition from Diocletian and Maximian, and for a while he was left in charge of Britain because Maximian was too preoccupied with raids across the Rhine to be able to deal with the problem. In an attempt to claim equality with the two Augusti, Carausius issued coins with portraits of all three of them on the obverse, accompanied by the legend CARAUSIUS ET FRATRES SUI, Carausius and his brothers.[18] He held his little Empire for six years, until his assassination in 293 by his subordinate Allectus, who ruled Britain for another three years.

The reigns of Carausius and Allectus probably did not deeply affect the northern British provinces. The troops that Carausius commanded while he had control of Gaul included vexillations from *II Augusta* and *XX Valeria Victrix*, which are named on his coinage. *VI Victrix* is conspicuously absent.[19] It is possible that Carausius made arrangements for the defence of the northern frontier and entrusted this task to the governor of Britannia Inferior, if a governor was still in post, and the military commanders. There seems to have been no resistance to him in the north, and he was acknowledged at least in the immediate vicinity of Carlisle where a milestone was set up in his name. The stone had an interesting history in that it already had an inscription in the centre when it was reused for Carausius, and then it was uprooted and turned over to receive a new inscription for the *nobilissimus* (most noble) Caesar Constantine, dated to 306 or 307, though it has been argued that it was Constantius who was honoured, not his son. Constantius I held the rank of Caesar in 296 when he recovered control of Britain, being made Augustus in 305. It could be the case that Carausius' milestone was quickly re-carved as soon as the province became part of the Empire again thanks to Constantius in 296. Constantius led an expedition to Britain, and Allectus was defeated by Constantius' Praetorian Prefect Asclepiodotus. A magnificent medallion was issued, showing Constantius riding to the right, with the personification of London kneeling to him in gratitude. The legend runs REDDITOR LUCIS AETERNAE, restorer of the eternal light.[20]

Britain under the Tetrarchs and the Rise of Constantine

The Tetrarchic government of the four British provinces could now be applied from 296 onwards. In the fully evolved version, the two British provinces were divided into four, with new names, Britannia Prima and Maxima Caesariensis probably being carved out of Britannia Superior, and Britannia Secunda and Flavia Caesariensis created from Britannia Inferior. The boundaries of these new provinces are not well elucidated and their capital cities and administrative centres are not certain, except that Maxima Caesariensis was the only one of the original four provinces to be governed by a consular, as attested in the *Notitia Dignitatum*.[21] It is thought that Britannia Secunda comprised the territory north of the Humber, and Flavia Caesariensis the lands to the east and north east of London.[22] A problem which has not been solved is the location of a province called Valentia, which according to the *Notitia* also had a consular governor, listed after the governor of Maxima Caesariensis and therefore contemporary with him, and indicating a separate province.[23] It is not certain whether it was a new name for an existing province, or a new extent of territory carved out from one of the four, or less probably, a new area just taken over outside the existing provinces. Valentia was a late creation. Referring to the fighting in 367–68 in Britain, Ammianus Marcellinus says that Theodosius, known as Count Theodosius in works on Britain, won back territory that had been overrun by the enemies of Rome, and a governor was installed in the area, which was renamed Valentia by order of the Emperor. Territory overrun by the tribes is most likely to have been in the north, and the relevance of this elusive province to Hadrian's Wall is that it has been suggested that Valentia was the new name for an area that had been part of Britannia Secunda, encompassing the Wall zone, with the consular governor's headquarters at Carlisle.[24]

The final version of the newly divided provinces probably did not come into operation until the reign of Constantine. The four provincial names are attested in the Verona list, called the *Laterculus Veronensis*, which is a catalogue of the provinces compiled somewhere between 303 and 314. In contrast to the first two centuries of Roman rule, epigraphic evidence for the governors and other officials virtually disappears in the fourth century, so very little is known of the governors of the British provinces. Although a *vicarius* was probably appointed as soon as the division into four provinces was planned, the first *vicarius* of Britain is not attested until 319. He was Lucius Papius Pacatianus, and his name is preserved because while he was in charge of the British provinces, he had addressed a query to Constantine about the laws of land tenure, and Constantine's reply of 20 November 319 is preserved in the *Codex Theodosianus*.[25] The governors of the four provinces in the years before the reign of Constantine held the title of *praeses*, though only one is known, Aurelius Arpagius, named on the Tetrarchic inscription from Birdoswald.[26] The inscription does not give the name of his province, but Arpagius was most likely the governor of Britannia Secunda, where Birdoswald and the Wall forts were located in the new provincial scheme.

The restoration of some forts and sections of the Wall perhaps belongs to Constantius' recovery of Britain. The inscription from Birdoswald recording the rebuilding of the headquarters, the commanding officer's house and the baths is dated by the mention of Diocletian and Maximian as Augusti.[27] Since these Emperors retired in the spring of 305, allowing the two Caesars Constantius and Galerius to take their places as Augusti, the work at Birdoswald must belong to the period between Constantius' victory over Allectus in 296 and the retirement of Diocletian and Maximian in 305. In that same year Constantius returned to Britain as Augustus for his campaign in the north. Another inscription, very fragmentary, was also set up before the spring of 305, at Housesteads. It is a dedication to Diocletian and Maximian, probably referring to the repair of some building or buildings, though it is not certain what was being built or rebuilt, or where it was.[28] Extensive rebuilding took place at South Shields after a disastrous fire in the later third century, some years before 296 or 297. A coin of Carausius or Allectus was found in the demolition layer of the headquarters building.[29] The rebuilding work is not closely dated, being placed somewhere between 286 and 318. The southern half of the interior of the fort was rebuilt on a different plan which shows similarities to other late Roman forts and to Diocletian's Palace at Split. The northern sections may have been retained as a supply base.[30] The rebuilding on a new plan could have been instigated under Constantius as Caesar from 296 onwards, or anywhere in the decade between his recovery of Britain and his campaign of 305, or even in the years thereafter.

The fateful date of 296–97 was once regarded as a horizon between Wall periods, because it was assumed that Allectus had brought troops southwards to fight for his survival, and lost most of them along with his life. The Wall was envisaged as almost deserted, tempting the northern tribes to invade, so that any signs of destruction were automatically dated to this alleged episode without benefit of proof that such an invasion had occurred and without any other dating evidence. The troubles of 296–97 are now discounted, but the reasons for the campaign of summer 305 are not clear, and there is an almost complete lack of information about it. Constantius was said to have reached the far north of the island, and he may have been accompanied by ships up the east coast, possibly reusing the Severan bases at Cramond and Carpow. None of the temporary camps revealing the various marches of armies into Scotland and beyond have been assigned to Constantius. Possibly the early fourth-century army in Britain did not build camps. Nothing more is known of Constantius' activities in the north, except that the few sources describe how the Romans crossed marshes and penetrated woods, which for the terrain of northern England and for Scotland does not narrow the choices for the location of the campaign. Constantius was victorious, and earned the title Britannicus Maximus, which is attested by January 306, not long before his death in York in July of the same year.

This campaign was presumably fought against the Picti, who are first recorded in the panegyrics addressed to Maximian and Constantine in 307, and to Constantine alone in 310, each referring to his father's achievements.[31] A new tribal name does not necessarily imply that a new people had arrived in the north. The Picts, or painted men, were most probably an amalgamation of the Caledonians and the Maeatae, the Britons whom Severus fought in the early third century. Herodian describes how the northern tribes of Severus' day tattooed their bodies with various figures and pictures of animals, and went without clothes so as not to obscure the designs.[32] The name Picti was probably a new label for an old established group of people, or perhaps more than one group. Some vestige of the Caledonians probably remained outside the group, since the Verona list mentions them separately from the Picts, and the Dicalydones and Verturiones are attested later in the work of Ammianus; these were probably separate branches of the Pictish nation.[33] As Collins points out, the Romans probably used the label Picts for all or most of the tribes north of the Wall, without bothering themselves about ethnic accuracy.[34]

The British Provinces in the Fourth Century

When Constantius died at York, a new era was about to begin, although it would be several years before this would become clear. Probably on 25 July 306, though the date is disputed, the troops in northern Britain declared Constantine Emperor. It may not have been as spontaneous as the sources suggest. Constantine may have encouraged the soldiers as soon as it was obvious that Constantius was not going to recover, and it is recorded that more encouragement came from Crocus, the Alamannic king who led his own tribesmen as part of Constantius' expeditionary army. The Tetrarchic principle was all very well, but dynastic succession was not dead as far as the troops were concerned. Whatever the truth of this episode, Constantine celebrated his *dies imperii* on 25 July from then onwards, and he favoured Germanic troops throughout his reign, possibly because of the loyalty shown by Crocus. It would take nearly two decades for Constantine to become sole Emperor, and there would be civil wars and upheavals on the frontiers on the way. Constantine's elevation was a direct challenge to the Tetrarchic system. Constantius as Augustus had appointed Flavius Valerius Severus as his Caesar, and the other Augustus, Galerius had appointed Galerius Maximinus, better known as Maximinus Daia. Galerius was now the senior Augustus, and Constantine wrote to him to explain that he had no choice but to abide by the wishes of the soldiers. Galerius compromised and offered to make Constantine Caesar. There was a complication in October 306 in Rome when the Praetorians combined with some senators to declare for Maxentius, the son of the former Augustus Maximian. In 307 Constantine married Maximian's younger daughter Fausta, and allegedly part of the deal was that Maximian, who had no authority because he had retired in 305, made Constantine Augustus. Whether or not it was an official appointment hardly matters, since Constantine was determined to be Augustus by any means whatsoever, and from this time onwards he counted himself as such.

Constantine may have returned to Britain, possibly more than once, in 307 and at some point before 312, and again in 314. The evidence for these visits derives from coins celebrating the ADVENTUS AUG., or arrival of Augustus, dated from the middle of 310 to the latter part of 312, and again between 313 and 315. Constantine may have arrived *c.* 311 probably to gather troops for the planned campaign against his main rival Maxentius, who had been in power as Augustus in Rome since 306. Zosimus says that for this campaign Constantine assembled his army from conquered barbarians, Germans and other tribes, and the troops that he collected from Britain.[35] It is not known where he found the British troops, or whether he took legionaries, auxiliaries, or newly recruited Britons, or a combination of all three. Casey links the coins of 310–12 with passages in Eusebius' *Life of Constantine* describing campaigns against the Britons, after which Constantine arranged terms with them. Part of the peace terms may have stipulated that the defeated tribes must contribute troops for the

Roman army, and Constantine perhaps included some or all of them in his army of 312.[36] A postulated visit by Constantine in 314 is also supported by Adventus coins, and in 315 Constantine took the title Britannicus Maximus, so it is possible that the campaigns noted by Eusebius belong to this period and not the visit before the confrontation with Maxentius in 312.

It has been suggested that the assembly of Constantine's campaign force for 312, and/or his possible campaigns and peace treaty in 314, are connected with the abandonment of the outpost forts north of Hadrian's Wall. The evidence will bear that interpretation, since the abandonment is now dated by coin evidence to some point between 312 and 314. The units from Risingham and High Rochester, respectively *cohors I Vangionum milliaria equitata* and *cohors I Fida Vardullorum milliaria equitata civium Romanorum*, are not attested after the first four decades of the third century, and nor are the *exploratores* that were with them in the first decade.[37] The *numerus exploratorum* at Bowes in the *Notitia Dignitatum* is too vaguely named to be certain that it must be a descendant of the units from the outposts. This lack of evidence for the whereabouts of the above-named units from the eastern outposts may simply be a result of the decline in the habit of setting up inscriptions from the later third century onwards, but neither of the cohorts appear in the British sections of the *Notitia* and they are not attested anywhere else. On the west side of the province, evidence for units in occupation in the late third century at the outposts of Birrens and Bewcastle is doubtful, and *cohors I Aelia Hispanorum* at Netherby is not attested epigraphically after 216, but it is the only unit from the outposts that possibly survives long enough to be included in the *Notitia*. It is listed at Stanwix, but in reality this is probably a mistake and the unit was possibly located at Bowness.[38]

The probable date when the outposts were abandoned and the disappearance from the record of two units, both of them nominally 1000-strong, with a contingent of cavalry, could be explained by the fact that Constantine removed them, mixed units like these being especially useful on campaigns, and he needed an army, larger than the troops that he already had at his disposal in Gaul, to deal with Maxentius in Rome, first having to besiege Verona on his way there. Maxentius was defeated at the battle of the Milvian Bridge in 312.

The repair work on the Wall forts under Constantius as Caesar, attested at Birdoswald and Housesteads, may have been more extensive than epigraphic or archaeological evidence suggests, and perhaps it was an ongoing programme, though if it was, it is devoid of further evidence for building. Nonetheless, Constantine may have picked up where Constantius left off. The northern campaign under Constantius as Augustus may have been as effective as that of Severus and Caracalla a century earlier. No one knows what arrangements Constantius had made with the tribes, but perhaps he had secured the allegiance of Lowland peoples to combat the northern tribes and keep them quiet, and the campaigns of 314 by Constantine, as described by Eusebius, may have been conducted to reinforce the terms or impose new ones.

It may be as part of an initial plan formulated by Constantius, continued by Constantine, that the forts in the hinterland of Hadrian's Wall were reoccupied after some of them had apparently been abandoned, probably in the last quarter of the third century.[39] None of the sparse evidence for this reoccupation can be unequivocally linked with Constantius or Constantine and the early fourth century. The only source is the *Notitia Dignitatum* which records the situation of these forts nearly a hundred years after Constantine's alleged visits to Britain, so the units could have arrived in these forts at any time between the early and the late fourth century. There are clues that Constantine may have had something to do with the reorganisation. The units attested in the hinterland forts are new-style *numeri* and *equites* instead of the old-style *alae* and cohorts, but one unit is called *ala Herculea* after Maximian, who was associated with Hercules just as Diocletian was associated with Jupiter. The *Notitia* records this unit at Olenacum, which could possibly be Ilkley, but perhaps more likely it is related to Olicana of Ptolemy's *Geography*, designated as a *polis* of the Brigantes, which Rivet and Smith assign to Elslack in North Yorkshire.[40] The unit may have been raised, not necessarily in Britain, before Maximian retired and ceased to be Augustus in 305. Constantius may have brought the *ala* to Britain in 296 to help in the battle against Allectus, or possibly in 305 for the northern campaigns. At least the unit name most probably dates to some point before 310. As mentioned above, Constantine married Maximian's younger daughter Fausta in 307, but in 310 Maximian tried to seize power again by staging a coup while Constantine was on the Rhine fighting against the Franks. He was foiled and captured but not punished, and then he allegedly tried to enlist the help of his daughter Fausta to rid the world of Constantine. The story goes that when the plot was revealed to Constantine by his loyal young wife, Maximian hung himself, conveniently. A new *ala* was hardly likely to have been named in honour of the disgraced Maximian after 310, but it may have retained its name with Constantine's acquiescence. Another unit connected with Constantine was the *equites Crispiani,* listed in the *Notitia* at a place called Danum, which may be Doncaster, or possibly Jarrow.[41] The unit was named for Crispus, Constantine's son by his first wife. He was made Caesar in 317, and executed by his father for reasons not perfectly understood in 326. It is not impossible that the *equites Crispiani* were raised, or formed from an existing unit and given a new name in his honour, before Crispus was made Caesar, and like the *ala Herculea* the unit may not have been raised in Britain.

On present evidence it is not possible to say with confidence that the *Notitia* of the late fourth or early fifth century represents Constantine's troop dispositions in the early years of the century. It is very likely that this Emperor paid close attention to the northern frontier and the forts of the hinterland, protecting the provinces of Britannia Secunda and Flavia Caesariensis from incursions from the north and also from the sea, but there could have been changes in the hundred years between his organisation and that of later emperors, in response to an escalation or a diminution of hostilities from different sources. It is not known if Constantine appointed the first *dux Britanniarum*, nor can it be discerned when the first *comes litoris Saxonici* came into being. To resort to the vernacular again, a lot of water passed under the bridge between Constantine's organisation of Britain and the scenario presented in the *Notitia*, so it will be convenient to review what happened in the intervening years, in so far as the sources allow. Only the high points in the history of Britain are briefly documented in the literary evidence. The emphasis is on the Roman world, in which Britain was not especially important, so the exploits of the emperors and the great generals receive some attention but the internal history of the British provinces remains obscure.

After Constantine's visits to Britain, the Roman world was

involved in external and internal wars for almost another two decades. In 324 Licinius, the last of Constantine's rivals who had ruled the eastern provinces, was eliminated, and Constantine emerged at last as the sole Emperor. He put into effect several changes, moving his capital to Byzantium where he was closer to the Danube and the east, the major sources of trouble in the rest of his reign. He altered the religious base of the whole Empire by making Christianity the official state religion, without entirely renouncing his allegiance to Sol Invictus, the Unconquered Sun. Soldiers now swore allegiance not just to the Emperor, but to God, Christ and the majesty of the Emperor, and churches or Christianised religious areas began to appear in forts. When Constantine died in 337, all three of his sons succeeded him, partitioned the Empire, and immediately began to squabble. Constantius II ruled the east, and most of the west was originally assigned to Constantine II. In 340 Constantius II attempted to take over the territories of Constans, the youngest of the brothers, but instead he was killed in the ensuing struggle. Constans took over the west, and in 343 he came to Britain. The reasons for his arrival are not clear. The section of Ammianus' history that covered this event is lost, but he makes reference to Constans in later passages concerning the expedition of Count Theodosius in 367. Ammianus explains that he has already described the position of Britain and the ebb and flow of the tides when he wrote about the Emperor Constans, and in another passage he says that Theodosius dismissed the *areani*, whom he had previously discussed in his account of the expedition of Constans.[42] In this passage Ammianus says that the *areani* were a group of men established long ago (*genus hominum a veteribus institutum*) and their function was to patrol backwards and forwards over large areas and report to the Roman commanders about any signs of threatening behaviour among neighbouring peoples. When Constans arrived in Britain, the *areani* had obviously been in existence for some time. Perhaps four decades could be classified as a long time, so it is possible that the *areani* had been recruited and installed beyond Hadrian's Wall by Constantine, in part to compensate for abandoning the outpost forts and withdrawing the troops. In the lost passages of Ammianus' narrative, it can be assumed that Constans had to deal with trouble on the northern frontier, and the trouble had something to do with the *areani*, but at that time it is possible that the *areani* had carried out their functions properly, and given adequate warning to the Roman generals that something was brewing among the northern tribes. The *areani* were retained until they failed in their tasks in 367, and Theodosius dismissed them.

Constans may possibly have been responsible for dividing Britannia Secunda, and creating a new province in the frontier zone, the original name of which is not known, but which some years later was eventually given the name Valentia, when Count Theodosius campaigned in Britain. Ammianus says that after the disaster of 367, the Romans recovered the province that had fallen under the control of the enemies, and it then received a regular governor and was called Valentia by the decision of the Emperor, which strongly implies that it was a province that already existed, and was upgraded and renamed. The problem is that no one really knows where it was.[43]

There is no mention of a *dux Britanniarum* during the campaign of Constans, but he may have appointed the elder Gratianus, the father of the Emperors Valentinian and Valens, as *comes rei militaris*, probably in charge of a contingent of the central field army as well as troops from Britain and perhaps from Hadrian's Wall. The post was not a regular or permanent one, and Gratianus' title is not even certain. Ammianus says that Gratianus had been *comes* in Africa, but only mentions that later he commanded troops in Britain, without giving him an official title. Since Gratianus died in 351 the most likely slot for command of an expeditionary army in Britain is under Constans in 342–43.[44]

From 350 to 353 the British provinces were controlled by the usurper Flavius Magnus Magnentius who was proclaimed at Autun. Constans was killed in 350, and Magnentius took over and held the west until August 353, when Constantius II defeated him. Magnentius had appointed his own officials, none of whom are known in Britain, but an immediate replacement by Constantius II was the *vicarius* Martinus in 353. Constantius also sent Paulus, nicknamed Catena, the Chain, to Britain to organise the witch-hunt for Magnentius' followers, and Martinus became a casualty. Trying to put a stop to Paul's zeal for rooting out supposed opponents of Constantius, Martinus tried to kill him, but failed and killed himself instead in 354.

In 360, the Picts emerge again, together with the Scotti, or the Attacotti. According to Ammianus, these tribes attacked places close to the frontier during the winter.[45] Winter raids resonate very closely with cattle raiding during the period of the Border reivers, when the best time to steal cattle was in the winter, because the beasts were 'in full meat', having grazed someone else's lands for the summer, and in winter the nights were long, helping to avoid detection, and even the bogs were frozen, so that escaping with the stolen animals was not hindered. Comparison with other periods of history is considered to be of no use by Breeze, but raids probably had a purpose behind them other than violence and destruction, and cattle would be a worthy goal.[46] Julian, Caesar to Constantius II, sent his *magister equitum* Flavius Lupicinus to deal with the attacks, while the Caesar himself was preoccupied with the incursions of the Alamanni. Lupicinus took with him units of Heruli, Batavi and Moesiaci, but nothing is known of his actions, which presumably concerned the northern frontier zone.

This episode prefigures the so-called barbarian conspiracy of 367, in the reign of Valentinian I. Ammianus reports that the *comes maritimi tractus* Nectaridus was killed and the *dux* Fullofaudes was surrounded, which probably means that he was killed as well. It is debated whether or not the title *comes maritimi tractus*, count of the coastal region, is a literary version of *comes litoris Saxonici*. It has been suggested that the post was concerned with the protection of the west coast, but this has not gained acceptance.[47] Valentinian sent two generals in succession to Britain, first the *comes domesticorum* Severus, and then Jovinus, *magister equitum*, but seemingly they were not effective. Only when Flavius Theodosius took over was there any success against the Britons, but his achievements as reported by Ammianus require a cautionary approach, because Theodosius was the father of Theodosius I, who was declared Emperor in January 379, and it was under this Emperor that Ammianus wrote his history. It is generally accepted that Theodosius was appointed as *comes rei militaris*, usually rendered in English as count, but Ammianus does not use this title, instead calling him *dux*, meaning leader, which is not to be confused with *dux Britanniarum*.[48]

Count Theodosius arrived at Richborough, and four units of the Continental field army followed him to Britain. Ammianus lists them as the Heruli, Jovii, Batavi and Victores.[49] Two of these, the Batavi and Heruli, had featured in the army of Lupicinus in 360, also recorded by Ammianus, who describes these units as light-armed forces.[50] The arrival of Lupicinus and Theodosius is described in very similar terms. They both arrived at Boulogne, crossed the Channel in calm seas to Richborough, and marched straight towards London, now called Augusta.[51] According to Ammianus, Theodosius had much to do before he entered the city. His operations seem to have been wide-ranging, covering large areas of the country, but it is not known exactly where he operated. He employed separate detachments to round up the bands of raiders, who were weighed down with their booty, including prisoners in chains and cattle. Theodosius defeated the raiders, rescued the stolen goods and restored most of them to their owners, saving a small amount to reward the soldiers. He issued an amnesty to all deserters to encourage them to return to the army, indicating that desertion was particularly problematic at this time. Most of the soldiers returned to the army. Theodosius then asked for Civilis to be appointed to govern Britain as deputy of the Prefect, meaning the Praetorian Prefect, which means Civilis was to be the *vicarius*. Theodosius also asked for the *dux* Dulcitius to be sent, possibly as *dux Britanniarum*, but this is not stated.[52] Probably in the following year, 368, he moved against the tribesmen. He had already learned, by questioning prisoners and deserters, that the way to deal with the scattered groups of men from different tribes was to make surprise attacks and lay ambushes for them, so this he proceeded to do. Ammianus says that the tribesmen were attacking what was Roman, which probably embraces cities, towns and forts. Having defeated the tribesmen, Theodosius restored and fortified cities and forts that had 'suffered damage of many kinds'. Ammianus says that this repair work gave the inhabitants peace for a long time.[53] In another passage Ammianus repeats that Theodosius restored cities, put garrisons into forts and fortified the frontiers.[54]

These non-specific statements by Ammianus have converted Theodosius into a late Roman version of Gnaeus Julius Agricola. Just as Agricola was once credited with building every fort north of Chester, the work of Theodosius was recognised in all building and repairs of vaguely the right date. He was usually credited with blocking some of the gates in forts on Hadrian's Wall, but it is now known that some gates were blocked in the second century, in some cases before the Wall was finished, and several were probably completely or partially blocked in the third century. However, there does seem to be a renewed spate of gate blocking in the late fourth century.[55] It was not only in Britain that access to forts was restricted by blocking them up in the fourth century. Probably under Constantine and his successors some forts on the Danube had their gates sealed by the construction of semi-circular or rectangular towers, projecting beyond the walls, built out across the entrance and also the original flanking towers of the gates. In some cases the usual four gates were reduced to only one. This and the projecting towers can be seen in the plans of Ulcisia Castra (modern Szentendre north of Budapest), and Drobeta (modern Turnu Severin, Romania).

Collins provides useful tables for Hadrian's Wall and the hinterland forts, showing that in the Wall forts, one or more of the gates were blocked, not necessarily under Theodosius, at South Shields and Wallsend, and at all the forts from Rudchester to Birdoswald, perhaps significantly all along the central sector, but further excavation at other forts may reveal that gates were blocked at nearly every fort at some point in the third or fourth centuries.[56] A possible exception to the rule is South Shields, where a gate that had been disused in the third century, when the fort ditch was dug out right across the entrance, was reopened in the fourth century, by which time the ditch had silted up. A paved road was laid out over the ditch, and timber posts were fitted into the gate, presumably to receive wooden doors.[57] In the hinterland, gate blocking has been found at Lanchester, Piercebridge, Malton, Ilkley, Ribchester, Burrow in Lonsdale and Watercrook.

The repair work carried out by Theodosius on the frontier, documented by Ammianus, shows that he was active in the frontier zone and at least some of the forts that he repaired and garrisoned were presumably on the Wall. He dismissed the *areani* because they had betrayed the Romans by giving information to the tribesmen about what was happening on the Roman side of the frontier. Dismissal sounds a little too lenient, and no punishment is mentioned. Were they paid by the Romans, the withdrawal of cash or gifts being punishment enough? Perhaps their numbers were not large enough to cause trouble, however resentful they may have felt. The perennial problem of Valentia surfaces again. According to Ammianus, Theodosius reported to the Emperor Valentinian I, who renamed the province Valentia, as if in celebration of a triumph, and installed a regular governor.[58] In the *Notitia* the governor was a consular.[59]

Probably while Theodosius was occupied in the north, a Pannonian called Valentinus, who had been exiled to Britain, stirred up the other exiles, presumably with the aim of making himself Emperor, but Theodosius foiled him. He ordered the *dux* Dulcitius to execute Valentinus and some of his associates, but forbade any enquiry into the plot in case it caused more trouble in the provinces which had just been pacified.[60] Theodosius went on to fight against the Alamanni as *magister equitum* from 370–72, and from 373 to 375 he quelled a Moorish rebellion in Africa. Shortly after the death of Valentinian I in November 375, he was executed, probably by Valentinian's younger brother Valens, for reasons unknown.

By the 380s, the Picts and Scots were causing trouble once again and in 382 they were repelled by Magnus Maximus, who is the Macsen Wledig of Welsh legend. His status is not clear. Since he operated in the north he was probably *dux Britanniarum* but it is also suggested that he was *comes litoris Saxonici*. Whatever his official appointment, he was declared Emperor by the troops and quickly left Britain for the Continent in 383. His motives have been examined by several authors. The east was ruled by Theodosius I, the son of Count Theodosius. He had been made *magister militum* by Gratian in 378 after the disastrous battle of Adrianople in which the Goths defeated the Romans and killed the Emperor Valens. In 379 Theodosius was made Emperor and in the 380s he made a treaty with the Goths, settling some of them in Thrace. The eastern part of the Empire and its army recovered from the battle of Adrianople, but although it was the eastern army that had been defeated it was the western army that suffered. The west was ruled by Gratian and Valentinian II, sons of Valentinian I by different mothers. They had been made Emperors while they were children, Gratian at the age of eight in 367, and Valentinian II at the age of four in 375. In 383 they were respectively twenty-four and twelve years old, and all was not going well. Magnus Maximus perhaps considered that he had a mission to save the west, and it has been suggested that he needed to set everything right in order to secure and maintain Imperial patronage whereby British produce, especially from the farmlands of the south-west, had a steady market on the Continent to feed the armies and the administrative staff based there. In other words, Maximus was trying to save the British economy.[61] Whatever his purpose, he defeated and killed Gratian, but it is not known what he achieved with regard to Britain in his five year rule. In 388 Theodosius I defeated him and had him executed.

From the defeat of Maximus to the end of Roman Britain, the sources are more numerous but fragmentary and not particularly illuminating. In January 395 Theodosius I died, and bequeathed the Empire to his two sons, Arcadius aged eighteen or nineteen taking charge of the east and Honorius aged ten in the west. Emperors as young as these could not rule entirely alone and could not hope to lead armies, but the emperors had already ceased to lead campaigns in person, entrusting the conduct of wars to the increasingly powerful generals, many of them of tribal origin. The real power behind both Arcadius and Honorius at first was the Vandal, Stilicho, who was probably *magister militum*. He insisted that Theodosius had entrusted both his sons to his care, and he spent some time fighting against the Goths in the east, and fending off the ambitious eastern Praetorian Prefect Rufinus. Power struggles such as this took attention away from the British provinces, which were not of the foremost importance in Imperial policies at this time. Between 388 and 398, the Picts raided, probably in the north and possibly along the east coast, and the Irish tribes came from the west. Nothing is known of how the British commanders dealt with these problems. Probably in 398 Stilicho sent extra troops to Britain, but did not come in person. He may have installed the *comes Britanniarum*, commanding a small field army, consisting primarily of cavalry units with some infantry. It was probably based in one of the more important cities, but no one knows where it might have been housed. The field army remained in Britain until the end of Roman rule.[62]

It is usually stated that Stilicho took troops from Britain in 401 for the army he commanded against Alaric the Goth at the battle of Pollentia in the following year, but the source is a poem, declaring that Stilicho's army included a legion from far-off

Britain. Birley suggests this is fantasy, and the troop withdrawals should be attributed to the Emperor Constantine III, raised by the armies in Britain probably at the beginning of 407. This was shortly after the soldiers had declared for two candidates in quick succession, Marcus and Gratianus, and had found each of them unsuitable. This was of course a death sentence. Constantine III possibly owed his elevation to his name Constantinus, and the fact that just over a hundred years earlier, Constantine I had been proclaimed at York. He added Flavius Claudius to his name, and the late authors Sozomen and Orosius point out that he gave the people hope, because it was expected that he would be a strong Emperor by association with the first Constantine.[63] The mutiny in Britain is said to have been a result of barbarian invasion across the Rhine into Gaul, probably at the end of 405. The troops in Britain thought that they would be attacked as well, and therefore chose their own Emperors. This implies that there was no faith in the central government to assist if attacks did occur from Gaul. Where were the *dux* and the two *comites* in all this turmoil? Who, apart from Constantine, formed a plan to take the army to Gaul to pre-empt attacks rather than fortify the island any further? Constantine obviously took troops with him, but from where, and which ones, is not clear. Nor is it known what arrangements he made for the protection of Britain, but it is possible that he left the northern frontier more or less intact and took the small field army with him and troops from the south. As Collins points out, there is no archaeological evidence to prove that forts of the northern frontier were suddenly abandoned at the time of Constantine's usurpation.[64]

Honorius at Ravenna recognised Constantine III as Augustus, because he had little choice, but his general Sarus defeated and killed Constantine's *magister militum*. Constantine took over Spain and may have protected Gaul with success, but everything soon began to go wrong. There was an attack on Britain by the Saxons in 408 or 409, possibly not just one event but a recurring problem, perhaps causing more damage because there were fewer troops to repel the attacks.

In 408 Arcadius the eastern Emperor died, and Honorius became suspicious of his best general Stilicho, who was accused of being too friendly with Alaric and the Goths. Instead of defeating Alaric in a military action Stilicho had bought him off. This was probably the best course to follow until Stilicho felt ready to go on the offensive, but Honorius executed Stilicho, so there was now for a short time no strong military leader who could pull everything back together. A Briton called Gerontius rebelled against Constantine III, holding out against him from 409 until 411, then committed suicide, and Constantine himself was captured and killed by Honorius. According to tradition, Honorius wrote to the Britons in 410 telling them that they must look to their own defence, but it could be the case that this letter was sent to Bruttium, telling the inhabitants that he could not help them to fight against Alaric, who was in Liguria by this time. The place names Bruttium and Britannia may have been mixed up by the historians.[65] In actuality, if such a letter was ever sent, the Britons had probably anticipated Honorius' decision, and broken away from the Empire in the previous year. Whatever group of men possessed any authority in Britain had decided to take the government into their own hands, allegedly expelling Roman officials. Probably this means the men in command decided to eject the officials who disagreed with the intention to detach Britain from the Empire. The higher officials would have come from other provinces to take up their posts in Britain, and perhaps they were simply allowed to return to their homes, rather than being forcibly bundled onto ships at Richborough with their households and belongings.

No names are recorded, so it is not known if a candidate was chosen as Emperor in Britain, or invested with power under another title. Initially the setup may have been similar to the Gallic Empire of the third century, an independent part of the Roman Empire but governed in parallel fashion on Roman principles. The Britons had never been as closely involved in government as the natives of Gaul had been, but there was hopefully a core of individuals with some experience who could take charge for a while. Did the Britons know it was the end? We have textbooks that tell us that Roman Britain came to an end in 410, but the people who witnessed this so-called end perhaps did not construe it as such, because their lives had to continue beyond 409 and they had to create a future for their descendants. We know that the western Empire itself had not long to live, just a generation or two, but did the Britons have any sense that Goths would rule in Rome and the Empire was going to be replaced by individual kingdoms? Assuming that there was a *dux Britanniarum* in 409, did he remain in post and try to organise the frontier in the new circumstances? Or if there was no officially appointed *dux*, was there an overall leader for the frontier who could coordinate defence, supplies, repair work, recruitment, at least for a while? These questions will probably never be answered but will be revisited below in this chapter.

Fourth-Century Forts in the North and the Notitia Dignitatum

The *Notitia Dignitatum* is an invaluable document because in the absence of epigraphic evidence and detailed literary accounts it is the only source that provides any information about the forts and the units in them under the *dux Britanniarum* in the north and the *comes litoris Saxonici* in the south. From about 398, or possibly earlier, there was also an additional small field army under the *comes Britanniarum*, probably brought in by Stilicho. The date of the *Notitia* is disputed, but there is some agreement, not universal by any means, that it was compiled in 395 and incorporates amendments up to about the middle of the 420s, which creates an instant problem because Britain ceased to belong to the Empire traditionally *c.* 410. Doubt has also been cast on the date and authenticity of the British sections of the *Notitia* because the units on the Wall are mostly the same as those attested in the second and third centuries, implying that the information must be hopelessly out of date. But more recently it has been shown that there are other provinces where units from the second and third centuries are still listed in their forts in the *Notitia*, notably Egypt and Armenia, where these troops are listed together with fourth-century units.[66]

Under the heading *per lineam valli*, the command of the *dux Britanniarum* included all the Wall forts and the west coast installations, plus Ribchester, Elslack and Bainbridge. Listed separately, before the Wall forts, the command also included VI legion, without its title Victrix and minus any location, and the forts in the hinterland in Durham, Yorkshire and Cumbria. The garrisons of the forts *per lineam valli* are nearly all cohorts commanded by tribunes, and *alae* commanded by prefects, with the exception of the *numerus Maurorum Aurelianorum* at Burgh-by-Sands, commanded by a prefect, and the *cuneus Sarmatarum* at Ribchester with no mention of any commanding officer at all. The units in the hinterland forts are all *equites* or *numeri*, all commanded by prefects.[67]

Although most of the place names in the *Notitia* can be identified with known forts, especially on the Wall, there are a few in the hinterland which are uncertain, and a further complication is that there are several forts which are known to be occupied in the fourth century, but these are not listed in the *Notitia*. At least a small number of these occupied forts must be the same as a handful of the unidentified sites in the list, but since the *equites* and *numeri* in the hinterland are all new-style units, the match cannot be made on the basis of unit names. So far there have been no discoveries of inscriptions naming one of these fourth-century units which would make it clear to which of the unidentified sites it belongs. It has been suggested that the *Notitia* lists only the headquarters of each unit where all the records would be kept, and ignores sites where only detachments of units were located.[68] Since the numbers of men in the new-style units are not known, it is possible that one unit could have sent detachments to more than one fort, which would account for several of the sites which are thought to be occupied but which do not appear in the *Notitia*. To speculate beyond the evidence, if the large fourth-century fort at Newton Kyme near York was still occupied in the late period it may have been garrisoned by legionaries of *VI* legion. The fort at Greta Bridge, which is thought to have been occupied after 369 but was not mentioned in the *Notitia*, could have held a number of soldiers from the *numerus exploratorum* at nearby Bowes. Ebchester has yielded very little evidence of occupation at the beginning of the fifth century, but it could have held soldiers from the *numerus Longovicanorum* at Lanchester. Even if this could be shown to be correct, it would not account for all the forts thought to be occupied but not listed in the *Notitia*.

The troop withdrawals under Magnus Maximus in 383 may have changed the dispositions of the units in northern Britain. One late Roman author working in Constantinople in the fifth century says that Maximus raised a large army of Britons, Gauls and other tribesmen.[69] It is not possible to pinpoint with accuracy which troops Maximus took with him from Britain. Probably none of them returned. There is a notable lack of fort names in the western Pennines in the *Notitia*. Although the forts at Papcastle and Ilkley were rebuilt *c.* 369 presumably as part of the clearing up and reoccupation after 367, these two forts do not feature in the *Notitia*. Nor does the list include the forts at Ebchester, Low Borrow Bridge and at Ambleside, though it has been suggested that Ambleside may be Glannibanta in the *Notitia*, the name previously assigned to Ravenglass. These forts were occupied after 369, but perhaps did not survive after 383. It has been suggested that Magnus Maximus took the troops and abandoned these sites, and this is why they do not appear in the *Notitia*.[70] There is a possibility that the forts which show signs of occupation in the later fourth century, but do not merit inclusion in the *Notitia*, were garrisoned by tribal levies such as the *laeti*, who were known in Gaul and Italy. These were tribesmen who had been settled on lands set aside for them by the Romans, on condition that they contributed recruits. A law of 399 refers to *terrae laeticae*, and several *praefecti laetorum* are listed in Gaul in the *Notitia Dignitatum*.[71] But no such troops are mentioned in the British sections of the *Notitia*. Despite this lack of confirmation it is still suggested that Maximus could have brought in units similar to the *laeti* to replace the regular troops that he took away. If he stripped the Wall forts of troops it is not known which units were affected. There is no evidence for wholesale abandonment of forts, so if Maximus did take troops he probably chose only a detachment from various units. On the other hand he may sensibly have left the northern garrisons intact to protect the province while he embarked on his bid for power.

Other considerations are that signs of occupation of a site in the archaeological record do not necessarily signify military use, and even if military use can be ascertained there are still some problems, as demonstrated by the fortress at Chester, which was not under the command of the *dux Britanniarum*, but it serves to illustrate the difficulties of interpreting the *Notitia*. The fortress was well maintained into the 350s, but its legion XX *Valeria Victrix* is not attested after the end of the third century, and the *Notitia* makes no mention of the site.[72] The years between the early to mid-third century and the compilation of the *Notitia c.* 395 are especially devoid of information, so it is virtually impossible to discern what was happening in the forts of the hinterland of Hadrian's Wall during this time. It is quite likely that Constantine I had something to do with the dispositions of the units in the hinterland but it is unlikely that his arrangements remained unchanged until the end of the fourth century. The *Notitia* records the finished product, but the stages by which the units arrived at various forts are unclear. In the years between the early fourth century and the beginning of the fifth, forts could have been abandoned and reoccupied more than once, according to the needs of the moment. In the last quarter of the fourth century, several forts seem to have been abandoned, and probably not all of them were put back into commission. Units from the field armies could have been located for short periods close to the frontier, and then moved on. There was probably a reorganisation after 367, put into effect by Theodosius, who may have been responsible for establishing in these forts units or parts of units from the field armies, which feature in the *Notitia* in the first section of the command of the *dux Britanniarum*, listed before the Wall units. It is not known how extensive the reorganisation would have been. Rob Collins discusses the *Notitia* and its problems much more fully and in greater detail than is feasible in just one chapter in this book.[73]

Fourth-Century Forts and the Army in the North

There were many changes in the army and forts from the late third century onwards, largely driven by changed circumstances. Not least was the emergence of new threats. On the frontiers the native peoples and the Romans influenced each other in several different ways, sometimes producing a blend of cultures through trade and by recruiting tribesmen into the army. But one of the main attractions for some tribes beyond the frontier was the material wealth of the provinces. In the fourth century it seems that the northern tribes were no longer restricted to land-based infiltration, and Britain had come to the notice of other tribes across the seas. The army had to take steps to meet the new problems.

It has been noted that the fourth-century forts are located in the best places to protect communications, and they reflect a new situation in Britain, with new enemies from new areas.[74] The preponderance of forts on or near the northern frontier indicates that the threat from the Picts was taken seriously, and the ill-documented campaigns by Constans in the mid-fourth century had not solved the problem. It has been suggested that there may have been an attempt to make alliances with pro-Roman tribes of the Lowlands in the last quarter of the fourth century, so that they could help to control the Pictish incursions. This was a normal Roman practice, and the theory is based on the Roman origins of the names of the early tribal kings, such as Cluim and Cinhill, rulers of the kingdom of Strathclyde, whose names derive from Clemens and Quintilius in Latin. One of the kings of the Votadini, usually considered pro-Roman from the earliest times, was Pesrut, which refers to a red cloak or possibly a red shirt or tunic, implying that this individual was perhaps acting in an official capacity authorised by the Romans. On the other hand the names may simply indicate that the rulers had become Christians and adopted tribal versions of Roman names, and the lack of fourth-century Roman goods in the territory of the tribes argues against gift giving or subsidies.[75]

During the fourth century the Cumberland Coast was strengthened, with the fort at Burrow Walls added to the system, and occupation probably continued at Maryport and Moresby, and definitely at Ravenglass. Possibly some of the milefortlets were reoccupied.[76] These measures were presumably directed against raids across the sea from Ireland, by the tribe known in the sources as Scotti, and possibly the Attacotti, but it is not certain whether these people came from Ireland or Scotland. Not much is known about the kind of ships that the Irish tribes used; Collins speculates that although the raiders probably used oared ships which were highly labour intensive, the larger boats could have been fitted with masts and sails, and arrival and escape in these ships would have been more rapid, requiring less energy.[77] In the fourth century, forts similar to the massive Saxon Shore forts were built to protect the west coast, at Cardiff, at Caer Gybi on Anglesey, and at Lancaster. There is no mention of these forts in the extant version of the *Notitia*, though it is possible that a section covering Wales has been lost. Without the assistance of the *Notitia* it is not possible to decide whether these forts were under the command of the *comes litoris Saxonici*, or the *dux Britanniarum*.

On the east coast a series of large towers or fortlets was constructed, perhaps by Theodosius. They are known from Filey to Huntcliffe, but may have extended further north, perhaps up to the Tyne, and also further south, though the coast has been eroded and there are probably no traces to be found of further fortlets. Erosion may also account for the lack of any evidence of military installations on the lower reaches of the River Tees and the Wear, though Dictum of the *Notitia*, where the *numerus Nerviorum Dictensium* was stationed, has been tentatively identified with Wearmouth, despite the lack of evidence for a fort there. Dating evidence for the towers can only point to a date after 367, so it is possible that Magnus Maximus established the fortlets in the 380s.[78] The towers were stone built, surrounded by an outer stone wall and an external ditch. Clearly there was a threat to the east coast from the sea, which required observation posts and most probably an early warning system, though how it worked is not known. Nor is the nature of the threat understood. Collins points out that there is no evidence for Germanic raiders coming to this part of Britain across the North Sea, and the target even if there were such raiders was more likely the south-east coast, where the forts of the Saxon Shore were established to combat such raids, probably by operations on land and sea.[79] If it was not the German tribes who threatened the east coast in the territory under the *dux Britanniarum*, was it seaborne Picts?

The fourth-century army that had to protect and defend the frontier and the hinterland is generally supposed to have been much smaller than its second-century counterpart. From the mid-third century onwards the barracks in some forts were reduced in size, with fewer *contubernia*, which has been taken to imply a reduction in the size of individual centuries. Whether or not this applied to all forts is debatable, a problem that can be solved only by extensive investigation at all the Wall forts and those of the hinterland. The number of *contubernia* in the barracks is not standardized, varying from five to eight. It is estimated that five soldiers would inhabit each of the five compartments or individual chalets in the new-style barracks, producing a total of twenty-five men under one centurion, or a maximum of forty-eight men by estimating that six men inhabited each compartment of an eight-roomed barrack. There is no way of confirming these estimates and they probably do not apply to all units at all times. It is estimated that the late Roman fort at South Shields could have accommodated a unit of about 300 to 400 men, and that this same number of men could have been housed in other Wall forts in the first half of the fourth century.[80] Another change concerned the terminology, *contubernia* being replaced by *familia*, which is used in the legal documentation.[81]

Various estimates have been made of the total forces on the northern frontier and in the hinterland, under the command of the *dux Britanniarum*. The figures range from nearly 5000 men to just over 19,000. Once again there is not enough evidence to confirm any of these estimates.[82] In any case the full complement of the army of the Wall and the hinterland forts will have varied over time, especially if troops from the Wall were taken away to support various attempted coups of the later fourth century.

Apart from the changes in appearance and size of the barracks, the layout and use of the buildings of fourth-century forts began to depart from the second-century norm. Archaeological excavations show that there had always been some variations in the plans of forts, but in the fourth century a whole range of changes can be discerned, succinctly summarised by Rob Collins, to whom readers are referred for detailed discussion.[83]

The blocking of fort gates has already been mentioned above in connection with the work of Theodosius, to whom all such developments were once attributed, but it is now understood that blocking of gates was not limited to the fourth century. In some forts, the guard chambers, or the redundant gateway itself, were converted to living space or industrial usage such as metalworking. There seems to have been no consistency in the choice of gates to be blocked up, so the decision was probably dependent upon the topography and the opinion of the fort commanders. In the absence of gates which had previously been open, not only access into and out of the forts changed, but there was also an impact on the direction of movement inside the forts.[84]

The ramparts of the forts changed in their appearance, as did the internal buildings which also changed in the way in which they were used. Construction techniques varied and became more localised as a form of vernacular architecture and building style developed. In some places the perimeter walls of forts were refaced in stone, to varying standards of workmanship, but in other instances the ramparts were built up in earth, sometimes with a revetment in stone or in timber, differing from the normal construction in which a free-standing stone wall was given an earthen rampart back. The defences therefore may have appeared to be somewhat ramshackle, but since forts were regularly built of earth and timber in the early Roman Empire, the defensive capabilities would be just as effective as stone walls, the only difference being that repairs might have been necessary on a more frequent basis. It is notable that the construction of earthen ramparts was not widely adopted in the hinterland forts, and it is suggested that on the Wall the practice may have been directed by a central policy.[85] If this type of repair work dates to the fourth century the decision presumably emanated from the offices of the *dux Britanniarum*, but a major problem is that these repairs are very difficult to date and could belong anywhere between the fourth and the sixth century. There was an increased use of timber in repairs, not only in fort buildings but also on parts of the Wall curtain, where gaps caused by collapse of the Wall were filled with timber instead of stone. At Housesteads the stone towers were rebuilt in timber.

In the earlier forts, although there was never a completely uniform plan in internal layout, the buildings generally had designated uses. The *praetorium* was where the commander lived with his family for his tour of duty lasting for about three years, and the *principia* was the administrative centre with offices at the back, together with the shrine of the standards and the underground strongroom where the fort's cash and perhaps important documents would be kept. There would have been a number of clerical staff working in the offices, keeping records up to date concerning pay, soldiers' savings, the outlay of cash for various items, and duty rosters, a strength reports and copies of correspondence sent to the governor's headquarters. In the late fourth century this all changed. Where excavations have been conducted in the *praetoria* it has been shown that up to the last quarter of the fourth century, commanders' houses were well appointed, comparable with the very best villa accommodation and revealing recognisable links with contemporary Mediterranean house architecture.[86] It is suggested that fort commanders of the late period had much more responsibility than their predecessors, perhaps being in charge of the government and administration of a designated area around their forts as well as commanding the military units.[87] There may also have been well-appointed *praetoria*

at Chesters and Binchester, but they have not been excavated as
extensively as those at Housesteads, Vindolanda and South Shields.
Judging from the results of these three major examples, which
admittedly do not necessarily apply at all commanders' houses at
all forts, it seems that the *praetoria* were maintained up to about
360 or 380 at the latest, then in the final years of the fourth century
the use of the buildings altered. Rooms were subdivided, and new
stone floors of inferior workmanship were laid at Vindolanda and
South Shields. Metalworking has been detected in the *praetorium*
at South Shields, and at Binchester the *praetorium* appears to
have been in use for various purposes until the middle of the sixth
century, with evidence for slaughter and butchering of animals,
and of ironworking.[88] In some forts the *principia* was converted to
residential and/or industrial use, and for storage. All three kinds
of activity were found in the *principia* at Housesteads.[89] It appears
that record-keeping and clerical work had either been extremely
simplified or such tasks were no longer required, perhaps as early
as the attempted usurpation of Magnus Maximus, and certainly
after about 407.

After Constantine promoted Christianity as the official religion,
paganism was not stamped out for some time. Temples were not
normally built inside forts, but were usually located within the
vicinity and built at private expense by an individual or a group of
people. It is likely that not all the frontier soldiers were Christianized
in the early fourth century, but there is no evidence to prove the
survival of pagan worship. The same private enterprise may have
continued with regard to churches, erected by Christian members
of the garrison. Some of the internal space within the ramparts may
have been reserved for churches, or individual buildings may have
been converted. At South Shields a church was established in the
forecourt of the headquarters building.[90] A building identified as
a church at Vindolanda was erected in the courtyard of the partly
demolished commander's house. It had an apse at the western end
and nothing else inside it such as ovens or hearths that would
have served to interpret it as living accommodation. The date is
estimated at somewhere between the end of the fourth century and
the beginning of the fifth.[91] Churches have also been identified at
Housesteads and Birdoswald, located in the north-western areas of
each fort.[92]

The granaries at some forts were either reduced in size or truncated, and the use of the space changed. One end of the Benwell granary was taken down and reduced to a paved area at an indeterminable date, and of the double granaries at Housesteads the southern one was divided into two parts, one probably for storage and the other for residential use. Another structure at Housesteads, labelled Building XV, has been identified as a store.[93] Metalworking has been detected in the granary at Newcastle. At Birdoswald there is more vivid evidence for reuse of the granaries well beyond the end of the fourth century. Around 350, the south granary had its floor filled in and a new one laid out on top. It was re-floored several times thereafter, revealing evidence for hearths, indicating its use probably as a hall. During the lifetime of this hall the roof of the northern granary collapsed, the stones were removed and rubbish was dumped on the site. At some point after the end of the fourth century the roof of the south granary also fell down, and at some unknown time after that two successive timber halls were built over the foundations of the north granary. The implication of the reuse of the granaries is that there were not as many soldiers to feed, so there was no need to store large quantities of food, and also it would seem that a centralized supply system was no longer operative. To date, although there is evidence for arable agriculture at Housesteads and at other forts, there is no accompanying evidence for cereal crops.[94] Local farmers may have contributed to military supply. In Britain in general, not necessarily in the frontier zone, there was a surplus of grain in previous centuries which was regularly shipped to the Rhine, a practice which had lapsed by the mid-fourth century, and which the Emperor Julian revived in 359. It is perhaps unlikely that he starved the inhabitants of Britain to death in favour of supplying the Rhine army and the devastated towns, since it would perhaps have been noticed and commented upon by Ammianus Marcellinus, who is one of the sources for Julian's revival of the transhipment of grain.[95] In the later fourth century it has been noted that agriculture, especially cereal production, was extended into areas that would not normally have been considered suitable for cultivation, such as floodplains, hill slopes and upland areas.[96] This may represent an even greater increase in cereal production to feed the army in Britain, a sort of Dig for Victory campaign anticipating the similar extended land use of the 1940s. Nevertheless even if food was produced in fields near to the forts, and local farmers produced more than they needed in order to send the surplus to the army, after the grain harvest, storage would have to be organised somewhere and the goods would have to be protected, not just from rodents and other pests, but from theft or deliberate destruction. One of the buildings at Housesteads, labelled Building XV, has been interpreted as a store for local produce, and/or produce from a wider area to supplement the food supply, but it is not known whether the food that may have been stored in this building was intended for the fort garrison or for distribution to other forts.[97] Livestock, whoever owned the animals, could be put out to grazing in the summer and culled for the winter, but fodder would be required from the hay and straw harvest to support some animals through the winter for breeding, and especially to support the horses of a cavalry unit. Were the men and horses accommodated together, as in the earlier cavalry barracks, with loft space above for hay? How many horses did a late fourth-century unit possess? Where did replacements come from? Was someone, military or civilian, breeding horses and draught animals for the army in the Wall zone?

A relatively recent discovery in some Wall forts is the evidence for market activity, which according to coin studies seems to have flourished from the last quarter of the third century to the last quarter of the fourth. There is no evidence that such activity continued beyond this time slot, but if it was converted to some form of non-coin based transactions or barter it would be more difficult to detect activity that might be connected with trade. The spread of coins indicates that there was a designated area for the market to be held, for instance at the west gate and the road in front of the granaries at Vindolanda and the minor west gate at Wallsend.[98] At Carlisle it appears that items such as dress accessories and pottery were brought to these markets.[99] This implies personal consumption rather than corporate demand.

The production of pottery was probably engendered or at least encouraged by the army, and although the central organisation of earlier times declined, on a regional basis the army could provide the transport to make production worthwhile and profitable.[100] The Crambeck kilns in East Yorkshire attest to lively private enterprise. Pottery had been produced at Crambeck for some time but at the end of the 360s, perhaps significantly after the disaster of 367, the rate of production exploded, probably because other small producers had been put out of business. From the 370s onwards Crambeck ware and pottery from Huntcliff dominate at military sites, accounting for about ninety per cent of the pottery finds.[101] The main routes by which products reached the frontier appear to be by sea up the east coast, and on the roads east of the Pennines. High-status goods were also reaching the frontier up to the fifth century, though this was probably organised on a private basis, by wealthy individuals maintaining their contacts with suppliers.

Late Roman Soldiers

Who were the soldiers in the late fourth century and where did they come from? Diocletian had made military service hereditary and compulsory, but after the decline of the *vici* outside the forts, where were the soldiers' sons? There is no documentation to show how many fourth-century soldiers regularly formed associations with, or actually married local women, nor can it be estimated how many of them actually had sons to follow them into the military units. The whereabouts of civilians in general and woman and children in particular are not clear in the fourth century. It is not certain if all the *vici* of the Wall forts were in decline or deserted by the late third century, but it is not certain where any of the civilians lived after this period. The older theory that civilians moved into the forts in the fourth century cannot be sustained because the presence of non-military personnel inside the forts of the Wall and the hinterland is very difficult to prove. On the other hand, a civilian presence has been detected in some forts in Germany, at Eining, Regensburg and Strasbourg.[102] The German frontiers were more highly pressurized than the British frontier, but for the civilians of the Wall zone the danger may have seemed severe, so where did they go for protection?

The towns at Corbridge and Carlisle, each with a military establishment, may have been the places where many of the civilians congregated. In the third century it is thought that the town at Carlisle that had grown up around the fort was upgraded to a *civitas* capital, which bestowed legal status on the settlement

as the centre for local government of the tribe of the Carvetii.
In the south of Britain the *civitas* capitals had been established
much earlier, some of them not long after the Romans arrived.
Silchester was one of the earliest, called Calleva Atrebatum,
combining the place name with the tribal name of the Atrebates.
On this pattern, Carlisle ought to have been called by its place
name Luguvalium Carvetiorum, but it seems to have been known
as Civitas Carvetiorum. A self-governing town may have attracted
the people of the abandoned *vici*, some of whom could perhaps set
up businesses in the *civitas* capital, or manufacturing and trading
establishments possibly geared to the requirements of the army.

Given that soldiers probably did marry and produce sons, was
local recruitment sufficient to fill all the gaps, and if not, were
Germanic soldiers, or men from a variety of tribes, drafted in by
the central government and sent to Britain? If the information in
the *Notitia* really is up to date and is a true picture of the situation
at the beginning of the fifth century, it is to be expected that the
command structure was still operative, with the forts' commanders
reporting to the *dux Britanniarum*, who in turn was responsible
to the *magistri militum*. Provincial governors would approach the
vicarius and through him the Praetorian Prefects. In the frontier
army, unit strength returns would perhaps still be sent to the
relevant offices and the need for recruits identified and remedied.
But the late fourth-century changes of use in the headquarters
buildings at some forts probably testifies against this procedure,
unless the space devoted to clerical work and record-keeping at the
forts was squeezed into a small section of the headquarters building
while the rest of it was converted to residential use and other
functions. One of the duties of the *dux* concerned recruitment, so
assuming that someone was in post in the late fourth century, did
full responsibility rest with this officer? When the post of *dux* was
abandoned, was there an officer in command of the Wall zone for a
while, or did control devolve quite rapidly onto the men in charge
at each fort?

The appearance of soldiers and their dress, armour and equipment
began to change in the third and fourth centuries, with less reliable
documentation to elucidate study of the details.[103] The clothing
of soldiers in the fourth century included long-sleeved tunics
and trousers, and the old-style hobnailed open sandals gave

way to various types of closed laced-up shoes. One of the more controversial aspects is the apparent decline of metallic body armour, which is supported by the lack of finds of such armour after the third century. The very latest depictions of the familiar segmented metal armour appear on the arch of Severus in Rome, in the early third century. The late Roman author Vegetius endorses the disappearance of body armour in his statement that after the reign of Gratian, who was killed in 383 by the British usurper Magnus Maximus, the soldiers did not wear body armour and helmets. Sculptural evidence also seems to suggest that soldiers did without armour, as for instance on the arch of Constantine in Rome. Running around the entire monument there is a narrow frieze, which is Constantinian in date, in contrast to most of the decoration which was looted from other monuments. Some of the soldiers depicted on this frieze wear tunics instead of body armour, and felt hats instead of helmets, like the headgear of the Tetrarchs on the statue from Venice. Bishop and Coulston suggest that from the later third to the fifth century, body armour was still necessary, pointing out that there are other artistic representations which do show body armour, and Ammianus Marcellinus writing in the 390s mentions the use of helmets and armour.[104] Feugère says that it is hard to accept that all the soldiers in the later Empire did without armour, and refers to archaeological finds of chainmail coats of the fourth century, and pictorial representations of such coats complete with mail hoods.[105] Helmets of the late Empire range from highly decorated examples of high quality workmanship to simple functional designs that could be made very quickly in large numbers, the bowl often formed from two separate half-bowls, riveted to a central spine, with a projecting neck guard and simple cheek pieces. Paintings and sculptural evidence show that shields were no longer half-cylindrical rectangles like the older legionary versions, but oval or round, and usually only slightly concave or flat. A highly decorated round shield of the third century was found at Dura Europos in Syria, and soldiers depicted on the arch of Constantine are shown besieging Verona, some of them wielding large round shields.

Weapons of late Roman soldiers include the long sword called the *spatha*, which replaced the short stabbing sword or *gladius* of the first two centuries of the Empire. An example of a fourth-century *spatha* comes from Cologne, measuring twenty-eight inches in length and two inches in width, with straight sides and a rounded point at the end.[106] These long swords were worn on the left side, and the fourth- and fifth-century scabbards did not end in a point like the scabbards of the *gladii* but were rectangular, made of wood with a metal chape attached to the end by three copper alloy or bronze studs or rivets.[107] The statue of the Tetrarchs in Venice shows them clearly, and all the Tetrarchs' swords have eagle-headed pommels. The new-style scabbards were simpler to manufacture and therefore quicker to produce. Missile weapons and spears used for thrusting were used throughout the history of the Roman army, the *pilum* being the most familiar missile weapon, with different sizes and shapes of iron head. By the fourth century, according to Vegetius, the name for this type of weapon was *spiculum*, for which he gives dimensions of nine to twelve Roman inches for the triangular metal head.[108] The wooden shaft was about five feet long. Archaeological finds show that the heads of such weapons in the late army tended to be larger and more substantial than the first- and second-century examples. A long-shanked barbed head was found at Carvoran, but it is not dated, and could belong anywhere between the third century and the post-Roman period.[109] Some of the soldiers may have been trained as archers, probably using the flexible composite bow that was used in the late period, made from wood, bone, horn and sinew. At Housesteads a large number of tanged triangular-bladed heads were found in the headquarters building, underneath stone tiles which had fallen from the roof.[110]

From Hadrian's reign onwards the Romans employed heavy armoured cavalry units called *cataphractarii*, which were not as mobile as the lighter-armed mounted units, and were soon exhausted by too much exertion, but they served their purpose as shock troops, when armed with the *contus* or long lance. Both the man and the horse were armoured, the horse being clad in barding or scale armour, like a blanket covering the horse's body and reaching half way down its legs, with a cut out section in the centre for the saddle. There is some dispute as to whether *cataphractarii* and *clibanarii* were synonymous terms for the same kind of horseman. *Clibanarius* literally means 'oven', graphically describing how it felt to wear the heavy armour in a hot climate. Some authors suggest that the *clibanarii* were purely eastern troops from Parthia and Palmyra, still qualifying as cataphracts. Other scholars have suggested that the distinction in terminology reflects the respective armament styles, the *cataphractarii* being armed with the lance and shield in the western tradition, while the *clibanarii* adopted the eastern tradition of bow and lance. Though the *cataphractarii* were more common in the eastern provinces than in the west, the *Notitia* lists a *praefectus equitum cataphractorium* at a place called Morbium, which is considered to be either Piercebridge or Ilkely.[111] Piercebridge would be a better choice for heavy-armoured cavalry to operate, though how they were employed is not known.

How the soldiers on the Wall were armed and equipped in the fourth century is hard to say because of a lack of a broad spectrum of finds. As self-sufficiency increased, soldiers probably wore whatever armour they could get, and probably used a variety of weapons. The Germanic tribesmen recruited into the army often brought their own weapons with them, such as the throwing axe used by the Franks, and Vegetius says that some of the infantry drawn from tribal levies used a *bebra*, similar to the *spiculum*. The tribesmen usually carried three of these weapons into battle, which suggests that they were used for throwing.[112] Repairs and even manufacture of weapons and armour probably took place inside individual forts, and the evidence for metalworking that has been detected in the interior buildings of forts could be associated with such work. But recycling can only go so far, and eventually someone would have to locate and extract iron-ore deposits, for which there is little evidence. This would surely be the responsibility of the *dux* for as long as such an officer was in post. Later, it may have been a free-for-all.[113]

The Final Frontier

There is no documentary evidence that provides sufficient detail about what happened to the forts of Hadrian's Wall and the frontier forces of the *limitanei* after the expulsion of the Roman government officials *c.* 409. The older view was that Honorius recalled the troops to the Continent, probably to help in the defence of Gaul and Italy. Even if this was correct, the soldiers on the Wall would probably have stayed where they were, being for the most part highly localised in the region, identifying themselves with their immediate areas before they identified with Rome and the Empire. When it was realised that the British provinces were now on their own, who would be left to punish the soldiers if they refused to obey an order to leave? Except for some of the commanders, probably none of the soldiers had ever seen Rome. Were the officers who wanted to leave, if there were any, allowed to depart? If some of the officers did leave, were replacements appointed from among the soldiers? How long did a corporate command structure survive?

The main difference between being part of the Empire and being outside it was the cessation of military pay. In the changed circumstances after 409, the priorities for all the fort garrisons would be to ensure that there was enough to eat, that there was shelter, and protection from whatever enemies were still out there. This would require cohesion and discipline, which automatically implies that officers of some description would have to exercise authority, or else there would be a disorganised scramble for food and resources. Since the soldiers would be already geared up during the last years of the fourth century to take care of all the priorities mentioned above, the absence of pay perhaps did not affect them as badly as redundancy affects people today. If surplus local produce was being directed to the forts in the later years of the fourth century, by 409 the system was probably already functioning as well as it could. For an unknown period of time this may have been centrally directed, by an officer called *dux* or identified by some equivalent title. From 370 onwards it would appear that there was central control over the distribution of pottery brought to the Wall zone, and this organisation may have continued into the post-Roman era, even if pottery and other goods had to be procured from new sources.

What seems certain is that there is no evidence for a wholesale withdrawal of military forces from the Wall in the late fourth or early fifth century.[114] The Wall forts were occupied in the sub-Roman period, but archaeology cannot elucidate who the occupiers were, and as Wilmott points out, continuous occupation does not mean continuous occupation of the same type.[115] It is not known how long the vestiges of the military organisation lasted. In the third century the Gallic Empire had survived for not quite fifteen years, relying on its own resources and a restricted pool of men from whom to appoint government officials and military officers. Internal squabbling began after about nine years, when Laelianus rebelled against the first Gallic Emperor Postumus. Carausius had governed Britain for not quite seven years when he was assassinated by Allectus. Perhaps there is a psychological norm for the amount of time that a leader can hope to hold everything together in adverse circumstances. In other words how long was it before the leaders of the communities at forts on the Wall decided to take charge of their own areas, gathering resources for themselves at the expense of others? It has been suggested that the *limitanei* of the Wall forts were transformed into the war-bands of the fifth century, presumably controlled by a warlord who provided for his men's needs and most probably their families, and enabled them to ensure their own protection.[116] The appearance of some fifth-century warlords may not always have been due to selfish actions or power-mad ambitious commanders. Eventually there would probably have been a time when there was no surviving higher authority to whom a fort commander was responsible.[117] This may be how coordinated control and actions ceased along the frontier zone, with forts subsequently experiencing different fortunes, some of them surviving longer than others. The fact that Anglo-Saxon colonisation was slower in the Wall zone than in other areas may mean that there was cohesion in military and political organisation for some time among the Wall garrisons which helped to fend off encroachments in the territory. The preponderance of sixth-century Anglo-Saxon material is found east of the Pennines, but K. and P. Dark have argued that there was a sixth-century reoccupation of the Wall.[118] By the seventh to ninth centuries the Anglo-Saxon material had infiltrated as far as the forts of the Stanegate or those relating to the road network.[119] By this time the Wall was no longer Roman, and the northern kingdoms had developed, Deira and Bernicia in the east and Rheged in the west. It is not possible to say exactly when individual forts ceased to be occupied. The two main dating tools, coins and pottery, were no longer being delivered to the Wall, so the last dated versions of coins do not necessarily mean that occupation ceased immediately after those coins were lost.[120] There would be no single event when all the forts were deserted at the same time, and small pockets of inhabitants may have hung on for as long as they could. Occupation of the south-west gate at South Shields was considered to have continued until the middle of the fifth century.[121] At Birdoswald the timber halls have already been mentioned, but the west gate at this fort remained as a house into the middle ages.[122] But there was presumably a day at some of the forts when the last people closed their doors and rode or walked away to a different future, leaving the Wall to stone robbers, outlaws, Border reivers, and finally archaeologists and tourists.

10

How Did the Wall Work?

The short answer to the question posed in the title of this chapter is that nobody knows how the Wall worked. There are too many imponderables for anyone to be pedantic about how the Wall functioned at any period of its long history. Everyone is entitled to an opinion and there have been long debates, still ongoing, about some aspects of the Wall, but in the end opinions are all that can be offered, modified slightly when new discoveries come to light.

The Nature of the Enemy

One of the major problems is that only half the picture is available to archaeologists and historians. The structures of the Wall are readily apparent, thanks to the work of the archaeologists and conservators who have laboured on them for many decades. It is a stone barrier eighty Roman miles long, equipped with turrets and milecastles, and then forts were added. It was built mostly by legionaries and manned by the auxiliary soldiers of the Roman army, and much is known about how the auxiliary units and the legions were organised. But the other half of the picture is missing because no one knows what the native people on either side of the Wall were truly like, except in so far as they were Iron Age tribes and some tribal names are recorded. In the Wall zone the Brigantes lived in the Pennines and possibly close to or even beyond the western side of the frontier, and the Votadini lived on the eastern side. The boundaries of the tribal territories of these two main tribes is not established, so it is still not known for certain whether the Wall cut through their territory, a problem which has occasioned much discussion in the past. It was suggested that the northern boundary of the Brigantes extended beyond the frontier, largely because the dedication to the goddess Brigantia by Amandus the architect was found at Birrens, but the theory that worship of the goddess signified tribal territory has been dismissed, and the cult of Brigantia has been assigned to the efforts of Severus to syncretise Roman and native religion.[1] The text of Amandus' inscription does hint that he set up the dedication by order of someone important.[2] The northern boundary of the Brigantes is complicated by the presence around Carlisle of the Carvetii, once interpreted as a sub-group of the Brigantian people, but the Carvetii probably constituted a separate tribe. The southern boundary of the Votadini may lie somewhere in Northumberland, which probably places the tribe just beyond the Wall.[3] If there is this much uncertainty about tribes within the vicinity of the Wall, there is even more uncertainty about the tribes further north.

The threat posed by tribes living close to the Wall, and the threat from tribes beyond them, cannot be elucidated without knowing the social organisation, the ethos by which the people lived, their attitudes towards each other, and to the Romans. Some tribes may have been peaceable and tractable, but other tribes could change the balance of power by passive influence, active infiltration, or aggressive domination. This would have happened without the added complication of the presence of the Romans. Tribal names come and go. The British tribes named by Julius Caesar in 55 and 54 BC are not attested a century later when the Roman conquest began, and the Empire-building tendencies of the Catuvellauni at the expense of their neighbours in the early first century ultimately provided the excuse for Claudius to invade and annexe Britain. In the third century Dio says that smaller tribes were subsumed by the Maeatae and the Caledonians. On the northern European frontiers, the name of the Alamanni simply means 'all men' suggesting a federation of different tribes under one heading if not under one leader. What these amalgamations meant for the people of the smaller, less powerful tribes is not known. Much depends on the nature of the takeover, whether it was assimilation or annihilation. The arrival of the Romans could not fail to alter the balance of power among the tribes. The Romans took over tribal lands, then they settled down in the areas they had conquered, in close proximity to tribes not yet under Roman control, but they extended their influence beyond their boundaries by means of gifts and subsidies to favoured leaders, and by occasional aggressive action against intractable people who did not conform to the Roman ideal. The northern British tribes would know about the Romans before they reached the north, and by the time the Wall was built they would have had first-hand experience of them under Agricola and his successors, probably up to the northern limits of the island. Whatever the attitude of the tribes had been before this first contact, it would probably have changed afterwards, and when the Wall was established it may have changed again. The history of the Wall involves forays beyond it into Scotland, the first of which under Antoninus Pius resulted in occupation for twenty years or so, and the results of the second under Severus, more difficult to assess, may have caused changes in tribal organisation. The third expedition under Constantius is virtually unknown, except in so far as it happened.

A north–south divide has been detected after the Wall was built.[4] This runs counter to the accepted orthodoxy that frontier zones usually display a meld of cultures instead of a sharp distinction between the people living on one side and the people living on the other. Up to a point, there may have been a blending of cultures in the areas immediately north of the Wall, where settlements have been discovered which may be contemporary with the Roman occupation of the frontier. Under the wing of the Roman army, settlers close to the Wall may have felt almost as secure as those living behind it. But Roman influence and control extended only so far north, probably not far beyond the outpost forts. It is notable that *vici* have not yet been found at High Rochester and Bewcastle. This lack of settlement could one day be overturned by new discoveries, and the annexe found outside the fort at High Rochester could eventually prove to have been inhabited, but in general these sites are considered too remote and unprotected for civilian settlement to flourish. Tribes of the far north continued to develop as Iron Age societies uncontrolled by Rome, playing out inter-tribal rivalries, and not in the least affected by Roman organisation except in so far as the Romanized areas offered a source of portable wealth which would enhance a warrior leader's standing. This is what was important to the tribes. It was how they had lived for centuries and if the Romans had never arrived they would probably have lived in the same way for many more centuries, but the Romans did arrive, and after finding it impractical or impossible to hold the entire island and slowly assimilate the northern tribes, the Romans and natives had to oppose each other. South of the Wall, although the Britons did not become fully Romanized, the protection that the Wall afforded from aggressive action from the north, combined with the peacekeeping exercises of the Roman army in the southern Wall zone and the hinterland, helped to promote settlements supported by agriculture, and encourage markets to develop for exchange of goods, all of which was more or less free from inter-tribal rivalries and hazards to communications. In this way if not in any other, the Wall was doing a good job.

The evidence accumulated so far from the native settlements north of the Wall reveals that many of them were probably not occupied beyond the later second or early third century. Roman finds on native sites are not abundant, but in general there is a marked absence of early third-century material. Further north in Scotland, traditional Iron Age settlements also begin to change around the beginning of the third century. This has been linked to the probable cessation of Roman subsidies and the consequent replacement of the old elite with a new social organisation, in which late Roman material starts to appear.[5] Hodgson suggests that this new society, 150 to 250 kilometres to the north of the Wall, may be one of the sources of the raids on the frontier zone.[6] It is tempting to add that what happened in the early third century, probably the start of the disruption and change in northern tribal society, was Septimius Severus.

Roman Perceptions

There are no contemporary records to help with reconstructing the mindset of the various British tribes when the Wall first appeared, and apart from the physical remains of the Hadrianic frontier, and a brief passage about separating the Romans from the barbarians in the *Historia Augusta*, there is no record of the Roman mindset either.

The brief derogatory references in the Vindolanda tablets reveal that at least in the early years the Romans had no respect at all for the Britons. The actual threat from the natives cannot be assessed, but more important and equally obscure is the way in which the Romans perceived this threat. The two things need not be the same, as demonstrated by recent military history. Perceived threat is all that military planners have to go on, and even if they gather intelligence rather than relying on hearsay, their interpretation of the results, which motivates their response, need not be a correct assessment.

If it was Hadrian who planned the Wall in detail, entirely according to his own perceptions or with assistance from the army officers on the spot, it is still not known what he was trying to combat. If the Emperor's thought processes were known, the first plan for the Wall would be clearer to modern audiences, but without such assistance it is not known why the Wall was equipped with so many small installations in the form of turrets and milecastles, and what they were intended to do. Then the fort decision altered the picture, but whatever it was that triggered this decision, a war *c.* 123–24 perhaps, or difficulties in operating the frontier, can only be surmised. With forts actually on the Wall, some but not all of them projecting to the north, the troops could be more rapidly assembled beyond the Wall instead of marching them from the Stanegate and filtering them through the milecastles. Was this the prime concern of the military planners, or was there some other consideration besides this common-sense move?

Hadrian created other frontiers as well as the British one, but can it be assumed that he was trying to achieve the same ends in the same way with all of them? Once again lack of detailed knowledge concerning the social organisation and political development of the tribes on the other side of the frontiers renders it difficult to assess whether the Hadrianic frontiers were built to satisfy the same criteria. Hodgson compares and contrasts the Upper German frontier with the Raetian version. The Upper German frontier was strongly held with towers and Kleinkastelle, the equivalent of milecastles, and forts up to two kilometers behind the palisade.[7] Significantly in the Wetterau region, the forts were placed on routes through the area and on valleys where infiltration was easier, and significantly the Taunus–Wetterau area is where the largest concentration of military and civilian sites were damaged in the invasions of the 230s, which could indicate that the Romans were right all along and this was an area where the threat was at greatest intensity. The Raetian frontier was more lightly held. It was not of uniformly Hadrianic date, and it was not built in uniform style, parts of it being constructed as a sort of fence, and its western end did not initially join up with the eastern end of the Upper German frontier until the later second century. There were fewer military installations on this frontier, and the towers were further apart than the German ones, until the third century when serious incursions began, and in response it was more strongly fortified.[8]

This slow development of the Raetian frontier, with changes to the degree of fortification in response to altered circumstances, raises another question about the Wall: did it function in the same way at all times? Or was it adapted to circumstances, its role being redefined when necessary?[9] The Hadrianic concept of frontiers may not have dictated the function and use of the Wall throughout its history. Simply because the Wall was there, any adaptations to the running barrier, the turrets, milecastles and forts would be limited in scope to a few alternatives, such as discontinuing the use of certain features, blocking doorways or even dismantling some structures, or conversely reinstating use of previously abandoned features. But routines and procedures could be adapted, and new ways of dealing with the natives could be instituted, using the Wall as reinforcement to current policy. Reconsideration of the ways in which the Wall could be used goes some distance to dispelling Mann's concept of inertia among the Roman high command, who have been accused of simply accepting the frontiers and failing to think of any alternatives.

If the role of the Wall changed in order to deal with altered circumstances, does this mean that the Wall served only one purpose at a time, or was it always, or only sometimes, multifunctional? It has been described as a symbolic and psychological boundary, a customs barrier, and a defensive or protective frontier. As a symbol, the Wall is somewhat over the top, but there is probably no doubt about the psychological effect of a stone barrier from sea to sea, with its forts and huge manpower, backed up by even more manpower in the hinterland and three legions in fortresses further south. A frontier also operating as a customs barrier is feasible, since there is no doubt that customs were levied at the boundaries between provinces and on the frontiers, but it may not have been a primarily military responsibility. A customs station has been discovered at Porolissum in Dacia, in a building that looks like a fort on the frontier line, but it is clear from the inscriptions found nearby that the collectors of the dues were not military men but civilian officials.[10] The British frontier may have had a secondary or incidental function as a customs barrier, but the assumption that there was considerable commercial traffic passing through the Wall lacks the benefit of absolute proof. As for protection, this was probably the prime function of the Wall, but it can be asked, is it possible to protect, without sometimes having to defend?

This reverts to the level of perceived threat, and the degree and nature of contact between Romans and natives. Roman goods passed through some parts of the Imperial frontiers to the tribes beyond, but this was not uniform across all frontiers. On the middle Danube, Roman artefacts are found in native territory from the first to the fourth century, but the dwellings of the British tribes north of the Wall are bereft of such Roman goods. Sometimes, judging from dating evidence of the Roman goods in *barbaricum* there was a hiatus in supply, or possibly in demand, which may indicate a change in Roman attitudes to the natives, for instance in putting a stop to subsidies, or a change of leadership of a tribe and a consequent change in attitudes of natives to Romans and vice versa. Particularly in the Hadrianic and Antonine era the European Roman frontiers seem to have prevented the infiltration of Roman material, which is found to be more abundant in the eras before and after this period, indicating just such changed attitudes.[11]

The little that can be discerned about the northern British tribes cannot answer the question whether they readily attacked the Wall in large numbers, or limited their activity to raids with a small band of warriors in the hope of carrying off portable wealth. It is generally agreed that no Roman frontier was capable of withstanding determined attack by hordes of tribesmen, nor were they designed to do so. No frontier was impermeable.

An Open or Closed Frontier?

In Britain the cultural relationship between Romans and the natives of the north seems to have been mutually exclusive, and remained so throughout the centuries of Roman occupation, in contrast to the British tribes of the south, some of whom were already accustomed to receiving Roman goods before the Claudian conquest. Towns such as Silchester were quickly founded and became tribal administrative centres or *civitas* capitals, and self-government, trade and industry flourished with the Roman framework. Such assimilation did not take hold in the areas north of the Wall, and was not widespread among the natives to the south of it, despite the more recent discoveries in the hinterland of villa sites, some local industries such as pottery manufacture, and the third-century elevation of the civil settlement at York to the status of a *colonia*. Does this mutual exclusivity mean that the natives of the north simply resisted Romanization, or is it an indication that the frontier as established by Hadrian, and as used by his successors, was closed?

This is a question that has occasioned much debate and interchange of arguments in print. Was the frontier designed to stop movement completely, or conversely was it the intention to allow free movement at the gates through the milecastles if not through the forts? Or was movement channelled through a few restricted points, controlled and supervised, and only prevented if necessary?

The most extreme view, that all movement between the north and south was initially prevented, gains some support from the presence of the Vallum south of the Wall, continuous all along the frontier, except along the eastern sector from Newcastle to Wallsend where the River Tyne substituted for it. The Vallum has been described by more than one author as a formidable barrier, which indeed it was. In the Hadrianic period, when the Vallum was complete, it would have been difficult enough for northbound pedestrians to cross the south mound, the south berm, scramble several feet down the south slope, climb up the north slope and clamber over the north mound, and drivers of wheeled vehicles or even horsemen would not even contemplate trying to follow suit. The Vallum has puzzled Hadrian's Wall scholars for generations. Several suggestions have been made as to why it was dug and what purpose it served. Protection for builders of the Wall was probably not one of its functions, because it would have hindered transport, and it may not have been completed until after the Wall and the forts were completed. The creation of a military zone between the

Wall and the natives to the south is feasible but some natives, such as the people living in the houses at Milking Gap, appear to have been allowed to remain in their settlements in the proposed military zone. Perhaps they had entered into some agreement with the army. The Antonine Wall was not accompanied by a continuous ditch to the south, but most forts had an annexe attached to them, so the Hadrianic Vallum may have served as one long annexe to store carts and wagons and to protect livestock and crops. The Vallum would have been highly effective if complete closure of the frontier was intended, and if the frontier really was completely closed, it may explain why trouble in Britain featured so prominently in the history of the province. Even if the Britons did not need to travel regularly across the zone where the Wall was built, the fact that the Romans possibly forbade them to do so would cause discontent.

On the other hand, it has been suggested that the Vallum may not have been intended to close off the frontier to everyone except the military. Causeways across the Vallum, complete with gates, existed opposite the forts, but were they also provided at each and every milecastle? This provision would be demanded if the Wall was open to civilian traffic through all of them or some of them, as proposed by Breeze and Dobson.[12] An investigation of the Vallum opposite thirty-one milecastles by H. Welfare showed that there had been causeways at some of them, namely milecastles 23, 25, 26, 29, 32, 33 and 34. If it was intended to allow civilians to cross the Vallum into the milecastles, there would also be a need for gaps in the north mound of the Vallum, but although such gaps were found opposite milecastles 20, 30 and 42, there was a frustrating lack of evidence that causeways also existed at these locations, so a coordinated system combining causeways with gaps in the north mound cannot yet be proposed.[13] It is likely that causeways were provided only at places where they were considered necessary.[14] If such was the case, the provision was not permanent, since it was discovered that the causeways had been removed or cut through at a later date to render them unusable, and a mound had been built across the northern end of the causeways at four of the milecastles which had been investigated.[15] The building of obstructions to the north of these causeways may have been carried out at the same time as they were cut through, since both measures would render them useless as crossing points. The alterations to the causeways may also coincide with the narrowing of some milecastle gateways to allow only pedestrian access and egress. If civilians had once been allowed through the milecastles, the use of the narrowed northern gates may now have been limited to soldiers, excluding the civilians altogether. One of the drawbacks in making any statement about the milecastles is that not all of them have been excavated, so it is not known if all gates were narrowed, but if they were, this restricted access to the milecastles, coupled with the destruction of causeways across the Vallum, would convert the frontier into a closed barrier.

Routes leading from the Wall to the north are not abundant, and as Johnson points out, it is hardly likely that there was a road from each and every milecastle, which would total eighty separate routes across the Wall.[16] Hardy British tribesmen perhaps did not require established routes to and from the north, but if every milecastle was an access point, ideally there should also be eighty causeways across the Vallum, eighty gaps across the north mound of the Vallum, and eighty causeways or possibly bridges across the northern ditch as well, and none of this can be proven.[17] Probably access to the north, for soldiers and perhaps also for civilians in the early years, was provided at only a few selected milecastles. Opposite milecastle 50 on the stone Wall, less than a mile to the west of Birdoswald, a paved area was traced between the north gate and the edge of the northern ditch, but no causeway was found.[18] A timber bridge across the ditch cannot be ruled out, and although the route to the north passes very close by, through the fort at Birdoswald, there could possibly have been a crossing point at the milecastle to allow traffic to bypass the fort and join the route to go north or divert from it to come south. At milecastle 54 further west, a cobbled area outside the north gate led to the ditch, and stones were found in the bottom of the ditch in line with the cobbles. This suggests that there was once crossing, which had eventually been removed.[19] Given that gates do exist in the northern walls of the milecastles, with the exception of Sewingshields, where no north gate has been found, were they used only by the soldiers for going out onto the berm to check the condition of the Wall and the northern ditch, and effect repairs when and where they were necessary?[20]

After the return from the Antonine Wall, the Vallum was not put back into its pristine state. The gaps that had been deliberately cut in the mounds on the north and south sides of the great ditch were not filled in, and it seems that there was no effort to dig out the infill where the sides had collapsed. On the other hand the Vallum was not completely obliterated all along its length, and it may be at this point where the causeways that probably existed at some milecastles were cut. This looks like confused thinking about what purpose the Vallum was intended to fulfil. It may mean that strict protection from the south was no longer necessary, which it turn possibly implies that the natives south of the Wall were once hostile but were now more settled. It may also have been at this period that the *vici* started to develop outside forts, implying a more relaxed attitude on the part of the Romans towards the population behind the Wall. Civil settlements spread over the Vallum at Halton Chesters, Castlesteads and Birdoswald. There seems to have been no effort to clear the area immediately north of the Wall, where some settlement was allowed, and there seems to have been no protection for the water supply to Halton Chesters, Chesters, Corbridge and Great Chesters, which was led in from the north beyond the Wall via aqueducts. These were not massive multi-arched structures like some Roman aqueducts, but channels in the ground, engineered to keep the flow steady. The Great Chesters aqueduct started only just over two miles north of the fort as the crow flies, but to avoid the tributaries of the Caw Burn it had to follow an erratic course, adding several miles to its length.[21] Perhaps the Romans knew that the natives who were likely to attack the Wall zone had no interest in cutting the water supply, because they were only intent on raiding, seizing goods and getting away again at speed.

If the frontier was open to traffic in its early years, it seems that it was closed probably after the return from the Antonine Wall, and in contrast to the relaxation of firm control behind the Wall and immediately in front of it, the attitude to natives to the far north of the Wall was not relaxed, and entry points through the Wall from the north were now more rigidly controlled. Passage through the Wall was probably limited to designated crossing points, which may also have served as checkpoints and customs stations at the same time. Portgate on Dere Street north of Corbridge is one such gateway, on the main north–south route on the eastern side of the country. It was a stone-built structure straddling the Wall, but its full plan is not known.[22] There may have been another access point at Newcastle. On the western side, Stanwix is proposed as a gateway, and east of Housesteads there is the gap at the Knag Burn.[23] There may be more crossing points where routes existed, but there is little except speculation to illustrate how many there may have been and how these gates worked and who manned them.

Design and Operation of the Wall

When the Wall was first designed, with milecastles every mile and two turrets in between, it is not known how the Romans intended to man them. Soldiers would perhaps have been brought from the Stanegate forts, possibly by rota, but how many? In the past the number of soldiers intended to garrison the milecastles was overestimated. Milecastle 48 at Poltross Burn, which was excavated in 1909, was divided into two halves by a road through the centre, and flanking the road there were two buildings, divided into four in the first phase and then into three. The layout and capacity of these buildings suggested that there could have been about thirty to thirty-two men in garrison. But this does not apply to all the milecastles, only nine of which are yet known to contain internal buildings, and the buildings are only about half the size of the Poltross Burn examples. This could mean that there was a greater need for protection in the west, as is sometimes suggested, or alternatively that all milecastles were intended to be the same size as the western examples, but before the plan for the Wall was completed it was decided to reduce the size of the milecastles and their internal buildings. It is suggested that there were eight men in each milecastle, but their functions are not known.[24] The turrets could have been operated by two or three men on a rota basis, but the full complement for the milecastles and turrets along the whole Wall would still have involved a considerable number of personnel who were presumably intended to come from the Stanegate forts. The decision to add forts to the Wall does not elucidate, and in fact complicates, the question of how the milecastles were manned, though the function and use probably changed when so many more soldiers were present actually on the frontier. Even the proposed eight men per milecastle may not have applied after the forts were added to the Wall.

What was the function of the men in the milecastles and turrets? The obvious answer to modern audiences, if not to the Romans, is surveillance, possibly to the north and also the south in the early period before the advance to the Antonine Wall. Reconstructions of milecastles usually show one tower over the gate on the north side, but it has been suggested that milecastles had a tower over the south gate as well, because the foundations for both gates are the same and if one set of foundations could support a tower, so could the other. Nothing survives to a sufficient height to be certain that there were any towers over any of the gates, but the surveillance theory positively demands that there were. With regard to the milecastle towers and the turrets, it is not known how high they would have been or how far they extended above the top of the Wall. Up to a point, the higher the tower the further observers can see, but there is a limit to human eyesight beyond which elevation cannot help. Foglia has suggested that the turrets were concerned with local surveillance, not long-distance observation and early warning systems.[25]

Most controversial of all, it is not known if there was a wall-walk with parapet and possibly crenellations. As already mentioned in the chapter on building the Wall, Breeze briefly summarises the arguments for and against a wall-walk in the fourteenth edition of the *Handbook to the Roman Wall*, and in 2014 he wondered why the Romans would need a wall-walk at all, since whoever approached from the north would be kept at a considerable distance away from it, probably beyond the range of missiles thrown from the Wall. Although it cannot yet be shown that the obstacles on the berm existed all the way along the frontier works, even without them hostiles would be at least sixteen metres away from the Wall and probably three metres below it, and would have to cross the northern ditch.[26] Bidwell made a good, even impassioned, case for the existence of a wall-walk, tackling the various points raised in objection to the wall-walk theory.[27]

The Wall is considered by some scholars to be wide enough, even at the reduced width of the Narrow Wall, to have accommodated a stone-fronted wall-walk. It has been pointed out that no other stone-built Roman frontiers were as wide as Hadrian's Wall, and could not have accommodated a wall-walk. The Raetian wall, built later than the British frontier, is much narrower, like the stretches of stone walls in the African provinces. The African walls are better preserved in the hot climate, and where they survive to full height, they end in a stone triangle, so there is no question of a wall-walk on this frontier. It is suggested that the differences between the frontiers imply that Hadrian entertained different solutions for different provinces, and he may have conceived of a wider wall to accommodate a wall-walk for surveillance of the north. But Breeze and Dobson point out that if there was a parapet of about two Roman feet wide, then there would be a platform varying from eight Roman feet on the Broad Wall to six or even four Roman feet on the Narrow Wall and the later repairs, which they consider would not be wide enough for soldiers to move around, pass each other, or carry casualties off the Wall.[28] In response Bidwell pointed out several examples of Narrow wall-walks as attested at forts in Germany. Another argument for a patrolling platform on the Wall is that when turrets were removed, the recess left in the frontier wall was built up, so that the wall-walk could be carried across, but this was decried as merely strengthening for the Wall in the absence of the demolished turrets, nothing more. Bidwell countered that there was no need for strengthening the Wall, because the rear walls of the turrets were strong enough, so there must have been another reason to go to the trouble of building them up.[29]

Dimensions of Hadrian's Wall alone are not a conclusive argument for a wall-walk, but it has been suggested that the footbridges accompanying the main bridges across rivers strongly imply that there was also a walkway on top of the Wall.[30] Not everyone agrees that this proves the existence of a wall-walk, especially as there seems to have been no access to the top of the Wall from the forts, for example there is no evidence for stairs at the junction of fort walls and the Wall itself.[31] But what happened where the forts and milecastles joined the Wall? At milecastle 48 at Poltross Burn the first few steps of a staircase survive in the north-east corner and it is assumed, without proof, that all milecastles possessed them. The steps show that there was access at least to the top of the eastern wall of the milecastle at Poltross Burn, and there was possibly a wall-walk around all four sides. The northern wall of each milecastle was formed by the Wall itself, so did the milecastle have a wall-walk round all four sides that was blocked off where the east and west sides joined the Wall, or was there a gap giving onto a walkway along the Wall, perhaps with a door or gate? This is the arrangement shown in a reconstruction drawing of a milecastle by M. Moore in *The Northern Frontiers of Roman Britain*.[32] And if the forts had a wall-walk all around their perimeters, which is usually assumed for free-standing forts, in the case of forts which utilized the Wall itself as its northern defence, what happened on that northern wall? Were the soldiers limited to walking around the east, south and west sides of the fort rampart tops, but not the northern wall, or was there an isolated stretch of fort-length northern wall-walk, closed off from the rest of the frontier because the Wall itself did not have a wall-walk? Does the lack of stairs at the points where the fort joined the Wall mean that not only was there no wall-walk on the frontier Wall, but also there was none for the fort on its northern side, or did a fort wall-walk exist which was reached from a wooden stairway or even a ladder in an interval tower or a corner tower? If this was the arrangement for getting up to the fort rampart top, then it could have enabled soldiers to pass along the fort wall to reach the hypothetical wall-walk of the frontier Wall as well. In the case of forts which projected north of the Wall, which usually joined the fort at the south tower of the double-portal gateway on the east and west sides, the fort wall-walk, if such there was, could pass over the gate and continue around the projecting sector of the fort, while the Wall that joined the south tower could remain without a wall-walk. Since nothing remains of the topmost sections of either the Wall or the forts the presence or absence of a wall-walk has to remain theoretical. But it is interesting to ask the questions and thump tables.

Another question concerning the wall-walk, if there was one, is did the Wall have crenellations with gaps or embrasures for visibility and merlons for protection? There is a hint that there may have been such features on the Wall, derived from the decoration on the metal skillets or pans known as the Rudge cup and the Amiens skillet, mentioned above in connection with the Staffordshire Moorlands pan. The Rudge cup shows a schematised Wall with what seem to be regularly spaced towers, possibly representing turrets, and at the tops of each one there are rudimentary crenellations. While artistic representations do not always depict the absolute truth, the decoration supports the idea that crenellations existed on at least some parts of the Wall. An argument against this is the fact that among the many finds from the Wall there is a marked absence of capping stones for the tops of the merlons. So far, South Shields is the only fort, not only in the Wall zone, but in Britain, where such stones have been found, but there are examples from forts in Germany.[33] The absence of capstones from the Wall area may simply mean that the Romans used flat stone slabs set at an angle, or possibly concrete, to finish off the tops and protect them from weathering.[34] Another supporting factor for the existence of crenellations is the discovery of chamfered string-course stones on some parts of the northern face of the Wall, which are usually associated in other Roman defensive works with crenellations.[35] The argument is important because it does not simply concern the appearance, structure and total physical form of the Wall, but also its function. The existence of a wall-walk and crenellations imply that soldiers, possibly from the turrets and maybe from the milecastles, patrolled along the Wall and watched for anyone approaching, thus validating the reconstructions that show turrets with an upper-storey doorway leading to the top of the Wall.

There can be no doubt that Hadrian's Wall scholars are polarised on the subject of the wall-walk. If the existence or non-existence of such a feature could be solved beyond doubt, it would help to determine, but not conclusively prove, the way in which the Wall functioned. If there was a wall-walk linking the turrets and milecastles at their top levels, this would support the surveillance theory, with soldiers covering the entire length of the Wall and watching for any approach with peaceful or hostile intent, or in places where there is dead ground, or in the dark, listening for any approach with whatever intent. This would be labour intensive and would require at least two shifts, and it is still not known how turrets and milecastles were manned. But one fiercely argued point about a wall-walk, if such existed, is whether soldiers fought from the top of the Wall as if it were a very elongated castle. This is hotly denied by several Hadrian's Wall scholars, but revisited by Hodgson, who argued for assembling on the wall top as a delaying tactic in the case of attack, while forces were mustered to deal with it.[36]

Breeze and Dobson always maintained that forts and frontiers had different functions, forts to protect the province and its inhabitants, and the frontiers to control movement.[37] If the two elements happened to be joined together as they are on Hadrian's Wall, does this impinge on their separate functions? Discussing the Antonine Wall, Breeze and Dobson detect a more flexible approach to the siting of forts than on Hadrian's Wall, and they regard this as a further stage towards the dispersal of forts along the frontier lines, rather than positioning them in concentrated groups, the optimum disposition for military operations.[38] In the second century what kind of military operations were necessary? Major wars involved the Emperor or a delegated general and probably the temporary import of extra troops. The function of the Wall with its forts could have embraced dual-purpose frontier defence and small-scale military operations beyond the frontier. Graafstal describes it as an anti-raiding barrier and a springboard for further action.[39]

It is repeatedly stated that the Romans preferred to fight in the open, rather than defending military installations from the inside. Can it be assumed that for the first three centuries the Romans were always in the ascendancy, that they were always able to choose their own battleground, and that the sheer psychological deterrent of their presence meant that they were never attacked directly in their forts? Probably not. The frequent mention of trouble in Britain in the ancient sources could indicate that once or twice the Britons succeeded in overpowering defences, as suggested in the 180s, when Dio says that the natives crossed the Wall, an event that is now linked to damage at three forts in the west at Corbridge, Halton Chesters and Rudchester. The mention of Caledonians and Maeatae in Dio's account suggests that the tribesmen came from the far north. Did they bypass Dere Street unobserved, hide in the undergrowth some distance from the point where this route crossed the Wall at Portgate, send a few men under cover of darkness to creep up behind the guards, slit their throats and steal their clothes and armour, as in war films which use the same scenario in many different costumes. The conjecture is not entirely ridiculous, because no one has any inkling of what the Romans were up against. How did the tribesmen cross the Wall and go on the rampage at the nearest forts? How often did emergencies arise on, or in advance of, the Wall, and how were they dealt with? Did messengers come from the outposts to the nearest fort commanders, reporting on signs of unauthorised massing of tribesmen, or did patrols come back with similar observations?

Closer to the Wall, if the milecastles, turrets, and possibly the Wall itself were used as observation platforms, and something was observed that had not been reported from the outposts, consequently requiring immediate action, the observers would have to tell someone. They could do this by using torches or smoke signals, which could only convey a few prearranged messages, which with too many relays are subject to misinterpretation at both the transmission and receiving ends. Polybius' system of using flags to send messages letter by letter may well have been effective, and detailed messages could be sent, but only slowly. Another means of spreading an alert would be by trumpet, and one was found near a watchtower on the German frontier. Trumpets can be more effective than torches because a prearranged combination of long and short notes could convey different messages, and sound is still effective in the dark or in fog. There would still be the problem of misinterpretation as to the nature and location of the trouble being reported. Who would signals be sent to? Woolliscroft examined the visual signalling techniques available to the Roman army, and the capacity of the installations along the Stanegate and the Wall to transmit and receive signals.[40] The Wall forts are not intervisible, so would be dependent on relays to receive signals from most of the initial sources. Using extant signal towers in conjunction with hypothetical ones, Woolliscroft detected a system whereby a number of turrets and milecastles in a particular sector could signal to individual towers, which could then serve as relay stations, but as he admits it is difficult to prove that such a system was ever in use.[41] On the other hand it would be difficult to prove that it was never used.

Having received messages or signals, what do the recipients do afterwards? Breeze and Jilek question the procedure: do commanders contact the governor, and send messages to the legate at York, or was there a senior commander in the Wall zone?[42] The erstwhile theory that the commander of the milliary *ala* at Stanwix was the commander of the Wall zone on account of his seniority cannot be proven, and in any case a fort commander faced with an attack at Wallsend or any fort in the eastern zone could not expect instant assistance from Stanwix, nor from York for that matter. How much autonomy did the fort commanders possess, and how did they coordinate their actions and responses with other fort commanders, if at all? In emergencies demanding an immediate turnout at one or several forts, it would take some time to ascertain what was happening and where, and while this was being dealt with, assembly of troops would be the next priority. Numbers turning out may not have been large. Probably half the men were not actually stationed in the fort, being out on errands and detached duties as listed in the military records. Some of the horses of an *ala* or part-mounted unit would probably be out to grass, and it would take time to get them together and equip them. Was there a *turma* or two, and a century or two, held in perpetual readiness, with horses and men fit and ready for action as a rapid-response team?

For the purposes of observation of the natives, patrolling is more or less taken for granted. Austin and Rankov point out that there would be a limit to how far a patrol could penetrate into tribal lands beyond the frontier, because the soldiers would either have to return to their forts each evening, or camp out in potentially hostile territory, where a small force would be at risk.[43] Horsemen could obviously range further and faster than foot soldiers, but though they could cover more territory, the patrol could only deal with any threat as and when it occurred, and try to get messages back to the forts.[44] The outpost forts of the third century were occupied by milliary *cohortes equitatae*, where the horseman would be best suited to patrolling, but there were also the units of *exploratores*, translated as scouts, which implies that these soldiers regularly went out into the countryside to check on what the natives were doing, but there is no proof that this is how they were employed.

It is often stated that one of the roles of the army on the Wall was policing. What exactly did police work entail? Did it involve dealing with low intensity squabbles between the natives, to maintain law and order, and if so, did soldiers from the Wall operate south of the frontier zone as well as north of it? Were soldiers sent out to track and apprehend thieves and murderers and escort them to the fort commander who then dispensed justice or passed the accused criminals to higher authorities? Some fort commanders were also in charge of the region, as attested at Ribchester where the officers were legionary centurions, and there may have been a similar officer at Carlisle. There is no evidence that the suggested policing functions on the Wall involved government of the area around the fort, but the commander of a fort would probably be the authority to whom civilians would appeal for help, even if he only acted as an intermediary between them and higher authorities. In all hypothetical instances like this, evidence is usually brought in from the archive of Flavius Abbinaeus, the fourth-century *praefectus alae* at the fort of Dionysias in Egypt, though his proper title did not impress itself on the natives, who addressed him as *praepositus*. Abbinaeus' correspondence is full of appeals from the civilians, one of whom asked him to extract his brother-in-law from the draft for the army, or if that could not be achieved, to save him from going abroad with the field army. Another civilian asked him to grant five day's leave to her son serving in the army.[45]

One of the policing functions probably involved supervision of any gatherings of tribesmen, which would have to be authorised by the Roman government. From military records from other provinces, it is known that soldiers were sent to supervise and guard markets. It is also known that the Romans controlled tribes beyond their frontiers by dictating where and when they could hold meetings which perhaps served as tribal assemblies. Dio describes the arrangements that Commodus made with the Marcomanni and Quadi in the Danube region, after the death of Marcus Aurelius. Commodus withdrew from the territory beyond the Danube, but first stipulated that the tribesmen should not meet frequently in any part of the country, but only once a month in a designated place, in the presence of a Roman centurion.[46] The officer would hopefully be accompanied by at least some men of his century. Similar arrangements for the northern tribes beyond the Wall were proposed by Richmond, who interpreted the list of British place names in the seventh-century *Ravenna Cosmography* as the designated meeting places.[47] This document contains a long list of British place names, not brilliantly organised, but in the seventh century, Britain had long since ceased to be Roman, and the author or compiler would have to use sources which were ancient even in his own day. The place names thought to represent the designated meeting places for the northern tribes are listed under the heading *sunt autem in ipsa Britannia diversa loca*, and if the locations are correctly identified, they are all in the north beyond Hadrian's Wall. *Locus Maponi* has been related to the Clochmabenstane or Lochmaben in Dumfries and Galloway, which may have been a religious cult centre before Romans arrived.[48] *Segloes* is identified with the tribe of the Selgovae, *Daunoni* or *Dannoni* with the Damnonii, and *Taba* is identified with Tava, meaning the Tay. *Panovius* may be the River Nith or somewhere in its vicinity, but *Mixa* and *Minox* cannot be identified with certainty. *Manavi* is possibly to be identified as Manau at the head of the Forth of Firth, as in modern place names Clackmannan and Slamannan. Rivet and Smith interpret *Manau* as the Isle of Man, and do not subscribe to the theory that these *loca* are designated meeting places, dismissing them simply as different places, as the description *diversa loca* indicates, which the cosmographer forgot to include in his main lists. Mann restated the case for permitted native assemblies, referring to Dio's references to treaties and similar arrangements for the Danube region.[49] Richmond dated the inception of the meeting places to the treaty with the Britons made by Caracalla after the death of Severus, but Breeze and Dobson preferred an earlier date, after the withdrawal from the Antonine Wall.[50]

The Wall was supported by forts in the hinterland guarding routes and communications and probably policing their areas in whatever ways were necessary. In the first half of the third century there is some evidence from epigraphic sources about the garrisons of some of these forts. The latest inscription discovered so far comes from Lancaster, recording rebuilding of the baths and the basilica in the 260s.[51] This work was done under the Gallic Emperor Postumus, whose name was chiselled out, most probably after Aurelian reclaimed the western provinces in 274, which means that the fort at Lancaster was still extant and the inscription still in place at that time. By the time that the *Notitia Dignitatum* was compiled, more than a century later, there had been several changes in the hinterland, which are not dated and may not have happened all at once. With the exception of the *numerus Maurorum Aurelianorum* at Burgh-by-Sands, and the *numerus Barcariorum Tigrisiensium* at South Shields, the Wall units listed in the *Notitia* are still styled *alae* or *cohortes*. By contrast in the hinterland only five cohorts, one *ala* and a *cuneus Sarmatarum* remain, while ten *numeri* and three units of *equites* occupy forts once held by *alae* or *cohortes*. Breeze and Dobson consider that the forts where the new units are attested had been abandoned in the later third century.[52] This may mean that there was little need for so many military units in the hinterland at that time, but the situation deteriorated in the fourth century, and so the forts were reoccupied by new-style units, perhaps in piecemeal fashion which is not reflected in the *Notitia* because it can only display the final version. Some of the units comprised soldiers from the field armies, so these may have been the last to arrive, probably after the troubles of 367.[53]

There are problems in trying to marry up the entries in the *Notitia* with the archaeology of the hinterland forts, because there are more sites yielding signs of occupation in the fourth century than are listed in the document. Collins enumerates the possible reasons for this. One explanation could be that although fourth-century occupation is attested at some forts, without exact dating it is possible that some of the forts may have been abandoned before the document was drawn up, and another explanation could be that occupation need not be military. It is possible that only unit headquarters were listed in the *Notitia*, and the others which were occupied but not mentioned, could have been held by detachments.[54] The salient point about the units listed in the *Notitia* is that reorganisation of the hinterland had been considered necessary but not of the Wall garrisons, except at its eastern and western ends, where *numeri* were installed, possibly to guard against attacks from the sea.

If the function of the Wall in the first three centuries is not clear, it is even less so in the later Roman period, but continuing repairs to the curtain wall in stone or more commonly timber and earth show that some people though it worthwhile to try to maintain it in the most effective manner that they could achieve. In the sub-Roman period, the psychological values of the Wall may have reverted to the people living behind it instead of displaying power and dominance to the people beyond it.

Notes

1 Before the Wall: c. 55 BC to AD 122

1. Maxwell 2004, 77–8.
2. Tacitus *Annals* 3.36.
3. Tacitus *Histories* 3.45.
4. Todd 2004b, 53; 57.
5. Todd 2004b, 57.
6. Birley 2005, 36; 237 no. 6.
7. Tacitus *Annals* 12.40; see also Birley 2005, 61 n.6, referring to D. Braund *Britannia* 15, 1984, 1–6.
8. Tacitus *Histories* 3.40.
9. Todd 2004b, 57.
10. Statius *Silvae* 5.2.144–8.
11. Tacitus *Annals* 14.32.
12. Tacitus *Agricola* 17.1.
13. Tacitus *Agricola* 5.1; Birley 2005, 73.
14. Tacitus *Agricola* 7.3.
15. Tacitus *Agricola* 8.2.
16. See Birley 2005, 77–8 (appropriate page numbers) for a succinct discussion of the chronology.
17. Tacitus *Agricola* 18.2.
18. R. Birley 2009, 42.
19. Tacitus *Agricola* 22.
20. Breeze 1982, 53 summarises the possible alternative scenarios based on Tacitus' brief description of the third season.
21. See Hanson 2007, 23–6 for discussion of the problems.
22. Hanson 2007, 29–32.
23. Woolliscroft and Hoffman 2006, 178 summarise the sparse dating evidence for the towers.
24. Woolliscroft and Hoffman 2006, 193–4.

25. Breeze 1982, 53 admits the possibility that Ardoch and Strageath may have been established by Agricola in the third season.
26. Hodgson 2000.
27. Jones and Woolliscroft 2001, 27–32; Birley 2005, 84; Fields 2005, 20; for a full description of the Gask, see Woolliscroft and Hoffman 2006.
28. Woolliscroft and Hoffman 2006, 179–80.
29. Breeze 1982, 53; Jones and Woolliscroft 2001, 27 suggests that the initial establishment of the Gask belongs to Agricola's earliest activities. Woolliscroft and Hoffman 2006, 185; 193–4 for the possibility that the Roman occupation of Scotland may have predated Agricola.
30. Woolliscroft and Hoffman 2006, 193, referring to Ogilvie and Richmond 1962, 192.
31. Tacitus *Agricola* 23.
32. Hanson 2007, 22 says that the halt in the fourth season was deliberate policy of Titus.
33. Breeze 1982, 45.
34. Tacitus *Agricola* 24.
35. Tacitus *Agricola* 25.3.
36. Tacitus *Agricola* 27.2.
37. Tacitus *Agricola* 30.3.
38. Tacitus *Agricola* 33.3; 33.6; Birley 2005, 89, referring to Henderson *Classical Views*, 1985, 330 argues for a battle in the far north, possibly between Ben Loyal and the sea.
39. Tacitus *Agricola* 38.2–4; 40.3.
40. Breeze 1982, 51–4 discusses possible contexts for the glen forts.
41. Hanson 2007, 34–6, fig.1.
42. Tacitus *Histories* 1.2.1.
43. Jones 1991.
44. Jones and Woolliscroft 2001, 34–5; Bidwell 1999, 12.
45. See Poulter 1998.
46. Bidwell 1999, 111–13; Hodgson 2009a, 13.
47. Hill 2006, 17.
48. Jones and Woolliscroft 2001, 62.
49. Jones and Woolliscroft 2001, 63.
50. Breeze and Dobson 2000, 51.
51. Austen 1994, 52–3; Bidwell 1999, 25; 178–9; Jones and Woolliscroft 2001, 62–6; Hodgson 2009a, 151–4.
52. Breeze and Dobson 2000, 22; 39; Jones and Woolliscroft 2001, 65.
53. Biggins et al. in Hodgson 2009a, 151–4.
54. Jones and Woolliscroft 2001, 66–7.
55. The original air photo was taken by J. K. St Joseph, reproduced in Jones and Woolliscroft 2001, 58; see also Hodgson 2009a, 11–13.
56. Hill 2006, 18.
57. Hodgson 2009a, 13.
58. Woolliscroft 2001; see also Southern 1990.
59. Jones and Woolliscroft 2001, 34; Birley 2002, 54.

60. Jones and Woolliscroft 2001, 37–8; 62–71.
61. Hodgson 2009a, 14.
62. Breeze and Dobson 2000, 22.
63. Jones and Woolliscroft 2001, 34–5; Hodgson 2009a, 14.
64. Birley 2002, 54.
65. Birley 2002, 95; Bowman 2003, 23.
66. On the *numeri* see Southern 1989.
67. *ILS* 1338.
68. Birley 2002, 95–6; 2005, 321–2; Hodgson 2009a, 14–15.
69. *HA Hadrian* 5.5.2.
70. Fronto *De Bello Parthico* 2.
71. *ILS* 2726; Birley 1997, 123 says that the expedition can only be Hadrianic.
72. *ILS* 2735.
73. See Birley 2005, 307–9 for Agrippa's career, his service in Britain, and the date when he acted as host for Hadrian.
74. Fields 2003, 10; Birley 1997, 130; 2005, 118 n. 30 says that the trouble was surely caused by the Brigantes, possibly reaching as far as southern Scotland.
75. *Censitor*: *ILS* 1338; Birley 2002, 95; 2005, 321–2; Bowman 2003, 23; Hodgson 2009a, 14–15.
76. Birley 2005, 114–19.
77. *RIB* I 1051; Birley 1997, 132–3.
78. *BMC* III Hadrian 1723; Birley 1997, 140–1, plate 19.
79. *RIB* I 665.
80. Pollard and Berry 2012, 98.
81. *HA Hadrian* 10.1 for the German visit; 12.6 for the frontiers; Birley 1997, 116.
82. *HA Hadrian* 11.2.

2 *The Man Who Put Hadrian into Hadrian's Wall*

1. Birley 1997, 12.
2. *HA Hadrian* 1.3; 2.1.
3. *HA Hadrian* 1.4.
4. *HA Hadrian* 1.2.
5. Birley 1997, 25.
6. *HA Hadrian* 2; in the Loeb edition the post is rendered as *decimvir litibus iudicandis*.
7. Birley 1997, 29.
8. *HA Hadrian* 2.
9. *ILS* 308.
10. Birley 1997, 30.
11. Birley 1997, 30.
12. *HA Hadrian* 2.3–5.

13. Birley 1997, 31.
14. Pollard and Berry 2012, 194–6.
15. Birley 1997, 318 nn.12–13 argues that *II Adiutrix* was at Aquincum by 89; Pollard and Berry 2012, 195 argue for 106.
16. *HA* Hadrian 2.3; *ILS* 308.
17. Birley 1997, 32–3.
18. Birley 1997, 32.
19. Birley 1997, 37.
20. *HA* Hadrian 2.6.
21. *HA* Hadrian 2.10.
22. *HA* Hadrian 2.10.
23. *HA* Hadrian 2.7.
24. *HA* Hadrian 3.1
25. The Athens inscription *ILS* 308 gives Hadrian's title in full as *quaestor imperatoris Traiani.*
26. *HA* Hadrian 3.2.
27. Birley 1997, 47.
28. *HA* Hadrian 3.3.
29. *HA* Hadrian 3.8.
30. Birley 1997, 49.
31. *ILS* 308.
32. *HA* Hadrian 3.6.
33. *ILS* 308.
34. *HA* Hadrian 4.10.
35. *HA* Hadrian 4.10; Birley 1997, 53.
36. *HA* Hadrian 4.10.
37. Dio 69.17.3.
38. Birley 1997, 51 favours Trajan as the champion of Servianus.
39. *HA* Hadrian 23.2.
40. *HA* Hadrian 1.5.
41. Birley 1997, 64.
42. *ILS* 308.
43. Sartre 2005, 87.
44. See Birley 1997, 66–7 on the various new appointments.
45. *HA* Hadrian 4.1.
46. Dio 68.29.1–2.
47. Birley 1997, 73.
48. Dio 68.29.3.
49. Dio 68.29.4.
50. Dio 68.30.3.
51. Dio 68. 33.1–2.
52. Birley 1997, 74; 324 n.21.
53. Dio 68.31–1–4.
54. Dio 68.33.3.
55. Dio 68.33.2.
56. *HA* Hadrian 4.6–7.

57. Dio 69.1.1–4.
58. *HA* Hadrian 4.10.
59. *HA* Hadrian 4.9.
60. Dio 69.1.1–2.
61. Dio 68.17–33.
62. *HA* Hadrian 5.2.
63. Dio 69.2.2; *HA* Hadrian 6.1–4, listing the honours which were offered but which he refused.
64. Birley 1997, 81; 83 plate 6 showing *BMC* III Hadrian no.8.
65. *HA* Hadrian 5.5.
66. Birley 1997, 78.
67. *HA* Hadrian 7.1; Birley 1997, 87–9.
68. Dio 69.2.5; *HA* Hadrian 7.1–3.
69. *HA* Hadrian 5.8.
70. Dio 69.2.5.
71. *HA* Hadrian 7.2.
72. Dio 69.2.6; *HA* Hadrian 7.3.
73. Dio 69.2.4; *HA* Hadrian 7.4.
74. *HA* Hadrian 5.2.
75. *HA* Hadrian 5.3.
76. Birley 1997, 81.
77. *HA* Hadrian 6.7.
78. Platorius Nepos as a friend of Hadrian: *HA* Hadrian 4.2; see also Birley 1997, 84.
79. Dio 68.13.
80. Birley 1997, 90–1.
81. Birley 1997, 90; 2005, 114–19.
82. *ILS* 2726.
83. *AE* 1951.88.
84. *HA* Hadrian 5.2; Fronto *De Bello Parthico* 2.
85. Dio 69.8.1; *HA* Hadrian 7.6; Birley 1997, 97.
86. *HA* Hadrian 7.5–12.
87. *HA* Hadrian 12–14 documents his journeys.
88. Dio 69.9.1–5; *HA* Hadrian 10–11.
89. *HA* Hadrian 11.3.
90. *HA* Hadrian 11.5.
91. *HA* Hadrian 13.1–4.
92. *HA* Hadrian 13.10.
93. Birley 1997, 197–200.
94. *HA* Hadrian 13.4–6.
95. Dio 69. 11.2; *HA* Hadrian 13.6; Birley 1997, 247–8.
96. Dio 69.12. 1–2; *HA* Hadrian 14.2; Birley 1997, 268–76.
97. Dio 69.14.1–2.
98. Dio 69.17.1; *HA* Hadrian 23.10–11.
99. Dio 69.20.1; *HA* Hadrian 23.16.
100. Dio 69.21.1; *HA* Hadrian 24.1–7; Birley 1997, 294–5.

101. Dio 69.2.6; 17.1–2; *HA* Hadrian 25.8.
102. Birley 1997, 302; 357 n.6 noting the medical evidence.
103. Dio 69.23.2.
104. Dio 69.2.5; 6.1.
105. Dio 69.11.4.
106. *HA* Hadrian15.2–10.
107. Dio 69.5.2; 7.4; *HA* Hadrian 15.1.
108. *HA* Hadrian 7.5–12.
109. Dio 69.7.4.
110. *HA* Hadrian 15.13.

3 Protecting the Empire

1. *HA* Hadrian 55.2.
2. Dio 69.5.2; *HA* Hadrian 13.5.
3. Cities: Dio 69.5.2–3; disasters: *HA* 21.5–7.
4. *CIL* 8.18042=*ILS* 2487; 9133–9135; for English version see Sherk 1988, 187–9 no. 148.
5. Dio 69.9.5–6; *HA* Hadrian17.10–12; 21.14.
6. *HA* Hadrian 6.8.
7. Dio 69.9.5.
8. Rankov 2005, 181.
9. Tacitus *Histories* 4. 64.
10. *RIB* I 2091.
11. Breeze and Dobson 2000, 46; Breeze 2005, 13–16; Hodgson 2009, 15.
12. Crow 2004b, 116–18.
13. Tacitus *Germania* 37.3.
14. For more detailed information on the Gask frontier see Woolliscroft and Hoffman 2006. 15. Breeze 1982, 61–2.
16. Intercisa: *ILS* 8913; Aquincum: *ILS* 395.
17. See Shotter 1996, 41.
18. Birley 2005, 84.
19. Dobson 1986, 2; Hodgson 2009a, 13.
20. Hodgson 2009a, 11–14 discusses the different points of view about the Stanegate as a frontier.
21. Hodgson 2000.
22. Crow 2004b, 126–9.
23. Daniels, 1978; Bidwell 1999, 20.
24. Hodgson 2009a, 15.
25. *HA* Hadrian 12.6.
26. Birley 2005, 118–19 n. 82 quoting Schallmayer 2003, 12.
27. *HA* Hadrian 11.2.
28. Stevens 1966, 39, 62.
29. Bennett 2002, 825–34; see also Hodgson 2009a, 17.
30. Graafstal 2012.

31. *CIL* 16.69, a diploma found at Brigetio; Birley 2005, 114.
32. Birley 2005, 118.
33. The earliest finds are *RIB* I 1637 and 1638, the first one being found in two broken sections, the left-hand part in *c.* 1715, and the right-hand section in 1829; *RIB* I 1638 was found at an unspecified date in the 1750s. See also *RIB* 1340 found at Benwell in 1937; *RIB* I 1427 found at Halton Chesters in1936; *RIB* I 1634 found reused as a flooring stone at Housesteads milecastle in 1851; *RIB* I 1666 from Cawfields milecastle, found in 1847; *RIB* I 1935, a fragment of an oak panel from a Turf Wall milecastle, found in 1934.

4 *Building the Wall: AD 122 to* c. *AD 142*

1. *RIB* I 2034.
2. Hodgson 2009a, 20–2.
3. First proposed by Stevens 1966, 39; 62; see also Graafstal 2102.
4. Breeze 2009.
5. *CIL* 8.18042=*ILS* 2487; 9133–9135; for English version see Sherk 1988, 187–9 no. 148.
6. Birley 2005, 122 n.90 citing Bowman and Thomas 1994, 344.
7. Hill 2006, 37.
8. Hill 2001; Breeze 2006, 57–8.
9. Breeze and Hill 2001.
10. Bennett 2002; see also Symonds 2005.
11. Hodgson 2009a, 17–19.
12. Symonds 2005.
13. Graafstal 2102.
14. *RIB* I 2091
15. Breeze and Dobson 2000, 46 concede that worship of Brigantia was not necessarily confined to her own territory, but still advance the theory that some part of the tribe was excluded by the Wall.
16. *RIB* I 627.
17. Breeze and Dobson 1987, 33; 2000. 46; Breeze 2005, 13–16; Hodgson 2009a, 15.
18. Hill 2006, 22.
19. Maps: Hill 2006, 36 referring to Sherk 1974. Plans: Taylor 2003, 27–9.
20. *Digest* 50.6.7.
21. *ILS* 2421.
22. Webster 1985, 119.
23. Hill 2006, 53–4.
24. *RIB* I 1816; 1818; 1820.
25. Breeze and Dobson 2000 66; 78.
26. *RIB* I 1340.
27. *RIB* I 1361, 1362, 1364, 1365, 1367, 1368, 1369.

28. *RIB* I 1365.
29. Hill 2006, 113.
30. Lepper and Frere 1988, plate XII, scene XI; Coarelli 1999, 55 Tav. 11, scenes XI-XII/X-XII. The scene numbers of Trajan's Column vary slightly in different publications.
31. Hill 2006, 114–16.
32. Crow 2004b, 121.
33. Hill 2006, 113–14; *RIB* I 1672, 1673 recording work by the Durotriges from their tribal capital at Lendiniae, which may be Ilchester; *RIB* I 1843, 1844 recording the Dumnonii, whose tribal capital was at Exeter; *RIB* I 1962 recording work by Tossodio of the Catuvellauni of Verulamium, modern St Albans; *RIB* I 2022 found in the eighteenth century but now lost, recording work by the Brigantes; *RIB* I 2053 recording work by Vindomorucus, but without listing the tribe.
34. Rebuilding the Turf Wall: Fulford 2006; Severan campaigns: Bidwell 1999, 25 also suggesting that the circular buildings found at Vindolanda when the first stone fort was replaced were houses for the British members of the *civitates* who were called in by Severus; see also Hodgson 2009a, 32–3.
35. Johnson 1989, 39–40.
36. Breeze and Dobson 2000, 82–3.
37. *RIB* I 1024; on surveying in general see Dilke 1971; for Hadrian's Wall and northern Britain see Poulter 2005; 2008; 2009.
38. Breeze 2014b.
39. *CIL* 8.18042=*ILS* 2487; 9133–9135; Sherk 1988. 187–9, no. 148.
40. Webster 1985, 180 fig. 30.
41. Webster 1985, 179–80; Breeze and Dobson 2000, 31; Bidwell 2007, 44–6.
42. Turf phases in general: Bidwell 1999, 21; Stanwix: Dacre 1985; Birdoswald: Wilmott 1997, 53.
43. Breeze 2014a, 74.
44. Turf Wall milecastle 53: Breeze 2014a, 74 referring to Simpson and Richmond 1933, 263; Turf Wall milecastle 72: Breeze and Dobson, 2000, 32; turf or cobble foundations: Breeze 2014a, 74; Burgh-by-Sands: Austen 1994, 39–40.
45. Crow 2004b, 122; Breeze 2006.
46. Breeze 2014a, 85–90.
47. Breeze 2014a, 87–8.
48. Breeze and Dobson 2000, 49–51; 60; 85.
49. Wilmott 1999, 147–8.
50. Breeze and Dobson 1987, 33.
51. Crow 2004a, 30.
52. Johnson 1989, 36.
53. Shotter 2008,110.
54. Milecastles: Symonds 2005; Stanegate: Hodgson 2009a, 19 referring to Hill 2002.

55. Breeze and Dobson 2000, 31 fig. 6 provide a map of known quarries; Hill 2006, 40 provides a list.
56. Crow 1991b; G. Johnson 1997; see also Hill 2006, 39–62 on quarrying and working the stone.
57. Breeze 2014a, 87, referring to excavations at Hare Hill by Hodgson and McKelvey 2006, 52.
58. Crow 2004b 120; 122.
59. Johnson 1989, 35 fig. 21.
60. Breeze and Hill 2013, 110.
61. Breeze and Hill 2013, 106.
62. Vitruvius *Ten Books of Architecture* 3.4 translated by M. H. Morgan page 86.
63. Breeze and Dobson 2000, 81.
64. Hill 2006, 95–7.
65. Breeze and Hill 2013.
66. Richmond 1947, 187–8; Johnson 1989, 77.
67. Crow 1991a, 55–7.
68. Hill 2006, 69.
69. Adam 1994, 83, fig. 181.
70. Hill 2006, 24; 68–76.
71. Breeze and Dobson 2000, 75–6.
72. Breeze and Dobson 2000, 68.
73. Hill 2006, 26–8 on milecastle gateways and legionary building styles.
74. Breeze and Dobson 2000, 68.
75. Breeze 2006, 66; 286–7.
76. Breeze and Dobson 2000, 34–8.
77. Foglia 2014, 29.
78. Hodgson 2009a, 24–5 referring to Wilmott 2006 and Welfare 2004.
79. Breeze and Dobson 2000, 30.
80. For a summary of the arguments see Hodgson 2009a, 16–17.
81. Maenius Agrippa: *CIL* 11. 5632=*ILS* 2735; Sabinus CIL 10.5829=ILS 2726; see Birley 2005, 118; 307–9.
82. Frere 2000.
83. Dio 69.13.2; Birley 2005, 130.
84. Stevens 1966; Breeze 2003.
85. Casey 1987, 71.
86. Hodgson 2009a, 16.
87. Breeze and Dobson 2000, 47; 76–9.
88. Crow 2004b, 122 referring to Hill and Dobson 1992, 28.
89. Crow 2004b, 126–30; see also Hodgson 2009a, 19–20.
90. Crow 2004b, 124; 127 fig. 8.4.
91. Bidwell 1999, 21.
92. Breeze and Dobson 2000, 47; 78–9.
93. Austen 2008.
94. Breeze and Dobson 2000, 78–9.
95. Crow 2004b, 126.

96. Benwell: *RIB* I 1340; Halton Chesters: *RIB* I 1427.
97. Breeze and Dobson 2000, 78 favour the date of 126; see Birley 2005, 123–5.
98. Breeze and Dobson 2000, 50, table 2.
99. Breeze and Dobson 2000, 51.
100. Wilmott 2009, 119.
101. Breeze 2014a, 140 referring to Swinbank 1954; Heywood and Breeze 2008; Welfare 2013, 96.
102. Heywood 1965, 89–90.
103. Breeze and Dobson 2000, 58.
104. Breeze and Dobson 2000, 58.
105. Bidwell 1999, 22; Wilmott 2008, 124–5; Hodgson 2009a, 28.
106. Wilmott 2008, 124.
107. Welfare 2000; Breeze 2014a, 115.
108. *RIB* I 974; it was seen and recorded in 1601, but lost by the later eighteenth century.
109. *RIB* I 995; Horsley 1732, 270, under 'Beaucastle'.
110. Breeze and Dobson 2000, 46; 81.
111. Breeze 2008, 3.
112. Altar: *RIB* I 1778; building work: *RIB* I 1818; 1820.
113. Breeze and Dobson 2000, 6–87.
114. Crow 2004a, 30.
115. de la Bédoyère, 1998, 21–2.
116. Bidwell 2005b; 2008b; Breeze 2006, 110.
117. Callwell 1906, 280–1.
118. Hodgson 2009a, 25–7, fig. 4.
119. Bidwell 2005b.
120. Peel Gap: Crow 1991b, 46, fig. 8.2; whitewash: Crow 2004b, 123; Bidwell 1999, 18.
121. Bidwell and Watson 1996, 23–8, figs. 18–20.
122. For poor building techniques see Hill 2006.
123. Bidwell 2007, plate 4.

5 Antonine Interlude: c. AD 142 to c. AD 165

1. Pausanias *Description of Greece* 8. 43.3.
2. Breeze 1982, 97; Breeze and Dobson 2000, 88–9.
3. Salway 1991, 200–1.
4. Hind 1977.
5. Rivet and Smith 1979, 47.
6. *HA* Pius 5.4.
7. *ILS* 340; Birley 2005, 137.
8. Breeze 1982, 98–9.
9. Breeze and Dobson 2000, 90.
10. Birley 2005, 137.

11. *RIB* I 1147; 1148.
12. *RIB* I 1276.
13. *RIB* I 2191; 2192.
14. *HA* Antoninus Pius 5.4.
15. Tacitus *Agricola* 23; Salway 1991, 196.
16. On the *numeri* in general see Callies 1964; Southern 1989.
17. Baatz 1973.
18. *CIL* 13. 6502; 6511; 6514; 6517; 6518.
19. Hodgson 2009a, 34 referring to Bidwell 2005b.
20. Salway 1991, 197; Breeze and Dobson 2000, 94.
21. Gillam 1958, 66–7.
22. Salway 1991, 197.
23. Dio 77.13.1.
24. Hanson 2004, 143.
25. *RIB* I 2313; Birley 2005, 142.
26. Original plan for six forts: Breeze and Dobson 2000, 100 quoting Gillam 1975.
27. Fields 2005, 40; Hill 2006, 116.
28. Breeze and Dobson 2000, 98.
29. Maxwell 1974; Breeze and Dobson 2000, 98.
30. *RIB* I 2139.
31. Breeze and Dobson 2000, 102.
32. Breeze and Dobson 2000, 96.
33. Bidwell 1999, 22.
34. Breeze 1982, 108 fig. 24; Shotter 1996, 91.
35. Shotter 1996, 89.
36. Breeze and Dobson 2000, 94.
37. Fields 2005, 38; Johnson 1989, 71.
38. Gillam 1975.
39. Breeze and Dobson 2000, 101–2.
40. Keppie and Walker 1981.
41. Shotter 1996, 87.
42. Steer 1957.
43. For a reconstruction drawing see Breeze 1982, 104–5, fig. 22; on signalling generally see Woolliscroft 2001; 2008; signalling on the Antonine Wall: Woolliscroft 1996.
44. Breeze and Dobson 2000, 110–13; and 111 table 9.
45. Breeze and Dobson 2000, 111–13, table 9.
46. Shotter 1996, 93 says that troops were withdrawn from Lanchester; Breeze and Dobson 2000, 92 describe Lanchester as a replacement between Ebchester and Binchester.
47. Birley 2005, 144.
48. Breeze and Dobson 2000, 91.
49. *RIB* I 1582; 1583.
50. *BMC* IV Antoninus Pius nos.1971ff and 1993ff.
51. *AE* 1997.1001; Birley 2005, 147.

52. *RIB* I 1322.
53. Breeze and Dobson 2000, 118–19.
54. Birley 2005, 147–8 n. 50.
55. *RIB* I 2110.
56. *RIB* I 283.
57. *RIB* I 1388; 1389.
58. *RIB* I 1389.
59. *RIB* I 1388.
60. Hodgson 2011, 66.
61. Breeze and Dobson 2000, 123.
62. Breeze 1982, 120–1; Shotter 1996, 9–95.
63. Corbridge: *RIB* I 1137; 1149; Vindolanda: *RIB* I 1703; Carvoran: *RIB* I 1792; 1809; Ribchester: *RIB* I 589; Hardknott: *RIB* I 793.
64. Hodgson 1995.
65. Hartley 1972.
66. Hodgson 2011, 192.
67. *RIB* I 2110.
68. Breeze and Dobson 2000, 129–30.
69. Hodgson 2009b, 192.
70. Hodgson 1995.
71. Hodgson 2009b, 187–8.
72. Millett 1990.
73. Ptolemy *Geography* 2.3.1; Rivet and Smith 1979, 425–6.
74. Hodgson 2009b, 189 n.21 referring to Wilson 2003, 113–14.
75. Hodgson 2009b, 189 n.21 referring to Bruhn 2008, 208.
76. Robertson 1978, 209–11; Hanson 2004, 141–2 and fig. 9.3.
77. Trading only during occupation: Hanson 2004, 142.
78. Hodgson 2009b, 187; Wilson 2003, 119; Birley 2005, 360 n.29.
79. Breeze 2014a, 139–40.
80. Hodgson 2009b, 189.
81. Rivet and Smith 1979, 425.
82. Hodgson 2009b, 189 n. 21 referring to Wilson 2001, 88–9; Birley 2005, 356–7.
83. Breeze 2014a, 140.
84. Dio 72.16.2.
85. Hodgson 2009b, 187 nn.11–12.
86. Keppie 2009, 245 n.35 quoting Campbell 2003, 28.
87. Keppie 2009, 243.
88. Keppie 2009, 245.
89. Steer 1964, 24.
90. Campbell 2003.
91. Keppie 2009, 249.
92. R. J. A. Wilson 2002, 567–8.
93. *HA* Marcus Aurelius 22.1.
94. Hodgson 2009b, 192.
95. *HA* Antoninus Pius 12.7.

96. Birley 1987, 121.
97. *BMC* 1273; Kent 1978, 296 and plate 87 no.306.
98. *HA* Antoninus Pius 10.6.
99. Dio 69.15.1.
100. *HA* Antoninus Pius 10.7.
101. *HA* Antoninus Pius 10.7; Marcus Aurelius 8.6.
102. *ILS* 1076.
103. Birley 1987, 121.
104. Dio 71.2.1.
105. *RIB* I 665.
106. Pollard and Berry 2012, 98.
107. Hodgson 2009b, 190–1.
108. Mann 1974.
109. Breeze 2008, 1.

6 Hadrian's Wall from Marcus Aurelius to Severus: AD 161 to AD 211

1. Birley 2005, 150–1 *CIL* 16.130=*RIB* II 2401.12.
2. *HA* Marcus Aurelius 8.7.
3. *HA* Marcus Aurelius 8.8.
4. Birley 2005, 156–7.
5. *RIB* I 589.
6. *RIB* I 793.
7. Carvoran: *RIB* I 1792; 1809; Vindolanda: *RIB* I 1703.
8. *VI Victrix*: *RIB* I 1137; *XX Valeria Victrix*: *RIB* I 1149.
9. See Hodgson 2008b on the development of Corbridge.
10. Bidwell 1999, 24; 97–9; Bidwell in Hodgson 2009, 83–4.
11. *RIB* I 1328, an altar to Antenociticus, who was worshipped at Benwell, set up by the prefect Cassianus; Hodgson 2008a, 15 n.11.
12. A centurion of *II Augusta* dedicating to Antoninus Pius before 161: *RIB* I 1330. A centurion of *XX Valeria Victrix* dedicating to the gods of the Emperors, which presumably refers to Marcus and Lucius Verus after 161: *RIB* I 1327; also *RIB* I 1338 records a centurion of *XX Valeria Victrix*, but with no name or date.
13. Breeze and Dobson 2000, 256–7.
14. Hodgson 2008a, 15 n.11 accepts the possibility.
15. Hodgson 2008a, 15.
16. *RIB* I 1463.
17. Prefect of cavalry: *RIB* I 1329.
18. Hodgson 2009a, 31.
19. *Cohors VI Nerviorum*: *RIB* I 1731; *cohors Raetorum*: *RIB* I 1737; *cohors II Asturum*: *RIB* I 1738.
20. *RIB* I 1792; 1809.
21. Breeze and Dobson 2000, 272.
22. McCarthy in Bidwell 1999,163.

23. Breeze and Dobson 2000, 265.
24. Hodgson 2009a, 31; 152–4.
25. Johnson 1989, 75.
26. Wilmott 2008, 122–5; Daniels 1978, 33.
27. Wilmott 2008, 125, with note 68 referring to excavations by Heywood 1965, 91–3; see also Hodgson 2009a, 28–9 on the Vallum and marginal mound.
28. Breeze 2014a, 87–8.
29. Bidwell 1999, 23.
30. Hassall 1984, 242–4.
31. Aurelius Victor *de Caesaribus* 20.18; Eutropius *Breviarum* 8.19.
32. Breeze 2104, 90 quoting Frere 1987, 152 n.24.
33. M. Bowden for RCHME in Bidwell 1999, 137–9.
34. Bidwell 1999, 2; 119–20.
35. *RIB* III 3480.
36. *RIB* I 995.
37. *RIB* I 1227, an elaborate dedication to the deities of the Emperors, who are not named, but they are most probably Marcus Aurelius and Lucius Verus. The inscription is contained within an octagon enclosed within a square, each side of the octagon decorated by carved leaves and fruit. Two figures flank the inscription, Victory on the left and Mars on the right. The appearance is reminiscent of the distance slabs of the Antonine Wall.
38. Breeze and Dobson 2000, 262; *RIB* I 837; 838; 842; 843.
39. Lanchester: a dedication set up by the 1000-strong, part-mounted *cohors I Vardullorum* under the governor Antistius Adventus, c. 172–4: *RIB* I 1083; Ilkley: an inscription found in the seventeenth century, reused in one of the buttresses of the parish church, drawn but since lost, a dedication for the welfare of Marcus Aurelius and Lucius Verus, therefore dated between 161 to 169 when Verus died: *RIB* I 636; Brough-on-Noe: *RIB* I 283.
40. *RIB* I 583: Aelius Antoninus, centurion of *VI Victrix*; *RIB* I 587: Titus Floridius Natalis, centurion of an unnamed legion.
41. Dio 72.16.2.
42. *RIB* I 583 names the *numerus equitum Sarmatarum*; *RIB* I 594, origin not recorded, now lost, is attributed to Ribchester because of the mention of the *ala Sarmatarum*, which is actually attested at this fort by *RIB* I 595, which was found in the vicinity.
43. Dio 72.33–34.
44. Dio 73.2.2–3.
45. Dio 73.8.1.
46. Dio 73.8.3–6.
47. Birley 2005, 166.
48. *RIB* I 1329.
49. *RIB* I 1463 records the installation of a water supply at Chesters fort under Ulpius Marcellus; see also *RIB* I 1464, which is fragmentary,

naming Marcellus but no mention of the Emperor, which may have
been in the missing section.

50. Birley 2005, 164.
51. Hodgson 2009a, 31–32.
52. Breeze and Dobson 1972, 200–8; Breeze and Dobson 2000, 134;
    Birley 2005, 167; Hodgson 2008b on the development of Corbridge;
    2009a, 32 on the destruction layers at Halton Chesters, and the
    excavation report by John Dore, published posthumously in 2009.
53. *RIB* I 1142.
54. Birley 2005, 168.
55. Rivet and Smith 1979, 322.
56. Dio 77.12.1.
57. *RIB* I 2034.
58. Birley 2005, 167; 263–4, pointing out that the possible dating for this
    inscription can only fall into a few time slots: it has to belong to a
    period when Hadrian's Wall was occupied as the frontier, between *c.*
    122 and 142, or after the abandonment of the Antonine Wall; but it
    must be before *c.* 216 by which time the legate of *VI Victrix* was also
    the governor of Lower Britain, Britannia Inferior, the northern part of
    Britain.
59. *RIB* I 946.
60. Dio 73.9.2: the passage at 9.2 consists of fragments surviving in the
    works of different authors, grouped together; *HA* Commodus 8.4.
61. Dio 73.8.6.
62. *HA* Commodus 8.4.
63. Dio 73.9.2–10.1.
64. Birley 2005, 170–1.
65. *HA* Pertinax 3.5.
66. Risingham: *RIB* I 1227; Vindolanda: *RIB* I 1705, under Caracalla; see
    also *RIB* I 1686; 1687; 1706; 1710.
67. *RIB* I 1234.
68. Breeze and Dobson 2000, 134.
69. Mason 2001, 155–7.
70. *RIB* I 1912; Wilmott 1999, 152–3; see Donaldson 1990 for a
    reinterpretation of this inscription.
71. Wilmott 1999, 151; Breeze and Dobson 2000, 223.
72. Hodgson 2009a, 36 referring to Halton Chesters as re-evaluated by
    Dore 2009.
73. For an illustration of how this was done see Johnson 1989, 75 fig. 50.
74. Breeze and Dobson 2000, 136.
75. Breeze and Dobson 2000, 136.
76. *RIB* I 1909.
77. *RIB* I 1337.
78. *RIB* I 1329; Breeze and Dobson 2000, 135.
79. *RIB* I 1463.
80. Breeze and Dobson 2000, 136.

81. *HA* Pertinax 12.8 says that Pertinax did not replace governors appointed by Commodus, so Albinus could have been governor of Britain even earlier than 192: see Birley 2005, 177.
82. Dio 74.14.3.
83. Dio 74.15.1–2; Herodian 2.15.3–5 says that Severus was only pretending to honour Albinus, who was convinced that Severus was sincere.
84. Dio 76.4.1–76.7.4 and Herodian 3.7.1–7 describe the campaign and reprisals.
85. Breeze and Dobson 2000, 122.
86. Salway 1991, 221.
87. Birley 1972; Salway 1991, 221 n.3.
88. Dio 76.5.4; the numbering of books and chapters of Dio's work is not clear here, see pages 216–17 in volume 9 of the Loeb edition of Dio.
89. Herodian 3.8.2.
90. Breeze and Dobson 2000, 232.
91. Birley 2005, 333 for the date and the move of *II Adiutrix*.
92. Dio 55.23.2 and 55.23.6; Birley 2005, 333 nn. 2 and 3, referring to *CIL* 8.5180 and 17266 for *VI Victrix* in Britannia Inferior, and *CIL* 8.2080 for *XX Valeria Victrix* and *II Augusta* in Britannia Superior.
93. Birley 2005, 336 citing *AE* 1922.116.
94. Birley 2005, 333–6 discusses the ideas that were formulated about the division of Britain, shamelessly looted and outlined here: one suggestion was that the successive consular governors appointed after 197 were operating in the north only temporarily, and another suggestion was that Britannia Inferior was governed from Carlisle by a procurator, whose remit excluded York and *VI Victrix*. A. J. Graham in *Journal of Roman Studies* 56, 1966, 92ff called attention to an inscription from Ephesus recording a man who met Severus in Britain and Caracalla in Upper Germany, the absence of any distinction between Upper or Lower Britain indicating that during Severus' campaigns Britain was still a single province. J. C. Mann and M. G. Jarrett replied in the same journal for the following year, *Journal of Roman Studies* 57, 1967, 61ff, that Germany had to be distinguished as the Upper province because otherwise it could have been construed as Free Germany, and it was suggested that at first Lower Britain was a consular province, including not only York and *VI Victrix* but also Chester and *XX Valeria Victrix*, and Superior was a praetorian province with one legion, *II Augusta*. Shortly afterwards Caracalla adjusted the boundaries *c.* 213, just as he did in Pannonia, and thereafter *XX Valeria* belonged in Britannia Superior. This accommodates Herodian and the seemingly anomalous presence of consular governors in the north after 197.
95. Lupus: *RIB* I 730; Senecio: *RIB* I 740.
96. Birley 2005, 186; 188–9; *RIB* III 3215.
97. *RIB* I 722; 723 and see addenda page 772 in *RIB* I.
98. *RIB* I 1234.
99. *RIB* I 1243.

100. Birley 2005, 211–12, citing *AE* 1967.250.
101. *RIB* I 746.
102. *RIB* I 1337.
103. Chesters: *RIB* I 1462; Birdoswald *RIB* I 1909.
104. *RIB* I 1163.
105. Birley 2005, 211; *RIB* I 1151.
106. *RIB* I 1143.
107. Dio 78.14.1; 79.8.2; Birley 1988, 171.
108. Birley 2005, 312–13.
109. Rankov 1987, 248–9; *RIB* I 1234 for Adventus at Risingham; *RIB* I 1235 for the *exploratores*.
110. Austen and Rankov 1995, 137; 194.
111. Birley 1988, 171–2.
112. Lollius Urbicus: *RIB* I 1147 and 1148; Calpurnius Agricola *RIB* I 1137; 1149.
113. Under Lollius Urbicus building was carried out at High Rochester: *RIB* I 1276, and at Balmuildy: *RIB* I 2191 and 2192, but the formula used is *sub*, not *sub cura*. At Carvoran Calpurnius Agricola is named as the governor but building was done *sub cura* Licinius Clemens, the prefect: *RIB* I 1792; 1809. At Ribchester and at Hardknott (the restoration of the text is uncertain) Agricola is acknowledged as the consular governor but he did not supervise the work: Ribchester: *RIB* I 589; Hardknott: *RIB* I 793.
114. Breeze 2006, 58.
115. Breeze 2006, 105–6.
116. Breeze 2006, 256.
117. Breeze 2006, 442; R. Birley 2009, 138.
118. R. Birley 2009, 139–40.
119. *RIB* I 1672; 1673; 1843; 1844; 1962; 2022; Bidwell 1999, 25; Hodgson 2009, 32–3. Another suggestion concerning these inscriptions, put forward by Fulford 2006, is that civilians were called in to help to replace the Turf Wall in stone in the 160s, in which case the *civitates* that contributed the men would have had nothing to do with the round structures at Vindolanda.
120. Bidwell 1985, 28–31.
121. Rivet and Smith 1979, 152; 162–3.
122. Margary 1967, 371- 374, route 72a; 401–3, route 72b; 416–17, route 28c.
123. *RIB* I 1265: a dedication to Caracalla; *RIB* I 1272 records that something built or rebuilt from the ground up (*a solo*) under the tribune Lucius Caecilius Optatus, who is also mentioned on *RIB* I 1265, a dedication set up in the reign of Caracalla.
124. *RIB* I 1243.
125. *RIB* I 976 for the dedication; *RIB* I 978 for the cavalry exercise hall. See also *RIB* I 977 for something built from the ground up; *RIB* I 979 for the rebuilding of a temple which had fallen down through old age.

126. *RIB* I 1143; 1151; 1163.
127. Breeze 2006, 116–18.
128. Hodgson 2001; 2009a, 32; largest collection: Breeze 2006, 120.
129. Breeze 2006, 120 with line drawing.
130. *Codex Theodosianus* 7.4.3.
131. Birley 1988, 173.
132. Birley 1988, 175; 255 n.9 citing *CIL* 6.1643.
133. Dio 77.10.6.
134. Dio 77.10.5; Birley 1988, 169.
135. *RIB* I 1337.
136. Herodian 3.14.1.
137. Herodian 3.14.2.
138. Birley 2005, 192.
139. Dio 77.11.1; Herodian 3.14.2.
140. Dio 77.13.1; Birley 1988, 171; 173.
141. *CIL* 13. 3496; Loeb ed. Herodian, vol. I p.357 n.3.
142. Herodian 3.14.3.
143. Herodian 3.14.4.
144. Dio 77.12.1.
145. Dio 77.12.1–4.
146. Herodian 3.14.6–8.
147. Birley 1988, 180; Breeze and Dobson 2000, 140.
148. Swamps: Dio 77.13.1–4; pontoons: Herodian 3.14.5; Traiectus coins: Birley 1988, 179; 255 n.16 quoting *BMC* V 353.
149. Birley 1988, 181.
150. Herodian 3.14.10.
151. Dio 77.13.3.
152. Dio 77.13.4.
153. Birley 1988, 182.
154. Dio 77.15.1.
155. Dio 77.11.1–2.
156. Dio 77.15.2.
157. Dio 78.1.1.
158. Ireland 1996, 115 no. 190 and line drawing; *RIC* IV.1 p.291 no.483c.
159. Birley 2005, 202 n.53.
160. Dio 77.13.1.
161. Aurelius Victor *de Caesaribus* 20.18; Eutropius *Breviarum* 8.19.1.
162. Orosius 7.17.
163. Birley 1988, 188.

7 *Living on the Wall: Soldiers and Civilians*

1. Watson 1969, 22; Goldsworthy 2003, 51.
2. Bassus: *RIB* I 1501; *hastatus prior*: *RIB* I 2091.

3. *RIB* I 1542 from Carrawburgh, a dedication to Minerva by Quintus, with no other name; *RIB* I 2091 from Birrens, recording Amandus, who set up a dedication to the goddess Brigantia; *RIB* I 2096 also from Birrens, a dedication to the goddess Harimella, by a man called Gamidiahus.
4. *Notitia Dignitatum* Occ. 40.34.
5. *Notitia Dignitatum* Occ. 40.36.
6. See Southern 2014, 255 for the supporting evidence for sixteen *turmae* and 512 men per quingenary *ala*.
7. *Notitia Dignitatum* Occ. 40. 22.
8. Breeze and Dobson 2000, 268.
9. Risingham: *RIB* I 1231 names the unit in full and also the commander: *cohors I Vangionum equitata milliaria cui praeest Marcus Peregrinius Super. RIB* I 1214, 1216, 1217 name the unit; 1208, 1210, 1212, 1213, 1220, 1221, 1222, 1223, 1234, 1237, 1241 mention the tribunes; High Rochester: *RIB* I 1262; 1263; 1265; 1267; 1268; 1270; 1272; 1280; 1281; 1286.
10. Bowman 2003, 51–2; 71–3.
11. Dixon and Southern 1992, 192–4, figs. 69–72.
12. For plans of both forts at different periods see Hodgson 2009a, 63 fig. 5 for South Shields cavalry barracks; 74 fig. 11 for Wallsend.
13. *RIB* I 1523.
14. Birley 2002, 47.
15. Bowman 2003, 104.
16. *RIB* I 1480.
17. Messorius Magnus: *RIB* I 1433; Nigrinus *RIB* I 2140.
18. Birley 2002, 47.
19. *RIB* I 1172.
20. *RIB* I 1247.
21. *RIB* I 1560.
22. *RIB* I 871.
23. *RIB* I 1171.
24. *RIB* I 1065.
25. Julius Pastor: *RIB* I 1795; Crescens: *RIB* I 769.
26. *RIB* I 1596.
27. *RIB* I 1619 and addendum page 787 on the name Leubasnus.
28. Vindolanda: Bowman 2003, 108 text no. 8 line 1= *Tab. Vindol.* II 182; Carrawburgh: *RIB* I 1559.
29. Bowman 2003, 138 text no. 35=*Tab. Vindol.* II 301.
30. Bowman 2003, 104–6, text 6=*Tab. Vindol.* II 180.
31. *ILS* 2427.
32. *RIB* I 1134.
33. Justus: *RIB* I 507; Julius Gr...nus: *RIB* I 1101.
34. Bowman 2003, 17; 101–2.
35. See *RIB* II Fascicule 4, 43–6 for discussion of stamps, and nos 2446.1 to 2446.31 for examples from Britain.

36. Lewis and Rheinhold 1990, 472–3, no. 147, Berlin Papyrus 1.564, dated to AD 138.
37. Birley 2002, 79; British Museum Papyrus 2851 in Fink 1971 no. 63, 217–25; clothing: 224 line 18 in Latin; 227 line 18 for translation.
38. Fink 1971 no. 63, 217–25, 224 and 227, lines 19 and 20.
39. Fink 1971, 108–9 line 7; 113.
40. Fink 1971, 186 line 9; 188 line 9.
41. Bowman 2003, 107–8 text no. 7=*Tab. Vindol.* II 181.
42. Birley 2002, 64.
43. Crow 2004a, 34; Breeze 2006, 236.
44. *RIB* I 583; *Notitia Dignitatum* Occ. 40.54.
45. Saddington 2005, 64.
46. Saddington 2005, 66.
47. Crow 2004a, 78.
48. Tacitus *Agricola* 29.2; 32.1 Tacitus invents a speech for the British leader Calgacus, who refers to British tribes expending their blood for the alien tyranny.
49. *RIB* I 2142.
50. *ILS* 1338; Birley 2005, 320–1.
51. Saddington 2009, 84 points out that recruiting during the Republic was the responsibility of provincial governors.
52. *RIB* III 3332; Birley 2009, 144–5; 155 fig. 91.
53. Bidwell 2005b.
54. Vegetius *Epitoma rei Militaris* 2.5.
55. Vegetius *Epitoma rei Militaris* 1.11–2.
56. Vegetius *Epitoma rei Militaris* 1.10; Vindolanda inscription: *RIB* III 3355.
57. *RIB* I 1049.
58. Tacitus Annals 13.54.
59. British Museum Papyrus 2851 known as Hunt's Pridianum in Fink 1971, no.63 217–27, especially 225 lines 31 and 33 in Latin; 227 lines 31 and 33 for translations.
60. Bowman 2003, 104–7 text no. 6=*Tab. Vindol.* II 180.
61. Davies 1971, 126–8; 138–41; table 1.
62. Banna: *RIB* I 1905; prefect of *ala Sebosiana*: *RIB* I 1041.
63. Bowman 2003, 138–9 text no. 36=*Tab. Vindol.* II 302.
64. Bowman 2003, 64–5.
65. Applebaum 1972, 109.
66. Haselgrove 1982, 83.
67. Southern and Dixon 1996, 116–17; Caerleon: Coulston 1985, 227–9; 268; Corbridge: Coulston 1985, 268; Housesteads: Crow 2004a, 96.
68. On artillery see Southern and Dixon 1996, 152–60; Wilkins 2003.
69. Bowman 2003, 147–8 text no. 44=*Tab. Vindol.* II 346.
70. Bowman 2003, 66–7.
71. Crow 2004a, 54; Breeze 2006, 137.
72. *RIB* I 1028.

73. *RIB* I 1618.
74. Hyginus *De Metatione Castrorum* 4.
75. Alston 1994.
76. Fink 1971, no. 68, 243–9 classifies the two men as legionaries.
77. Fink 1971, no. 117, 422–9.
78. Bowman 2003, 33–4; 104–5, text no. 5=*Tab. Vindol.* II 174–5.
79. *RIB* I 1544; 1545; 1546.
80. For a list of sites see de la Bedoyere, 1999, 166; 188.
81. Birley 2002, 163; 174 n.9.
82. Crow 2004a, 63; Birley 2009, 162.
83. Nectovelius: *RIB* I 2142.
84. Crow 2004a, 73.
85. Crow 2004a, 85.
86. Crow 2004a, 87 referring to Wilmott 2001, 82–3.
87. Bidwell in Hodgson 2009a, 71.
88. Crow 2004a, 73.
89. Hancke et al. in Hodgson 2009a, 168.
90. Iron Age: Crow in Bidwell 1999, 189; probable *vicus*: Hodgson 2008, 15; fort annexe: 2009a, 35.
91. *RIB* III 3503.
92. *RIB* I 1616; Crow 2004a, 74; 75 fig. 41.
93. *RIB* I 1700.
94. *RIB* I 899.
95. Hassall 1976, 111; Rivet and Smith 1979, 406.
96. Crow 2004a, 74; 76 figs. 40 and 42.
97. *CIL* 3.10505 attests a soldier on the Danube frontier calling himself *interpres Germanorum officii consularis*, and *CIL* 3. 14349.5 attests an *interprex Sarmatarum*.
98. Birley 2009, 167.
99. Birley 2009, 26; 167.
100. Crow 2004a, 77.
101. Birley 2009, 137.
102. Birdoswald: Wilmott 1997, 198–201; Vindolanda: Birley 2009, 150; 157; other forts: Bidwell 2007, 88–9.
103. Bidwell 2007, 89.
104. Bidwell 2007, 127; Hodgson 2009a, 37–8; Birley 2009, 150.
105. Hodgson 2003, 14–18; Bidwell 2007, 87; Hodgson 2009a, 76.
106. Biggins and Taylor 2004; Hodgson 2009a, 35; 113.
107. Hodgson 2009a, 35.

8 *The Wall from Caracalla to the Accession of Diocletian: AD 211 to AD 284*

1. Whittaker 1994, 210–14.
2. Hodgson 2008a, 14 and fig. 3.

3. Herodian 3.15.1; 3.15.6; Dio 77.14.1–6.

4. Dio 78.9.5.

5. Dio 78.9.3 complained that Caracalla demanded provisions for celebrations but gave most of the supplies to the soldiers.

6. Herodian 3.8.2.

7. Birley 2005, 334.

8. Birley 2005, 333.

9. Birley 2005, 342–4; *CIL* 13.3162 from Thorigny.

10. Breeze and Dobson 2000, 152.

11. Breeze and Dobson 2000, 152 relate the title to the recovery of the Gallic Empire; Birley 2005, 366 n.127 referring to E. Kettenhofen *Tyche* 1, 1986, 138ff accepts that the title has been misread.

12. Birley 2005, 337.

13. *RIB* I 605; Birley 2005, 337; 365–6.

14. *RIB* I 311 Caerwent honouring Tiberius Claudius Paulinus former legate of *II Augusta*, then governor of Britannia Inferior in 220; *RIB* I 316 Caerleon Titus Flavius Postumius Varus, legatus; *RIB* I 334 Vitulasius Laetinianus, *legatus legionis*.

15. *RIB* I 980.

16. John Zant in Hodgson 2009a, 147.

17. *RIB* III 3460; Birley 2005, 336 n.14 referring to the section on new inscriptions in *Britannia* 20, 1989, 331f for the altar; Breeze 2006, 460; 463.

18. Hodgson 2009a, 32.

19. *RIB* III 3253.

20. *RIB* I 1022.

21. Hodgson 2008a, 16–17 n.17.

22. M. R. McCarthy in Bidwell 1999, 170.

23. Hodgson 2008a, 17.

24. *RIB* I 747.

25. *RIB* I 745 found not far from the confluence of the River Greta with the River Tees, reproduced by Horsley in *Britannia Romana* and since lost.

26. *RIB* I 1696; Birley 2005, 336 n.14.

27. Austin and Rankov 1995, 196; 203–4.

28. Birley 2005, 345.

29. Bidwell 1999, 26; Crow 2004a, 69.

30. Bidwell 1999, 28 referring to Casey and Savage 1980 on High Rochester; Austen 1991 on Bewcastle.

31. *RIB* I 2298; Birley 2005, 203; 207. Newcastle: *RIB* III 3284; Vindolanda: *RIB* I 1705; Birley 2005, 204; South Shields: *RIB* III 3272; Old Carlisle in Cumbria: *RIB* I 905; Whitley Castle in the Pennines: *RIB* I 1202.

32. Newcastle: *RIB* III 3284; Vindolanda: *RIB* I 1705; Birley 2005, 204; South Shields: *RIB* III 3272; Old Carlisle in Cumbria: *RIB* I 905; Whitley Castle in the Pennines: *RIB* I 1202.

33. Birley 2005, 203.
34. *RIB* I 1265.
35. *RIB* I 1235.
36. *RIB* I 1272.
37. *RIB* I 1265.
38. *RIB* I 1279, dated by Caracalla's nineteenth year of *tribunicia potestas*.
39. *RIB* I 1280.
40. *RIB* I 1281; the date is not established, but on the inscription the presence of AUGG, with the second letter G inserted inside the first one, indicates that two Emperors were involved. This may mean that the work was done in 235, when Severus Alexander was killed in March and Maximinus Thrax became Emperor, so the extra letter G was carved to represent the new Emperor: Birley 2005, 352.
41. Crow in Bidwell 1999, referring to Campbell 1984, 84 and Donaldson 1990, 211.
42. *RIB* I 1262; 1263; 1272; 1279–81; 1285; 1288.
43. *RIB* I 1270.
44. *RIB* I 1262.
45. Crow in Bidwell 1999, 191; 192 fig. 64 for preliminary plan of the fort, based on an amalgamation of the nineteenth-century plan and geophysical survey.
46. *RIB* I 1234.
47. *RIB* I 1216; 1217; 1230; 1231; 1234; 1235; 1241; 1243.
48. *RIB* I 1241.
49. *RIB* I 1242.
50. *RIB* I 1243; see also 1244.
51. Vexillations of *Raeti Gaesati* are attested at Jedburgh, or more likely from the small fort at Cappuck nearby, and at Great Chesters on the Wall: *RIB* I 2117; 1724; tribune Aemilianus: *RIB* I 1216; Victor: *RIB* I 1217; three units together, *Vangiones*, *Raeti Gaesati* and *exploratores Habitancenses*: *RIB* I 1235. *RIB* I 1216; 1217. See also Southern 1989, 109.
52. *RIB* I 988; 989.
53. *RIB* I 977.
54. *RIB* I 980; the inscription was recut in modern times and the reading is not certain; see Birley 2005, 341.
55. *RIB* I 978 *sub cura* Marius Valerianus.
56. Wallsend: Breeze 2006, 133–4; Hodgson 2009a, 73; Halton Chesters: Breeze 2006, 179–81.
57. Vegetius *Epitoma Rei Militaris* 2.23.
58. Dixon and Southern 1996, 220–5.
59. *RIB* I 968; 976–80.
60. Breeze and Dobson 2000, 148.
61. *RIB* I 1299–1301.
62. *Notitia Dignitatum* Occ. 40.33.

63. Breeze 2006, 133–4; Hodgson 2009a, 73.
64. Breeze 2006, 133–4; Hodgson 2009a, 73–4.
65. *RIB* III 3281.
66. Breeze 2006, 134.
67. Bidwell 1989; Hodgson and Bidwell 2004, 150; Hodgson 2008a, 18.
68. Hodgson 2009a, 35; 76.
69. Bidwell in Hodgson 2009, 83–4.
70. *RIB* III 3284; Birley 2005, 206.
71. *Notitia Dignitatum* Occ. 40.34.
72. *RIB* I 1337.
73. *RIB* I 1334.
74. *RIB* I 1348; *Notitia Dignitatum* Occ. 40.35.
75. Breeze 2006, 168; *Notitia Dignitatum* Occ. 40.36; RIB I 1523.
76. *RIB* I 1433.
77. *Notitia Dignitatum* Occ. 40.37.
78. Breeze 2006, 179–81.
79. *RIB* I 1462–65; 1480.
80. *RIB* I 1465, the dedication specifically dated to the third day before the Kalends of November in the consulships of Gratus and Seleucus, ie: 30 October 221.
81. *RIB* I 1467 dated to 223, when Claudius Xenophon was governor; Birley 2005, 345–6.
82. *RIB* I 1466.
83. *Notitia Dignitatum* Occ. 40.38.
84. *RIB* I 1534–36; 1544–45; 1553; 1559–60; 1562.
85. *RIB* I 1544.
86. *Notitia Dignitatum* Occ. 40.39.
87. *RIB* I 1553 under Maximinus Thrax.
88. Breeze 2006, 220.
89. Breeze 2006, 222.
90. Breeze 2006, 223.
91. Crow 2004a, 63–4.
92. Hodgson 2009a, 31 argues for 158; see also Hodgson 2011 for the significance of the date of 158.
93. *RIB* I 1578–80; 1584–86; 1591; 1598; 1618–19; *Notitia Dignitatum* Occ. 40.40.
94. Breeze 2006, 235.
95. Crow 2004a, 104.
96. Crow 2004a, 69–70.
98. Crow 2004a, 100–1, fig 57 for plans; Hodgson 2008a, 19, fig.6 for comparative plans of chalet type barracks from different forts drawn to the same scale.
99. Crow 2004a, 102–3.
100. *RIB* I 1594.
101. *RIB* I 1593.
102. *RIB* I 1576.

103. Crow 2004a, 79; 149 n.4.
104. Bidwell 1999, 125; Hodgson 2008a, 15 n.16; Hodgson 2009a, 35, 113.
105. *RIB* I 1738 in the governorship (*regente*) of Maximus, who may be the governor whose name has not survived distinctly enough to be read with certainty on *RIB* I 1467 from Chesters.
106. *RIB* I 1751, only a small fragment, with only the letters REGN in the bottom line, but interpreted as *regente* followed by the name of the governor which is missing from the stone; the same letters REGNT is the formula used on *RIB* I 1738 recording the repair of the granary at the same fort. The governor was probably Maecilius Fuscus; Birley 2005, 357–8.
107. *Notitia Dignitatum* Occ. 40.42; Breeze and Dobson 2000, 294; Breeze 2006, 270.
108. *RIB* I 1737.
109. *RIB* I 1778; 1780 to the goddess Hammia; 1792; 1810; on *RIB* I 1818, the unit name is missing but the prefect is Flavius Secundus, as on *RIB* I 1778, Titus Flavius Secundus.
110. *RIB* I 1791.
111. *RIB* I 1795; Breeze 2006, 280. *Notitia Dignitatum* Occ. 40.43.
112. *RIB* I 1872; 1874–96; 1898; 1904; 1909; 1914; 1921.
113. Breeze and Dobson 2000, 294–6; Rivet and Smith 1979, 220–1 quoting amendment by Hassall 1976, 113.
114. Wilmott in Hodgson 2009a, 127.
115. *RIB* I 1909.
116. *RIB* I 1914; Breeze 2006, 302.
117. *RIB* I 1922 dated to the consulships of Maximinus and Africanus.
118. Wilmott in Bidwell 1999, 152.
119. *Notitia Dignitatum* Occ. 40.44.
120. *RIB* I 1981–83; 1999.
121. *RIB* I 1983.
122. *RIB* I 1999.
123. Breeze 2006, 331.
124. *RIB* I 2027.
125. *RIB* I 2028.
126. *Notitia Dignitatum* Occ. 40.48.
127. Breeze 2006, 353.
128. Breeze 2006, 369.
129. *RIB* I 1059; 1060; *RIB* III 3272.
130. Breeze 2006, 115; Tomlin et al 2009, 275 in connection with *RIB* III 3272.
131. *RIB* III 3272.
132. *RIB* III 3284.
133. *RIB* I 1060 *curante* Marius Valerianus, under Severus Alexander with *tribunicia potestas* for the first time, in 222.
134. Hodgson in Bidwell 1999, 76–8.

135. *RIB* I 1060; Breeze 2006, 117–18.
136. Bidwell in Hodgson 2009, 67.
137. *Notitia Dignitatum* Occ. 40.22.
138. *RIB* I 1151.
139. Breeze 2006, 423.
140. Hodgson 2008b.
141. *RIB* I 1127.
142. *RIB* I 1705, dated by Caracalla's sixteenth year of tribunician power.
143. *RIB* I 1706.
144. R. Birley 2009, 144.
145. Bidwell 1999, 182; 184.
146. Breeze 2006, 385–7.
147. Bidwell 1999, 184–5.
148. *RIB* I 814–17; 821–3; 827–30.
149. *RIB* I 821; 827.
150. *Cohors I Delmatarum RIB* I 810; 832; *cohors I Baetasiorum* 837; 838.
151. *RIB* I 812; Breeze and Dobson 2000, 262.
152. *Notitia Dignitatum* Occ. 40.53.
152. *Notitia Dignitatum* Occ. 40.53.
153. For history of the fort see I. Caruana in Bidwell 1999, 184–6; Breeze 2006, 397–407.
154. Breeze 2006, 409–10.
155. Hodgson 2009a, 165; *RIB* I 806.
156. *RIB* I 798; 800.
157. *RIB* I 797 attests the unit as *equitata*; *RIB* I 803; 804.
158. *Notitia Dignitatum* Occ. 40.50 for Gabrosentum; Breeze 2006, 410.
159. Woolliscroft 1994, 57.
160. *Notitia Dignitatum* Occ. 40.51.
161. Old Carlisle: *RIB* I 905; Whitley Castle: *RIB* I 1205.
162. Old Carlisle: *RIB* I 897; Old Penrith: *RIB* I 929.
163. *RIB* I 741.
164. Baths: *RIB* I 1091; headquarters: *RIB* I 1092.
165. *RIB* I 587.
166. *RIB* I 605.
167. Hodgson 2003, 150–2; 2008a, 15.
168. Chesters: *RIB* I 1463; South Shields: *RIB* I 1060.
169. Crow 2004a, 102–3.
170. Hodgson 2008a 18–20 with comparative plans of new-style barracks.
171. Hodgson 2008a 22 and note 51 with references to depleted garrisons in Germany.
172. *RIB* I 1235; see also *RIB* I 1216 and 1217 for further records of the Raeti.
173. *ILS* 451.
174. Great Chesters: *RIB* I 1724; Cappuck: *RIB* I 2117.
175. *RIB* I 1594.

176. *RIB* I 1262; see also *RIB* I 1270 with no dating evidence.
177. *RIB* I 2042.
178. *Numerus Hnaudifridi*: *RIB* I 1576; *cives Tuihanti RIB* I 1593.
179. Hodgson 2009a, 34.
180. *Duplicarii*: *RIB* I 1270.
181. Fulford 2004, 323.
182. Hodgson 2003, 14–18; 2008a 15; 2009a 76.
183. Housesteads: Biggins and Taylor 2004; Biggins and Taylor in Hodgson 2009a, 112–13; High Rochester: Hancke 2004; Hodgson 2009a, 168–70.
184. Hodgson 2009a, 35.
185. Hodgson 2009a, 76.
186. Crow 2004a, 109.
187. R. Birley 2009, 150; 175.
188. Casey and Hoffman 1998.
189. Hodgson 2009a, 36 referring to Cool and Mason 2008.
190. Hodgson and Bidwell in Hodgson 2009a, 67–8.
191. Hodgson 2009a, 35.
192. Millett 1990, 106.
193. Fulford 2004, 321.
194. Hodgson 2008a, 22.
195. Fulford 2004, 314–15.
196. Millett 1990, 162–3.
197. *RIB* I 344.
198. Mainz: *CIL* 13.6780; Sirmium: *CIL* 3.3228= *ILS* 546.
199. Birley 2005, 363–4.
200. *Notitia Dignitatum* Occ. 28.18.
201. Johnson 1979, 65–6; 69; Pearson 2002, 90; 147.
202. Drinkwater 1987, 168–9.
203. Birdoswald: *RIB* I 1883; 1886; Lancaster: *RIB* I 605; Birley 2005, 364.
204. Drinkwater 1987, 229.
205. Fulford 2004, 322.
206. Wilmott in Bidwell 1999, 152–4.
207. Breeze and Dobson 2000, 230.
208. *RIB* I 1912.
209. Bidwell 1999, 26–7.
210. Thomas and Witshcel 1992.

9 The Wall from the Late Third to the Mid-Fifth Century: AD 284 to c. AD 450

1. Aurelius Victor *de Caesaribus* 39.
2. Potter 2013, 17.
3. James 1988, 269; Southern and Dixon 1996, 89–90.

4. Zosimus 2.34.
5. *Codex Theodosianus* 7.20.4.
6. Ammianus Marcellinus 39.3.7.
7. *Notitia Dignitatum* Occ. 28.23; 36.7; O'Flynn 1983, 4.
8. *Notitia Dignitatum* Or. I.6–8; VII-IX.
9. Southern and Dixon 1996, 59 referring to Grosse 1920, 158.
10. Grosse 1920, 163.
11. *Codex Theodosianus* 15.1.13.
12. Ammianus Marcellinus 27.8.1–2.
13. Ammianus Marcellinus 28.3.6.
14. Birley 2005, 439.
15. Eutropius *Breviarum* 9.21.
16. *CIL* 12.686=*ILS* 2911 from Arles is the last record of the Classis Britannica; see also Cleere 1989, 22.
17. Casey 1994, 103.
18. Kent 1978, 322; plate 149 no. 570.
19. Casey 1994, 93.
20. Kent 1978, 322; plate 152, no. 585 obverse and reverse.
21. *Notitia Dignitatum* Occ. 23. 9–10.
22. Birley 2005, 398.
23. *Notitia Dignitatum* Occ. 23. 9–10.
24. Birley 2005, 400 n.8 referring to J. C. Mann *Antiquity* 35, 1961, 320, and E. Birley *Quintus Congressus Limitis Romani 1961*, 85, (Fifth International Congrees of Roman Frontier Studies held in Yugoslavia and published 1963).
25. *Codex Theodosianus* 11.7.2; Birley 2005, 413.
26. *RIB* I 1912.
27. *RIB* I 1912.
28. *RIB* I 1613.
29. Breeze and Dobson 2000, 226.
30. Hodgson 2008a, 21; 2009a, 67; 70.
31. Birley 2005, 388; 406–7.
32. Herodian 3.14.7.
33. Ammianus Marcellinus 28.8.4.
34. Collins 2012, 67.
35. Zosimus 2.15.1.
36. Birley 2005, 411–12, n.4 referring to an article by J. P. Casey in *Collectanea Londiniensis: studies presented to R. Merrifield*. 1978; Eusebius *Life of Constantine* 1.8.2; 1.25.2; 4.50.
37. *Cohors I Vangionum*: latest epigraphic evidence *RIB* I 1235 dated to 213; 1237 less certain but possibly dated to 211–17; there are undated inscriptions at Benwell: *RIB* I 1328 and Chesters: *RIB* I 1482, a tombstone for the daughter of the tribune Fabius Honoratus. *Cohors I Vardullorum*: latest epigraphic evidence *RIB* I 1262 dated to the 240s; there is an undated inscription from Hadrian's Wall recording the building of a temple *RIB* I 1421.

38. *Notitia Dignitatum* Occ. 40.49.
39. Breeze and Dobson 2000, 230.
40. *Notitia Dignitatum* Occ. 40.55; Rivet and Smith 1979, 430–1.
41. *Notitia Dignitatum* Occ. 40.20.
42. Ammianus Marcellinus 27.8.3; 28.3.8; Birley 2005, 414–16; 436.
43. Ammianus Marcellinus 28.3.7; Birley 2005, 399–400; 416.
44. Ammianus Marcellinus 30.7.3; Birley 2005, 416–17.
45. Ammianus Marcellinus 20.1.1.
46. Breeze 2104, 132.
47. Birley 2005, 428 n. 50 referring to K. M. Martin *Latomus* 28, 1969, 408ff.
48. Birley 2005, 439.
49. Ammianus Marcellinus 27.8.7.
50. Ammianus Marcellinus 20.1.3.
51. Ammianus Marcellinus 27.8.7; 28.3.1.
52. Ammianus Marcellinus 27.8.10.
53. Ammianus Marcellinus 28.3.2.
54. Ammianus Marcellinus 28.3.7.
55. Collins 2012, 77.
56. Collins 2012, 79–80 tables 4.1 and 4.2.
57. Collins 2012, 83.
58. Ammianus Marcellinus 28.3.7.
59. *Notitia Dignitatum* Occ. 23.11.
60. Ammianus Marcellinus 28.3.4–6.
61. Fulford 2004, 324.
62. Breeze and Dobson 2000, 245.
63. Birley 2005, 459.
64. Collins 2012, 158.
65. Birley 2005, 463–4.
66. Hodgson 1991, 85; Collins 2012, 38–9.
67. *Notitia Dignitatum* Occ. 40.17–56.
68. Frere 1987, 217–24.
69. Birley 2005, 445 quoting Sozomenus.
70. Frere 1987, 222–3.
71. *Codex Theodosianus* 13.11.10; *Notitia Dignitatum* Occ. 42. 33–44.
72. Mason 2000, 210–11.
73. Collins 2012, 38–54.
74. Breeze and Dobson 2000, 230; Collins 2012, 46–7.
75. Breeze and Dobson 2000, 242–3.
76. Breeze and Dobson 2000, 230.
77. Collins 2012, 69.
78. Breeze and Dobson 2000, 243–4.
79. Collins 2012, 69–70.
80. On late Roman barracks see Bidwell 1991; numbers of soldiers: Hodgson 1999; Hodgson and Bidwell 2004; Hodgson 2009a, 33–4; 36.

81. Collins 2012, 52 referring to Nicasie 1998, 53.
82. Collins 2012, 52, table 3.4.
83. Collins 2012, 74–96, especially 79–80, tables 4.1 and 4.2.
84. Collins 2102, 88.
85. Collins 2012, 85–6.
86. Esmonde-Cleary 2004, 417; Hodgson 2009a, 36–7.
87. Esmonde-Cleary 2000, 90.
88. Collins 2012, 92–3.
89. Crow 2004a, 96; Collins 2012, 90.
90. Collins 2012, 105 referring to Bidwell and Speak 1994, 103–4.
91. R. Birley 2009, 152.
92. Collins 2102, 105 referring to Crow 2004a, 114–18 for Housesteads and Wilmott 2009, 395 for Birdoswald.
93. Collins 2012, 95 referring to Rushworth 2009, 171–4.
94. Collins 2012, 97.
95. Ammianus Marcellinus 18.2.3–4; Birley 2005, 423–4 for other sources.
96. Esmonde-Cleary 2004, 414.
97. Collins 2102, 95; 160 referring to Rushworth 2009, 171–4; 307–9.
98. Vindolanda: Birley 2009, 150; Wallsend: Hodgson 2009a, 37.
99. Collins 2102, 98 referring to Zant 2009, 463–5.
100. Esmonde-Cleary 2004, 429–32.
101. Collins 2012, 100.
102. Eining and Regensburg: W. Czysz et al. (eds.) *Die Romer in Bayern*. Stuttgart: Theiss, 1995, 368–9; 434–5; 507; Strasbourg: H. Cuppers *Die Romer in Rheinland-Pfalz*. Stuttgart: Theiss, 1990, 139 describes how the fortress sheltered civilians.
103. On arms, armour and equipment in general see Bishop and Coulston 1993, 160–82; Southern and Dixon 1996, chapter six by Karen Dixon, 89–126; Feugère 2002, 183–98.
104. Bishop and Coulston 1993, 167.
105. Feugère 2002, 190 and figure 253.
106. Bishop and Coulston 1993, 162–4, fig. 116.
107. See Southern and Dixon 1996, 110 fig. 38 for an illustration of how the ends were attached by three rivets.
108. Vegetius *Epitoma Rei Militaris* 2.15.
109. Dark 1992; Wilmott 2000, 15; Collins 2012, 104.
110. Southern and Dixon 1996, 116–17; Caerleon: Coulston 1985, 227–9; 268; Corbridge: Coulston 1985, 268; Housesteads: Crow 2004a, 96.
111. *Notitia Dignitatum* Occ. 40.21.
112. Vegetius *Epitoma Rei Militaris* 1.20.
113. Collins 2012, 161 on iron ore deposits.
114. Collins 2012, 139; 161.
115. Wilmott 2005, 132.
116. Wilmott 1997, 224–31; see also Wilmott and Wilson 2000.
117. Collins 2012, 163.
118. Dark 1992; Dark and Dark 1996.

119. Collins 2012, 166–7.
120. Breeze 2014a, 137–8.
121. Bidwell and Speak 1994, 46.
122. Breeze 2014a, 137.

10 How Did the Wall Work?

1. Allason-Jones 2009, 220 referring to Jolliffe 1941.
2. *RIB* I 2091.
3. Allason-Jones 2009, 221–2.
4. Hodgson 2009a, 49–50; Allason-Jones 2009, 219–20.
5. Hodgson 2009a, 47, referring to Fraser Hunter *Beyond the Edge of the Empire: Caledonians, Picts and Romans.* Rosmarkie 2007.
6. Hodgson 2009a, 47.
7. Hodgson 2005, 186.
8. Hodgson 2005, 185–6.
9. Hingley 2008, 27; Collins 2012, 26.
10. Hodgson 2005, 186.
11. Breeze and Jilek 2005,145 referring to M. Erdrich *Rom und die Barbaren.* Romish-Germanische Forschungen 58. Mainz, 2001.
12. Breeze and Dobson 2000, 40.
13. Wilmott 2008, 124.
14. Welfare 2000; Breeze 2014a, 115.
15. Welfare 2000.
16. Johnson 1989, 59.
17. Bidwell 1999, 34–5.
18. Breeze 2006, 314–15.
19. Breeze 2006, 325.
20. Sewingshields: Johnson 1989, 59; Breeze 2006, 227–8.
21. Breeze 2006, 275.
22. Breeze 2006, 184.
23. Hodgson 2005, 184.
24. Breeze 2006, 66; 286–7.
25. Foglia 2014, 29.
26. Breeze 2006, 110; 2014, 122–3.
27. Bidwell 2008b.
28. Breeze and Dobson 2000, 42.
29. Bidwell 2008b, 133.
30. Bidwell 1999, 18; for the footbridges see Bidwell and Holbrook 1989, 134–5.
31. Breeze and Dobson 2000, 48.
32. Breeze 1982, 81 fig.14.
33. Bidwell 2008b, 138 and fig. 12.
34. Flat stones: Hill and Dobson 1992, 32; concrete: Bidwell 1999, 18; crenellations and merlons: Bidwell 2008b, 138–9.

35. Crow 2004b, 128; 130 and fig. 8.5, a photograph showing a stack of the chamfered stones; Bidwell 2008b, 134–5; 138–9; fig. 7 showing the same photograph as in Crow 2004; Hodgson 2009a, 44.
36. Hodgson 2009a, 45.
37. Breeze and Dobson 2000, 62.
38. Breeze and Dobson 2000, 107.
39. Graafstal 2012, 160–1.
40. Woolliscroft 2001.
41. Woolliscroft 2001, 155.
42. Breeze and Jilek 2005, 143.
43. Austin and Rankov 1995, 180.
44. Austin and Rankov 1995, 183.
45. Dixon and Southern 1996, 69; 86; *Abbinaeus Archive* letters 19 and 34.
46. Dio 73. 2.4.
47. Richmond, 1940, 96.
48. Salway 1991, 685.
49. Rivet and Smith 1979, 212; Mann 1992.
50. Richmond, 1940, 96; Breeze and Dobson 2000, 144; see also Breeze 2014a, 127–8.
51. *RIB* I 605.
52. Breeze and Dobson 2000, 221–2.
53. Hodgson 1991, 87; Collins 2012, 43–4.
54. Collins 2012, 48–51.

Abbreviations

AA Archaeologia Aeliana
AE Année Epigraphique
BMC Coins of the Roman Empire in the British Museum
BRGK Bericht der Römisch-Germanisch Kommission
CIL Corpus Inscriptionum Latinarum
HA Historia Augusta = Scriptores Historiae Augustae
ILS Inscriptiones Latinae Selectae. ed. H. Dessau. Berlin. 3 vols
JRS Journal of Roman Studies
JRS Journal of Roman Archaeology
Notitia Dignitatum Occ./Or. = partis Occidentis; partis Orientis
RIB Roman Inscriptions in Britain:
Vol. I: *Inscriptions on Stone.* R. G. Collingwood and R. P. Wright. Addenda and Corrections by R. S. O. Tomlin. Alan Sutton Publishing, 1995
Vol II. *Instrumentum Domesticum.* Eight Fascicules and Index. Alan Sutton Publishing, 1990–95.
Vol. III *Inscriptions on Stone.* R. S. O. Tomlin, R. P. Wright, and M. W. C. Hassall. Oxbow Books, 2009.
RIC Roman Imperial Coinage (1923-)

Bibliography

Ancient Sources

Abbinaeus Archive: papers of a Roman officer in the reign of Constantius II. Edited by H. I. Bell *et al.* Clarendon Press 1962.

Ammianus Marcellinus. Loeb. 3 vols.

Aurelius Victor *de Caesaribus.*

Codex Theodosianus=The Theodosian Code and Novels and the Sirmondian Constitutions. Translated by C. Pharr. New York: Greenwood Press.

*Digest of Justinian.*Translated by A. Watson. University of Pennsylvania Press 1985.

Dio *Roman History.* Loeb. 9 vols.

Eutropius *Breviarum.* Translated with commentary by H. W. Bird. Liverpool University Press 1993.

Fronto *Correspondence* Loeb. 2 vols.

Herodian. *History of the Empire.* Loeb. 2 vols.

Historia Augusta. Loeb. 3 vols.

Hyginus *de Metatione Castrorum.*

*Notitia Dignitatum.*Edited by O. Seeck 1876, reprinted 1962.

Orosius *Histories Against the Pagans.*

Statius *Silvae.* Loeb.

Tacitus Agricola; *Germania; Dialogus.* Loeb.

Tacitus *Histories* and *Annals.* Loeb. 4 vols.

Vegetius Epitoma Rei Militaris. Translated by N. P. Milner. Liverpool University Press, 1993.

Vitruvius *On Architecture.* Loeb 2 vols.

Vitruvius *Ten Books of Architecture* translated by M. H. Morgan. Dover Publications 1960, first published by Harvard University Press 1914.

Zosimus *New History.* Translated and with commentary by R.T. Ridley. Australian Assoc. for Byzantine Studies, 1982.

Modern Sources

Adam, J.-P. 1994, *Roman Building: materials and techniques*. Batsford.

Allason-Jones, L. 2009, 'Some problems of the Roman Iron Age in N England', in Hanson 2009, 217–24.

Alston, R. 1994, 'Roman military pay from Caesar to Diocletian', *JRS* 84, 113–23.

Applebaum, S. 1972, 'Roman Britain' in Finberg 1972, 3–27.

Austen, P. S. 1991, *Bewcastle and Old Penrith: a Roman outpost fort and a frontier vicus, excavations 1997–8. Cumberland and Westmorland Antiquarian and Archaeological Society* Research series 6.

Austen, P. S. 1994, 'Recent excavations on Hadrian's Wall at Burgh-by-Sands', *Transactions of the Cumberland and Westmorland Antiquarian and Archaeological Society* second series, vol. 94, 35–54.

Austen, P. S. 2008, 'Some problems of projecting forts on Hadrian's Wall', in Bidwell 2008a, 113–18.

Austin, N. J. E. and Rankov, N. B. 1995, *Exploratio: military and political intelligence in the Roman world from the second Punic war to the battle of Adrianople*. Routledge.

Baatz, D. 1973, *Kastell Hesselbach und andere Forschungen am Odenwaldlimes*. Limesforschungen 12.

Bellhouse, R. l. 1989, *Roman Sites on the Cumberland Coast*. Cumberland and Westmorland Antiquarian and Archaeological Society Research Series 3.

Bennett, J. 2002, 'A revised programme and chronology for the building of Hadrian's Wall', in Freeman *et al* 2002, 825–34.

Bidwell, P. T. 1985, *The Roman Fort of Vindolanda*. HBMCE Archaeological Report no.1.

Bidwell, P. T. 1991, 'Later Roman barracks in Britain', in Maxfield and Dobson 1991, 9–15.

Bidwell, P. T. (ed) 1999, *Hadrian's Wall 1989–1999: a summary of recent excavations and research prepared for the Twelfth Pilgrimage of Hadrian's Wall, 14–21 August 1999*. Cumberland and Westmorland Antiquarian and Archaeological Society and Society of Antiquaries of Newcastle upon Tyne.

Bidwell, P. T. 2005a, 'Connections between the military units of Spanish origin in Britannia and their homelands', in Fernandez-Ochoa, C. and Garcia Diaz, P. 2005, Unidad y diversidad en el Arco Atlantico en época romana. Oxford: British Archaeological Reports S1371, 35–8.

Bidwell, P. T. 2005b, 'The systems of obstacles on Hadrian's Wall: their extent, date and purpose', *Arbeia Journal* 8, 53–76.

Bidwell, P. 2007, *Roman Forts in Britain*. Tempus.

Bidwell, P. T. 2008a, *Understanding Hadrian's Wall*. Kendal.

Bidwell, P. T. 2008b, 'Did Hadrian's Wall have a Wall-walk?', in Bidwell 2008a, 129–43.

Bidwell, P. T. and Holbrook, N. 1989, *Hadrian's Wall Bridges*. English Heritage Archaeological Report no. 9.

Bidwell, P. T. and Speak, S. 1994, *Excavations at South Shields Roman Fort, Volume I*. Society of Antiquaries of Newcastle upon Tyne.

Bidwell, P. T. and Watson, M. 1996, 'Excavations on Hadrian's Wall at Denton, Newcastle upon Tyne, 1986–89. *AA* fifth series, vol. 24, 1–56.

Biggins, J.A. and Taylor, D. J. A. 2004, 'A geophysical survey at Housesteads Roman fort, April 2003', *AA* fifth series, vol. 33, 51–60.

Biggins, J.A. et al, 2014, 'Survey of the Roman outpost fort at Risingham (*Habitancum*), Northumberland', *AA* fifth series, vol. 43, 47–72.

Birley, A. R. 1987, *Marcus Aurelius: a biography*. Routledge. Revised edition.

Birley, A. R. 1988, *Septimius Severus: the African Emperor*. Routledge. Revised edition.

Birley, A. R. 1997, *Hadrian: the restless Emperor*. Routledge.

Birley, A. R. 2002, *Garrison Life at Vindolanda: a band of brothers*. Tempus.

Birley, A. R. 2005, *The Roman Government of Britain*. Oxford University Press.

Birley, R. 2009, *Vindolanda: a Roman frontier fort on Hadrian's Wall*. Amberley.

Bishop, M. C. (ed.) 1985, *The Production and Distribution of Roman Military Equipment: proceedings of the second Roman Military Equipment Seminar*. British Archaeological Report S275.

Bishop, M. and Coulston, J. C. N. 1993, *Roman Military Equipment from the Punic Wars to the Fall of Rome*. Batsford.

Bowman, A. K. 2003, *Life and Letters on the Roman Frontier: Vindolanda and its people*. British Museum Press.

Bowman, A. K. and Thomas, J. D. 1994, *The Vindolanda Writing Tablets: Tabulae Vindolandenses II*. British Museum.

Breeze, D. J. 1982, *The Northern Frontiers of Roman Britain*. Batsford.

Breeze, D. J. 2003, 'Warfare in Britain and the building of Hadrian's Wall', *AA* fifth series, vol. 32, 13–16.

Breeze, D. J. 2005, 'Why was Hadrian's Wall built across the Tyne Solway isthmus?', in Beutler, F. and Hameter, W. (eds.) *Eine ganz normale inschrift und ähnliches zum Geburtstag von Ekkehard Weber am 30 April 5005*. Vienna.

Breeze, D. J. 2006, *Handbook to the Roman Wall*. Society of Antiquaries of Newcastle upon Tyne. 14th ed.

Breeze, D. J. 2008, 'To study the monument: Hadrian's Wall 1848–2006', in Bidwell 2008a, 1–4.

Breeze, D. J. 2009, 'Did Hadrian design Hadrian's Wall?', *AA* fifth series, vol. 38, 87–103.

Breeze D. J. 2014a, *Hadrian's Wall: a history of archaeological thought*. Cumberland and Westmorland Antiquarian and Archaeological Society, extra series no. XLII.

Breeze, D. J. 2014b, 'The marking out of Hadrian's Wall', *AA* fifth series, vol. 43, 19–26.

Breeze, D. J. and Dobson, B. 1972, 'Hadrian's Wall: some problems', *Britannia* 3, 182–208; reprinted in Breeze and Dobson 1993, 404–30.

Breeze, D. J. and Dobson 1987, *Hadrian's Wall*. Penguin, 3rd ed.

Breeze, D. J. and Dobson, B. 1993, *Roman Officers and Frontiers*. Stuttgart: Theiss.

Breeze, D. J. and Dobson, B. 2000, *Hadrian's Wall*. Penguin, 4th ed.

Breeze, D. J. and Hill, P. R. 2001, 'Hadrian's Wall began here', *AA* fifth series, vol. 29, 1–3.

Breeze, D. J. and Hill, P. R. 2013, 'The foundations of Hadrian's Stone Wall', *AA* fifth series, vol. 42, 101–14.

Breeze, D. J. and Jilek, 2005, 'Strategy, tactics, operation: how do frontiers actually work', in Visy 2005, 141–6.

Bruce, J. C. 1978, *Handbook to the Roman Wall with the Cumbrian coast and outpost forts*.13th ed. edited and enlarged by Charles Daniels.

Bruce, J. C. 2006, *Handbook to the Roman Wall with the Cumbrian coast and outpost forts*.14th ed. edited and revised by D. J. Breeze.

Bruhn, J. 2008, *Pluralistic Landscapes of Northern Roman Britain: a GIS multiscalar approach to archaeology*. PhD thesis, Durham University.

Callies, H. 1964, 'Die Fremden Truppen in Römischen Heer des Prinzipats und die sogenannten Nationalen Numeri', *BRGK* 45, 130–227.

Callwell, C. E. 1906, *Small Wars*. HMSO, 3rd ed. Reprinted by Bison Books, University of Nebraska, 1996.

Campbell, D. B. 1984, '*Ballistaria* in mid-third century Britain: a re-appraisal', Britannia 15, 75–84.

Campbell, D. B. 2003, 'The Roman siege of Burnswark', *Britannia* 34, 19–33.

Casey, P. J. 1987, 'The coinage of Alexandrian and the chronology of Hadrian', in Huvelin et al. (eds.) *Mélanges de Numismatique offerts à Pierre Bastien a l'occasion de son 75 anniversaire*. Wetteren.

Casey, P. J. and Hoffman, B. 1998, 'Rescue excavations in the vicus of the fort at Great Bridge, Co. Durham, 1972–74', *Britannia* 29, 111–83.

Casey, P. J. and Savage, M. 1980, 'The coins from the excavations High Rochester in 1852 and 1855', *AA* fifth series, vol. 8, 75–87.

Clack, P. and Haselgrove, C. 1982, *Rural Settlement in the Roman North*. Council for British Archaeology, Regional Group 3.

Cleere, H. 1989, 'The *Classis Britannica*', in Maxfield 1989, 18–22.

Coarelli, F. 1999, *La Colona Traiana*. Editore Colombo.

Collins, R. 2012, *Hadrian's Wall and the End of Empire: the Roman frontier in the 4th and 5th centuries*. Routledge.

Cool, H. E. M. and Mason, D. P. 2008, *Roman Piercebridge: excavation by D. W. Harding and Peter Scott, 1969–1981*. Architectural and Archaeological Society of Durham and Northumberland, Research Report 7.

Coulston, J. N. C. 1985, 'Roman archery equipment', in Bishop 1985, 220–336.

Coulston, J. N. C. 1988, *Military Equipment and the Identity of Roman Soldiers*. Proceedings of the Fourth Military Equipment Conference. Oxford: British Archaeological Reports S394.

Crow, J. G. 1991a, 'A review of current research on the turrets and curtain of Hadrian's Wall', *Britannia* 22, 51–63.

Crow, J. G. 1991b, 'Construction and reconstruction in the central sector of Hadrian's Wall', in Maxfield and Dobson 1991, 44–7.

Crow, J. 2004a, *Housesteads: a fort and garrison on Hadrian's Wall*. Tempus. 2nd ed.

Crow, J. 2004b, 'The Northern Frontier of Britain from Trajan to Antoninus Pius: Roman builders and native Britons', in Todd 2004, 114–35.

Daniels, C. M. (ed.) 1978, *Handbook to the Roman Wall with the Cumbrian coast and outpost forts*.13th edition. Newcastle upon Tyne: Harold Hill and Son.

Dacre, J. A. 1985, 'An excavation on the Roman fort at Stanwix, Carlisle', *Transactions of the Cumberland and Westmorland Antiquarian and Archaeological Society* second series, vol. 85, 53–69.

Dark, K. 1992, 'A sub-Roman re-defence of Hadrian's Wall?' *Britannia* 23, 111–20.

Dark, K. 2000, *Britain and the End of the Roman Empire*. Tempus.

Dark, K. and Dark, P. 1996, 'New archaeological and palynological evidence for a sub-Roman re-occupation of Hadrian's Wall', *AA* fifth series, vol. 24, 57–72.

Davies, R. W. 1971, 'Rhe Roman military diet', *Britannia* 2, 122–42.

De la Bédoyère, G. 1998, *Hadrian's Wall: history and guide*. Tempus.

De la Bédoyère, G. 1999, *Companion to Roman Britain*. Tempus.

Dilke, O. A. W. 1971, *The Roman Land Surveyors: an introduction to the agrimensores*. David and Charles.

Dixon, K. R. and Southern, P. 1992, *The Roman Cavalry from the first to the third century AD*. Batsford.

Dobson, B. 1986, 'The function of Hadrian's Wall', *AA* fifth series, vol. 14, 1–30.

Donaldson, G. H. 1988, 'Thoughts on a military appreciation of the design of Hadrian's Wall', *AA* fifth series, vol. 16, 125–37.

Donaldson, G. H. 1989, '*Tormenta*, *auxilia* and *ballistaria* in the environs of Hadrian's Wall', *AA* fifth series, vol. 17, 217–19.

Donaldson, G. H. 1990, 'A reinterpretation of *RIB* 1912 from Birdoswald', *Britannia* 27, 207–14.

Dore, J. N. 2009, *Excavations Directed by J. P. Gillam at the Roman fort of Haltonchesters, 1960–1961*. Oxbow Books.

Drinkwater, J. F. 1987, *The Gallic Empire: separatism and continuity in the north-western provinces of the Roman Empire A.D. 260–274*. Franz Steiner Verlag.

Esmonde-Cleary, S. 1989, *The Ending of Roman Britain*. Routledge.

Esmonde-Cleary, S. 2000, 'Summing up' in Wilmott and Wilson 2000, 89–94.

Esmonde-Cleary, S. 2001, 'The Roman to medieval transition', in James and Millett 2001, 90–97.

Esmonde-Cleary, S. 2004, 'Britain in the fourth century' in Todd 2004, 409–27.

Everitt, A. 2009, *Hadrian and the Triumph of Rome*. Random House, republished by Head of Zeus, 2013.

Feugère, M. 2002, Weapons of the Romans. Tempus.

Fields, N. 2003, *Hadrian's Wall AD 122–410*. Osprey.

Fields, N. 2005, *Rome's Northern Frontier AD 70 -235: beyond Hadrian's Wall*. Osprey.

Finberg, H. P. R. (ed.)1972, *Agrarian History of England and Wales Vol. I part II AD 43–1042*.

Fink, R. 1971, *Roman Military Records on Papyrus*. Case Western Reserve University for the American Philological Association.

Foglia, A. B. 2014, 'Turrets as watchtowers on Hadrian's Wall: a GIS and source based analysis of appearance and surveillance capabilities', *AA* fifth series, vol. 43, 27–46.

Freeman *et al* (eds.) 2000, *Limes XVIII: Proceedings of the XVIII International Congress of Roman Frontier Studies, Amman, Jordan, 2000*. Oxford: BAR international Series 1084, 2 vols.

Frere, S. S. 1987, *Britannia*. London. 3rd ed.

Frere, S. S. 2000, 'M. Maenius Agrippa, the *expeditio Britannica* and Maryport', *Britannia* 31, 23–8.

Fulford, M. 2004, 'Economic structures', in Todd 2004, 309–26.

Fulford, M. 2006, 'Corvées and *civitates*', in Wilson 2006, 65–71.

Gillam, J. P. 1958, 'Roman and Native, AD 122–97', in Richmond (ed.) 1958, 60–90.

Gillam, J. P. 1975, 'Possible changes in plan in the course of the construction of the Antonine Wall', *Scottish Archaeological Forum* 7, 51–6.

Goldsworthy, A. 2003, *The Complete Roman Army*. Thames and Hudson.

Goodburn, R. and Bartholomew, P. 1976, *Aspects of the Notitia Dignitatum*. Oxford: British Archaeological Reports S15.

Graafstal, E. 2012, 'Hadrian's haste: a priority programme for the Wall', *AA* fifth series, vol. 41, 123–84.

Grosse, R. 1920, *Römische Militärgeschichte von Gallienus bis zum Beginn der Byzantinischen Themenverfassung*. Wiedmannsche Buchhandlung.

Gudea, N. 1999, *Proceedings of the XVII International Congress of Roman Frontier Studies1997*. Zalau, Romania.

Hancke, T. (et al.) 2004, 'Geophysical survey at High Rochester Roman fort', *AA* fifth series, vol. 33, 35–50.

Hanson, W. S. 2004, 'Scotland and the northern frontier: second to fourth centuries AD', in Todd 2004, 136–61.

Hanson, W. S. 2007, *A Roman Frontier Fort in Scotland: Elginhaugh*. Tempus.

Hanson, W. S. (ed.) 2009, *The Army and Frontiers of Rome: papers offered to David J. Breeze on the occasion of his sixty-fifth birthday and his retirement from* Historic Scotland. *JRA* supplementary series number 74.

Hartley, B. R.1972, 'The Roman occupations of Scotland: the evidence of the samian ware', *Britannia* 3, 1–55.

Haselgrove, C. 1982, 'Indigenous settlement patterns in the Tyne-Tees lowlands', in Clack and Haselgrove 1982, 57–104.

Hassall, M. 1976, 'Britain in the Notitia', in Goodburn and Bartholomew (eds.) 1976, 103–17.

Hassall, M. 1984, 'The date of the rebuilding of Hadrian's Turf Wall in stone', *Britannia* 15, 242–4.

Heywood, B. 1965, 'The Vallum – its problems restated', in Jarrett and Dobson 1965, 85–94.

Heywood, B. and Breeze, D. J. 2008, 'Excavations at Vallum causeways on Hadrian's Wall in the 1950s', *AA* fifth series, vol. 37, 93–126.

Hill, P. R. 2001, 'Hadrian's Wall from MC0 to MC9', *AA* fifth series, vol. 29, 3–18.

Hill, P. R. (ed.) 2002. *Polybius to Vegetius: essays on the Roman Army and Hadrian's Wall presented to Brian Dobson*. Hadrianic Society private publication.

Hill, P. R. 2006, *The Construction of Hadrian's Wall*. History Press.

Hill, P. R. and Dobson. B. 1992, 'The design of Hadrian's Wall and its implications', *AA* fifth series, vol. 20, 27–52.

Hind, J. G.F. 1977. 'The 'Genounian' part of Britain' *Britannia* 8, 229–34.

Hingley, R. 2008, 'Hadrian's Wall in theory: pursuing new agendas', in Bidwell 2008a, 25–8.

Hodgson, N. 1991, 'The *Notitia Dignitatum* and the later Roman garrison of Britain', in Maxfield and Dobson 1991, 84–92.

Hodgson, N. 1995, 'Were there two Antonine occupations of Scotland?', *Britannia* 26, 29–49.

Hodgson, N. 1999, 'The late Roman plan at South Shields and the size and status of units in the late Roman army', in Gudea 1999, 547–54.

Hodgson, N. 2000, 'The Stanegate: a frontier rehabilitated'. *Britannia* 31, 11–22.

Hodgson, N. 2001, 'The origins and development of the Roman military supply base at South Shields: an interim report on the results of the excavations in the eastern quadrant and the central area', *Arbeia Journal* 6–7 for 1997–98, published 2001, 25–36.

Hodgson, N. 2003, *The Roman Fort at Wallsend: excavations in 1997–8*. Tyne and Wear Museums Archaeological Monographs no. 2.

Hodgson, N. 2005, 'Gates and passage across the frontiers: the use of openings through the barriers of Britain, Germany and Raetia', in Visy 2005, 183–7.

Hodgson, N. 2008a, 'After the Wall-Periods: what is our historical framework for Hadrian's Wall in the twenty-first century', in Bidwell 2008a, 11–23.

Hodgson, N. 2008b, 'The development of the Roman site at Corbridge from the first to the third centuries AD', *AA* fifth series, vol. 37, 93–126.

Hodgson, N. 2009a, *Hadrian's Wall 1999–2009: a summary of excavation and research prepared for the Thirteenth Pilgrimage of Hadrian's Wall 8–14 August 2009*. Cumberland and Westmorland Antiquarian and Archaeological Society and Society of Antiquaries of Newcastle upon Tyne.

Hodgson, N. 2009b, 'The abandonment of Antonine Scotland: its date and causes', in Hanson 2009, 185–93.

Hodgson, N. 2011, 'The provenance of RIB 1389 and the rebuilding of Hadrian's Wall in 158', *Antiquaries Journal* 91, 59–72.

Hodgson, N. and Bidwell, P. 2004, 'Auxiliary barracks in a new light: recent discoveries on Hadrian's Wall', *Britannia* 35, 121–57.

Hodgson, N. and McKelvey, J. 2006, 'An excavation on Hadrian's Wall at Hare Hill, Wall mile 53, Cumbria', *Transactions of the Cumberland and Westmorland Antiquarian and Archaeological Society* third series, vol. 6, 45–60.

Horsley, J. 1732, *Britannia Romana, or the Roman antiquities of Britain*. Facsimile edition with introduction published by Frank Graham, Newcastle upon Tyne, 1974.

James, S. 1988, 'The *fabricae*: state arms factories of the later Roman Empire', in Coulston 1988, 257–332.

James, S. and Millett, M. (eds.) 2001, *Britons and Romans: advancing an archaeological agenda*. Council for British Archaeology.

Jarrett, M. G. and Dobson, B. (eds.) 1965, *Britain and Rome: essays presented to Eric Birley*. Kendal.

Jarrett, M. G. 1976, 'An unnecessary war', *Britannia* 7, 145–51.

Johnson, G. A. L. 1997, *The Geology of Hadrian's Wall*. Geological Association Guide no. 59.

Johnson, S. 1979, *The Roman Forts of the Saxon Shore*. Book Club Associates. 2nd edition.

Johnson, S. 1989, *English Heritage Book of Hadrian's Wall*. Batsford.

Jolliffe, N, 1941, 'Dea Brigantia', *Archaeological Journal* 98, 36–61.

Jones, G. D. B. and Woolliscroft, D. J. 2001. *Hadrian's Wall from the Air*. Tempus.

Kent, J. P. C. 1978, *Roman Coins*. Thames and Hudson.

Keppie, L. J. F. 2009, 'Burnswark Hill: native space and Roman invaders', in Hanson 2009, 241–52.

Keppie, L. J. F. and Walker, J. J. 1981, 'Fortlets on the Antonine Wall at Seabegs Wood, Kinneil and Cleddans', *Britannia* 12, 143–62.

Lepper, F. and Frere, S. 1988, *Trajan's Column*. Alan Sutton.

Lewis, N. and Rheinhold, M. 1990, *Roman Civilization: selected readings vol. II: The Empire*.Columbia University Press. Third edition.

McGuire, M. 2013, 'Barcombe Hill quarries and the Thorngrafton find', *AA* fifth series, vol. 42, 115–28.

Mann, J. C. 1974, 'The frontiers of the Roman Principate', *Aufstieg und Niedergang der Römischen Welt II Principat* vol. 1 (ed. H. Temporini) Berlin, 508–33.

Mann, J. C. 1990, 'The function of Hadrian's Wall', *AA* fifth series, vol. 18, 51–4.

Mann, J. C. 1992, '*Loca*'. *AA* fifth series, vol. 20, 53–6.

Margary, I. D. 1967, *Roman Roads in Britain*. John Baker. Revised edition.

Mason, D. J. P. 2001, *Roman Chester: city of the eagles*. Tempus.

Maxfield, V. A. (ed.) 1989, *The Saxon Shore*. Exeter University.

Maxfield, V. A. and Dobson, M. J. (eds.) 1991, *Roman Frontier Studies 1989: Proceedings of the XV International Congress of Roman Frontier Studies*. Exeter.

Maxwell, G. S. 1974, 'The building of the Antonine Wall', *Actes du IXieme Congrès Internationale d'Etudes sur les Frontières Romaines*. Bucharest 327–32.

Maxwell, G. 2004, 'The Roman penetration of the north in the late first century AD', in Todd 2004, 75–90.

Millett, M. 1990, *The Romanization of Britain*. Cambridge University Press.

Nicasie, M. J. 1998, *Twilight of Empire: the Roman army from the reign of Diocletian to the battle of Adrianople*. Gieben.

O'Flynn, J. M. 1983, *Generalissimos of the Western Roman Empire*. University of Alberta Press.

Ogilvie, R. M. and Richmond, I. A. R. 1962, *Cornelii Taciti de Vita Agricolae*. Oxford University Press.

Pearson, A. 2002, *The Roman Shore Forts*. Tempus.

Pollard, N. and Berry, J. 2012, *The Complete Roman Legions*. Thames and Hudson.

Potter, D. 2013, *Constantine the Emperor*. Oxford University Press.

Poulter, J. 1998, 'The date of the Stanegate, and a hypothesis about the manner and timing of the construction of Roman roads in Britain', *AA* fifth series, vol. 26, 49–56.

Poulter, J. 2005, 'The direction and planning of the eastern sector of Hadrian's Wall and the Vallum, from the River North Tyne to Benwell, west of Newcastle upon Tyne', *Arbeia Journal* 8, 87–100.

Poulter, J. 2008, 'The direction and planning of the eastern sector of Hadrian's Wall: some further thoughts', in Bidwell 2008a, 99–104.

Poulter, J. 2009, *Surveying Roman Military Landscapes Across Northern Britain: the planning of Roman Dere Street, Hadrian's Wall and the Vallum, and the Antonine Wall in Scotland*. Oxford: British Archaeological Reports 492.

Rankov, N. 1987, 'M. Oclatinius Adventus in Britain', *Britannia* 18, 243–9.

Rankov, N. 2005, 'Do rivers make good frontiers? In Visy 2005, 175–82.

Richmond, I. A. R. 1940, 'The Romans in Redesdale', in *History of Northumberland* vol. XV. Newcastle.

Richmond, I. A. R. (ed.) 1947, *Handbook to the Roman Wall*. Newcastle upon Tyne. 10th ed.

Richmond, I. A. R. (ed.) 1958, *Roman and Native in North Britain*. Nelson.

Rivet, A. L. F. and Smith, C. 1979, *The Place-names of Roman Britain*. Batsford.

Robertson, A. S. 1978, 'The circulation of Roman coins in North Britain: the evidence of hoards and site finds from Scotland', in R. A. G. Carson and C. Kraay (eds), *Scripta Nummaria Romana*. London, 186–216.

Rushworth, A. 2009, *Housesteads Roman Fort- the Grandest Station: excavation and survey at Housesteads 1954–1995 by Charles Daniels, John Gillam, James Crow and others*. English Heritage.

Saddington, D. B. 2005, 'The Roman government and the Roman Auxilia', in Visy 2005, 63–70.

Saddington, D. B. 2009, 'Recruitment patterns and ethnic identities in Roman auxiliary regiments', in Hanson 2009, 83–9.

Salway, P. 1991, *Roman Britain*. Oxford: Clarendon Press.

Sartre, M. 2005, *The Middle East Under Rome*. Belknap Press Harvard University.

Schallmayer, E. 2003, *Denkmalpflege und Kulturgeschichte* 2, Landesamt für Denkmalpflege Hessens.

Sherk, R. K. 1974, 'Roman geographical exploration and military maps' *ANRW* II. Berlin.

Sherk, R. K. 1988, *The Roman Empire: Augustus to Hadrian*. Cambridge University Press.

Shotter, D. 1996, *The Roman Frontier in Britain: Hadrian's Wall, the Antonine Wall and Roman Policy in the North*. Carnegie Publishing.

Shotter, D. 2008, 'From conquest to frontier in the North West', in Bidwell 2008a, 105–12.

Simpson, F. G. and Richmond I. A. R. 1933, 'Report of the Cumberland excavation committee for 1932', *Transactions of the Cumberland and Westmorland Antiquarian and Archaeological Society* second series, vol. 33, 246–62.

Southern, P. 1989, 'The *numeri* of the Roman Imperial army', *Britannia* 20, 81–140.

Southern, P. 1990, 'Signalling versus illumination on Roman frontiers', *Britannia* 21, 233–42.

Southern, P. 1996, 'Men and mountains, or geographical determinism and the conquest of Scotland', *Proceedings of the Society of Antiquaries of Scotland* 126, 371–86.

Southern, P. 2014, *The Roman Army: a history 753 BC to AD 476*. Amberley.

Southern, P. and Dixon, K. R. 1996, *The Late Roman Army*. Batsford.

Steer, K. A. 1957, 'The nature and purpose of the expansions on the Antonine Wall', *PSAS* 90, 1956–57, 161–69.

Steer, K. A. 1964, John Horsley and the Antonine Wall', *AA* fourth series, vol. 42, 1–39.

Stevens, C. E. 1966, *The Building of Hadrian's Wall*. Kendal.

Swinbank, B. 1954, *The Vallum Reconsidered*. Unpublished PhD thesis, University of Durham.

Symonds, M. 2005, 'The construction and order of the milecastles on Hadrian's Wall', *AA* fifth series vol. 34, 67–81.

Taylor, R. 2003, *Roman Builders: a study in architectural progress*. Cambridge University Press.

Thomas, E. and Witschel, C. 1992, 'Constructing reconstruction: claim and reality of Roman building inscriptions from the Latin west, *Papers of the British School at Rome* 60, 135–77.

Todd, M. (ed.) 2004, *A Companion to Roman Britain*. Blackwell.

Tomlin, R. S. O. 2004, 'Inscriptions', *Britannia* 35, 344–5.

Visy, Z. (ed.) 2005, *Limes XIX: Proceedings of the XIX International*

Congress of Roman Frontier Studies Held in Pécs, Hungary September 2003. University of Pécs.

Watson, G. R. 1969, *The Roman Soldier*. Thames and Hudson.

Webster, G. 1985, *The Roman Imperial Army*. A. and C. Black.

Welfare, H. 2000, 'Causeways, at milecastles, across the ditch of Hadrian's Wall', *AA* fifth series, vol. 28,13–25.

Welfare, H. 2004, 'Variation in the form of the ditch, and of its equivalents, on Hadrian's Wall', *AA* fifth series, vol. 33, 9–23.

Welfare, H. 2013, 'A Roman camp, quarries, and the Vallum at Shield-on-the-Wall (Newbrough)', *AA* fifth series, vol. 42, 81–100.

Whittaker, C. R. 1994. *Frontiers of the Roman Empire: a social and economic study*. Johns Hopkins University Press.

Wilkins, A. 2003, *Roman Artillery*. Shire Publications Ltd.

Wilmott, T. 1997, *Birdoswald: excavations of a Roman fort on Hadrian's Wall and its successor settlements 1987–1992*. English Heritage Archaeological Reports 14.

Wilmott, T. 1999, 'Birdoswald-Banna' in Bidwell 1999, 145–57.

Wilmott, T. 2000, 'The late Roman transition at Birdoswald and on Hadrian's Wall', in Wilmott and Wilson 2000, 13–23.

Wilmott, T. 2001, *Birdoswald Roman Fort: 1800 years on Hadrian's Wall*. Tempus.

Wilmott, T. 2005, 'The end of Hadrian's Wall', in Visy 2005, 131–7.

Wilmott. T. 2006, 'The profile of the ditch on Hadrian's Wall', *AA* fifth series, vol. 35, 33–8.

Wilmott. T. 2008, 'The Vallum: how and why: a review of the evidence', in Bidwell 2008a, 119–28.

Wilmott. T. (ed.) 2009a, *Hadrian's Wall: archaeological research by English Heritage 1976–2000*. English Heritage.

Wilmott, T. (et al.) 2009b, 'Excavations on the Hadrian's Wall fort of Birdoswald (*Banna*), Cumbria', in Wilmott 2009a, 203–395.

Wilmott, T. and Wilson, P. 2000, *The Late Roman Transition in the North*. Oxford: British Archaeological Reports 299.

Wilson, A. 2001, 'The Novantae and Romanization in Galloway', *Transactions of the Dumfries and Galloway Natural History and Antiquarian Society* 75, 73–131.

Wilson, A. 2003, 'Roman and native in Dumfriesshire', *Transactions of the Dumfries and Galloway Natural History and Antiquarian Society* 77, 103–60.

Wilson, R. J. A. 2002, *A Guide to the Roman Remains in Britain*. Constable. 4th ed.

Wilson, R. J. A. (ed,) 2006, *Romanitas: essays on Roman archaeology in honour of Sheppard Frere*. Oxford.

Woolliscroft, D. J. 1994, 'Signalling and the design of the Cumberland coast system', *Transactions of the Cumberland and Westmorland Antiquarian and Archaeological Society* second series, vol. 94, 55–65.

Woolliscroft, D. J. 1996, 'Signalling and the design of the Antonine Wall', *Britannia* 27, 153–77.

Woolliscroft, D. J. 1999, 'More thoughts on the Vallum', *Transactions of the Cumberland and Westmorland Antiquarian and Archaeological Society* second series, vol. 99, 53–65.

Woolliscroft, D. J. 2001, *Roman Military Signalling*. Tempus.

Woolliscroft, D. J. 2008, 'Signalling on Roman frontiers', in Bidwell 2008a, 91–8.

Woolliscroft, D. J. and Hoffman, B. 2006, *Rome's First Frontier: the Flavian occupation of Northern Scotland*. The History Press.

Zant, J. 2009, *The Carlisle Millennium Project: excavations in Carlisle 1998–2001, Volume I: Stratigraphy*. Lancaster Imprints.

Index